T0325652

Video Surveillance Techniques and Technologies

Vesna Zeljkovic
New York Institute of Technology, Nanjing Campus, China

A volume in the Advances in Multimedia and Interactive Technologies (AMIT) Book Series

An Imprint of IGI Global

Managing Director:	Lindsay Johnston
Production Manager:	Jennifer Yoder
Publishing Systems Analyst:	Adrienne Freeland
Development Editor:	Allyson Gard
Acquisitions Editor:	Kayla Wolfe
Typesetter:	Christina Barkanic
Cover Design:	Jason Mull

Published in the United States of America by
Information Science Reference (an imprint of IGI Global)
701 E. Chocolate Avenue
Hershey PA 17033
Tel: 717-533-8845
Fax: 717-533-8661
E-mail: cust@igi-global.com
Web site: http://www.igi-global.com

Library of Congress Cataloging-in-Publication Data

Zeljkovic, Vesna, 1972-Video surveillance techniques and technologies / by Vesna Zeljkovic.
    pages cm
 Includes bibliographical references and index. ISBN 978-1-4666-4896-8 (hardcover) -- ISBN 978-1-4666-4898-2 (print & perpetual access) -- ISBN 978-1-4666-4897-5 (ebook) 1. Video surveillance. I. Title.
  TK6680.3.Z45 2013
  621.389'28--dc23
                                    2013032973

This book is published in the IGI Global book series Advances in Multimedia and Interactive Technologies (AMIT) (ISSN: 2327-929X; eISSN: 2327-9303)

British Cataloguing in Publication Data
A Cataloguing in Publication record for this book is available from the British Library.

All work contributed to this book is new, previously-unpublished material. The views expressed in this book are those of the authors, but not necessarily of the publisher.

For electronic access to this publication, please contact: eresources@igi-global.com.

Advances in Multimedia and Interactive Technologies (AMIT) Book Series

ISSN: 2327-929X
EISSN: 2327-9303

MISSION

Traditional forms of media communications are continuously being challenged. The emergence of user-friendly web-based applications such as social media and Web 2.0 has expanded into everyday society, providing an interactive structure to media content such as images, audio, video, and text.

The **Advances in Multimedia and Interactive Technologies (AMIT) Book Series** investigates the relationship between multimedia technology and the usability of web applications. This series aims to highlight evolving research on interactive communication systems, tools, applications, and techniques to provide researchers, practitioners, and students of information technology, communication science, media studies, and many more with a comprehensive examination of these multimedia technology trends.

COVERAGE

- Audio Signals
- Digital Games
- Digital Technology
- Digital Watermarking
- Gaming Media
- Internet Technologies
- Mobile Learning
- Multimedia Services
- Social Networking
- Web Technologies

IGI Global is currently accepting manuscripts for publication within this series. To submit a proposal for a volume in this series, please contact our Acquisition Editors at Acquisitions@igi-global.com or visit: http://www.igi-global.com/publish/.

Titles in this Series

For a list of additional titles in this series, please visit: www.igi-global.com

Video Surveillance Techniques and Technologies
Vesna Zeljkovic (New York Institute of Technology, Nanjing Campus, China)
Information Science Reference • copyright 2014 • 223pp • H/C (ISBN: 9781466648968) • US $175.00 (our price)

Techniques and Principles in Three-Dimensional Imaging An Introductory Approach
Martin Richardson (De Montfort University, UK)
Information Science Reference • copyright 2014 • 300pp • H/C (ISBN: 9781466649323) • US $180.00 (our price)

Computational Solutions for Knowledge, Art, and Entertainment Information Exchange Beyond Text
Anna Ursyn (University of Northern Colorado, USA)
Information Science Reference • copyright 2014 • 511pp • H/C (ISBN: 9781466646278) • US $180.00 (our price)

Perceptions of Knowledge Visualization Explaining Concepts through Meaningful Images
Anna Ursyn (University of Northern Colorado, USA)
Information Science Reference • copyright 2014 • 418pp • H/C (ISBN: 9781466647039) • US $180.00 (our price)

Exploring Multimodal Composition and Digital Writing
Richard E. Ferdig (Research Center for Educational Technology - Kent State University, USA) and Kristine E. Pytash (Kent State University, USA)
Information Science Reference • copyright 2014 • 352pp • H/C (ISBN: 9781466643451) • US $175.00 (our price)

Multimedia Information Hiding Technologies and Methodologies for Controlling Data
Kazuhiro Kondo (Yamagata University, Japan)
Information Science Reference • copyright 2013 • 497pp • H/C (ISBN: 9781466622173) • US $190.00 (our price)

Media in the Ubiquitous Era Ambient, Social and Gaming Media
Artur Lugmayr (Tampere University of Technology, Finland) Helja Franssila (University of Tampere, Finland) Pertti Näränen (TAMK University of Applied Sciences, Finland) Olli Sotamaa (University of Tampere, Finland) Jukka Vanhala (Tampere University of Technology, Finland) and Zhiwen Yu (Northwestern Polytechnical University, China)
Information Science Reference • copyright 2012 • 312pp • H/C (ISBN: 9781609607746) • US $195.00 (our price)

Multimedia Services and Streaming for Mobile Devices Challenges and Innovations
Alvaro Suarez Sarmiento (Universidad de las Palmas de Gran Canaria, Spain) and Elsa Macias Lopez (Universidad de las Palmas de Gran Canaria, Spain)
Information Science Reference • copyright 2012 • 350pp • H/C (ISBN: 9781613501443) • US $190.00 (our price)

www.igi-global.com

701 E. Chocolate Ave., Hershey, PA 17033
Order online at www.igi-global.com or call 717-533-8845 x100
To place a standing order for titles released in this series, contact: cust@igi-global.com
Mon-Fri 8:00 am - 5:00 pm (est) or fax 24 hours a day 717-533-8661

Table of Contents

Section 1
Moving Object Detection Algorithms

Section 2
Moving Object Detection Algorithms and its Applications under Various Conditions

Section 3
Shape Recognition Algorithms

Section 4
Object Identification Algorithms and their Applications

Section 5
Video Surveillance Applied in Industry and Quality Control

Section 6
Video Technology Overview

Section 7
Devices and Applications

Chapter 24

Preface

Video surveillance techniques and technologies have improved and matured drastically over the past several decades. Internet Protocol technology, digital video cameras, and intelligent video analytics have taken over analog tapes and security personnel. Especially tremendous advances in video surveillance technologies happened over the past few years, as well as significant decreases in the cost of those technologies. As a result, there has been an explosion in the use of video surveillance as this evolution provides organizations with significant opportunities to improve security and reduce operating costs.

Considering increased terroristic activities all around the world, public agencies are faced with a critical need to protect citizens and assets from possible threats with a security system that enables rapid response to security breaches and prompt investigation of events. Besides governmental institutions, various businesses, municipalities, agencies, educational institutions, mass transportation centers, financial institutions, utility plants, and medical centers must also plan for threats and protect the security of their assets, employees, and clients. The critical areas that need video surveillance are: public zones where increased threats have caused many government agencies to apply video surveillance systems, university and school campuses' entry and exit points which prevents vandalism, airports, seaports, and railways where mass transit businesses and agencies protect passengers, staff, and physical assets from terrorist threats and security breaches, retail stores where video surveillance reduces fraud, theft, and administrative errors, financial institutions with 24/7 human video surveillance requirements needed in order to reduce threats of robbery and fraud.

The oldest version of video surveillance systems and the most widely used is an analog video surveillance system that uses analog video cameras coupled with closed-circuit television. Closed-circuit television represents the first generation of visual surveillance. German scientists deployed it for the first time in 1942 for remote monitoring of rocket launches. In 1969, the London Metropolitan Police used two temporary cameras in Trafalgar Square to monitor Guy Fawkes Day activities, which represented its first "open-street" application. These systems are used for online monitoring and recording movement of people and property. The drawbacks of these systems are: huge amounts of video-tapes that must be manually viewed by security guards which is a tedious, boring, and inefficient task, the necessity of security personnel to monitor hundreds of cameras, poor image quality, storage and deterioration of videotapes, lack of the ability to distribute video information across the network and to automatically extract useful information.

Invention of digital video cameras, IP video cameras, networked video recorders, Web video, consumer cameras, video processing intelligent algorithms, and application of automated signal analysis and pattern recognition to video cameras and sensors introduced intelligent digital video surveillance systems. These systems automatically extract useful information from video and sensor streams in real-time by detecting security incidents. They eliminate the need for monitoring and reviewing videotapes and enable integration of multiple events captured from various video analytic technologies and non-video sensors simple and easy. These systems provide a wide range of queries on events that may or may not have been previously defined as alerts, remote monitoring and analysis of events, real-time alerts for known "threat conditions," events and patterns of the past to be used to help predict potential threats, capability to track human movement used to study and understand traffic patterns, capability to carry out efficient data analysis of video sequences, either in real-time or recorded video and real-world events via sensors (video cameras, radar, or audio inputs). Web networking gives these systems the functionality to virtually anytime and anywhere access real-time and historical event data.

Motion detection, movement and color analysis, and people counting are available as commercial off-the-shelf products with a decent track record, but the quality of these functionalities in commercial domain is difficult to determine. Intelligent video surveillance systems are applied in many domains on CCTV systems, either distributed on the cameras or centralized on dedicated processing systems. Implemented video analysis often coexists and complements audio analysis.

The terrorist attacks of 9/11 as well as the Boston marathon accident that happened more recently raised the public awareness of security issues as well as tremendously increased the importance of intelligent automated video surveillance systems placed in public spaces.

The book *Video Surveillance Techniques and Technologies* offers, described in detail, various original mathematical models and algorithms aimed at automatic video sequence analysis with the goal to detect, track, and identify moving objects based on a sequence of images. It also includes biometric algorithms for anthropometric measurements and iris recognition. The main value of this book lies in its practical implementation in numerous domains and wide spectra of applications like video surveillance, homeland security, military aircraft radar ISAR image analysis, healthcare, quality control, industry, safety, etc. These algorithms can be implemented as software either on general purpose machines or in specialized video processing units.

This book is aimed to be educational material for graduate students as well as a source of valuable information for high-level professionals who build intelligent automated video surveillance systems in the field of signal and image processing applied in static/moving object detection, tracking, and identification. The described mathematical algorithms are employed in security video surveillance systems with a wide variety of applications; some of them are of high priority and important: homeland security and national defense.

This book is the result of my years-long research efforts and acquired experience, which is published in numerous proceedings and journals. The early chapters offer original solutions and mathematical algorithms for the motion detection and object identification problem. They are research-oriented and highly theoretical with the offered simulation results and proofs. The last chapters are oriented towards more practical aspects such as proper digital video equipment selection and more detailed information regarding camera and other video equipment element description. The book also provides IP video surveillance systems data, its basic functions, the advantages of network video, and customizing surveillance applications. It provides explanations related to motion detectors that represent the physical realization and practical application of the algorithms and mathematical solutions offered in the early chapters. Information concerning design guidelines, hardware information, specific examples, and necessary parameters to be addressed while designing representative security video surveillance system applications is also presented.

SECTION 1: MOVING OBJECT DETECTION ALGORITHMS

A new, simple, fast, and effective method for moving object detection to an outdoor environment, invariant to extreme illumination changes, is presented as an improvement to the shading model method. It is based on an analytical parameter introduced in the shading model, background updating technique, and window processing.

A new improvement of a method for the detection of moving objects from image sequences is described. This improvement permits reliable detection of moving objects even in the case of large and fast changes of scene illumination.

A real time change detection technique is proposed in order to detect moving objects in real image sequence, independent of the illumination of the analyzed scene. It is based on comparison of corresponding pixels that belong to different frames and combines time and space analysis, which augments the algorithm's precision and accuracy.

The problem of edge-based classification of natural video sequences containing buildings and captured changing lighting conditions is addressed. A strategy is devised in which a fuzzy rule-based classification technique is combined with a method for changing region detection in outdoor scenes.

The efficiency of the described techniques is illustrated on a real world video sequence recorded under significant illumination changes.

SECTION 2: MOVING OBJECT DETECTION ALGORITHMS AND ITS APPLICATIONS UNDER VARIOUS CONDITIONS

An integrated multimedia supported intelligent video surveillance system is proposed. The system alleviates the disadvantages of the existing video-surveillance kits and provides advanced search, notification, visualization, and alarming functionality through integration of artificial intelligence, motion detection and tracking technology, multimedia databases, and Internet/cell phone connectivity.

The resistance of the improved moving objects detection algorithm to various types of additive and multiplicative noise is discussed as well. The algorithm's first phase contains the noise suppression filter based on spatiotemporal blocks including dimensionality reduction technique for a compact scalar representation of each block, and the second phase consists of the moving object detection algorithm resistant to illumination changes that detects and tracks the moving objects.

Performance of the moving objects detection algorithm on infrared videos is discussed. The algorithm has two phases that comprise the noise suppression filter based on spatiotemporal blocks including dimensionality reduction technique and the illumination changes resistant moving object detection algorithm that tracks the moving objects.

A technique that improves precision in classification results using information extracted from video features is introduced. It combines fuzzy rule-based classification with a method for changing region detection in outdoor environment, which is invariant to extreme illumination changes and severe weather conditions.

SECTION 3: SHAPE RECOGNITION ALGORITHMS

The natural process in automated video surveillance systems is to perform correct shape recognition and object identification after the desired moving object is correctly detected.

Two new model-based algorithms for shape recognition are proposed. The proposed algorithms are efficient and tolerate severe noise. They have the ability to identify the close match between the noisy polygon that has a significantly greater number of sides and the assigned polygon. They work for convex and concave polygons equally well. These algorithms are invariant under translation, rotation, change of scale, and are reasonably easy to compute. The proposed criterion is a metric. The polygonal shapes are compared based on their areas and gravity centers.

A two-step process for removing noise from polygonal shapes for the purpose of easier and more efficient shape recognition is presented in this chapter. A polygonal shape is presented as its turning function and then a nonlinear diffusion filter and triangle method are applied. The obtained results demonstrate that the proposed technique successfully removes vertices that should be dismissed as noise while preserving dominant vertices that can be accepted as relevant features and give a faithful description of the shape of the polygon.

SECTION 4: OBJECT IDENTIFICATION ALGORITHMS AND THEIR APPLICATIONS

Two different novel algorithms are offered that can identify aircraft categories from Inverse Synthetic Aperture Radar images that use both the radar reflection pulse shape and the Doppler shifts of different parts of the aircraft. The first method forms numerical equivalents to shape, size, and other aircraft features as critical criteria to constitute the algorithm for their correct classification. The second method compares each ISAR image to unions of images of the different aircraft categories. The obtained results indicate that in most parts of the holding pattern the category of the aircraft can be successfully identified with both proposed methods.

Automatic body detection and identification of a person is one of the most recent research topics that has gained a lot of attention from researchers. Automated systems that will store human biometrics along with personal information can be of a significant assistance in investigations and security issues.

Another topic in this section is a comparative study of the ability of two novel image retrieval algorithms to provide automated touch-free identification of persons by iris recognition. Numerical experiments on a real biometric database indicate feasibility of the presented approach as automated iris recognition tool without special image pre-processing.

SECTION 5: VIDEO SURVEILLANCE APPLIED IN INDUSTRY AND QUALITY CONTROL

The goal of automatic pattern classification of real metallographic images from the steel plant ArcelorMittal Ostrava is to monitor the quality process in the steel plant. The number and sizes of dark dots produced by the production procedure imperfections are automatically determined; that represents a measure of how imperfect each plate is.

Steel Companies use a ladle furnace refining process that refines under a non-oxidizing atmosphere and supports slag-metal reaction through stirring by Ar gas injection. The automatic software capable to analyze the homogeneity of the surface and characterize features of the molten steel level such as presence of slag clusters is developed.

A new heuristic algorithm for porosity segmentation for the colored petro-graphic images is proposed as well. The algorithm automatically detects the porosities that represent the presence of oil, gas, or even water in the analyzed thin section rock segment based on the color of the porosity area filled with dies in the analyzed sample.

A comparative study of the ability of the proposed novel image retrieval algorithms is performed to provide automated object classification invariant of rotation, translation, and scaling. Simple cosine similarity coefficient methods are analyzed. Numerical experiments on real database sets indicate the feasibility of the presented approach.

SECTION 6: VIDEO TECHNOLOGY OVERVIEW

The first chapter in the following section is a description of the technology with which we can: capture an image, transform the image to the video signal format, transmit this signal to a remote location's receiver, display the image on a monitor, and save the image and print it for preservation.

High definition television is becoming ever more popular, opening up the market to new high-definition technologies. Image quality and color fidelity have experienced improvements faster than ever. The video surveillance market has been affected by high definition television demand. Since video surveillance calls for large amounts of image data, high-quality video frame rates are generally compromised. However, a network camera that conforms to high definition television standards shows good performance in high frame rate, resolution, and color fidelity. High quality network cameras are a good choice for surveillance video quality.

Industry experts are predicting that the advancement of video security technology will lead to a general increase in demand for surveillance systems. Over the next ten years these technological advances will continue, improving existing equipment and generating new methods. The next chapter outlines technologies that are currently in their infancy but are expected to be integrated into security systems in the near future.

A video surveillance system design requires making decisions that demand knowledge of basic options and the rationale for selecting from different ones available on the market. One needs to face making the following key decisions:

1. Choosing the best video surveillance companies.
2. Camera types.
3. Camera connection to video management system.
4. Video management system types.
5. Storage type.
6. Video analytics type.
7. Surveillance video display.
8. Integrating video with other systems.

SECTION 7: DEVICES AND APPLICATIONS

The very first element in the video surveillance system is the device that captures the images, which is the camera. "Cameras" is very important chapter in the book as it discusses the concepts of analog and digital cameras, their various designs, and camera specifications. Proper camera choice as well as setting is a very important issue in video surveillance system installation and design.

The next chapter in this section is a summary of IP surveillance systems: basic functions, the advantages of network video, customizing surveillance applications, and possible legal concerns. The most important step one can take before installing an IP surveillance system is to define goals and requirements. Once these are determined, the video system can be set up. The required goals to be determined are the following: definition of the video surveillance system needs (installation plan, area of coverage, camera positioning, illumination conditions determination, camera cabling, the recording server positioning), network camera and/or video encoder selection (image quality, lens selection, network camera selection, Power over Ethernet [PoE], video motion detection, audio, accessories selection, testing), hardware (switches, additional light sources, power supplies, additional server for video management software, hard drives), software (software package selection, licenses, image quality and frame rate requirements, IP address range calculation, hard disk usage calculation, cameras configuration, video motion detection settings, user access definition), and maintenance.

The first five sections represent the foundation and offer various intelligent algorithms that are the basics for motion detectors and their realization. There are two classes of security system alarm triggers: physical motion sensor and visual motion sensors. Both analog motion detectors and digital motion detectors belong to the group of visual motion sensors. Digital motion detector systems should differentiate between activities that are acceptable and those that breach security. When security-breaching acts occur, the system should identify the individuals and instruct security personnel what to do. Motion detectors can surveil, detect, and assess, as well as analyze information and distribute information to security personnel. Motion detector systems drastically reduce the load of footage that guards must watch for a long period of time.

Automated motion detectors are now a standard for serious medium to large security installations; they are necessary for high detection capabilities. All security systems must have an alarming device to signal the guard of irregular motion in a scene, even systems that have a tiny or huge number of cameras.

The fact that video surveillance is such an effective system especially when one thinks of its widespread use attests to its low investment cost. The last chapter contains information about design guidelines, hardware information, specific examples, and necessary parameters to be addressed while designing representative security video surveillance system applications: protection of all assets and personnel, calculation of the overall cost of the video system, surveillance target (assets and/or personnel), surveillance timing schedule, type and number of cameras needed, camera placement, field of view required, console room monitoring equipment, number and types of monitors, number of displays per monitor, number and type of recorders, digital recording technology needed, type of video switchers, type of video printer, if additional lighting is required, if intensified or thermal IR cameras are required, if sensors at doors, windows, and perimeters that are integrated with video signals are needed, digital video motion detectors placement, IP cameras, type of signal and video transmission, type of digital transmission, type of 802.11 protocol, type of compression (MPEG-4 or H.264), and the necessity of encryption or scrambling.

Vesna Zeljkovic
New York Institute of Technology, Nanjing Campus, China

Acknowledgment

I would like to express my special thanks and sincere gratitude to my brother, Milos, who has been my constant support and given me tremendous motivation throughout the years.

Vesna Zeljkovic
New York Institute of Technology, Nanjing Campus, China

Section 1
Moving Object Detection Algorithms

A new, simple, fast, and effective method for moving object detection to an outdoor environment, invariant to extreme illumination changes, is presented as an improvement to the shading model method. It is based on an analytical parameter introduced in the shading model, background updating technique, and window processing.

A new improvement of a method for the detection of moving objects from image sequences is described. This improvement permits reliable detection of moving objects even in the case of large and fast changes of scene illumination.

A real time change detection technique is proposed in order to detect moving objects in real image sequence, independent of the illumination of the analyzed scene. It is based on comparison of corresponding pixels that belong to different frames and combines time and space analysis, which augments the algorithm's precision and accuracy.

The problem of edge-based classification of natural video sequences containing buildings and captured changing lighting conditions is addressed. A strategy is devised in which a fuzzy rule-based classification technique is combined with a method for changing region detection in outdoor scenes.

The efficiency of the described techniques is illustrated on a real world video sequence recorded under significant illumination changes.

Chapter 1
Illumination Independent Moving Object Detection Algorithm

ABSTRACT

A new, simple, fast, and effective method for moving object detection to an outdoor environment, invariant to extreme illumination changes, is presented as an improvement to the shading model method. It is based on an analytical parameter introduced in the shading model, background updating technique, and window processing.

1. INTRODUCTION

In recent years extensive investigations and analysis have been done in the domain of moving object detection. Detection of moving objects in video processing plays a very important role in many vision applications. The vision systems that include image processing methods are widely implemented in many areas as traffic control (Inigo, 1989), (Mecocci, 1989), (Rourke, 1990), video surveillance of unattended outdoor environments (Foresti, 1998), video surveillance of objects (Corall, 1991), etc.

The change detection algorithms implemented in these video systems provide low-level information that can be used by higher level algorithms to determine the information desired (the trajectory of an object, the control of traffic flow, etc). Methods for moving object detection must be accurate and robust so that complex video systems can operate successfully.

Most of the existing algorithms for moving object detection assume that the illumination in a scene remains constant. Unfortunately, this assumption is not valid, especially in outdoor environment. The efficiency of some of existing techniques diminishes significantly if the illumination varies.

There are two types of methods that realize moving object detection. One detects changes at pixel level and the other is based on feature comparison. The first method is better because of very fast detection of any kind of changes in the analyzed scene and it is implemented in the technique proposed in this paper.

Considering the fact that the image frequency in video sequence is 25 frames per second the real-time video processing demands simple and fast algorithms. Simple differencing methods or fixed background extraction realized by various operations related to threshold determination are thus dominating in applications. The efficiency

DOI: 10.4018/978-1-4666-4896-8.ch001

of these methods depends mostly on accuracy of background updating techniques and on the threshold choice.

A new, illumination independent method for moving object detection in outdoor environment, based on the shading model method (Faithy, 1995), is invented. Shading model method shows to be superior to other techniques if illumination is allowed to vary. The experiments were performed that apply this method to the whole image. Since this is time consuming, only two successive frames were included. There was just a slight illumination change between them and new objects appeared in the second frame.

In the new approach the shading model method is applied as a basis for moving object detection in video sequence with illumination changes. Two major improvements are proposed here:

- Processing of windowed segment of the image.
- Background updating technique.

Only windowed segments of images where the moving object is expected are processed. In this way the execution time is significantly reduced.

Background updating technique on a frame-by-frame basis is also introduced. According to the performed experiments, the shading model method is effective only when applied in parallel with background updating. An improvement of this method is introduced that makes it work well even when there is a moving object detected in the scene (when background updating is locked out which makes the algorithm susceptible to illumination changes in that period).

A range of experiments with different type of illumination changes has proven the efficiency of the proposed method.

2. THE SHADING MODEL METHOD

2.1. Moving Object Detection

Moving object detection algorithms usually take two consecutive images as input and return the locations where differences are identified. These differences can be caused by the motion of an object, (including its entering and leaving the scene), changes in illumination or noise. The aim of such an algorithm is to locate only the changes that are due to structural changes in the scene, i.e. a moving object. Moving object detection and extraction from the fixed background in the analyzed scene is mostly done by simple subtracting the current image and background image (that does not contain any moving objects), (Inigo, 1989), (Mecocci, 1989), (Rourke, 1990), (Foresti, 1998), (Corall, 1991), (Skifstad, 1989).

The applied subtracting operation finds an absolute difference for each pixel, thus detecting moving objects (that have brighter or darker gray value), which usually differ from the background. If the difference is below a certain threshold, there is no change in the scene and the observed pixel is regarded as if it belongs to the background. Otherwise, there has been a change and the pixel belongs to the moving object. The absolute subtracting algorithm can be presented by

$$\text{IF } D = \left| C - B \right| > T$$

$$O = 1 \text{ (object)}$$

$$\text{ELSE}$$

$$O = 0 \text{ (background)} \tag{1}$$

where C is the value of the corresponding pixel of the current image, B is the value of the corresponding pixel of the background image, D is the absolute difference of the current and background image and O is the binary difference image. T is the predefined threshold for image segmentation.

In the case of fixed threshold it can happen that a moving object with an average brightness, which is only slightly different than the background, cannot be detected. The value for threshold becomes very important because:

- If the threshold is too low, a sudden increase in background brightness due, for example, to a rapid change from overcast to sunshine, could cause a false detection.
- If the threshold is too high, a moving object with brightness close to the background will not be detected.

The optimal threshold value is usually determined by analyzing the histogram of difference image in a certain time interval, where the appearance of moving object in the scene causes the histogram of difference image to widen. However, this is a time consuming process that is not effective in real-time applications.

The main problem with difference technique is a variation in background brightness, mostly due to weather phenomena (clouds, rain, etc.) or artificial sources (illumination, car or plane headlights, shadows, etc.).

In order to make the background differencing technique more effective, the changes in ambient lighting must be compensated by some kind of background updating technique.

2.2. The Shading Model Method

The shading model method determines whether structural changes occurred in the scene. It is shown in the literature that the shading model method is superior to other techniques when the illumination is allowed to vary (Skifstad, 1989).

The shading model method models the intensity of pixel I_p in the analyzed image according to:

$$I_p = I_i S_p \qquad (2)$$

where I_i is the illumination value and S_p is the shading coefficient. Phong's shading model (Skifstad, 1989) is one of typical shading models used.

The main idea of the shading model is that it mathematically formulates the shading coefficient of every physical material, which is defined uniquely by the physical surface structure of the object and the reflectance of the surface material.

Unfortunately, it is not possible to calculate the shading coefficient for a given pixel without a priori knowledge of the surface structure. This task is very difficult, almost impossible to realize in real world applications. However, we do not need the exact value of the shading coefficient. We only need to detect a change in the shading coefficient to be able to indicate a change between the frames of the sequence. The shading model change detection algorithm uses the ratio of intensities recorded in a region of the two frames to detect this change. It is expressed by

$$\sigma^2 = \frac{1}{\text{card}\{A\}} \sum_{i \in A} \left(\frac{B}{C} - \mu_A \right)^2 \geq T \qquad (3)$$

where σ^2 is the variance of the intensity ratios, B is the background image that does not contain moving objects, C is the current frame of the scene, A is the observed region of interest of the processed image, $\text{card}\{A\}$ stands for the region size, T is predetermined threshold and μ_A is the average of the intensity ratio:

$$\mu_A = \frac{1}{\text{card}\{A\}} \sum_{i \in A} \frac{B}{C} \qquad (4)$$

Summation is performed pixel by pixel, over the region of interest.

If there are changes in the physical surface in the observed region (all the shading coefficients do not change in exactly the same manner), the average of the ratios' variance in that region is greater than zero.

To determine whether a change has taken place in a given region, one simply calculates the σ^2 in that region. If it is close to zero (less than certain threshold), there has not been any structural changes in the scene. Otherwise, we assume a structural change had occurred (the moving object has appeared in the image). The region of interest A should be large enough so that the statistics is indicative of the nature of the region. For the experiments, 3 x 3 regions is used because only small image segments of dimensions 60 x 5 are observed.

This technique detects changes in physical surface structure and is, roughly, illumination independent. The shading model method is rather insensitive to noise (Skifstad, 1989).

2.3. Improved Shading Model Method

Experiments, shown later in the text, with various illumination changes were performed considering the shading model method presented in the literature. It is concluded that this method works well as long as the illumination changes are within +/-20% difference between background and current image. This method is not working for larger luminance changes. Therefore, the background updating technique is introduced in every frame that contains no moving objects in the scene. After the appearance of a moving object, background updating is locked out.

This algorithm becomes again susceptible to luminance changes while the moving object is in the scene. If, for example, a cloud appears or disappears, illumination difference would cause significant changes in the ratio between corresponding pixels of background image and current picture.

This is the reason why we have introduced a modification to the existing method. Instead of using the variance of $\dfrac{B}{C}$ from (3), we introduced a new coefficient that measures the ratio between average pixel value of the first frame when the moving object entered the scene and average pixel value of every current frame while the moving object is in the scene, i.e. while the background updating process is locked out. Also median value of all pixels that belong to the region A is used, instead of mean value in the variance value calculation because this accelerates the whole algorithm. The comparison operation is faster then addition and division used for mean value calculation.

The mathematical expression of improved version of shading model method is given by

$$\sigma_I^2 = \frac{1}{\text{card}\{A\}} \sum_{i \in A} \left(\frac{B}{C} * \text{coef} - \text{median}_A \right)^2 \geq T$$

(5)

where σ_I^2 is the improved variance of the ratio of the background and the current frame (compared to σ^2 in (3)), and the *coef* is determined by

coef $= 1$ (the beginning coefficient value)

   IF

$$\sigma_I^2 = \frac{1}{\text{card}\{A\}} \sum_{i \in A} \left(\frac{B}{C} * \text{coef} - \text{median}_A \right)^2 \geq T$$

THEN

$$\text{coef} = \frac{\dfrac{1}{\text{card}\{A\}} \sum\limits_{i \in A} C_{ni}}{\dfrac{1}{\text{card}\{A\}} \sum\limits_{i \in A} C_{1i}} = \frac{\mu_n}{\mu_1}$$

ELSE coef $= 1$ (6)

Parameter μ_n is the average of the current frame while the moving object is present in the scene, μ_1 is the average value of the first frame after the moving object entered the scene, and T is a threshold which determines whether there was a structural change in the observed scene or not.

If σ_1^2 is greater than T, it is assumed that the moving object entered the observation window.

At that moment, the average value of the first window μ_1 is memorized just one frame before the moving object entered the scene so that it would not contain a contribution from the moving object. In all the following frames, while the moving object is present in the scene, the average value of every current window μ_n is computed and *coef* represents the ratio of these two mean values, i.e. it compensates possible illumination changes while background updating is locked out.

When σ_1^2 becomes less than predetermined threshold T, it means there are no more moving objects present in the observed scene, so the *coef is* set to 1. Background updating method functions again and there is no need for compensation using *coef*. The initial value of *coef is* set to one.

3. BACKGROUND UPDATING

Every change of illumination in the analyzed image demands an adequate background updating. However, the interruption of image processing in real-time for background updating is not always possible. Thus, the background updating method must be simultaneous with image processing.

The simplest algorithm for background updating is the moving averaging updating technique, described in literature (Faithy, 1995)

$$B_{n+1} = kB_n + (1-k)C_n \qquad (7)$$

where B_{n+1} is the updated background image, used for moving object extraction from the next image in the sequence, B_n is the previous background image and C_n is the current image, k is the constant that determines the updating rate. Typical values of k are ≈ 0.5 so that the influence of the current picture on background updating is equal to the influence of the previous background frame. The most important drawbacks of this method are the following:

1. The moving object appears in the background image.
2. The optimal choice of k is almost unsolvable problem.

Illumination changes in the scene are usually smaller then those due to the moving object in the analyzed image. This fact implies the possibility that the background updating is applied only to those segments of the analyzed scene that are not covered with the moving object. Pseudocode of this technique, applied on pixel level, is described by

$$\text{IF} \ (D_n = \left| C_n - B_n \right| > T)$$

$$O_n = 0 \ \text{(object)}$$

$$B_{n+1} = B_n \ \text{(no background updating, there is a moving object in the scene)}$$

ELSE

$$O_n = 1 \ \text{(background)}$$

$$B_{n+1} = kB_n + (1-k)C_n \ \text{(background updating, no moving objects in the scene).} \qquad (8)$$

This algorithm shows better results than the previous background updating algorithm. But the effectiveness and the quality of the selective background updating technique mostly depends on the proper choice of the threshold value T, which implies a compromise between background updating and moving object detection quality. If the threshold is not selected properly, the moving object pixels are misclassified as the background pixels. The background image becomes unusable.

Previously described techniques for background updating could be combined, giving selective background updating with averaging that provides new quality. Here, the background of the selected pixels is replaced by the average of the current and background picture pixels ($k = 0.5$), instead of directly replacing the background pixels by the current image pixels.

Selective background technique with averaging is implemented only in those frames where the average value of variance of the ratio of background and current picture gave binary picture which number of pixels that indicate the moving object exceeded certain threshold.

Before mentioned methods are combined into the following algorithm:

$$\text{coef} = 1 \text{ (the beginning coefficient value)}$$

IF

$$\left(\sigma_i^2 = \frac{1}{\text{card}\{A\}} \sum_{i \in A} \left(\frac{B}{C} * \text{coef} - \text{median}_A\right)^2 \geq T\right)$$

$$O_n = 0 \text{ (object)}$$

$$B_{n+1} = B_n \text{ (no background updating, there is a moving object in the scene)}$$

$$\text{coef} = \frac{\dfrac{1}{\text{card}\{A\}} \sum_{i \in A} C_{ni}}{\dfrac{1}{\text{card}\{A\}} \sum_{i \in A} C_{1i}} = \frac{\mu_n}{\mu_1}$$

ELSE

$$O_n = 1 \text{ (background)}$$

$$B_{n+1} = (B_n + C_n) / 2 \text{ (background updating, no moving objects in the scene)}$$

$$\text{coef} = 1 \tag{9}$$

4. EXPERIMENTAL RESULTS

The proposed algorithm is applied to the analysis of video sequence that shows a passenger plane rolling on the runway. The sequence contains 49 monochrome images, 640 x 480 pixels with 256 gray levels (8 bits). Video rate is 25 frames per second.

The images are too large for real-time implementation of the image processing algorithm.

Since it is not necessary to analyze and update the whole image, but just the segment, which is of interest, on the expected path of the moving object, this improvement is included into the proposed algorithm.

The section of interest is presented by rectangular window 5 pixels wide and 60 pixels high, perpendicular to the expected path of the moving object. Five windows of this shape have been analyzed, placed at distance of ten pixels along horizontal direction. They are placed at the horizontal range 21-25, 31-35, 41-45, 51-55 and 61-65, respectively and the vertical range is 171-230. The results obtained from each of these windows were used to get the final score. The height of these windows is some 10% larger than the expected height of the moving object. Windows are located so that the moving object passes through their center.

The proposed algorithm was tested under various lighting conditions gained artificially on real video sequences. The algorithm allows the user to define regions.

Figure 1 represents the background without moving objects and Figure 2 represents the airplane in the 45th frame.

Figures 3 and 4 show the result of processing the whole image with shading model method masks of size 3x3. Experiments with different mask size, for example 5x5, were made but the results obtained with larger masks did not compensate the significantly greater execution times.

The plain shading model method presented in the literature, the improved shading model method and selective background updating technique with averaging are applied. All images were post processed. The binary image obtained with the plain shading model method was first median filtered with the 7x7 mask and then treated with the dilation technique with 15x15 mask. This was inevitable to get the best possible results but this post processing is also very time consuming.

On the binary image obtained with the new algorithm was applied the dilation technique with 15x15 mask only.

Figure 3 represents the binary image obtained by the application of the plain shading model method (3) with 3x3 mask and the threshold level of 0.25. Figure 4 is the binary image that emphasizes the moving object obtained by the application of the new proposed method (9) with 3 x 3 mask and threshold level of 0.1.

Comparing Figures 3 and 4 with the video sequence, it is obvious that the proposed technique gives significantly better results. According to

Figure 1. Background image

Figure 2. 45ᵗʰ frame

Figure 3. The binary image obtained with the application of the shading model method (Skifstad, 1989)

Figure 4. The binary image obtained with the application of the improved shading model method

Figure 4, two moving objects are present in the scene, airplane (on the left) and the truck (in the lower right corner of the image), as seen in the video sequence.

The results reported here are obtained for the first window, located at the coordinates 21-25 horizontally and 171-230 vertically. The airplane enters the window in the 4th frame and leaves it in the 36th frame.

Several other experiments were done on this video sequence. It can be noticed that the moving object is brighter than the background. There were neither video sequences with sudden luminance change nor video sequences with the moving object darker than the background available. However, these conditions were simulated, the first one with illumination variations and the second one by inverting the original sequence.

Experiments were divided into two groups. The first group is performed on the original sequence of images where the moving object is brighter than background and the second one on the inverted video sequence where the moving object is darker than background.

Nine experiments were done, with eight different methods. Results are given in Table 1, column per each experiment.

1. Original video, column 1.
2. The luminance change began, continued and stopped while the moving object was permanently present in the observed scene. This experiment could simulate the real situation when cloud and its shadow appear while there is a moving object in the scene. The illumination change lasted 20 consecutive frames, from 11th to 30th frame (0.8 s). Five experiments of this kind have been conducted considering different levels of luminance changes. Illumination level has been decreased to 90%, 80%, 70%, 60% and 50% of the initial luminance level, respectively. Only the results with 50% luminance level change are shown here because they exhibit the extreme situations, column 2.
3. The illumination level is increased while the moving object was permanently in the scene from 50% to 100% of the initial luminance level, from 11th to 30th frame, column 3. The

Table 1.

Algor/Exp.	1.	2.	3.	4.	5.	6.	7.	8.	9.
I	100 / 0	100 / 0	100 / 0	100 / 0	100 / 0	100 / 0	100 / 0	100 / 0	100 / 0
II	96,97 / 0	96,97 / 81,25	75,76 / 75	96,97 / 81,25	51,52 / 0	84,85 / 0	66,67 / 81,25	96,97 / 0	54,55 / 25
III	87,88 / 0	100 / 81,25	100 / 81,25	100 / 81,25	100 / 81,25	100 / 81,25	100 / 81,25	87,88 / 62,50	87,88 / 62,5
IV	96,97 / 0	100 / 75	69,70 / 75	100 / 75	27,27 / 75	100 / 75	39,39 / 75	96,97 / 56,25	0 / 56,25
V	96,97 / 0	100 / 81,25	100 / 81,25	100 / 81,25	100 / 81,25	100 / 81,25	100 / 81,25	96,97 / 62,50	93,94 / 62,5
VI	81,81 / 12,5	90,90 / 56,25	60,60 / 0	90,90 / 56,25	72,72 / 0	90,90 / 56,25	66,67 / 0	81,81 / 50	81,81 / 0
VII	81,81 / 12,5	87,80 / 56,25	69,69 / 0	87,87 / 56,25	72,72 / 0	87,87 / 56,25	66,67 / 0	81,81 / 50	81,81 / 0
VIII	93,93 / 0	93,93 / 81,25	84,85 / 81,25	93,93 / 81,25	90,90 / 12,50	93,94 / 81,25	90,90 / 81,25	93,94 / 0	93,94 / 0

luminance increase was performed on the sequence where the illumination decrease was already done so the maximum illumination level was not violated.

4. The luminance decrease lasted 20 frames (0.8 s), starting while the moving object was in the scene (20th frame), until the 40th frame. This simulates the real situation when cloud and its shadow appear while there is a moving object in the scene and the shadow is still present after the moving object leaves the scene. Several luminance changes were performed as in previous experiments but only the results with the decrease of 50% are shown, column 4.

5. The luminance increase of 50% under the same conditions, from 20th to 40th frame, column 5.

6. Sudden luminance change (50% decrease) during the 20th frame (in 0.04 s), column 6.

7. Sudden luminance increase of 50% in 20th frame, column 7.

8. Sudden luminance decrease of 50%, when the moving object is not present in the observed scene, in the 40th frame, column 8.

9. Sudden luminance increase of 50%, also in the 40th frame, column 9.

The proposed algorithm gives good results in all experiments. The moving object was always detected and there were no false alarms.

For comparison, the same experiments were performed, with application of existing known methods.

The following eight methods are given in rows of Table 1.

- **I:** The new method.
- **II:** SMED operator (Faithy, 1995.)
- **III:** Inigo technique (Inigo, 1989.)
- **IV:** Improved version of differencing with selective background updating technique with averaging (Faithy, 1995.)

- **V:** Change detection method (Foresti, 1994.)
- **VI:** Skifstad and Jain method (Skifstad, 1989.)
- **VII:** Skifstad and Jain method applied only with introduced coefficient without background updating.
- **VIII:** The Skifstad and Jain method in parallel with the technique of background updating but without the coefficient.

For each method and experiment, two numbers are given. The first one describes the percentage of correct detection in the observed window. This calculation was realized by the division of the sum of the number of frames where the moving object was correctly detected, with the sum of all the frames in the observed sequence where the moving object really appears, multiplied with 100%. The second one indicates the percentage of false alarms in the observed window. This percentage was realized by the division of the sum of the number of frames where the moving object was incorrectly detected by the algorithm, with the sum of all the frames where the moving object does not appear, multiplied with 100%. As mentioned earlier, the moving object is present in 33 of total 49 frames, from 4th to 36th frame.

The superiority of proposed method over the existing techniques is obvious.

Some of the results are presented in the graphical form.

The x axis (time axis) in Figures 5 and 6 represents the ordinal number of the processed frame, in the range 1-49. The y axis shows the number of black pixels that represent the detected moving object in the observed window.

The following Figures illustrate more detailed representation of the mentioned methods under various illumination conditions. They show the absolute difference, of detected pixels that represent the moving object, between the normal sequence and the sequence with luminance change observed through frames, in other words, in time.

Figure 5. Results for the 2nd experiment, methods I, II, IV, V and VI

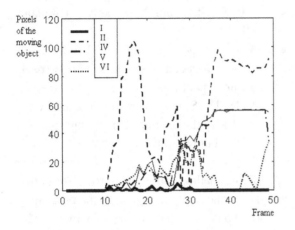

Figure 6. Results for the 7th experiment, methods I, II, IV, V and VI

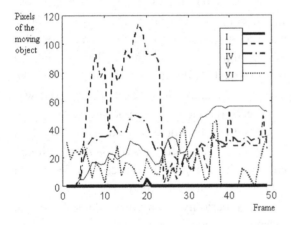

Figure 5 shows the absolute difference between the results in column 1 and column 2 for the following methods:

- I (marked with the solid line)
- II (plus line)
- IV (circle line)
- V (dashed line)
- VI (the star line)

The absolute difference means the difference between the number of correctly detected pixels

that really belong to the moving object in the first and the second experiment.

Figure 6 shows the absolute difference between the results from column 1 and column 7 for mentioned methods.

The superiority of the proposed method is quite obvious. It almost does not change its behavior with illumination changes, while other methods seriously deteriorate.

For the second group of experiments the inverted video sequence has been used.

Figure 7 shows the artificially processed, inverted background image and Figure 8 represents 45th frame that contains moving object, which is darker than the background.

The proposed algorithm is applied to these two images with 3x3 masks.

Figure 9 represents the binary image obtained by the application of the plain shading model method with the threshold level 0.25 and Figure 10 is the binary image that emphasizes the moving object obtained by the application of the proposed method with the threshold level 0.1.

Median filtering with 7x7 mask and dilation with 15x15 mask are also applied.

It is obvious that the new technique gives significantly better results with fewer false alarms. Comparing Figures 4 and 10 it is obvious, observ-

Figure 7. Inverted background image

Figure 8. Inverted 45ᵗʰ frame

Figure 9. The binary image with the application of the shading model method presented in the literature (Skifstad, 1989)

Figure 10. The binary image obtained with the application of the improved shading model method

ing the inverted video sequence experiment, that binary image is obtained, which better defines the moving object. For these reasons the process of dilation is not necessary.

The same nine experiments were repeated for the inverted images. The results for all experiments are very promising. The percentage of correctly detected moving object was 100% and there were no false alarms.

All these results show that the proposed algorithm is not sensitive neither to slow nor fast illumination changes.

For the comparison reasons the same experiments have been performed on the inverted sequence with application of existing known methods mentioned above. All these methods showed to be subtle to illumination changes, which is obvious from the Table 2.

The structure of the Table 2 is the same as for the Table 1 as well as the way the results are presented.

Some of the results are presented in graphical form.

In Figures 11 and 12 the x-axis represents the number of processed frame i.e. the time and y-axis shows the number of black pixels that represent the detected moving object in the observed window.

Figure 11 represents the graphic of absolute difference between the results from column 1 and column 5 for mentioned methods.

Figure 12 represents the absolute difference between the results from column 1 and column 9 for mentioned methods.

The previous Figures illustrate the superiority of the proposed method even in the case when the moving object is darker than the background. This technique remains resistant to illumination changes while other methods obviously fail. It also succeeds to handle the completely correct detection of the moving object under luminance variation while other techniques completely lose control.

It must be emphasized that the only reliable way to entirely check the effectiveness of this method would be the real-time testing. However,

Table 2.

Algorithm	1.	2.	3.	4.	5.	6.	7.	8.	9.
I	100 0	100 0	100 0	100 0	100 0	100 0	100 0	100 0	100 0
II	96,97 0	75,76 0	54,55 81,25	84,85 0	54,55 81,25	75,76 0	78,79 81,25	96,97 0	54,55 81,25
III	96,97 0	100 75	24,24 75	100 75	100 81,25	100 81,25	100 81,25	87,88 62,50	84,85 62,50
IV	96,97 0	100 81,25	100 81,25	100 81,25	24,24 75	100 75	51,52 75	96,97 56,25	0 56,25
V	96,97 0	100 81,25	100 81,25	100 81,25	100 81,25	100 81,25	100 81,25	96,97 62,50	90,90 68,75
VI	100 18,75	100 62,50	100 6,25	100 62,50	100 6,25	100 62,50	100 6,25	100 56,25	100 6,25
VII	100 18,75	100 62,50	100 6,25	100 62,50	100 6,25	100 62,50	100 6,25	100 56,25	100 6,25
VIII	100 0	100 81,25	100 0	100 75,00	100 0	100 81,25	100 0	100 0	100 0

Figure 11. Results for the 5th experiment, methods I, II, IV, V and VI

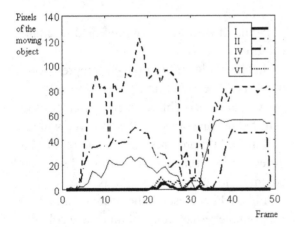

Figure 12. Results for the 9th experiment, methods I, II, IV, V and VI

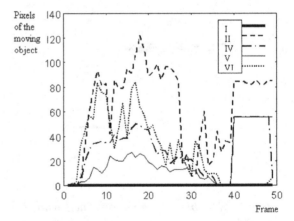

the presented simulations and experiments give very promising results.

5. CONCLUSION

The problems associated with the background-based moving object detection techniques are mainly due to the variations of ambient lighting. In this chapter an effective moving object detection algorithm is introduced, based on the shading model method with background updating technique under conditions where illumination cannot be controlled.

The new method is shown to be invariant to significant illumination changes and superior to other techniques when the illumination is allowed to vary.

In order to accelerate the execution time of the whole algorithm, only certain segments of images where the moving object is expected to be found are processed. Median value instead of mean value of the observed region A is also used, in calculating the variance because the comparison is faster then addition and division that are necessary for calculating the mean value.

The process of background updating in this technique is also introduced, along with the shading model method, applied at every frame. The shading model method has shown to be effective only when applied in parallel with background updating. That is why an improvement of this method is introduced that makes it function well even when there is a moving object detected in the scene (when background updating is locked out which makes the algorithm susceptible to illumination changes in that period).

The described algorithm was applied on three more video sequences and it also showed very good and promising results. One was also grey as the one used presented in this chapter, and two others were colored. One of the colored sequences had two moving objects. The proposed method succeeded to completely successfully detect the both moving objects in the scene independently of the luminance conditions. The results obtained from the one of the used sequences were shown that was the most convenient for the representation.

The proposed algorithm, invariant to external luminance changes, has been tested under various lighting conditions, artificially simulated on the computer and with the moving object brighter and darker than the background, and satisfactory and promising results have been achieved.

REFERENCES

Corrall, D. (1991). *VIEW: Computer vision for surveillance applications*. London: IEE.

Dragovic, R., & Zeljković, V. (2004). *Video conferences - The possibilities of application in judiciary*. Kopaonik, Serbia and Montengro: YU INFO.

Fathy, M., & Siyal, M. Y. (1995). An image detection technique based on morphological edge detection and background differencing for real-time traffic analysis. *Pattern Recognition Letters*, (16): 1321–1330. doi:10.1016/0167-8655(95)00081-X

Foresti, G. L. (1998). A real-time system for video surveillance of unattended outdoor environments. *IEEE Transactions on Circuits and Systems for Video Technology*, 8(6), 697–704. doi:10.1109/76.728411

Foresti, G. L., & Regazzoni, C. S. (1994). A change detection method for multiple object localization in real scenes. In *Proceedings of IEEE Conference*, (pp. 984-987). IEEE.

Inigo, R. M. (1989). Application of machine vision to traffic monitoring and control. *IEEE Transactions on Vehicular Technology*, 38(3), 112–122. doi:10.1109/25.45464

Mecocci, A. (1989). Moving object recognition and classification in external environments. *Signal Processing*, (18): 183–194. doi:10.1016/0165-1684(89)90049-2

Popović, M., & Zeljković, V. (2000). *Moving object extraction from image sequences using edge information*. Novi Sad, Yugoslavia: DOGS.

Rourke, A., Bell, M. G. H., & Hoose, N. (1990). *Road traffic monitoring using image processing*. London: Road Traffic Control.

Skifstad, K., & Jain, R. (1994). Illumination independent change detection for real world image sequences. *Computer Vision Graphics and Image Processing*, (46): 387–399.

Zeljkovic, V. (2010). *Illumination independent moving object detection in image sequences*. LAP Lambert Academic Publishing GmbH & Co. KG.

Zeljković, V., Dorado, A., & Izquierdo, E. (2004). Combining a fuzzy rule-based classifier and illumination invariance for improved building detection. *IEEE Transactions on Circuits and Systems for Video Technology*, 14(11), 1277–1280. doi:10.1109/TCSVT.2004.835145

Zeljković, V., Dorado, A., & Izquierdo, E. (2004). *A modified shading model method for building detection.* Lisbon, Portugal: WIAMIS.

Zeljković, V., Dorado, A., Trpovski, Ž., & Izquierdo, E. (2004). *A modified shading model method used for building extraction.* Cacak, Serbia and Montengro: ETRAN.

Zeljković, V., & Dragovic, R. (2004). *Moving object detection in video sequence independent of the scene illumination - Software solution.* Kopaonik, Serbia and Montengro: YU INFO.

Zeljković, V., & Dragovic, R. (2004). *Software solution for moving object detection in video sequence independent of the scene illumination.* Zabljak, Serbia and Montengro: IT.

Zeljkovic, V., Pokrajac, D., Dorado, A., & Izquierdo, E. (2006). *Application of the improved illumination independent moving object detection algorithm on the real video sequence.* Montreux, Switzerland: WIAMIS.

Zeljković, V., & Popović, M. (2000). *Illumination independent moving object extraction from video sequences.* Soko Banja, Yugoslavia: ETRAN.

Zeljković, V., & Popović, M. (2001). *Detection of moving objects in video signal under fast changes of scene illumination. Niš, Yugoslavia: TELSIKS.*

Zeljković, V., & Trpovski, Ž. (2002). *Moving object localization applying change detection.* Novi Bečej, Yugoslavia: DOGS.

Zeljković, V., & Trpovski, Ž. (2004). *Illumination independent moving object detection in real sequence.* Sombor, Serbia and Montengro: DOGS.

Zeljković, V., Trpovski, Ž., & Šenk, V. (2003). *Improved illumination independent moving object detection in real world video sequences.* Zagreb, Croatia: EURASIP. doi:10.1109/VIPMC.2003.1220508

Zeljković, V., Trpovski, Ž., & Šenk, V. (2004). *Improved illumination independent change detection for real world video sequences.* YUJOR.

Chapter 2
Improved Illumination Independent Moving Object Detection Algorithm

ABSTRACT

A real time change detection technique is proposed in order to detect the moving objects in a real image sequence. The described method is independent of the illumination of the analyzed scene. It is based on a comparison of corresponding pixels that belong to different frames and combines time and space analysis, which augments the algorithm's precision and accuracy. The efficiency of the described technique is illustrated on a real world interior video sequence recorded under significant illumination changes.

1. INTRODUCTION

Detecting important changes, i.e. moving objects in dynamic real scenes, has become very popular research area in recent years. First of all, this problem is present in several domains of image processing as well as in digital signal processing area. There is a great interest in this kind of systems because of its wide application and huge spectra of use. The systems have practical application in traffic regulation (Inigo, 1989), (Mecocci, 1989), (Rourke, 1990), (Fathy, 1995), video surveillance, securing different objects in interior or exterior, national security, etc (Corall, 1991), (Foresti, 1998), (Foresti, 1994).

Real time image processing algorithms should be fast, simple and computationally feasible in order to support practical applications. The most of the existing algorithms for change detection in real time use various techniques for segmentation of the fixed background, based on changing decision threshold. That is why the accuracy of these methods depends significantly on the appropriate choice of the adequate threshold as well as on the precision of the background updating technique.

Improved technique for moving object detection in real sequences independent of illumination variation, based on the method explained in the previous chapter, is presented. The new technique exploits information extracted from a sequence of images relying on time and space analysis performed in parallel. This augments the accuracy of the algorithm.

2. METHODOLOGY

Image sequence I consisting of N video frames is observed. The sliding mask A_i is applied on every frame.

DOI: 10.4018/978-1-4666-4896-8.ch002

Skifstad and Jain, (Skifstad, 1989), use the ratio of pixel intensities in mask A_i between two a reference and a current frame to estimate the pixel variance σ_i^2 as follows:

$$\sigma_i^2 = \frac{1}{\text{card}\{A_i\}} \sum_{m \in A_i} \left(\frac{B_m}{C_m} - \mu_{A_i} \right)^2, \; i = 1..n . \quad (1)$$

Here, pixel intensities within mask A_i are denoted with B_m for a reference, background frame that does not contain changing regions and with C_m for a current frame where moving objects are being identified. The mean of the pixel intensity ratio within A_i is denoted with μ_{A_i}. If $\sigma_i^2 \geq \varepsilon$ (where ε is a suitable threshold), the center of the mask A_i is marked as changing region.

Experiments in (Inigo, 1989), (Mecocci, 1989), (Rourke, 1990), (Fathy, 1995), (Corall, 1991), (Foresti, 1998), (Foresti, 1994) have shown that for significant illumination changes this method fails, i.e. some pixels are falsely assigned to changing regions. A modified technique based on adaptive coefficient for illumination compensation is proposed in this chapter. Pixel variance is estimated as:

$$\sigma_i^2 = \frac{1}{\text{card}\{A_i\}} \sum_{m \in A_i} \left(\frac{B_m}{C_m} K_i - \text{median}\{A_i\} \right)^2, \quad (2)$$

The median instead of mean value is used in order to reduce sensitivity on outliers. The illumination compensation coefficient is defined as

$$K_i = \frac{\sum_{m \in A_i} C_m}{\sum_{m \in A_i} C_{1m}} = \frac{\mu_i}{\mu_1}, \quad (3)$$

where C_{1m} is pixel intensity for the first frame in the sequence.

2.1 Improved Method

The modified shading model method illustrated in previous chapter is fairly robust to significant and sudden illumination changes (up to roughly 50% of change in comparison to the starting illumination level), due to the coefficient K_i that enables sensitivity suppression.

The improved version of the algorithm is proposed here to further improve the behavior of the existing method. It performs the analysis in time and space at the same time and improves resistance to the illumination changes and reduces the false detection, i.e. noise. It successfully detects the inner parts of the moving objects and the thicker edges as well.

In the technique proposed here, pixel variances for three successive pairs of frames are average estimated and its average value is thresholded in order to determine the presence of moving objects. This represents temporal analysis. The ratio of pixel intensities in A_i between two frames is used to estimate the pixel variance $^I\sigma_i^2$ for three pairs of successive frames. The estimation of pixel variance was done on following pairs of frames i-3 and i-2, i-2 and i-1 and i-1 and i, where i is the current frame. Thus, three pixel variances for three successive and corresponding variance pairs $^I\sigma_{i-2}^2$, $^I\sigma_{i-1}^2$ and $^I\sigma_i^2$ are obtained. Subsequently, the average value of these three variances is computed as follows:

$$^I\sigma_{mean}^2 = (^I\sigma_{i-2}^2 + {}^I\sigma_{i-1}^2 + {}^I\sigma_i^2) / 3, \quad (4)$$

After that, the mean value is subtracted from the pixel variance of the current and previous frame:

$$^I\sigma_{i'}^2 = {}^I\sigma_i^2 - {}^I\sigma_{mean}^2, \quad (5)$$

If $^I\sigma_{i'}^2 \geq \varepsilon$ (a suitable threshold), the center of A_i is marked as changing region, i.e. as moving object.

This algorithm performs analysis in three dimensions, two space dimensions and one temporal dimension. The time analysis, additionally to space analysis, helps with correct moving object detection and augments the precision of the algorithm. It could have been proposed that the increase of the analyzed dimensions in the algorithm, apart from the two space dimensions (height and width), can improve its performance. That is the third time dimension is introduced, in order to insure better precision of the method. It is quite understandable why this improved method, analyzing three dimensions, the inner parts of the moving objects and the thicker edges as well. It gives better and more efficient results than the modified shading model method.

It should be pointed out, as well, that this algorithm works with local intensity, and can be easily used for gray movies, i.e. BW movies. This is important because then this method could also work with IR movies.

3. EXPERIMENTAL RESULTS

The described improved illumination variation independent algorithm for moving object detection is applied on the real color video sequence recorded in interior ambience. The sequence depicts interior of a room where a person walks accross the scene while the artificial illumination is turned off and then turned on, again. This way the illumination changes during the course of the sequence: First it decreases for 50% and later it is increases to the previous level. The real video sequence contains 94 RGB frames with resolution of 352×288 pixels. The image frequency is 25 frames per second. The Figure 1 contains the first frame of the sequence showing background (chair, metal office furniture and the floor) without any moving object.

The following figures, Figure 2 and 3, illustrate the frames in which there were significant illumination changes. These frames present most

Figure 1. The 1st frame of analyzed video sequence

Figure 2. The 30th frame of analyzed video sequence

Figure 3. The 86th frame of analyzed video sequence

challenges for detection moving objects by illumination sensitive algorithms.

In the Figure 2 is shown the 30th frame of the sequence containing the moving object—the person moving across the observed scene. At this frame, the light in the room was turned off and the illumination decreased for about 50%.

The Figure 3 represents the 86th frame of the real sequence that also contains the person moving across the observed scene while the light in the room was again turned on and the illumination was doubled in one frame.

The improved moving object detection method, described with Equations (2) to (5), is applied on this sequence. The results of the proposed algorithm are compared with the results obtained with the application of the modified shading model method.

In these experiments, a sliding window A_i of 3×3 pixels was used for averaging. The optimal threshold was experimentally found to be $\varepsilon = 0.1$ for old and $\varepsilon = 0.01$ for new method.

The binary images of the very first frame of the processed sequence for both methods are presented in the Figures 4(a) and 4(b). In these and the subsequent figures, moving objects are marked with white pixels. The Figure 4(a) indicates the results obtained with the application of the new

improved method and the Figure 4(b) illustrates the modified shading model method. Similarly, in further Figures (a) will be reserved for the new improved method and (b) will indicate the modified shading model method.

It is obvious that both methods can identify the moving object, i.e. that part of the leg of the person that crosses the scene. The new improved method gives slightly better detection of the foot.

The Figures 5(a) and 5(b) represent the binary images of the thirtieth frame of the processed sequence for which there was sudden and significant illumination decrease of about 50%.

It is important to point out the difference between these two figures. As it can be seen the old method, illustrated by the Figure 5(b) has more false alarms. The Figure 5(b) contains the line on right edge which represents a false alarm and this is not the case with the new method, which is obvious from the Figure 5(a). The new improved algorithm gives better results with thicker moving object and in addition to edges this new technique is capable of identifying inner parts of moving object.

The Figures 6(a) and 6(b) represent the binary images of the 86th frame with the sudden illumination increase of about 100%, the light was again turned on. On the Figure 6(a), it can be seen that

Figure 4. 1ˢᵗ frame (a) new improved method; (b) modified method

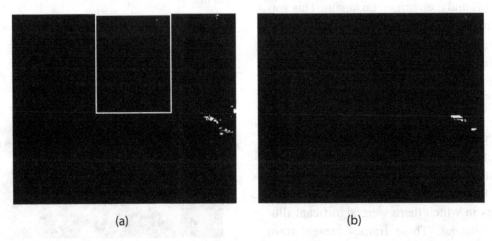

(a)   (b)

Figure 5. The 30th frame (a) the new improved method; (b) modified method

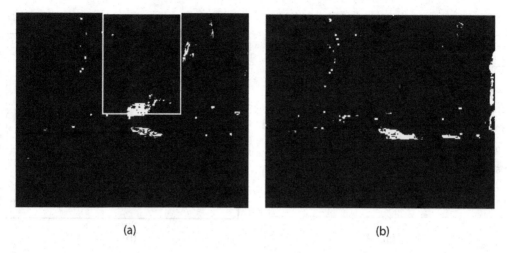

(a)   (b)

Figure 6. The 86th frame (a) the new improved method; (b) modified method

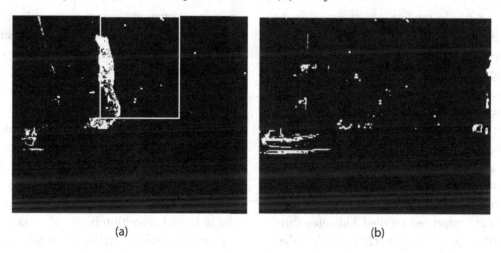

(a)   (b)

the detection is better, e.g., back part of the leg is better identified. The binary image also contains significantly less false alarms.

From the binary images shown above it is easy to observe one moving object that represents the person's legs crossing the scene. However, it can be noticed from the analyzed figures that there is some noise present, i.e. some pixels are misclassified as pixels that belong to the moving object. But the new improved method contains less misclassified pixels and the moving object is better segmented. The noise and ghost problem can be efficiently controlled with the appropriate choice

of the threshold used for segmentation. The increase of the threshold will reduce the noise and also the thickness of the moving objects.

In order to demonstrate the quality of the algorithm frame segment represented with the rectangular window is analyzed. When moving object appears, it gradually occupies the window and ultimately leaves it.

As an example to this mode of image analysis, the window of height 150 pixels and width 120 pixels, was placed in the processed video sequence. The upper left corner is placed at the coordinates (130,0). The height of the window is set so it can

Figure 7. Number of white pixels in the window a) the new improved method; b) modified shading model method

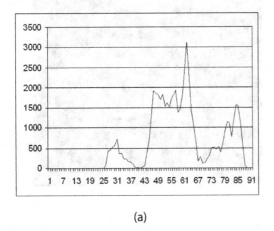

(a)

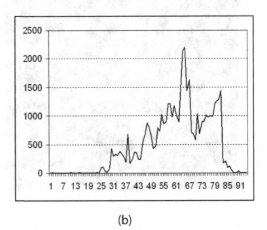

(b)

contain the whole moving object and that the moving object goes through its center.

These diagrams for both techniques, presented in the Figures 7(a) and 7(b), show the portion of window occupied by the moving object. The vertical axis represents the number of white pixels that represent the moving object, and horizontal axis shows the serial number of the processed frame in the sequence.

The movement of the feet can be clearly seen particularly from the diagram shown in the Figure 7a. The new improved method indicates three peaks, as the step is made, first from one leg, then the other leg moves and then at the end the first one moves again. These three phases are not so obvious from the diagram obtained with the application of the modified shading model method depicted in Figure 7b.

4. CONCLUSION

Improved version of the previous method described in this chapter for moving object detection independent of illumination changes is presented.

The proposed improvement is based on additional temporal analysis that, apart from two di-

mensional space analysis augments the precision, efficiency and accuracy of the proposed technique. The time analysis contributes to better moving object detection. The inner parts of the moving objects are also detected. The detected edges are thicker in comparison to the previous method presented in the last chapter. This technique is resistant to significant illumination changes. In most cases it succeeds to detect changing regions under luminance variation. If efficiency is considered as time required to perform the analysis, the proposed algorithm is slightly less efficient, but this overhead in efficiency is not significant considering very strong and powerful computers and specialized hardware for image processing that compensate this.

The further work related to this method is the focused on improving the noise reduction and on simplification and acceleration of the algorithm. It will be explained in the following chapters.

REFERENCES

Corrall, D. (1991). *VIEW: Computer vision for surveillance applications*. London: IEE.

Dragovic, R., & Zeljković, V. (2004). *Video conferences - The possibilities of application in judiciary*. Kopaonik, Serbia and Montengro: YU INFO.

Fathy, M., & Siyal, M. Y. (1995). An image detection technique based on morphological edge detection and background differencing for real-time traffic analysis. *Pattern Recognition Letters*, (16): 1321–1330. doi:10.1016/0167-8655(95)00081-X

Foresti, G. L. (1998). A real-time system for video surveillance of unattended outdoor environments. *IEEE Transactions on Circuits and Systems for Video Technology*, 8(6), 697–704. doi:10.1109/76.728411

Foresti, G. L., & Regazzoni, C. S. (1994). A change detection method for multiple object localization in real scenes. In *Proceedings of IEEE Conference*, (pp. 984-987). IEEE.

Inigo, R. M. (1989). Application of machine vision to traffic monitoring and control. *IEEE Transactions on Vehicular Technology*, 38(3), 112–122. doi:10.1109/25.45464

Iqbal, Q., & Aggarwal, J. K. (1999). Applying perceptual grouping to content-based image retrieval: Building image. In *Proceedings of IEEE Int'l Conf. on Computer Vision and Pattern Recognition* (pp. 42-48). IEEE.

Mecocci, A. (1989). Moving object recognition and classification in external environments. *Signal Processing*, (18): 183–194. doi:10.1016/0165-1684(89)90049-2

Popović, M., & Zeljković, V. (2000). *Moving object extraction from image sequences using edge information*. Novi Sad, Yugoslavia: DOGS.

Rourke, A., Bell, M. G. H., & Hoose, N. (1990). *Road traffic monitoring using image processing*. London: Road Traffic Control.

Skifstad, K., & Jain, R. (1994). Illumination independent change detection for real world image sequences. *Computer Vision Graphics and Image Processing*, (46): 387–399.

Vailaya, A., Figueiredo, M. A. T., Jain, A. K., & Zhang, H.-J. (2001). Image classification for content-based indexing. *IEEE Transactions on Image Processing*, 10(1), 117–130. doi:10.1109/83.892448 PMID:18249602

Wang, Y.-N., Chen, L.-B., & Hu, B.-G. (2002). *Semantic extraction of the building images using support vector machines*. Beijing, China: IEEE.

Zeljkovic, V. (2010). *Illumination independent moving object detection in image sequences*. LAP Lambert Academic Publishing GmbH & Co. KG.

Zeljković, V., Dorado, A., & Izquierdo, E. (2004). Combining a fuzzy rule-based classifier and illumination invariance for improved building detection. *IEEE Transactions on Circuits and Systems for Video Technology*, 14(11), 1277–1280. doi:10.1109/TCSVT.2004.835145

Zeljković, V., Dorado, A., & Izquierdo, E. (2004). *A modified shading model method for building detection*. Lisbon, Portugal: WIAMIS.

Zeljković, V., Dorado, A., Trpovski, Ž., & Izquierdo, E. (2004). *A modified shading model method used for building extraction*. Cacak, Serbia and Montengro: ETRAN.

Zeljković, V., & Dragovic, R. (2004). *Moving object detection in video sequence independent of the scene illumination - Software solution*. Kopaonik, Serbia and Montengro: YU INFO.

Zeljković, V., & Dragovic, R. (2004). *Software solution for moving object detection in video sequence independent of the scene illumination*. Zabljak, Serbia and Montengro: IT.

Zeljkovic, V., Pokrajac, D., Dorado, A., & Izquierdo, E. (2006). *Application of the improved illumination independent moving object detection algorithm on the real video sequence.* Montreux, Switzerland: WIAMIS.

Zeljković, V., & Popović, M. (2000). *Illumination independent moving object extraction from video sequences.* Soko Banja, Yugoslavia: ETRAN.

Zeljković, V., & Popović, M. (2001). *Detection of moving objects in video signal under fast changes of scene illumination.* Niš, Yugoslavia: TELSIKS.

Zeljković, V., & Trpovski, Ž. (2002). *Moving object localization applying change detection.* Novi Bečej, Yugoslavia: DOGS.

Zeljković, V., & Trpovski, Ž. (2004). *Illumination independent moving object detection in real sequence.* Sombor, Serbia and Montengro: DOGS.

Zeljković, V., Trpovski, Ž., & Šenk, V. (2003). *Improved illumination independent moving object detection in real world video sequences.* Zagreb, Croatia: EURASIP. doi:10.1109/VIPMC.2003.1220508

Zeljković, V., Trpovski, Ž., & Šenk, V. (2004). *Improved illumination independent change detection for real world video sequences.* YUJOR.

Chapter 3
Application of Improved Illumination Invariance Algorithm in Building Detection

ABSTRACT

The problem of edge-based classification of natural video sequences containing buildings and captured under changing lighting conditions is addressed. The introduced approach is derived from two empiric observations: In static regions the likelihood of finding features that match the patterns of "buildings" is high because buildings are rigid static objects, and misclassification can be reduced by filtering out image regions changing or deforming in time. These regions may contain objects semantically different to buildings but with a highly similar edge distribution (e.g., high frequency of vertical and horizontal edges). Using these observations, a strategy is devised in which a fuzzy rule-based classification technique is combined with a method for changing region detection in outdoor scenes. The efficiency of the described techniques is implemented and tested with sequences showing changes in the lighting conditions.

1. INTRODUCTION

The classification of "building images," or images in which a substantial part of the scene consists of man-made buildings, is an important problem in image processing. It has applications in several areas of technology including remote sensing, pattern recognition and automatic annotation of video for categorization and retrieval. The work leading to this section has been originated in the latter application. The aim is to automatically classify and annotate shots in video sequences using medium level descriptions or genre. Genre extraction refers to a generic classification and it is an important step toward more specific semantic annotation of video data. According to their type

images and video shots can be cataloged into indoor, outdoor, vegetation, human faces, man-made objects, landscapes, buildings, etc. The focus here is on the classification of video sequences containing buildings and captured under natural outdoor lighting conditions. Existing approaches for classification of building images use a Bayesian framework to exploit image features by perceptual grouping, (Iqbal, 1999), binary Bayesian hierarchical classifiers, (Vailaya, 2001), or perform building semantic extraction using support vector machines (Wang, 2002), which are all described in the literature. The approach presented in this study exploits automatically extracted low-level features and specifically edge descriptors to achieve the classification process.

DOI: 10.4018/978-1-4666-4896-8.ch003

The proposed technique has been inspired by a few empiric observations. In static image regions the likelihood of finding edge features that match the pattern of "buildings" is high because buildings are rigid and static objects. As a consequence, misclassification can be reduced by filtering out image areas changing or deforming in time. These regions can contain objects semantically different to buildings but with a highly similar edge distribution. However, in natural outdoor scenes varying lighting conditions severely influence the accurate detection of changing image areas. To deal with this problem illumination invariant detection of areas changing in time is required. Later in the text, a preprocessing step is described in which an improved filter is used to detect changing or deforming image regions. The results of this filtering process are combined with a fuzzy rule-based classifier aimed at automatic and accurate detection of a building. Selected experimental results are reported.

2. ILLUMINATION INVARIANT DETECTION OF CHANGING IMAGE AREAS

The approach proposed in this section requires a preprocessing phase to filter out image areas changing in time. The results of this initial filtering are fed into the classifier to improve the detection rate and reduce the probability of misclassification. Most existing algorithms for detection of changing regions in video sequences do not consider illumination changes inherent to exterior conditions (Fathy, 1995), (Skifstad, 1989), (Zeljkovic, 2003). For this reason the algorithms frequently fail when applied to natural outdoor scenes. The model presented in this section initially assumes that the background is static. However, this limitation has been released in the actual implementation by assuming that global motion parameters of background objects are known. Motion compensation is applied using conventional approaches. Under this assumption the outcome of the preprocessing technique described below is the same if global motion parameters are used to compensate global changes of rigid background objects.

The preprocessing filter is a modification of the shading model method described in (Zeljkovic, 2003). I. It achieves invariance to extreme illumination changes at pixel level. If single frames in the video sequence are denoted by I, a window W of fixed size and position is superimposed on I and a sliding mask A_i, i=1,...,n which performs scanning of W in each frame.

2.1. Skifstad and Jain's Method

Skifstad and Jain use the ratio of pixel intensities in A_i between two frames to estimate the pixel variance σ_i^2 as follows:

$$\sigma_i^2 = \frac{1}{\text{card}\{A_i\}} \sum_{m \in A_i} \left(\frac{B_m}{C_m} - \mu_{A_i}\right)^2, \; i = 1..n \quad (1)$$

where B_m is a reference frame called *background* which does not contain changing regions, C_m is the current frame; B_m and C_m are pixel intensities within A_i, and μ_{A_i} is the mean of the pixel intensity ratio within A_i.

If $\sigma_i^2 \geq \varepsilon$ the center of A_i is marked as changing region, where ε is a suitable threshold.

Experiments have shown that for fast and large illumination changes this approach fails, i.e. some pixels are falsely assigned to changing regions, as explained in more details earlier in this section.

2.2 The Proposed Method

To overcome this shortcoming an improved and simplified version of the shading model method for changing region detection is applied. This version is invariant to extreme illumination changes at pixel level. The pixel variance $^I\sigma_i^2$ is defined as:

$$'\sigma_i^2 = \frac{1}{\text{card}\{A_i\}} \sum_{m \in A_i} \left(\frac{B_m}{C_m} K_i - \text{median}\{A_i\} \right)^2,$$

$$(2)$$

where $\text{median}\{A_i\}$ estimates median of all pixel belonging to A_i and K_i is an adaptive coefficient to avoid falsely assignment of pixel to changing region for fast and large illumination changes. K_i is defined as

$$K_i = \frac{\sum_{m \in A_i} C_m}{\sum_{m \in A_i} C_{1m}} = \frac{\mu_i}{\mu_1},$$

$$(3)$$

where C_{1m} is pixel intensity for the first frame in the sequence. If $'\sigma_i^2 \geq \varepsilon$ the center of A_i is marked as changing region.

Changing region detection uses I_b to apply a filter on each pixel of current image I_m as follows

$$\hat{I}_m(x,y) = \begin{cases} 255 & \text{if } I_m^b(x,y) = 255 \\ I_m(x,y) & \text{otherwise} \end{cases},$$

$$(4)$$

where $\hat{I}_m$ contains static regions only. In this way, changing regions are located and used to obtain a binary image I_b that contains white and black pixels to represent changing and static regions, respectively.

2.3. Comparative Analysis with Other Methods

While the Skifstad and Jain's shading model method described in more details in the literature (Skifstad, 1989), is robust to illumination changes up to a certain point (roughly 10% of change) the coefficient k_i ensures sensitivity suppression far beyond mentioned level (up to 50%).

The modified shading model method for changing region detection was applied for analyzing video sequences containing about 49 monochrome images of 640×480 pixels with 256 gray levels (8 bits). The video rate is 25 frames/s and a window W of 5×60 pixels.

A sliding window A_i of 3×3 pixels was used for averaging. The larger windows have caused significantly greater execution times with negligible improvement. The optimal threshold was experimentally found to be $\varepsilon = 0.1$.

In order to evaluate the modified method, several experiments with various illumination changes were performed. Selected results are depicted in Figure 1. For example, the dashed line 3 in the second diagram shows a luminance increase from 50% to 100% of the original. The changing region is detected between frame #11 and frame #30. Besides, a comparison with representative methods was performed. The obtained results are summarized in Table 1. Figure 2 illustrates the behavior of the mentioned methods under various illumination conditions for a selected experiment.

Table 1 Comparison between representative methods:

Figure 1. Illumination changes detection (in %). The horizontal axe represents the ordinal number of the processed frame, in the range 1-49. The vertical axe shows the luminance changes.

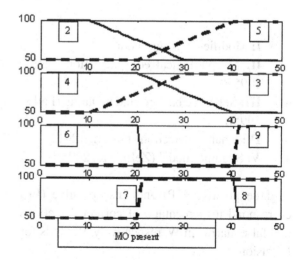

Table 1.

Result[%]	I	II	III	IV	V
TP	100	96.97	100	100	90.90
FP	0	81.25	75	81.25	56.25
P	100	54.41	57.14	55.17	61.77

Figure 2. Results for a selected experiment under different illumination conditions. The horizontal axe represents the ordinal number of the processed frame, in the range 1-49. The vertical axe shows the absolute difference of number of detected changing regions pixels in W between the normal sequence and sequence with the observed luminance change.

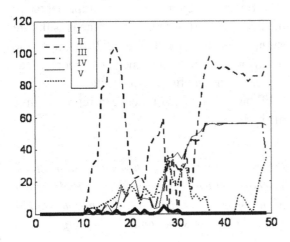

- **I:** Modified shading model.
- **II:** Morphological edge detection (Fathy, 1995.)
- **III:** Selective background updating (Fathy, 1995.)
- **IV:** Change detection (Foresti, 1994.)
- **V:** Shading model (Zeljkovic, 2003.)

True positive (TP) and false positive (FP) correspond to percentage of correct detections and false alarms in W, respectively. P stands for Precision.

The proposed modified method always detected changing regions and there were no false alarms.

3. BUILDING DETECTION PROCESS

3.1. Building Image Classification

Edge-based building image classification can be found in the literature mentioned in the references. This work addresses the problem of classification of low level features extracted from video sequences for detecting and classifying building images.

Let $x = (x_{11}, x_{12}, ..., x_{1N}, x_{2N}, ..., x_{MN})$ be an image or video frame, $f = \{f^{(1)}, ..., f^{(n)}\}$ be feature sets where f is a function of the image x, $E^t = (e_1^t, ..., e_5^t)$ be a pattern extracted from a feature vector $f^{(t)}$, and $Y = \{B, NB\}$ be a class set (B: Building, NB: Non Building). The building image classification problem is stated as learn a function

$$g(x) = E^t \mapsto Y, \qquad (5)$$

where Y are symbols identifying classes and representing semantic interpretations of pattern E^t. $g(x)$ can be decomposed into K single-class specialized classifiers

$$g_j(x) = E^t \mapsto y_j, \ 1 \leq j \leq K \qquad (6)$$

Subsequently, a fuzzy model is extracted from feature set $f^{(t)}$ in order to approximate each function $g_j(x)$ by a set $R_j = \{{}'R_{j1}, ..., R_{jc}\}$ of C if-then rules which has the following structure:

$$^w R_{jk}: \text{If } e_i^t \text{ is } A_i^k \text{ then } Y \text{ is } y_j \qquad (7)$$

e_i^t is associated with a specific type of edge and A_i^k is a linguistic label used to transform values from a continuous to a discrete domain. Therefore, $g_j(x)$ is summarized by a rule base R as follows:

$$g(x) \approx R = \bigvee_{j=1,k=1}^{M,C} {}^w R_{jk} \qquad (8)$$

where $w \in [0, 1]$ is the weight of rule R_{jk}.

After several experiments, it was identified that most of the misclassifications of building images in real-world videos were due to objects with a similar edge distribution of buildings but semantically different. Most of them were moving non-rigid objects. Therefore, the technique was improved by integrating a pre-processing method to detect changing regions.

3.2. Classification and Detection Process

The building image classifier uses a set of if-then rules and a fuzzy reasoning method. The rules have a number of antecedents and a consequent according to Equation (7).

The fuzzy reasoning method consists of three stages:

1. The Fuzzification stage transforms feature values from a continuous to a discrete domain using membership functions.
2. The Inference stage combines fuzzy sets and uses fuzzy rules to determine the class for these features. This combination requires a T-Norm operator. The importance of the rules is adjusted assigning weights to each one. If a class appears in more than one rule a T-Conorm operator is required.
3. Finally, in the Defuzzification stage the result is transformed from fuzzy to real domain.

Figure 3 summarizes the whole building classification and detection process.

Figure 4 depicts the building image classification and detection process. The video frame is partitioned into 16 sub-images which are classified using the fuzzy classification process mentioned above. According to the number of sub-images classified as building, the whole image is or is not classified as "Building".

3.3. Improved Building Detection

The process results are improved using a pre-processing step to filter, select and extract suitable low level features. Changing regions are not considered to avoid misclassification as is shown in Figure 5.

Figure 3. Classification and detection process

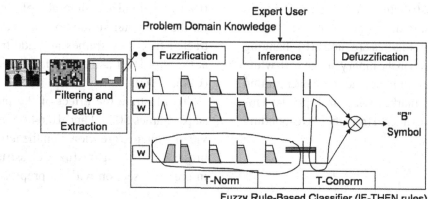

Figure 4. Building Image classification and detection process

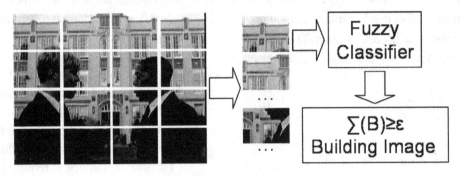

Figure 5. Improved building image classification and detection process

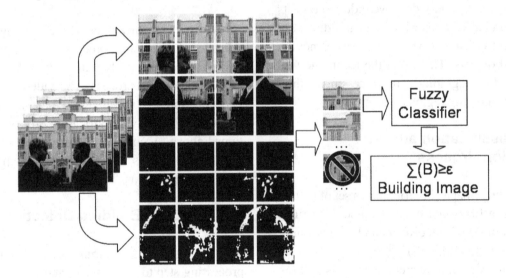

As an example, frames 50389 and 10647 showed in Figures 6(a) and 7(a), respectively, are classified as "building image". Looking at Figures 6(b) and 7(b) that represent edge histograms of sub-images contributing to classification results have similar distribution. This shortcoming is sorted out by using the proposed method.

As is shown in Figures 8(a) and 8(b) changing regions are marked in the binary image with white pixels and the rest of it, i.e. the static background or foreground is marked with black pixels. This information was extracted from the corresponding video sequences.

4. EXPERIMENTAL RESULTS

To validate the introduced approach, several experiments were conducted using the video test corpus of the TRECVID forum. Over 3000 frames from a set of videos randomly selected were used for the computer simulations. Features were extracted from key frames and additional frames at the shot level using an edge-based descriptor (Choi, 2002).

To illustrate the effect of the preprocessing steps, frames 50,389 and 10,647 of a TRECVID video sequence are shown on the left side of Figures 6 and 7. Using the fuzzy classifier described in previous section without preprocessing, both

Figure 6. Example of building image is a) the video frame 50389; b) the edge histogram of sub-image at row 1 and column 3

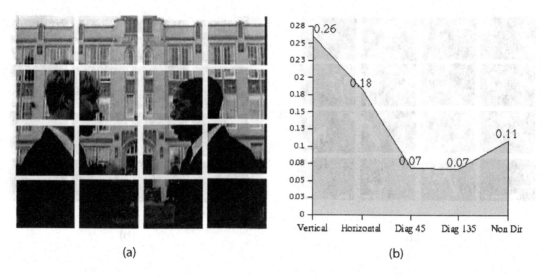

(a) (b)

Figure 7. Example of building misclassification is a) the video frame 50389; b) the edge histogram of sub-image at row 4 and column 3

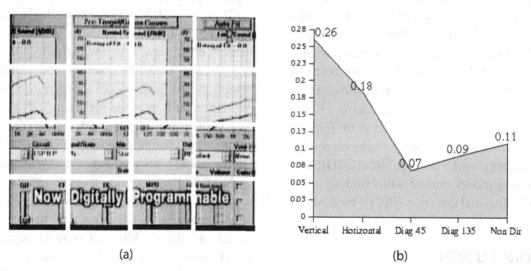

(a) (b)

frames were classified as "building image." Clearly, the picture in Figure 7 was misclassified. The images on the right of Figures 6 and 7 display the distribution of edge histograms of sub-images contributing to the classification result. It can be observed that these sub-images are very similar. As a consequence it becomes almost impossible to assign the right genre to the second image without using additional information.

The shortcoming illustrated in Figures 6 and 7 can be overcome by applying the proposed preprocessing to filter out moving and deformable objects in the scene. Figure 8 shows detected changing regions in these images. In this representation moving image regions are displayed with white while the static areas are marked with black pixels.

Figure 8. Changing region detection using shading model method. Figure a and b depict binary images for video frames 50389 and 10647, respectively

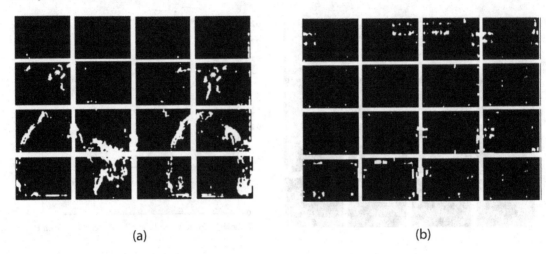

(a)   (b)

Building image classification was applied to over 3000 frames from a set of videos randomly selected from TRECVID video repository. Features were extracted from key- and additional- frames at the shot level using an edge-based descriptor (Choi, 2002). A statistical performance evaluation based on the amount of imagery correctly classified and marked as True Positive, TP or misclassified, marked as False Positive, FP, was conducted. The results are shown in Table 2. Precision is significantly improved by combining changing region detection algorithm (CRD) based on shading model method with building image classification and detection (BICD) method.

5. CONCLUSION

A technique for improving classification of building images is presented. It exploits additional information extracted from a sequence of images and applies a fast, simple and effective shading model method for detecting changing regions.

The modified shading model method has been tested on real video sequences under various lighting conditions. It is insensitive to illumination changes, while the other methods seriously deteriorate. It always succeeds to detect changing regions under luminance variation.

By filtering out features extracted from pixels belonging to changing regions, misclassification is reduced and precision is significantly increased.

Next chapter describes integrated multimedia supported intelligent video surveillance aimed to alleviate the disadvantages of the existing video-surveillance kits and provide advanced search, notification, visualization and alarming functionality through integration of artificial intelligence, motion detection and tracking technology, multimedia databases and Internet/cell phone connectivity. The effectiveness and feasibility of the proposed concept is proven through experimental results on a real-life video sequence. The resistance of the improved moving objects detection algorithm to various types of additive and multiplicative noise is discussed as well. The proposed method is evaluated on PETS repository

Table 2. Precision results (P) [%]

Method	TP	FP	P
EBIC	77.70	21.96	77.97
BICD+CRD	89.54	10.12	89.84

videos and substantial noise robustness is demonstrated. Performance of moving objects detection algorithm on infrared videos is also illustrated and evaluated on monochrome and multispectral IR videos. A technique that improves precision in classification results using information extracted from video features and combines fuzzy rule-based classification with a method for changing region detection in outdoor environment, which is invariant to extreme illumination changes and severe weather conditions is introduced in the second chapter as well.

REFERENCES

Corrall, D. (1991). *VIEW: Computer vision for surveillance applications*. London: IEE.

Dragovic, R., & Zeljković, V. (2004). *Video conferences - The possibilities of application in judiciary*. Kopaonik, Serbia and Montengro: YU INFO.

Fathy, M., & Siyal, M. Y. (1995). An image detection technique based on morphological edge detection and background differencing for real-time traffic analysis. *Pattern Recognition Letters*, (16): 1321–1330. doi:10.1016/0167-8655(95)00081-X

Foresti, G. L. (1998). A real-time system for video surveillance of unattended outdoor environments. *IEEE Transactions on Circuits and Systems for Video Technology*, 8(6), 697–704. doi:10.1109/76.728411

Foresti, G. L., & Regazzoni, C. S. (1994). A change detection method for multiple object localization in real scenes. In *Proceedings of IEEE Conference*, (pp. 984-987). IEEE.

Inigo, R. M. (1989). Application of machine vision to traffic monitoring and control. *IEEE Transactions on Vehicular Technology*, 38(3), 112–122. doi:10.1109/25.45464

Iqbal, Q., & Aggarwal, J. K. (1999). Applying perceptual grouping to content-based image retrieval: Building image. In *Proceedings of IEEE Int'l Conf. on Computer Vision and Pattern Recognition* (pp. 42-48). IEEE.

Mecocci, A. (1989). Moving object recognition and classification in external environments. *Signal Processing*, (18): 183–194. doi:10.1016/0165-1684(89)90049-2

Popović, M., & Zeljković, V. (2000). *Moving object extraction from image sequences using edge information*. Novi Sad, Yugoslavia: DOGS.

Rourke, A., Bell, M. G. H., & Hoose, N. (1990). *Road traffic monitoring using image processing*. London: Road Traffic Control.

Skifstad, K., & Jain, R. (1994). Illumination independent change detection for real world image sequences. *Computer Vision Graphics and Image Processing*, (46): 387–399.

Vailaya, A., Figueiredo, M. A. T., Jain, A. K., & Zhang, H.-J. (2001). Image classification for content-based indexing. *IEEE Transactions on Image Processing*, 10(1), 117–130. doi:10.1109/83.892448 PMID:18249602

Wang, Y.-N., Chen, L.-B., & Hu, B.-G. (2002). *Semantic extraction of the building images using support vector machines*. Beijing, China: IEEE.

Zeljkovic, V. (2010). *Illumination independent moving object detection in image sequences*. LAP Lambert Academic Publishing GmbH & Co. KG.

Zeljković, V., Dorado, A., & Izquierdo, E. (2004). Combining a fuzzy rule-based classifier and illumination invariance for improved building detection. *IEEE Transactions on Circuits and Systems for Video Technology*, 14(11), 1277–1280. doi:10.1109/TCSVT.2004.835145

Zeljković, V., Dorado, A., & Izquierdo, E. (2004). *A modified shading model method for building detection*. Lisbon, Portugal: WIAMIS.

Zeljković, V., Dorado, A., Trpovski, Ž., & Izquierdo, E. (2004). *A modified shading model method used for building extraction*. Cacak, Serbia and Montengro: ETRAN.

Zeljković, V., & Dragovic, R. (2004). *Moving object detection in video sequence independent of the scene illumination - Software solution*. Kopaonik, Serbia and Montengro: YU INFO.

Zeljković, V., & Dragovic, R. (2004). *Software solution for moving object detection in video sequence independent of the scene illumination*. Zabljak, Serbia and Montengro: IT.

Zeljkovic, V., Pokrajac, D., Dorado, A., & Izquierdo, E. (2006). *Application of the improved illumination independent moving object detection algorithm on the real video sequence*. Montreux, Switzerland: WIAMIS.

Zeljković, V., & Popović, M. (2000). *Illumination independent moving object extraction from video sequences*. Soko Banja, Yugoslavia: ETRAN.

Zeljković, V., & Popović, M. (2001). *Detection of moving objects in video signal under fast changes of scene illumination. Niš, Yugoslavia: TELSIKS*.

Zeljković, V., & Trpovski, Ž. (2002). *Moving object localization applying change detection*. Novi Bečej, Yugoslavia: DOGS.

Zeljković, V., & Trpovski, Ž. (2004). *Illumination independent moving object detection in real sequence*. Sombor, Serbia and Montengro: DOGS.

Zeljković, V., Trpovski, Ž., & Šenk, V. (2003). *Improved illumination independent moving object detection in real world video sequences*. Zagreb, Croatia: EURASIP. doi:10.1109/VIPMC.2003.1220508

Zeljković, V., Trpovski, Ž., & Šenk, V. (2004). *Improved illumination independent change detection for real world video sequences*. YUJOR.

Section 2
Moving Object Detection Algorithms and its Applications under Various Conditions

An integrated multimedia supported intelligent video surveillance system is proposed. The system alleviates the disadvantages of the existing video-surveillance kits and provides advanced search, notification, visualization, and alarming functionality through integration of artificial intelligence, motion detection and tracking technology, multimedia databases, and Internet/cell phone connectivity.

The resistance of the improved moving objects detection algorithm to various types of additive and multiplicative noise is discussed as well. The algorithm's first phase contains the noise suppression filter based on spatiotemporal blocks including dimensionality reduction technique for a compact scalar representation of each block, and the second phase consists of the moving object detection algorithm resistant to illumination changes that detects and tracks the moving objects.

Performance of the moving objects detection algorithm on infrared videos is discussed. The algorithm has two phases that comprise the noise suppression filter based on spatiotemporal blocks including dimensionality reduction technique and the illumination changes resistant moving object detection algorithm that tracks the moving objects.

A technique that improves precision in classification results using information extracted from video features is introduced. It combines fuzzy rule-based classification with a method for changing region detection in outdoor environment, which is invariant to extreme illumination changes and severe weather conditions.

Chapter 4
Multimedia Supported Intelligent Video Surveillance System

ABSTRACT

An integrated multimedia supported intelligent video surveillance system is proposed. The system alleviates the disadvantages of the existing video-surveillance kits and provides advanced search, notification, visualization, and alarming functionality through integration of artificial intelligence, motion detection and tracking technology, multimedia databases, and Internet/cell phone connectivity. The effectiveness and feasibility of the proposed concept is proven through experimental results on a real-life video sequence.

1. INTRODUCTION

Nowadays, the expansion of inexpensive video surveillance technology is present on the market, such as wireless digital cameras, motion sensors, etc. Therefore, the equipment, once having dominated corporate security market, becomes available to average homeowners. Typical systems, currently installed at a homeowner's premise, consist of one or several analog or digital cameras, video tape recorder and a monitor (Remagnino, 2002), (Fathy, 1995), (Foresti, 1994). If properly installed, such systems can provide customers with forensic evidence of potential intrusions into property and also may serve as deterrent against potential intruder. However, such systems also have significant drawbacks:

1. The surveillance systems have limited or no interaction with other media, including World-Wide Web and e-mail.
2. The systems do not have any artificial intelligence capable of analyzing the recorded scene.
3. The video storage is bulky and may require an operator to manipulate tapes.
4. Long periods of no activity are unnecessary recorded and stored.
5. Search of sequential storage media is difficult and cannot be automatic.

Recent progress in video and image processing has provided capability of performing intelligent video signal analysis, that includes scene analysis, motion detection, detection of events and tracking. Such systems have wide application and huge spectra of use (e.g., traffic regulation, securing objects in interior or exterior).

DOI: 10.4018/978-1-4666-4896-8.ch004

Current developments in object-relational and multimedia database technology can provide efficient linkage between textual and non-textual (image) information. Hence, contextual meaning of recorded visual information could be accomplished by properly coupling an intelligent video-surveillance system with such a database. On the other hand, pattern matching techniques make possible to couple an acquired image with those stored in the database, and thus provide identification of visitors.

Contemporary communication technologies, such as DSL/Cable permanent Internet links, and global mobile and satellite phone networks, make possible instant connectivity and relatively wide bandwidth for transmitting multimedia between homes and remote customers (homeowners). Information can be delivered to the remote user via standardized and universally available interface such as World Wide Web and e-mail.

An integrated multimedia supported intelligent video surveillance system aimed to alleviate the disadvantages of the current video-surveillance devices is described in this chapter. The proposed system encompasses available cutting-edge technologies and is based on recent advances in motion detection and tracking. At the same time, the system consists of inexpensive and easily accessible off-shelf hardware and is easy to implement, produce and maintain. The system configuration emphasizing the motion detection subsystem is discussed and the proof of proposed concept is provided on experimental video.

2. SYSTEM CONFIGURATION

2.1 Video Surveillance System Design Requirements

A video surveillance system design requires making decisions that demand knowledge of basic options and the rationale for selecting from different ones available on the market. One needs to face making the following key decisions:

1. Camera Types
2. Camera Connection To Video Management System
3. Video Management System Types
4. Storage Type
5. Video Analytics Type
6. Surveillance Video Display

Camera Types

Cameras represent the main input into the video surveillance system and the following is relevant to them:

1. **Physical position of used cameras:** Cameras have to be placed in critical areas in order to record relevant video. The critical places for proper camera placement are entrances, exits, hallway, driveways, etc in surveiled areas where there is a high density of people or vehicles. Also, camera placement can be related to the specific objects or areas that need security such as safes, merchandise areas, cash registers, parking spots, lobbies, banks, etc. Placing cameras at critical and adequate points is a very cost-effective way to document people and vehicles entering and exiting certain facility.

2. **The camera type being used:**
   a. A camera can be fixed when it is recording only one specific view or it can be PTZ camera that is moving left and right which is called panning, moving up and down which is called tilting and closer and farther away called zooming. PTZ cameras are generally used to cover wider fields of views. Most cameras used in video surveillance are fixed because they cost five to eight times less than PTZ cameras.

b. Color cameras are used during day time and highly lighted areas. During night time and obscure and poorly illuminated areas infrared or thermal cameras are used that produce black and white images. Thermal cameras are used under the conditions of complete light absence when they produce only contours of objects.

c. Cameras can be standard definition or high definition cameras that provide up to 16 MP resolutions.

d. There are analog and IP cameras. IP cameras digitize the video inside the camera and analog cameras', used as surveillance cameras, recordings are digitized on computers. Megapixel resolution is only provided by IP cameras. Video surveillance systems usually mix and match a number of different camera types.

Camera Connection to Video Management System

The video captured by cameras has to be transferred to the module of the video surveillance system called video management system which is recording and managing access to that video. There are two types of connectivity:

1. Video can be transmitted over the computer network IP or it can be sent as analog video. Both IP cameras and analog cameras can be transmitted over the computer network where IP cameras can connect directly to an IP network unlike analog ones that cannot directly connect to an IP network. In the case of analog cameras an encoder has to be installed in order to transmit analog video over IP. The encoder has an input for an analog camera video feed and outputs a digital stream for transmission over an IP network.

2. Depending whether IP or analog video camera is being used, the captured video can be sent over cables or though the air. Cables is generally the cheapest and most reliable way of sending video but, wireless is an important option for transmitting video as positioning wires can be cost-demanding for certain applications such as parking lots, fence lines, remote buildings, etc.

Video Management System

Video management systems are responsible for accepting the video captured by cameras, storing the video and managing video distribution to various viewers. Most video surveillance systems use one of four different video management systems:

1. Digital Video Recorder DVR is a security system device that records the video from surveillance cameras on a hard disk. The frame rate can be switched from real time to time lapse in order to save disk space. Digital recorders are more flexible than earlier analog VHS tape systems and the video can be easily transmitted over a computer network. Digital Video Recorders combine software, hardware and video storage. They only accept analog camera feeds and support remote viewing over the Internet.

2. HDVRs are hybrid Digital Video Recorders that support IP cameras. They have all the functionality of a Digital Video Recorder listed above plus they add support for IP and megapixel cameras.

3. Network Video Recorder NVR is a computer that records video transmitted over the network from multiple digital CCTV surveillance cameras. It only supports IP cameras. To support analog cameras with an NVR, an encoder must be used.

4. IP Video Surveillance Software is a software application that does not come with any hardware or storage. The user must load

and set up the PC/Server for the software which provides much greater freedom and potentially lower cost but at the same time it comes with significant more complexity and time necessary to set up and optimize the system. IP Video Surveillance Software is the most frequent choice for video systems that contain very large camera counts like hundreds or more.

Storage

Storage of the captured surveillance video is very important part of the video surveillance system. It is used for later retrieval and review of the surveillance video. The storage duration is determined by the cost of storage and the security threats specific for the application of the video surveillance system being used. For example, banks have great need for longer term storage because a major threat to it is the report of fraudulent investigations which are often reported 60 or 90 days after the incident. Unlike casinos that usually use much shorter storage duration for a few weeks because they know about potential issues right away.

Storage permanently holds digital data, until it is purposely erased. It is a repository that retains its content without power. Storage mostly means magnetic disks, solid state disks and USB drives. The term may also refer to magnetic tapes and optical discs like CDs, DVDs, etc.

Even though storage price is always decreasing, video surveillance system demands for amount of storage are increasing. Various techniques have been developed to optimize the use of storage because of its significant cost. There are three fundamental types of storage:

1. Internal Storage represents the hard drives that are built inside of a digital video recorder, network video recorder or server. It is the cheapest storage but tends to be less reliable and scalable. It is used the most frequently in video surveillance systems and can provide total storage of 2TB to 4TB.

2. Directly Attached Storage represents hard drives located outside of the digital video recorder, network video recorder or server. It is more expensive but has greater scalability, flexibility and redundancy.

3. Storage Clusters are IP based storage places specialized in storing video streaming from large number of cameras. They provide efficient, flexible and scalable storage.

Video Analytics

Video analytics addressed in this chapter encompasses the following tasks:

1. **Optimize Storage:** Storage optimization is realized based on the motion detection which is approached her. If the motion or moving object is detected in the observed scene the video management system can decide to store video or if it is not present in the scene not to store video or to store video at a lower frame rate or resolution. Cameras placed in hallways, staircases, buildings when they are closed, etc. capture long periods of inactivity. Motion analytics application can reduce storage consumption by 60% to 80% relative to continuous recording.

2. **Identify Threatening Events:** Video analytics used to identify threatening events is what is proposed in this chapter. Typical examples of threatening events identification are perimeter violation, abandoned objects detection, people counting and license plate recognition. The goal of these types of video analytics is to pro-actively and automatically identify security incidents, to alert the operator and to stop them while being in progress.

Viewing Video

Surveillance video captured by video surveillance systems is ultimately viewed by human beings, the most commonly used for historical investigations. Some surveillance video is viewed online continuously, generally in shops in order to catch shoplifters and in public surveillance to identify criminal threats. Some surveillance video is viewed online occasionally by the owner of the apartment or a condo who has a camera placed above her/his entrance door and connected through Internet to her/his PC or her/his cell phone, as proposed later in the text. There are four different ways for video viewing:

1. Local Viewing directly from the digital video recorder, the network video recorder or servers is ideal for monitoring small facilities on site most commonly used in retailers, banks and small businesses.
2. Remote PC Viewing through standard remote PCs to view live and recorded video using an installed application, powerful web viewing or only using a web browser.
3. Mobile Viewing allows immediate check of the captured surveillance video. It has

great potential in video surveillance systems. Mobile clients exist on the market for at least 5 years, but there are its implementation challenges with PDAs/phones. The introduction of the Apple iPhone has renewed interest and optimism related to mobile viewing.

4. Video Wall Viewing is typically used in large security operation centers that have hundreds or thousands of cameras under their jurisdiction. Video walls provide very large screens so that a group of people can simultaneously watch captured videos from numerous cameras. Video walls generally have abilities to switch between various video streams and to automatically display videos from locations where alarms have been triggered.

2.2 Proposed System Configuration

An intelligent motion-detection based multimedia supported video-surveillance system is proposed. The system takes advantage of the existing multimedia technologies and is enhanced with the proposed intelligent motion detection techniques. It is intended to protect apartments in apartment

Figure 1. The architecture of the proposed motion detection based multimedia supported intelligent video surveillance system

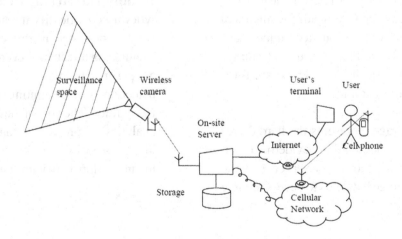

buildings or condos, but also can be extended to provide protection of private houses.

The system consists of the following parts shown in Figure 1:

1. Static wireless CCD RGB/IR camera.
2. Computational server with image storage and retrieval capabilities and DSL/cable modem permanent Internet connectivity.

The wireless camera can be wall or door-mounted and is positioned such that the surveillance space (the field of view) covers the area in front of the main entrance of a customer's apartment. The camera sends its signal through IEEE 802.11 wireless link to a computational server. The server gets real-time data from the camera, performs video analysis and motion detection, stores and identifies pictures of persons who appeared at the door and informs the customer (the owner of the apartment being under surveillance) about the events on his or her entrance door. The system sends two kinds of messages to the customer:

1. Information and alarm through permanent Internet connection (to the customer's terminal.)

2. Information and alarm through cell phone network (to a customer's cell phone.)

The essence of the system is an algorithm that determines the character of activities of a person in front of the door. The following scheme depicted in Figure 2 is proposed. When the moving object first time appears at the door (Event: moving object), the system identifies the movement and starts the timer. The system continues to trace the moving objects and records if and when the motion stops. At the particular moment, the system takes a snapshot (captures the digital photo) of the (now static) object and stores it at the server. When the moving object ultimately leaves the scene, the timer stops and the system records the elapsed time. If the elapsed time is larger than a pre-specified threshold, the system considers this as unusual situation (potential intruder or suspicious person at the door) and sends alarm to the customer.

As specified at Figure 3, the customer will be immediately called on his/her cell phone and will be able to assess the situation by observing the real-time video transmission from the entrance on a World Wide Web through the Internet. If the elapsed time is smaller than the threshold, the system will permanently store the photo of the

Figure 2. Algorithm for the characterization of moving object activities

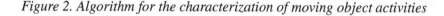
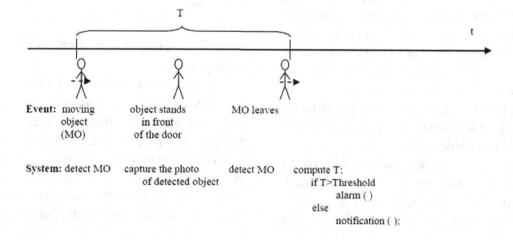

Figure 3. The system alarm and notification activities

```
notification ( )
    store photo;
    identify the person;
    notify the user;

alarm ( );
    ring cell phone;
    send on line video on the web;
```

potential guest, retrieve the identity of the person by comparing the person's picture with the pre-stored pictures from the database kept at the server, and notify the customer about the guest's identity. The notification can be performed by sending e-mail with day and time of visit and person's photo and related database records, using Internet or cell phone. Since the information of all visitors and potential intruders is stored at the server, the customer is able to off-line search for the people who visited his/her home, and, if desired, perform advanced queries about frequency of visit, usual days of person's visits, etc.

3. MOVING OBJECT DETECTION METHODS

To determine the existence and a character of motion at the scene, it is necessary to go beyond standard motion detection sensors (e.g., based on IR or ultrasound detection). Namely, the goal is not only to detect the existence of the object but also its size, relative position on the scene, etc. Also, the existence of the camera (that is also here to provide video feed for evidence and archival) makes the video signal a natural candidate for advanced motion detection.

To perform moving objects detection two novel and complementary approaches are suggested. The first method is pixel-based and resistant to significant and sudden illumination changes

(Zeljkovic, 2004). The second method is block-wise and resistant to high-intensity noise of various statistics (Pokrajac, 2003). The existence of the object, its size, relative position on the scene, etc are detected.

3.1 Pixel-Based Detection

Consider image sequence I consisting of N video frames. The sliding mask A_i is applied on every frame.

The pixel variance is calculated in order to estimate the potential movement in the observed area, as follows:

$$\sigma_i^2 = \frac{1}{card\{A_i\}} \sum_{m \in A_i} \left(\frac{B_m}{C_m} K_i - median\{A_i\} \right)^2,$$

(1)

where pixel intensities within mask A_i are denoted with B_m for a reference - background frame that does not contain changing regions and with C_m for a current frame (where moving objects are being identified). The estimated mean of the pixel intensity ratio within A_i is denoted with μ_{A_i}

The illumination compensation coefficient is defined as:

$$K_i = \frac{\sum_{m \in A_i} C_m}{\sum_{m \in A_i} C_{1m}} = \frac{\mu_i}{\mu_1},$$

(2)

where C_{1m} is pixel intensity for the first frame in the sequence.

The algorithm performs the analysis in time and space domains simultaneously, contributing to its resistance to the illumination changes and reducing the false detection, i.e. artifacts.

Estimated pixel variance values are averaged for three successive pairs of frames and the calculated average value is thresholded to determine the presence of moving objects. This represents temporal aspect of analysis. The ratio of pixel intensities in A_i between two frames is used to estimate the pixel variance $^1\sigma_i^2$ for the following three pairs of successive frames: frames i-3 and i-2, i-2 and i-1 and i-1 and i, where i is the current frame. Thus, three pixel variances for three successive and corresponding variance pairs $^1\sigma_{i-2}^2$, $^1\sigma_{i-1}^2$ and $^1\sigma_i^2$ are obtained. Subsequently, the average value of these three variances is computed as follows:

$$^1\sigma_{mean}^2 = (^1\sigma_{i-2}^2 + {}^1\sigma_{i-1}^2 + {}^1\sigma_i^2) / 3, \qquad (3)$$

After that, the mean value is subtracted from the pixel variance of the current and previous frame:

$$^1\sigma_{i'}^2 = {}^1\sigma_i^2 - {}^1\sigma_{mean}^2, \qquad (4)$$

If $^1\sigma_{i'}^2 \geq \varepsilon$ (a suitable threshold), the center of A_i is marked as changing region, i.e. as a moving object.

The proposed algorithm performs analysis in three dimensions, two spatial and one temporal. The time analysis, additionally to space analysis, helps with correct moving object detection and augments the precision of the algorithm. It should be pointed out, as well, that this algorithm works with local intensity and does not require color information. Hence, the method can easily be used for gray movies, i.e. BW movies or infra red monochromatic movies.

3.2 Block-Wise Detection

The proposed block-oriented technique (Pokrajac, 2003) for moving object detection consists of two major phases:

1.   Dimensionality reduction by spatiotemporal blocks.

2.   Detection of moving blocks using incremental learning of Gaussian distributions and outlier detection.

Given video is treated as three-dimensional (3D) array of gray pixels $p_{i,j,z}$, $i=1,\ldots,X$; $j=1,\ldots,Y$; $z=1,\ldots,Z$ with two spatial dimensions X, Y and one temporal dimension Z. Spatiotemporal (3D) blocks are used, represented by N-dimensional vectors $\mathbf{b}_{I,J,t}$, where a block spans $(2T+1)$ frames and contains N_{BLOCK} pixels in each spatial direction per frame ($N=(2T+1)\times N_{BLOCK}\times N_{BLOCK}$). To reduce dimensionality of $\mathbf{b}_{I,J,t}$ while preserving information to the maximal possible extent, principal component analysis is used. The resulting transformed block vectors $\mathbf{b}_{I,J,t}^*$ provide a joint representation of texture and motion patterns in videos.

For principal component analysis, sample mean and covariance matrix are estimated of representative sample of block vectors corresponding to the considered types of movies and use the first $N'=3$ s eigenvectors of the covariance matrix $\mathbf{S}$ (corresponding to the largest eigenvalues) to create the $N\times N'$ projection matrix used for dimensionality reduction.

The proposed algorithm for detection of moving blocks is a variant of the incremental EM algorithm for estimating the Gaussian mixtures extended by additional mechanism for detecting blocks corresponding to moving objects. The mixture consists of K components, and each component is specified by its estimated mean vector, a diagonal covariance matrix and a distributional prior. The squared Mahalanobis distances are computed of the block vector with respect to the distribution components the mixture estimated for all blocks that appeared at the same position at previous time instants. If the minimal squared distance is above a pre-specified threshold, the block is considered as outlier and labeled as 'moving'. Subsequently, the distribution component that has the smallest estimated prior probability at the moment is replaced by a new Gaussian

Figure 4. Frame 139 from the processed sequence indicating the window for motion detection

distribution. If the minimal squared Mahalanobis distance to one of distribution is small, the block still may belong to a moving object. Therefore, the second criterion for moving blocks detection is employed. First, it is checked whether an outlier has been detected within H frames preceding the current frame at the considered block position. If there were no outliers within the H previous frames, the block at the current frame is labeled as background. Otherwise, the block is labeled as moving if the closest distributional component has relatively large variance but small prior probability.

Since one of design goals of the proposed system is to reduce false alarm error rate, e.g., people ring on other doors, the following heuristics is introduced. The detected moving object needs to be large enough and has to fit into the window which represents the region of the scene where the moving object is expected to appear, in order to start the timer. See Figure 4 as an example.

4. EXPERIMENTAL RESULTS

The proposed system is demonstrated on the experimental video that accurately corresponds to a real- life situation. The video consists of 348 PAL video frames consisting of 576*768 RGB pixels per frame, at 25 frames per second taken from commercial low-cost camera. The video sequence consists of the following scenes taken indoors:

1. A person enters the field of view from left.
2. A person rings on the door twice.
3. A person leaves back to the left.

The described illumination resistant pixel based algorithm for moving object detection is applied on the described color video. Figure 5 depicts characteristic frames of the analyzed video sequence in correspondence to the motion statistics values calculated for the window [100, 300; 250, 450] indicated in Figure 4.

The subject enters the window at the frame 40 which corresponds to immediate increase of the computed statistics. The system successfully detects the presence of the moving object and starts the timer. The next significant instant, as denoted on the diagram, is the frame 78 when the person straightens her head and rings the bell. This corresponds to glitch on the motion statistics. On the frame 157, as detected by the algorithm, the subject moves the head and, at the frame 203, rings the bell again, which ends at the frame 245. Finally, after getting no answer, person moves the head again (the frame 278) and then leaves the scene (as seen on the frame 305 where the motion in the window is substantial). Person moves out of the spatial window at the frame 325 (when the timer is stopped) and leaves the scene at the frame 344.

The elapsed time between the person's appearance and leaving the window was 11.40s (from the 40th to the 325th frame at 25fps). Since the time was below the threshold that is preset to be 1 min = 60 s, the system sent notification to the customer.

The illustration of the proposed system is given in the following Figures 6(a)-(c). The figures show binary images obtained applying the pixel-based algorithm where pixels identified as belonging

Figure 5. Characteristic frames of an experimental surveillance video with corresponding events on a measured motion statistics in the window shown in Figure 4

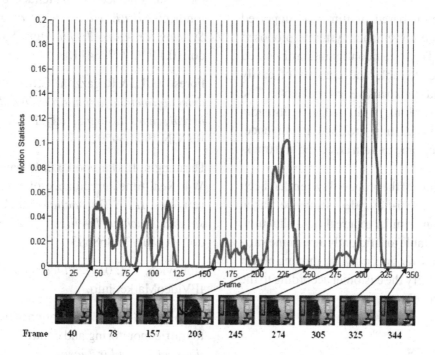

Figure 6. The (a) 40ᵗʰ; (b) 78ᵗʰ and (c) 305th frame of analyzed video sequence

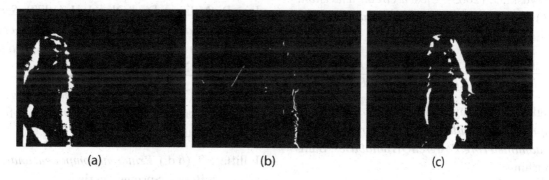

to the moving object are marked as white. Figure 6 a) shows the subject entering the scene which represents the first frame when subject appears in the analyzed window. As it can be seen, the edges of the moving object are visible. The precision and sensitivity of the proposed algorithm is obvious from the fact that the motion of the right hand was detected as well.

The frame 78 when person is straightening her hand and is ringing the first time is characterized by relatively smooth motion. Indeed, Figure 6(b) indicates slight motion of body and the edge of the person's right arm.

The frame 305 illustrates the person as leaving the scene and the video. The amplitude of motion is the highest as indicated in the binary image.

4. CONCLUSION

Motion detection based multimedia supported intelligent video surveillance system is proposed in this section. The system configuration discussed here is simple, feasible and consists of easily accessible and inexpensive components. The system itself exploits cutting-edge multimedia technologies integrating artificial intelligence, pattern matching and motion detection and tracking algorithms.

The feasibility of the proposed system has been illustrated on a real-life video sequence, taken under conditions similar to a real field situation. The system was able to efficiently determine various phases of the motion, track the moving object (person) and notify the customer according to the embedded algorithm.

REFERENCES

Cieszynski, J. (2003). *Closed circuit television: CCTV installation, maintenance and operation* (2nd Ed.). Newnes.

Corrall, D. (n.d.). *VIEW: Computer vision for surveillance applications*. London. *IEE*.

Douglas, K., & Douglas, S. (2003). *PostgreSQL-A comprehensive guide to building, programming and administering PostgreSQL databases*. Sams Publishing.

Duda, R., Hart, P., & Stork, D. (2001). *Pattern classification* (2nd ed.). Hoboken, NJ: John Wiley & Sons.

Dunckley, L. (2003). *Multimedia databases: An object-relational approach*. Pearson Education.

Fathy, M., & Siyal, M. Y. (1995). An image detection technique based on morphological edge detection and background differencing for real-time traffic analysis. *Pattern Recognition Letters*, (16): 1321–1330. doi:10.1016/0167-8655(95)00081-X

Foresti, G. L. (1998). A real-time system for video surveillance of unattended outdoor environments. *IEEE Transactions on Circuits and Systems for Video Technology*, 8(6), 697–704. doi:10.1109/76.728411

Foresti, G. L., & Regazzoni, C. S. (1994). *A change detection method for multiple object localizations in real scenes*. Bologna, Italy: IEEE. doi:10.1109/IECON.1994.397923

Haritaoglu, I., Harwood, D., & Davis, L. (2000). W4: Real-time surveillance of people and their activities. *IEEE Transactions on Pattern Analysis and Machine Intelligence*, 22(8), 809–830. doi:10.1109/34.868683

Honovich, J. (2011). *Video surveillance book*. IPVideoMarket.jnfo.

Inigo, R. M. (1989). Application of machine vision to traffic monitoring and control. *IEEE Transactions on Vehicular Technology*, 38(3), 112–122. doi:10.1109/25.45464

Jain, R., Militzer, D., & Nagel, H. (1977). *Separating nonstationary from stationary scene components in a sequence of real world TV images*. Cambridge, MA: IJCAI.

Jolliffe, I. T. (2002). *Principal component analysis* (2nd Ed.). Springer Verlag. Retrieved from ftp://pets.rdg.ac.uk/

Jolliffe, I. T. (n.d.). *Principal component analysis* (2nd Ed.). Berlin: Springer Verlag.

Mecocci, A. (1989). Moving object recognition and classification in external environments. *Signal Processing*, (18): 183–194. doi:10.1016/0165-1684(89)90049-2

Oliver, N. M., Rosario, B., & Pentland, A. P. (2000). A Bayesian computer vision system for modeling human interactions. *IEEE Transactions on Pattern Analysis and Machine Intelligence*, 22(8), 831–843. doi:10.1109/34.868684

Pokrajac, D., & Latecki, L. J. (2003). *Spatiotemporal blocks-based moving objects identification and tracking*. Nice, France: Proc. IEEE.

Remagnino, P., Jones, G.A., Paragios, N., & Regazzoni, C. S. (Eds.). (2002). *Video-based surveillance systems*. Kluwer Academic Publishers.

Rourke, A., Bell, M. G. H., & Hoose, N. (1990). *Road traffic monitoring using image processing*. London: Road Traffic Control.

Stauffer, C., & Grimson, W. E. L. (2000). Learning patterns of activity using real-time tracking. *IEEE Transactions on Pattern Analysis and Machine Intelligence, 22*(8), 747–757. doi:10.1109/34.868677

Wren, C., Azarbayejani, A., Darrell, T., & Pentland, A. P. (1997). Pfinder: Real-time tracking of the human body. *IEEE Transactions on Pattern Analysis and Machine Intelligence, 19*(7), 780–785. doi:10.1109/34.598236

Zeljkovic, V., & Pokrajac, D. (2006). *Motion detection based multimedia supported intelligent video surveillance system*. ELMAR. doi:10.1109/ELMAR.2006.329512

Zeljkovic, V., Pokrajac, D., Dorado, A., & Izquierdo, E. (2005). Application of the improved illumination independent moving object detection algorithm on the real video sequence. In *Proceedings of the 6th International Workshop on Image Analysis for Multimedia Interactive Services*. WIAMIS.

Zeljkovic, V., Trpovski, Z., & Senk, V. (2003). Improved illumination independent moving object detection in real world video sequences. In *Proceedings of the 4th EURASIP Conf. focused on Video/Image Processing and Multimedia Communications*. EURASIP.

Chapter 5
Improved Spatial–Temporal Moving Object Detection Method Resistant to Noise

ABSTRACT

The resistance of the improved moving objects detection algorithm to various types of additive and multiplicative noise is discussed. The algorithm's first phase contains the noise suppression filter based on spatiotemporal blocks including dimensionality reduction technique for a compact scalar representation of each block, and the second phase consists of the moving object detection algorithm resistant to illumination changes that detects and tracks moving objects.

1. INTRODUCTION

The performance of the improved moving object detection algorithm resistant to the additive Gaussian, Salt and Pepper and Speckle noise of various variances is presented and evaluated in this chapter. The main goal is to demonstrate that this novel technique is resistant to influence of various types of noise and to augment the reasons for such desirable behavior.

A common feature of the most common approaches for moving object detection is the fact that they are pixel based (Jain, 1977), (Haritaoglu, 2000), (Oliver, 2000), (Remagnino, 2002), (Wren, 1997). Recent approaches are however based on the spatiotemporal blocks. While the pixel based techniques are shown resistant to the illumination change they are prone to the influence of noise. On the other hand, block-based methods are shown resistant to noise. To combine these desirable prop-erties, both approaches are combined in the new improved method (Pokrajac, 2003). The novelty that is introduced is image preprocessing similar to that used in the block-based method. The pixel and region levels are combined to a single level texture representation with 3D blocks and the image processing is continued on such spatially-temporally filtered pixels. More precisely, a given video is decomposed into overlapping spatio-temporal blocks, e.g., 7x7x3 blocks centered at each pixel, and then a dimensionality reduction technique is applied to obtain a compact represen-tation of color or gray level values of each block as a single scalar value. The principal component analysis is applied and the dominant eigenvector (corresponding to the largest eigenvalue) is used to obtain the coefficients of three dimensional filter, employed on every current frame. Such filtered images are subsequently treated with the moving detection algorithm based on pixel value.

DOI: 10.4018/978-1-4666-4896-8.ch005

It should be noted that the standard input of pixel values that are known to be noisy and in this way the main cause of instability of video analysis algorithms are avoided. In contrast, the application of principal component projection instead of original pixels is expected to retain useful information while suppressing successfully the destructive effects of noise. Hence, it is anticipated that the proposed technique will provide motion detection robust to various types of noise that may be present in video sequence, including additive Gaussian, Salt and Pepper and Speckle noise. This chapter shows the practical approval of this theoretically asserted claim on a test video from PETS repository.

2. METHODOLOGY

The used technique for moving object detection consists of four major phases:

1. Extraction of the 3D filter coefficients with the PCA analysis.
2. Dimensionality reduction by spatiotemporal blocks.
3. Image filtering of a current frame with the noise removal filter.
4. Detection of moving objects applying the pixel based method for moving object detection resistant to illumination changes.

A given video is treated as three-dimensional (3D) array of gray pixels $p_{i,j,z}$, $i=1,\ldots,X$; $j=1,\ldots,Y$; $z=1,\ldots,Z$ with two spatial dimensions X, Y and one temporal dimension Z, which can be found in the literature mentioned in the references. Spatiotemporal (3D) blocks are used, represented by N-dimensional vectors $\mathbf{b}_{I,J,t}$, where a block spans $(2T+1)$ frames and contains N_{BLOCK} pixels in each spatial direction per frame ($N=(2T+1)\times N_{BLOCK}\times N_{BLOCK}$). To represent the block vector $\mathbf{b}_{I,J,t}$ by a scalar while preserving information to the maximal

Figure 1. Dimensionality reduction using spatial-temporal blocks

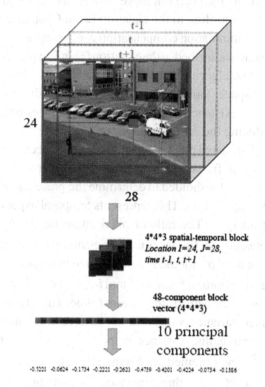

4*4*3 spatial-temporal block
Location I=24, J=28,
time t-1, t, t+1

48-component block
vector (4*4*3)

10 principal components

-0.5221 -0.0624 -0.1734 -0.2221 -0.2621 -0.4739 -0.4201 -0.4224 -0.0734 -0.1386

possible extent, principal component analysis is used. It is illustrated in Figure 1.

For principal component analysis, sample mean and covariance matrix are estimated of representative sample of block vectors corresponding to the considered types of movies and use the first eigenvector of the covariance matrix $\mathbf{S}$ (corresponding to the largest eigenvalue) that represents the coefficients of the 3D filter that suppresses the noise. In practice, the 3D filter can be emulated by three 2D filters applied on frames $z-1$, z and $z+1$.

The fourth phase of the proposed method implies the application of a pixel based algorithm for moving object detection and tracking, mentioned in Chapter 2.

Consider image sequence I consisting of N video frames. The sliding mask A_i is applied on every frame.

The pixel variance is calculated in order to estimate the potential movement in the observed area, according to the equation (2) in Chapter 2. The illumination compensation coefficient is defined as described in the equation (3) in Chapter 2.

The algorithm performs the analysis in time and space domains simultaneously, contributing to its resistance to the illumination changes and reducing the false detection, i.e. artifacts.

Estimated pixel variances for three successive pairs of frames are averaged and this average value is thresholded to determine the presence of moving objects. This represents temporal aspect of analysis. The ratio of pixel intensities in A_i between two frames is used to estimate the pixel variance $'\sigma_i^2$ for the following three pairs of successive frames: frames i-3 and i-2, i-2 and i-1 and i-1 and i, where i is the current frame. Thus, three pixel variance values for three successive and corresponding variance pairs $'\sigma_{i-2}^2$, $'\sigma_{i-1}^2$ and $'\sigma_i^2$ are obtained. Subsequently, the average value of these three variances is computed as explained in the equation (4) in Chapter 2.

After that, the mean value is subtracted from the pixel variance of the current and previous frame as written in the equation (5) in Chapter 2.

If $'\sigma_{i'}^2 \geq \varepsilon$ (a suitable threshold), the center of A_i is marked as changing region, i.e. as a moving object.

The proposed algorithm performs analysis in three dimensions, two spatial and one temporal. The time analysis, additionally to space analysis, helps with correct moving object detection and augments the precision of the algorithm. This algorithm, it should be pointed out, exploits local intensity and does not require color information.

3. EXPERIMENTAL RESULTS

The performance of the proposed approach is demonstrated on sequences from the Performance Evaluation of Tracking and Surveillance (PETS) repository.

Since the original sequences contain RGB colors, conversion from RGB to grayscale (PAL luminance) is performed. Video consists of 25 frames per second, 576×768 pixels per frame. The sequence contains 2688 frames. In the performed experiments $N_{BLOCK} = 7$ is used, thus the length of a block vector $\mathbf{b}_{I,J,t}$ is $N = 147 = 7 \times 7 \times 3$.

The experiments with additive Gaussian, noise with zero mean and different variances 0.1, 0.25 and 0.5 are performed. The result of the proposed approach on the frames 2500 and 2574 of *Outdoor video* sequence is illustrated in Figures 2 and 3, for three different noise variance values.

The experiments with Speckle noise of different variances 0.1, 0.25 and 0.5 are performed as well. The result of the proposed approach on the frames 2500 and 2574 of *Outdoor video* sequence is illustrated in Figure 4 and Figure 5, for three different noise variance values.

The experiments with Salt and Pepper noise of different variances 0.05, 0.1 and 0.2 are performed. In the realized experiments $N_{BLOCK} = 5$ is used, thus the length of a block vector $\mathbf{b}_{I,J,t}$ is $N = 75 = 5 \times 5 \times 3$. The result of the proposed approach on the frames 2500 and 2574 of *Outdoor video* sequence is illustrated in Figures 6 and 7, for three different noise variance values.

Images (a), (c) and (e) represent the noisy frames and the images (b), (d) and (f) are the binary images that contain the detected moving objects (white pixels). The pixels identified as moving are marked as white and the still background is marked as black.

Observing the binary images obtained by the application of the new method it is obvious that the proposed technique is able to successfully and precisely detect moving objects even in case of extremely strong noise, when even a human may have difficulties to actually identify a moving object. Observe that the examined, as any other algorithm, may introduce "false alarms". However, such effects are significant only for very large noise variances and can be successfully removed by median filters applied on the obtained binary images.

Figure 2. The 2500 frame of Outdoor video and binary images containing the detected moving objects of the 2500 frame under Gaussian zero-mean noise with (a), (b) variance 0.1; (c), (d) variance 0.25; (e), (f) variance 0.5

(a)   (b)   (c)

(d)   (e)   (f)

Figure 3. The 2574 frame of Outdoor video and binary images containing the detected moving objects of the 2574 frame under Gaussian zero-mean noise with (a), (b) variance 0.1; (c), (d) variance 0.25; (e), (f) variance 0.5

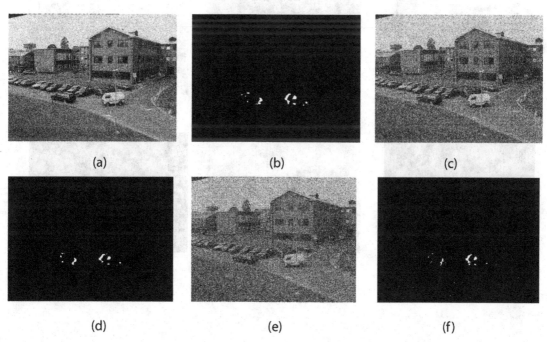

(a)   (b)   (c)

(d)   (e)   (f)

Figure 4. The 2500 frame of Outdoor video and binary images containing the detected moving objects of the 2500 frame under Speckle noise with (a), (b) variance 0.1; (c), (d) variance 0.25; (e), (f) variance 0.5

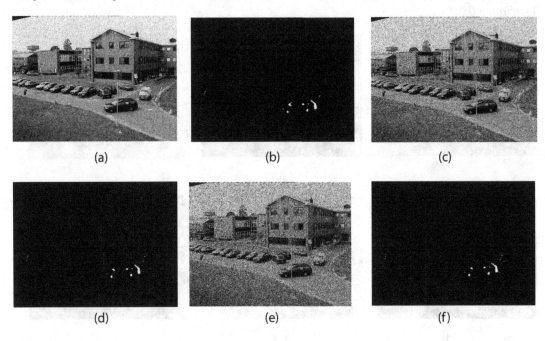

Figure 5. The 2574 frame of Outdoor video and binary images containing the detected moving objects of the 2574 frame under Speckle noise with (a), (b) variance 0.1; (c), (d) variance 0.25; (e), (f) variance 0.5

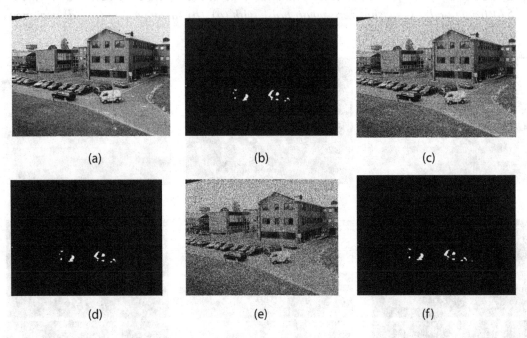

Figure 6. The 2500 frame of Outdoor video and binary images containing the detected moving objects of the 2500 frame under Salt and Pepper noise with (a), (b) probability 0.05 (c), (d) probability 0.1; (e), (f) probability 0.2

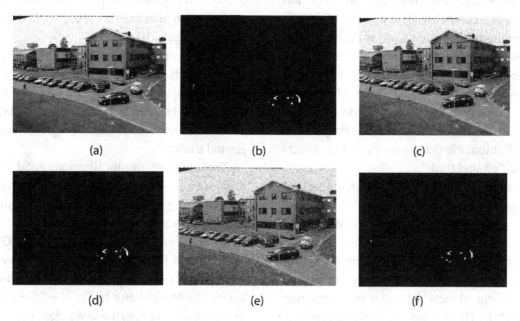

(a) (b) (c)

(d) (e) (f)

Figure 7. The 2574 frame of Outdoor video and binary images containing the detected moving objects of the 2574 frame under Salt and Pepper noise with (a), (b) probability 0.05; (c), (d) probability 0.1; (e), (f) probability 0.2.

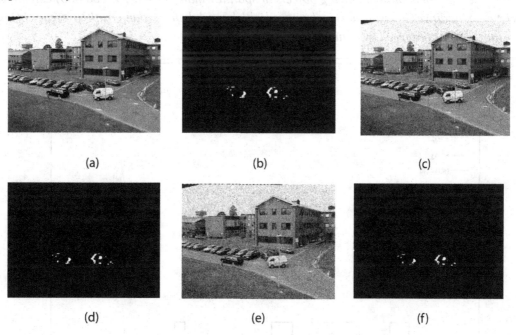

(a) (b) (c)

(d) (e) (f)

To demonstrate the influence of varying noise levels on the performance of the proposed algorithm, spatial-windows based on evaluation statistics are computed. The number of identified moving block within a pre-specified spatial window is counted and it is normalized with the number of spatial blocks in the same window. The observed spatial window is hand-labeled by denoting time intervals when a moving object is present in the window in order to compare the result of automatic detection of moving objects with the "ground truth".

The computed statistics for different levels of Gaussian noise (0.1, 0.25, 0.5) as well as ground truth moving objects detection in rectangular region (350, 510; 500, 600) is shown in Figure 8.

The computed statistics for different levels of Speckle noise (0.1, 0.25, 0.5) as well as ground truth moving objects detection in rectangular region (350, 510; 500, 600) is shown in Figure 9.

The computed statistics for different levels of Salt and Pepper noise (probabilities of 0.05, 0.1, 0.2) as well as ground truth moving objects detection in rectangular region (350, 510; 500, 600) is shown in Figure 10.

It can easily be observed that, in spite of increased levels of noise, it is still possible to detect a moving object in a window by properly thresholding the observed statistics. It should be also noted that such identification agrees with the ground truth.

The obtained results illustrate good performance of our combined technique since it reduces noise in background and can extract information about temporal change of texture.

In the performed experiments with Gaussian, Salt and Pepper, multiplicative ("speckle") and Poisson noise, $N_{BLOCK} = 5$ is used, thus the length of a block vector $\mathbf{b}_{I,J,t}$ is $N = 75 = 5 \times 5 \times 3$. The additive Gaussian noise was zero mean, with variance ranging from 0.1 to 0.5. The Salt and

Figure 8. Percentage of identified moving objects at spatial window (350,510; 500,600) calculated for various levels of additive Gaussian noise, compared with hand-labeled ground truth (presence of moving object in the video as observed by a human)

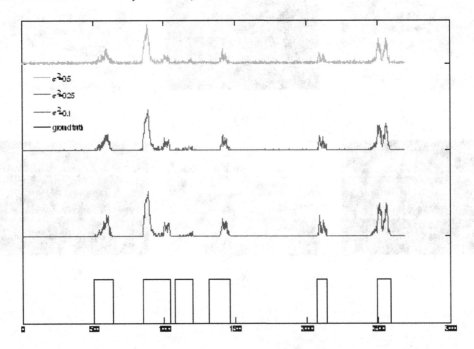

Figure 9. Percentage of identified moving objects at spatial window (350,510; 500,600) calculated for various levels of Speckle noise, compared with hand-labeled ground truth (presence of moving object in the video as observed by a human)

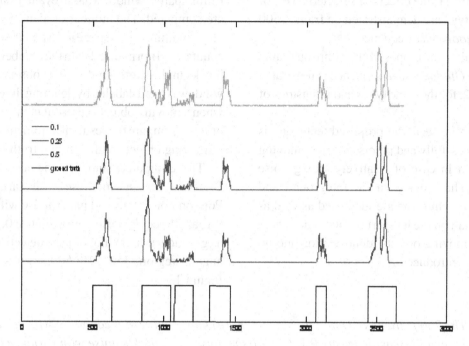

Figure 10. Percentage of identified moving objects at spatial window (350, 510; 500, 600) calculated for various levels of Salt and Pepper noise, compared with hand-labeled ground truth (presence of moving object in the video as observed by a human)

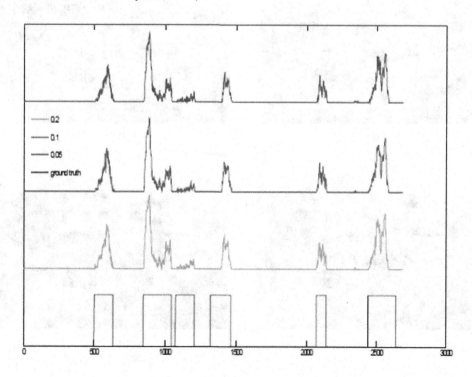

Pepper noise densities varied from 0.05 to 0.2. The variance of the speckle noise ranged from 0.1 to 0.5. In Figure 11, the effects of selected levels of each noise type are demonstrated on frame 2500 of the *Outdoor video* sequence.

The result of the proposed algorithm on Frame 2500 of the *Outdoor video* sequence is illustrated in Figure 12, for the same types and intensities of noise.

As it can be seen, the proposed technique is able to successfully and precisely detect moving objects even in case of relatively strong noise influence. The moving car in foreground and slow-moving white van are identified as well as the pedestrian on the left part of the scene. There is no false moving objects identification and no artifacts are introduced.

To demonstrate the influence of varying noise levels on the performance of the proposed algorithm, spatial-windows based evaluation statistics are computed. The number of identified moving block within a pre-specified spatial window is counted and normalized with the number of spatial blocks in the same window. The observed spatial window is hand-labeled by denoting time intervals when a moving object is present in the window in order to compare the result of automatic detection of moving objects with "ground truth".

The computed statistics for sequence with Gaussian zero-mean noise with variance 0.1, Poisson noise, Salt and paper noise with density 0.1, and Speckle noise with variance 0.1, as well as ground truth moving objects detection in rectangular region (350, 510; 500, 600) is shown in Figure 13.

Figure 11. The 2500ᵗʰ frame of Outdoor video under (a) Gaussian zero-mean noise with variance 0.1; (b) Salt and paper noise with density 0.1; (c) Poisson noise; (d) Speckle noise with variance 0.1

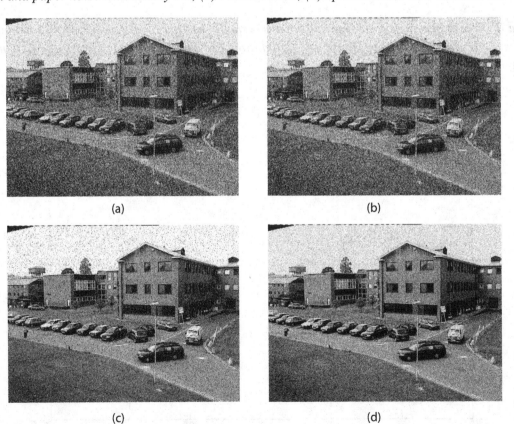

(a)

(b)

(c)

(d)

Figure 12. Detection of moving objects on frame 2500 of Outdoor video under (a) Gaussian zero-mean noise with variance 0.1; (b) Salt and paper noise with density 0.1; (c) Poisson noise; (d) Speckle noise with variance 0.1

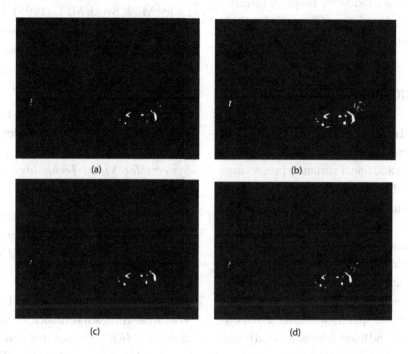

Figure 13. Percentage of identified moving objects at spatial window (350,510; 500,600) calculated for Outdoor video with Gaussian zero-mean noise with variance 0.1, Poisson noise, Salt and paper noise with density 0.1, Speckle noise with variance 0.1, compared with hand-labeled ground truth (presence of moving object in the video as observed by a human)

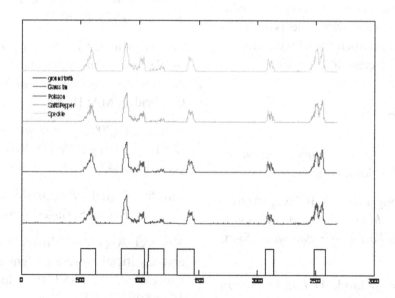

It can easily be observed that, in spite of various types of noise, it is still possible to detect a moving object in a window by properly thresholding the observed statistics. Observe also that such identification agrees with the ground truth.

4. CONCLUSION

It is demonstrated in this chapter that the proposed moving object detection algorithm based on spatiotemporal blocks and linear variance-preserving dimensionality reduction is resistant to the influence of strong additive Gaussian, Salt and Pepper and Speckle noise of various variances.

The performance of the applied algorithm is evaluated on benchmark videos from Performance Evaluation of Tracking and Surveillance (PETS) repository. As a performance measure, in addition to a visual evaluation, spatial-windows based on evaluation statistics and hand-labeled ground truth moving objects detection is used. The results indicate that a proper detection is still possible in spite of significant levels of additive or multiplicative noise. This can be explained by inherent capability of employed dimension reduction techniques to efficiently suppress a noisy component. In contrast, plain pixel-based moving objects detection methods become overwhelmed with the amount of noise present and cease to be useful.

REFERENCES

Corrall, D. (n.d.). *VIEW: Computer vision for surveillance applications*. London. *IEE*.

Douglas, K., & Douglas, S. (2003). *PostgreSQL-A comprehensive guide to building, programming and administering PostgreSQL databases*. Sams Publishing.

Duda, R., Hart, P., & Stork, D. (2001). *Pattern classification* (2nd ed.). Hoboken, NJ: John Wiley & Sons.

Dunckley, L. (2003). *Multimedia databases: An object-relational approach*. Pearson Education.

Fathy, M., & Siyal, M. Y. (1995). An image detection technique based on morphological edge detection and background differencing for real-time traffic analysis. *Pattern Recognition Letters*, (16): 1321–1330. doi:10.1016/0167-8655(95)00081-X

Foresti, G. L. (1998). A real-time system for video surveillance of unattended outdoor environments. *IEEE Transactions on Circuits and Systems for Video Technology*, 8(6), 697–704. doi:10.1109/76.728411

Foresti, G. L., & Regazzoni, C. S. (1994). *A change detection method for multiple object localizations in real scenes*. Bologna, Italy: IEEE. doi:10.1109/IECON.1994.397923

Haritaoglu, I., Harwood, D., & Davis, L. (2000). W4: Real-time surveillance of people and their activities. *IEEE Transactions on Pattern Analysis and Machine Intelligence*, 22(8), 809–830. doi:10.1109/34.868683

Inigo, R. M. (1989). Application of machine vision to traffic monitoring and control. *IEEE Transactions on Vehicular Technology*, 38(3), 112–122. doi:10.1109/25.45464

Jain, R., Militzer, D., & Nagel, H. (1977). *Separating nonstationary from stationary scene components in a sequence of real world TV images*. Cambridge, MA: IJCAI.

Jolliffe, I. T. (2002). *Principal component analysis* (2nd Ed.). Springer Verlag. Retrieved from ftp://pets.rdg.ac.uk/

Jolliffe, I. T. (n.d.). *Principal component analysis* (2nd Ed.). Berlin: Springer Verlag.

Mecocci, A. (1989). Moving object recognition and classification in external environments. *Signal Processing*, (18): 183–194. doi:10.1016/0165-1684(89)90049-2

Oliver, N. M., Rosario, B., & Pentland, A. P. (2000). A Bayesian computer vision system for modeling human interactions. *IEEE Transactions on Pattern Analysis and Machine Intelligence, 22*(8), 831–843. doi:10.1109/34.868684

Pokrajac, D., & Latecki, L. J. (2003). *Spatiotemporal blocks-based moving objects identification and tracking*. Nice, France: IEEE.

Pokrajac, D., & Zeljković, V. (2005). *Influence of the salt and pepper noise on spatial-temporal method for moving objects detection*. IASTED.

Pokrajac, D., Zeljković, V., & Latecki, L.J. (2005). *Noise-resilient detection of moving objects based on spatial-temporal blocks*. ELMAR.

Remagnino, P., Jones, G. A., Paragios, N., & Regazzoni, C. S. (Eds.). (2002). *Video-based surveillance systems*. Kluwer Academic Publishers. doi:10.1007/978-1-4615-0913-4

Rourke, A., Bell, M. G. H., & Hoose, N. (1990). *Road traffic monitoring using image processing*. London: Road Traffic Control.

Stauffer, C., & Grimson, W. E. L. (2000). Learning patterns of activity using real-time tracking. *IEEE Transactions on Pattern Analysis and Machine Intelligence, 22*(8), 747–757. doi:10.1109/34.868677

Wren, C., Azarbayejani, A., Darrell, T., & Pentland, A. P. (1997). Pfinder: Real-time tracking of the human body. *IEEE Transactions on Pattern Analysis and Machine Intelligence, 19*(7), 780–785. doi:10.1109/34.598236

Zeljkovic, V., & Pokrajac, D. (2006). *Improved spatial-temporal moving object detection method resistant to noise*. ICEST.

Zeljkovic, V., Pokrajac, D., Dorado, A., & Izquierdo, E. (2005). Application of the improved illumination independent moving object detection algorithm on the real video sequence. In *Proceedings of the 6th International Workshop on Image Analysis for Multimedia Interactive Services*. WIAMIS.

Zeljkovic, V., Pokrajac, D., & Latecki, L.J. (2005). *Noise robust spatial-temporal algorithm for moving objects detection*. XLIX ETRAN.

Zeljkovic, V., Trpovski, Z., & Senk, V. (2003). Improved illumination independent moving object detection in real world video sequences. In *Proceedings of the 4th EURASIP Conf. focused on Video/Image Processing and Multimedia Communications*. EURASIP.

Chapter 6
Improved Illumination Independent Moving Object Detection Algorithm Applied to Infrared Video Sequences

ABSTRACT

Performance of the moving objects detection algorithm on infrared videos is discussed. The algorithm consists of two phases: the noise suppression filter based on spatiotemporal blocks including dimensionality reduction technique for a compact vector representation of each block and the illumination changes resistant moving object detection algorithm that tracks the moving objects. The proposed method is evaluated on monochrome and multispectral IR videos.

1. INTRODUCTION

The performance of motion detection algorithm introduced in previous chapters is evaluated here. The main goal is to demonstrate that the novel technique is capable of successfully detecting moving objects in infrared videos.

Moving objects detection methods are in most of the cases pixel based (Jain, 1977), (Remagnino, 2002). Authors in (Stauffer, 2000) propose technique based on adaptive Gaussian mixture model of the color values distribution over time at a given pixel location. This approach is adopted but with a major difference that the computation is based on the spatiotemporal blocks. The standard input of pixel values are avoided as they are known to be noisy and the main cause of instability of video analysis algorithms. In contrast, the application of principal components instead of original vectors is expected to retain useful information while suppressing successfully the destructive effects of noise (Jolliffe, 2002). Consequently, the proposed technique (Pokrajac, 2003) provides motion detection robust to various types of noise that may be present in infra-red video sequences.

The pixel and region levels are combined to a single level texture representation with 3D blocks and the image processing is being performed on such spatially-temporally filtered pixels. A given video is decomposed into overlapping spatiotemporal blocks, e.g., 7x7x3 and 7x8x3 blocks centered at each pixel, and a dimensionality reduction technique is applied to obtain a compact representation of color or gray level values of each block as a single scalar value. The principal component analysis is applied and the dominant

DOI: 10.4018/978-1-4666-4896-8.ch006

eigenvector (corresponding to the largest eigenvalue) is used to obtain the coefficients of 3D filter that is employed on every current frame. Such filtered images are subsequently treated with the moving detection algorithm based on pixel value.

The application of principal component projection instead of original pixels is expected to retain useful information while suppressing successfully the destructive effects of noise. Proposed technique provides motion detection robust to various types of noise that may be present in infra-red video sequences.

2. IMPROVED NOISE RESISTANT ILLUMINATION INDEPENDENT MOVING OBJECT DETECTION ALGORITHM

The technique for moving object detection consists of two major phases:

1. Image filtering of a current frame with the noise removal filter coefficients extracted with the PCA analysis.
2. Detection of moving objects applying the pixel based method for moving object detection resistant to illumination changes.

A given video is treated as three-dimensional (3D) array of gray pixels with two spatial dimensions X, Y and one temporal dimension Z. We use spatiotemporal (3D) blocks represented by N-dimensional vectors, where a block spans $(2T+1)$ frames and contains N_{BLOCK} pixels in each spatial direction per frame $N = (2T+1) \times N_{BLOCK} \times N_{BLOCK}$, which can be found in the literature mentioned in the references. To represent the block vector by a scalar while preserving information to the maximal possible extent, principal component analysis is used. For principal component analysis, sample mean and covariance matrix of representative sample of block vectors corresponding to the considered types of movies are estimated and

the first eigenvector of the covariance matrix **S** (corresponding to the largest eigenvalue) is used that represents the coefficients of the 3D filter that suppresses the noise. The 3D filter can be emulated by three 2D filters applied on frames z-1, z and z+1.

The last phase of the proposed method implies the application of a pixel based algorithm for moving object detection and tracking. The pixel variance is calculated in order to estimate the potential movement in the observed area incorporating the illumination compensation coefficient. The algorithm performs the analysis in time and space domains simultaneously, contributing to its resistance to the illumination changes and reducing the false detection, i.e. artifacts. Estimated pixel variances for three successive pairs of frames are averaged and the obtained average value is thresholded in order to determine the presence of moving objects. This represents temporal aspect of analysis. The time analysis, additionally to space analysis, helps with correct moving object detection and augments the precision of the algorithm. Details of the algorithm are provided in previous sections.

3. EXPERIMENTAL RESULTS

The performance of the proposed approach on two infrared video sequences is demonstrated in this section. The first sequence, *RoofCam*, is obtained from Ohio State University Thermal Pedestrian Database. Video was captured using a Raytheon 300D thermal sensor core with 75 mm lens. Camera was mounted on an 8-story building overlooking a pedestrian intersection on the OSU campus. Image size is 360x240 pixels and was captured at varying sampling rates. The second sequence, *RocketLounch*, is false color thermal infrared sequence of Spitzer Telescope launch (25 August 2003 at 1:35:39 a.m. EDT from Cape Canaveral Air Force Station in Florida) taken from 3km distance.

The original 45s video shows the rocket passing through a cloud including cooling of the rocket plume after the rocket flies out of flame. In the experiments $T = 1$ and $N_{BLOCK} = 5$ is used for *RoofCam* and *RocketLaunch*.

Figure 1 contains two characteristic frames (40 and 194) with the results of the proposed moving objects detection for *RoofCam* video. The identified moving pixels are marked in red. In the frame 40, four pedestrians appear in the "red" color in the scene. The algorithm is able to identify all four moving objects. The algorithm successfully identifies again all four pedestrians in the frame 194.

It should be pointed out that the proposed algorithm worked with no false alarms in spite of the relatively high level of noise in the considered IR video.

Figure 2 contains two frames (350 and 450) of the *RocketLaunch* video sequence with indicated results obtained by the application of the proposed moving objects detection algorithm. The frames show two characteristic phases of rocket launch. In the frame 350, the clouds are reflecting the bright infrared light of the hot rocket engines below so that clouds appear to light up and come down to meet the rocket. In this frame, this reflection is

clearly identified by the algorithm (red-colored ellipsoid above the rocket top). The algorithm is also able to identify the base of the rocket flame in the frame 450, where the base of the jet appears through the cloud.

The proposed algorithm can identify movement in particular region of interest. To accomplish this, first rectangular spatial windows corresponding to the regions of interest are defined and the following spatial-windows based evaluation statistics is computed. The number of identified moving block within the spatial window is counted and it is normalized with the window size.

In Figure 3(a), the computed statistics for *RoofCam* sequence on the rectangular block [120:140, 110:130], annotated on Figure 1 is shown. Visual inspection of the video sequence indicates the existence of two moving objects in the block: one in frames 6-65 and another in the frames 242-284. The values of motion statistics correspond to these two intervals, indicating two peaks of motion activity. Observe that the motion statistics value in the frame 40 is large, corresponding to the moving objects actually appearing in the frame within the observed rectangular block, see Figure 1. It can be observed that the inertia of

Figure 1. Original frames (a) 40 and (b) 194 of RoofCam video with spatial block [120:140, 110:130] (yellow) and the result of moving objects detection (moving objects—red: background—navy)

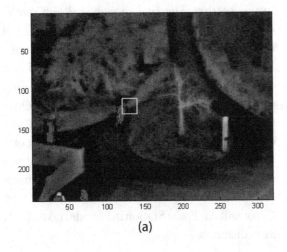 

(a)   (b)

Figure 2. Original frames (a) 350 and (b) 450 of RocketLaunch video with spatial block [70:140, 70:140] (yellow) and the result of moving objects detection (moving objects - red: background - blue)

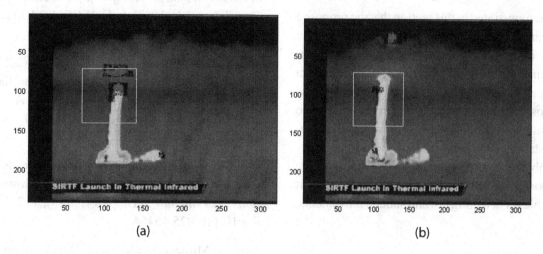

(a) (b)

Figure 3. Motion statistics: Percentage of identified moving objects-at spatial blocks (a) [120:140, 110:130] and (b) [70:140, 70:140] calculated for the RoofCam and RocketLaunch sequence, respectively

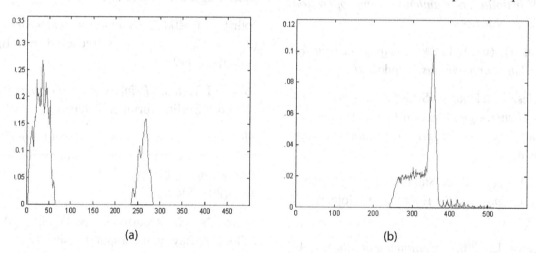

(a) (b)

the proposed method is minimal; moving blocks cease to be identified in the observed rectangular regions as soon as the actual motion stops. Also, by thresholding the motion statistics, it is possible to get clear indication of the factual presence of the moving object in the rectangular region.

In Figure 3(b), the computed statistics for *RocketLaunch* sequence on the rectangular block [70:140, 70:140], annotated on Figure 1 is shown. On frame 260, the base of the flame enters the

block, which results in increase of the motion statistics. On frame 342, the cloud reflection appears and grows which results with rapidly augmenting motion statistics value. The reflection disappears at frame 370 and the level of the motion statistics becomes negligible. As it can be seen, the proposed motion statistics not only could be used to accurately detect the presence/absence of the moving object in the frame but also to distinguish different *phases* of motion.

4. CONCLUSION

It is demonstrated in this section that the proposed illumination and noise-resistant moving object detection algorithm based on principal component filtering and spatiotemporal analysis can perform successful detection of moving objects in infrared videos. As a performance measure, in addition to a visual evaluation, spatial-windows based evaluation statistics and hand-labeled ground truth moving objects detection are used. The inertia of the proposed algorithm is negligible which makes it suitable for detecting fast and sudden movements.

REFERENCES

Cieszynski, J. (2003). *Closed circuit television: CCTV installation, maintenance and operation* (2nd ed.). Newnes.

Corrall, D. (n.d.). *VIEW: Computer vision for surveillance applications*. London. *IEE*.

Douglas, K., & Douglas, S. (2003). *PostgreSQL-A comprehensive guide to building, programming and administering PostgreSQL databases*. Sams Publishing.

Duda, R., Hart, P., & Stork, D. (2001). *Pattern classification* (2nd ed.). Hoboken, NJ: John Wiley & Sons.

Dunckley, L. (2003). *Multimedia databases: An object-relational approach*. Pearson Education.

Fathy, M., & Siyal, M. Y. (1995). An image detection technique based on morphological edge detection and background differencing for real-time traffic analysis. *Pattern Recognition Letters*, (16): 1321–1330. doi:10.1016/0167-8655(95)00081-X

Foresti, G. L. (1998). A real-time system for video surveillance of unattended outdoor environments. *IEEE Transactions on Circuits and Systems for Video Technology*, 8(6), 697–704. doi:10.1109/76.728411

Foresti, G. L., & Regazzoni, C. S. (1994). *A change detection method for multiple object localizations in real scenes*. Bologna, Italy: IEEE. doi:10.1109/IECON.1994.397923

Haritaoglu, I., Harwood, D., & Davis, L. (2000). W4: Real-time surveillance of people and their activities. *IEEE Transactions on Pattern Analysis and Machine Intelligence*, 22(8), 809–830. doi:10.1109/34.868683

Inigo, R. M. (1989). Application of machine vision to traffic monitoring and control. *IEEE Transactions on Vehicular Technology*, 38(3), 112–122. doi:10.1109/25.45464

Jain, R., Militzer, D., & Nagel, H. (1977). *Separating nonstationary from stationary scene components in a sequence of real world TV images*. Cambridge, MA: IJCAI.

Jolliffe, I. T. (2002). *Principal component analysis* (2nd Ed.). Springer Verlag. Retrieved from ftp://pets.rdg.ac.uk/

Jolliffe, I. T. (n.d.). *Principal component analysis* (2nd Ed.). Berlin: Springer Verlag.

Mecocci, A. (1989). Moving object recognition and classification in external environments. *Signal Processing*, (18): 183–194. doi:10.1016/0165-1684(89)90049-2

Oliver, N. M., Rosario, B., & Pentland, A. P. (2000). A Bayesian computer vision system for modeling human interactions. *IEEE Transactions on Pattern Analysis and Machine Intelligence*, 22(8), 831–843. doi:10.1109/34.868684

Pokrajac, D., & Latecki, L. J. (2003). *Spatiotemporal blocks-based moving objects identification and tracking*. Nice, France: IEEE.

Pokrajac, D., & Zeljković, V. (2005). *Influence of the salt and pepper noise on spatial-temporal method for moving objects detection*. IASTED.

Pokrajac, D., Zeljković, V., & Latecki, L.J. (2005). *Noise-resilient detection of moving objects based on spatial-temporal blocks*. ELMAR.

Remagnino, P., Jones, G. A., Paragios, N., & Regazzoni, C. S. (Eds.). (2002). *Video-based surveillance systems*. Kluwer Academic Publishers. doi:10.1007/978-1-4615-0913-4

Rourke, A., Bell, M. G. H., & Hoose, N. (1990). *Road traffic monitoring using image processing*. London: Road Traffic Control.

Stauffer, C., & Grimson, W. E. L. (2000). Learning patterns of activity using real-time tracking. *IEEE Transactions on Pattern Analysis and Machine Intelligence, 22*(8), 747–757. doi:10.1109/34.868677

Wren, C., Azarbayejani, A., Darrell, T., & Pentland, A. P. (1997). Pfinder: Real-time tracking of the human body. *IEEE Transactions on Pattern Analysis and Machine Intelligence, 19*(7), 780–785. doi:10.1109/34.598236

Zeljkovic, V., & Pokrajac, D. (2006). *Improved spatial-temporal moving object detection method resistant to noise*. ICEST.

Zeljkovic, V., Pokrajac, D., Dorado, A., & Izquierdo, E. (2005). Application of the improved illumination independent moving object detection algorithm on the real video sequence. In *Proceedings of the 6th International Workshop on Image Analysis for Multimedia Interactive Services*. WIAMIS.

Zeljkovic, V., Pokrajac, D., & Latecki, L. J. (2005). *Noise robust spatial-temporal algorithm for moving objects detection*. XLIX ETRAN.

Zeljkovic, V., Trpovski, Z., & Senk, V. (2003). Improved illumination independent moving object detection in real world video sequences. In *Proceedings of the 4th EURASIP Conf. focused on Video/Image Processing and Multimedia Communications*. EURASIP.

Chapter 7
Classification of Building Images in Video Sequences

ABSTRACT

A technique for detection of building images in real-world video sequences is presented. The proposed technique uses information extracted from video features to improve precision in classification results. It combines fuzzy rule-based classification with a method for changing region detection in outdoor environments, which is invariant to extreme illumination changes and severe weather conditions. It has been tested on sequences under various lighting conditions. Satisfactory and promising results have been achieved.

1. INTRODUCTION

The problem of edge-based building image classification in real-world video sequences is addressed in this section. The presented technique exploits information in video primitives to focus classification on features extracted from pixels belonging to static regions.

The introduced technique is based on two simple observations: In static regions the possibility of finding features that match the pattern of "building" is higher because buildings are rigid and static objects; and misclassification can be reduced removing pixels belonging to changing regions. These regions can contain objects semantically different to buildings but with an edge distribution highly similar, i.e. high frequency of vertical and horizontal edges.

Existing approaches for classification of building images use a Bayesian framework to exploit

image features by perceptual grouping (Iqbal, 1999), binary Bayesian hierarchical classifiers (Vailaya, 2001), or perform building semantic extraction using support vector machines (Wang, 2002).

2. EDGE-BASED BUILDING IMAGE CLASSIFICATION

Edge-based building image classification can be found in (Iqbal, 1999), (Vailaya, 2001), (Wang, 2002).

Let x be an image or video frame, $f = \{f(1), ..., f(n)\}$ be feature sets where f is a function of the image x, $Et = (e_1t, ..., e_5t)$ be a pattern extracted from a feature vector $f^{(i)}$, and $Y = \{B, NB\}$ be a class set (B:Building, NB:Non Building). Edge-based building image classification uses a function:

DOI: 10.4018/978-1-4666-4896-8.ch007

$$g(x): E^t \rightarrow Y \qquad (1)$$

where E^t is extracted from the description of x given by the MPEG-7 edge histogram descriptor.

This descriptor uses an 80-bin histogram to represent the local distribution of directional (vertical, horizontal, diagonal 45°, and diagonal 135°) and non-directional (isotropic) edges.

$g(x)$ is approximated with a set $R = \{R_1, \ldots, R_C\}$ of if-then fuzzy rules which has the following structure:

$${}^{W}R_k: \text{If } e_i^t \text{ is } A_i^k \text{ then } Y \text{ is } y_j \qquad (2)$$

where ${}^{w}R_k$ is a weighted rule, $w \in [0, 1]$ is the weight, e_i^t a specific type of edge, and A^k is a linguistic label used to transform values from a continuous to a discrete domain.

The fuzzy model has five input variables because of the semantics of edge histogram descriptor which uses five types of edges. Besides, a group of three fuzzy sets is associated with each variable. Thus, rule base is a multi-input single-output space as is depicted in Figure 1.

R_i and R_j are if-then rules associated with classes NB and B, respectively. H, M, L stand for High, Low, Medium, and Low.

Figure 1. Fuzzy model for edge histogram descriptor

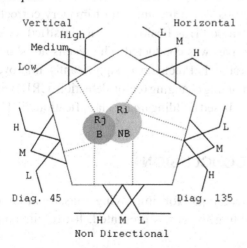

After several experiments, it was identified that most of the misclassifications of building images in real-world videos were due to objects with a similar edge distribution of buildings but semantically different. Most of them were moving non-rigid objects. Therefore, the technique was improved integrating a pre-processing method to detect changing regions.

3. CHANGING REGION DETECTION

A shading model method for moving object detection is applied in order to perform detection of changing regions. This version is invariant to extreme illumination changes at pixel level.

It uses the ratio of pixel intensities within a sliding mask A_i, $i = 1 \ldots N$, which performs scanning of a window W in each frame within a video sequence I. W has fixed size and position, the pixel variance ${}^I \sigma^2$ is defined as described in the Equation (2) in Chapter 2.

K_i is an adaptive coefficient to overcome falsely assignment of pixel to changing region for fast and large illumination changes. K_i is defined according to the equation (3) in Chapter 2.

In this way, changing regions are located and used to obtain a binary image I_b that contains white and black pixels to represent changing and static regions, respectively.

As an example, frames 50850 and 27172 showed in Figures 2(a) and (c), respectively, are classified as "building image". Looking at Figures 2(b) and (d), edge histograms of sub-images contributing to classification results have similar distribution. Rain drops present a high number of contiguous vertical edges. This shortcoming is sorted out using proposed method. As is shown in Figure 3(a) changing regions are marked in the binary image with white pixels and the rest of it, i.e. the static background or foreground is marked with black pixels. This information was extracted from the video sequence depicted in Figure 3(b).

Figure 2. Example of close edge distribution: a) Building image (frame 50850); b) Edge histogram Sub-image Row 1, Column 2; c) Non Building image (frame 27172); d) Edge histogram Sub-image Row 2, Column 1

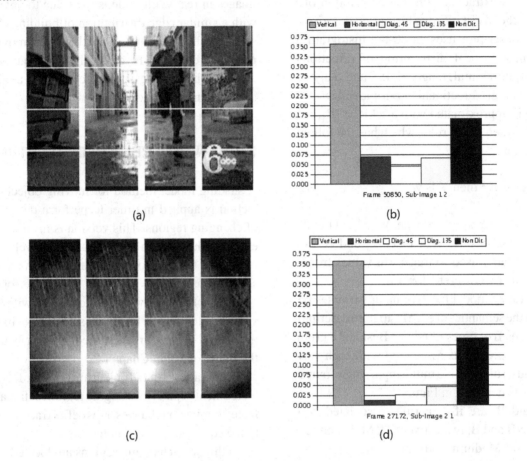

(a)

(b)

(c)

(d)

Changing region detection uses I_b to apply a filter on each pixel of current image I_m as follows:

$$\hat{I}_m(x,y) = \begin{cases} 255 & \text{if } I_m^b(x,y) = 255 \\ I_m(x,y) & \text{otherwise} \end{cases}, \quad (3)$$

where $\hat{I}_m$ contains static regions only.

4. EXPERIMENTAL RESULTS

Edge-based building image classification was applied on over 3000 frames from a set of videos randomly selected from TRECVID video repository. Features were extracted from key– and additional–frames at the shot level using edge histogram descriptor. A statistical performance evaluation based on the amount of imagery correctly classified (True Positive) or misclassified (False Positive) was conducted. The results are shown in Table 1. Precision is significantly improved combining changing region detection (CRD) with edge-based building image classification (EBIC).

5. CONCLUSION

A technique for improving classification of building images is presented. It exploits addi-

Figure 3. Changing and static regions detection: a) I_b binary image for image 27172; b) I video sequence (frames)

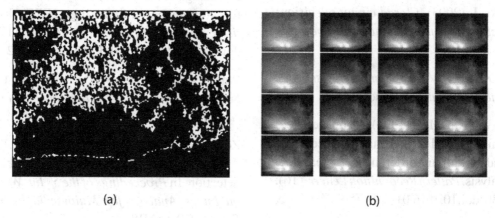

(a)   (b)

Table 1. Precision results (P) [%]

Method	TP	FP	P
EBIC	77.70	21.96	77.97
EBIC + CRD	89.54	10.12	89.84

tional information extracted from a sequence of images and applies a fast, simple and effective method for detecting changing regions. Filtering out features extracted from pixels belonging to changing regions, misclassification is reduced and precision is significantly increased.

The natural process in automated video surveillance systems is to perform correct shape recognition and object identification after the desired moving object is correctly detected. This is why the topic of the third chapter is shape recognition. Two new algorithms, optimal and sub-optimal solution algorithm, for shape recognition using geometric calculations are proposed. They are model based which means that shape from the data base which is considered as a model is compared with another shape that is extracted from the sequence of images, such as for example, a moving object. The proposed algorithms are efficient and tolerate severe noise. They have the ability to identify the close match between the noisy polygon that has a significantly

greater number of sides and the assigned polygon. They work for convex and concave polygons equally well. These algorithms are invariant under translation, rotation, change of scale and it is reasonably easy to compute.

A two step process for removing noise from polygonal shapes for the purpose of easier and more efficient shape recognition is presented in the next chapter as well. A polygonal shape is presented as its turning function and then a nonlinear diffusion filter and triangle method are applied on it. In the first step several different nonlinear diffusion filters are applied on the turning function and the performance of these filters is later compared. Nonlinear diffusion filters identify dominant vertices in a polygon and remove those vertices that are identified as noise or irrelevant features. The obtained results demonstrate that the proposed two step process successfully removes vertices that should be dismissed as noise while preserving dominant vertices that can be accepted as relevant features and give a faithful description of the shape of the polygon. In experimental tests of this procedure successful removal of noise and excellent preservation of shape thanks to appropriate emphasis of dominant vertices is demonstrated.

REFERENCES

Cieszynski, J. (2003). *Closed circuit television: CCTV installation, maintenance and operation* (2nd ed.). Newnes.

Corrall, D. (n.d.). *VIEW: Computer vision for surveillance applications*. London. *IEE*.

Fathy, M., & Siyal, M. Y. (1995). An image detection technique based on morphological edge detection and background differencing for real-time traffic analysis. *Pattern Recognition Letters*, (16): 1321–1330. doi:10.1016/0167-8655(95)00081-X

Foresti, G. L. (1998). A real-time system for video surveillance of unattended outdoor environments. *IEEE Transactions on Circuits and Systems for Video Technology*, 8(6), 697–704. doi:10.1109/76.728411

Foresti, G. L., & Regazzoni, C. S. (1994). *A change detection method for multiple object localizations in real scenes*. Bologna, Italy: IEEE. doi:10.1109/IECON.1994.397923

Inigo, R. M. (1989). Application of machine vision to traffic monitoring and control. *IEEE Transactions on Vehicular Technology*, 38(3), 112–122. doi:10.1109/25.45464

Iqbal, Q., & Aggarwal, J. K. (1999). Applying perceptual grouping to content-based image retrieval: Building image. In *Proceedings of the IEEE Int'l Conf. on Computer Vision and Pattern Recognition*, (pp. 42-48). IEEE.

Mecocci, A. (1989). Moving object recognition and classification in external environments. *Signal Processing*, (18): 183–194. doi:10.1016/0165-1684(89)90049-2

Rourke, A., Bell, M. G. H., & Hoose, N. (1990). *Road traffic monitoring using image processing*. London: Road Traffic Control.

Vailaya, A., Figueiredo, M. A. T., Jain, A. K., & Zhang, H.-J. (2001). Image classification for content-based indexing. *IEEE Transactions on Image Processing*, 10(1), 117–130. doi:10.1109/83.892448 PMID:18249602

Wang, Y.-N., Chen, L.-B., & Hu, B.-G. (2002). *Semantic extraction of the building images using support vector machines*. Beijing, China: IEEE.

Zeljkovic, V., Dorado, A., & Izquierdo, E. (2004). A modified shading model method for building detection. In *Proceedings of the 5th Int. Workshop on Image Analysis for Multimedia Interactive Services*. WIAMIS.

Zeljkovic, V., Dorado, A., & Izquierdo, E. (2004). Combining a fuzzy rule-based classifier and illumination invariance for improved building detection. *IEEE Transactions on Circuits and Systems for Video Technology*, (14): 1277–1280. doi:10.1109/TCSVT.2004.835145

Zeljkovic, V., Dorado, A., Trpovski, Ž., & Izquierdo, E. (2004). Classification of building images in video sequences. *IEEE Electronics Letters*, 40(3), 169–170. doi:10.1049/el:20040128

Zeljkovic, V., Pokrajac, D., Dorado, A., & Izquierdo, E. (2005). Application of the improved illumination independent moving object detection algorithm on the real video sequence. In *Proceedings of the 6th International Workshop on Image Analysis for Multimedia Interactive Services*. WIAMIS.

Zeljkovic, V., Trpovski, Z., & Senk, V. (2003). Improved illumination independent moving object detection in real world video sequences. In *Proceedings of the 4th EURASIP Conf. focused on Video/Image Processing and Multimedia Communications*. EURASIP.

Section 3
Shape Recognition Algorithms

The natural process in automated video surveillance systems is to perform correct shape recognition and object identification after the desired moving object is correctly detected.

Two new model-based algorithms for shape recognition are proposed. The proposed algorithms are efficient and tolerate severe noise. They have the ability to identify the close match between the noisy polygon that has a significantly greater number of sides and the assigned polygon. They work for convex and concave polygons equally well. These algorithms are invariant under translation, rotation, change of scale, and are reasonably easy to compute. The proposed criterion is a metric. The polygonal shapes are compared based on their areas and gravity centers.

A two-step process for removing noise from polygonal shapes for the purpose of easier and more efficient shape recognition is presented in this chapter. A polygonal shape is presented as its turning function and then a nonlinear diffusion filter and triangle method are applied. The obtained results demonstrate that the proposed technique successfully removes vertices that should be dismissed as noise while preserving dominant vertices that can be accepted as relevant features and give a faithful description of the shape of the polygon.

Chapter 8
Shape Recognition Methods Used for Complex Polygonal Shape Recognition

ABSTRACT

Two new algorithms, optimal and sub-optimal solution algorithm, for shape recognition using geometric calculations are proposed. They are mode-based, which means that shape from the data base which is considered as a model is compared with another shape extracted from the sequence of images, such as, for example, a moving object. The proposed algorithms are efficient and tolerate severe noise. They have the ability to identify the close match between the noisy polygon that has a significantly greater number of sides and the assigned polygon. They work for convex and concave polygons equally well. These algorithms are invariant under translation, rotation, change of scale, and are reasonably easy to compute. The proposed criterion is a metric. The polygonal shapes are compared based on their areas and gravity centers. One polygon is placed over the other one so that one polygon has a fixed center of area (gravity center). The area of the intersection of these two polygons is calculated after one of the polygons is rotated one degree at time. The angular position with the best match is recorded.

1. INTRODUCTION

A very important domain in video surveillance systems is object identification. This is a phase that comes after the moving object detection and moving object tracking blocks. After designing the intelligent software capable of extraction of moving objects from video sequence without any aside intervention, the next problem to be solved is how to train the system to identify the detected object and report its identification automatically. That is why shape recognition has its theoretical and practical importance in image processing and computer vision.

Many authors have done research in the shape resemblance domain (Schwartz, 1984), (Shapiro, 1982), (O'Rourke, 1985), (Hong, 1988), (Cox, 1989), (Avis, 1983), but these methods are position, range scale and orientation dependent. They are not metrics and are also complicated from computational point of view. Some of these methods (Schwartz, 1984) and (Cox, 1989), apply only to convex polygons and that additionally restricts the proposed algorithms. Huttenlocher and Kedem in (Huttenlocher, 1990) develop the method that computes a distance between two shapes based on the Hausdorff metric. Their metric compares polygonal shapes independently of affined transformation. Some of the proposed

DOI: 10.4018/978-1-4666-4896-8.ch008

algorithms as in (Wolson, 1987) use the curvature function as a shape signature. The methods presented in (Schwartz, 1984), (Shwartz, 1987) and (Arkin, 1991) have a similar approach. They are all based on convolution.

The authors in (Arkin, 1991) represent the simple polygon boundary with the turning function that measures the angle of the counterclockwise tangent as a function of the arc-length, measured from some reference point on polygon's boundary. The turning function represents the angle that the tangent at the reference point makes with some reference orientation associated with the polygon (such as the x-axis). It keeps track of the turning that takes place, increasing with left-hand turns and decreasing with right-hand turns. The metric proposed in (Arkin, 1991) turns out to be very problematic for noisy and destroyed shapes.

In this chapter it is proposed a model based shape recognition methods that compare a shape p_1, stored in a database as a model, with another shape p_2, extracted from the image sequence. If these compared shapes are similar enough, then the algorithms should give a report of a match and return a measure of how good that match is. This model based algorithms define and compute a similarity measure function $M\left(p_1, p_2\right)$ that measures the level of similarity between two compared shapes. The only difference between the proposed two optimal solution and sub-optimal solution techniques is that in optimal solution algorithm one of the compared polygons is translated and rotated and in sub- optimal solution method one of the polygons is only rotated while the gravity centers of both compared polygons are kept concurrent.

The attention is on two dimensional polygonal shapes with the known boundaries. The algorithms work both for convex and concave polygons equally well.

The proposed algorithms proceed as follows:

1. The polygons are entered into the program. The polygon's areas are computed.

2. The polygons' gravity centers are calculated along with the area calculation.

3. Both polygons are scaled to an arbitrary size that endows them with the same area.

4. One of the polygons is positioned so that its center of gravity is fixed while the other polygon is translated and rotated for optimal solution method.

5. Both polygons are positioned so that their centers of gravity are concurrent and one of the polygons is kept fixed while the other polygon is rotated. This is the sub-optimal solution method.

6. The measure by which the polygons match is computed by comparing the area of the intersection of the polygons. One polygon is translated along x and y axis for the arbitrary value, so it can cover all possible positions in the image, and rotated by an angle of 1 degree, which is an arbitrary value, for different positions of the polygon and the comparison is made each time until it has been rotated a total of 360 degrees and translated in both x and y dimensions. The other polygon remains still all the time. All angular and x-y dimensions positions and the corresponding intersection areas are recorded.

7. The best match corresponds to the largest intersection area.

8. Based on the best match value the similarity level between the two polygons can be concluded.

The authors in (Arkin, 1991) also propose a shape comparison metric. But, unlike in (Arkin, 1991) the proposed algorithm is very noise resistant. The applied technique based on intersection area measurements makes it highly tolerant of the noise that becomes compensated and minimized with this metric. This algorithm also successfully recognizes similar shapes with displaced gravity centers due to some deformations along one of the axes. This is realized by translation of a polygon along x and y axes.

2. METHOD OVERVIEW

2.1. Area Calculation

A 2D polygon can be decomposed into triangles. For computing area, there is a very easy decomposition method for simple polygons defined as polygons that are without self -intersections.

Let a polygon Ω be defined by its vertices $V_i = (x_i, y_i)$ for $i = 0, 1, 2, ..., n$ with $V_n = V_0$. Also, let P be any point; and for each edge $V_i V_{i+1}$ of polygon Ω, form the triangle $\Delta_i = \Delta(P, V_i, V_{i+1})$.

Then, the area of Ω is equal to the sum of the *signed* areas of all the triangles Δ_i for $i = 0, 1, 2, ..., n - 1$:

$$A(\Omega) = \sum_i B(\Delta_i) - \sum_i C(\Delta_i)$$

$$\text{where } \Delta_i = \Delta(P, V_i, V_{i+1}) \tag{1}$$

For a counterclockwise oriented polygon, when the point P is on the "inside" left side of an edge $V_i V_{i+1}$, then the area of Δ_i is positive; whereas,

when P is on the "outside" right side of an edge $V_i V_{i+1}$, then Δ_i has a negative area. B denotes the positive areas Δ_i when the point P is on the "inside" left side of an edge $V_i V_{i+1}$. C denotes negative areas Δ_i, when the point P is on the "outside" right side of an edge $V_i V_{i+1}$.

If instead the polygon is oriented clockwise, then the signs are reversed, and inside triangles become negative.

From the coordinates of the vertices we calculate the distances between vertices giving us the lengths of the sides of each triangle.

$$a_i = \sqrt{(x_i - x_{i+1})^2 + (y_i - y_{i+1})^2}$$

$$b_i = \sqrt{(x_i - x_{i+2})^2 + (y_i - y_{i+2})^2} \quad , \quad i = 0, 1, 2, ..., n - 2$$

$$c_i = \sqrt{(x_{i+1} - x_{i+2})^2 + (y_{i+1} - y_{i+2})^2} \tag{2}$$

x_i and y_i are the coordinates of the ith vertex of the polygon, where $i = 0, 1, 2, ..., n-2$.

The area of each triangle is calculated using the half perimeter of the triangle in accordance to the following formula:

$$p_i = \frac{a_i + b_i + c_i}{2}$$

$$C_i, B_i = \sqrt{p_i(p_i - a_i)(p_i - b_i)(p_i - c_i)} \tag{3}$$

2.2. Gravity Center Calculation

While the areas are being calculated the gravity center is calculated as well because it is also necessary in the algorithm. This requires the calculation of the gravity center of each triangle. The gravity center is defined as the intersection of gravity lines of that triangle. The gravity line is the line segment between one vertex and the midpoint of the opposite side. Each triangle has three gravity

Figure 1. Area calculation

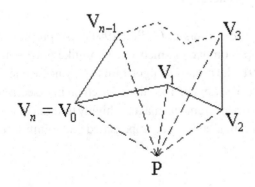

Figure 2. Gravity center calculation

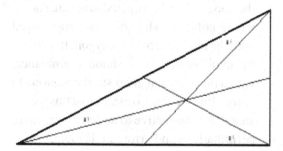

Figure 3. The mismatch area representation

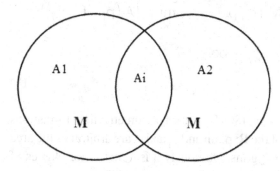

lines. The gravity center intersects each gravity line in proportion 2:1 calculated from the vertex.

However, only one gravity line is needed to calculate the gravity center of the triangle because the gravity center lies on each gravity line two-thirds the distance from the vertex to the opposite side. The gravity center of the triangle is calculated according to the formula:

$$gx_i = \frac{2}{3} gl_x$$
$$gy_i = \frac{2}{3} gl_y \qquad (4)$$

where g_i is the gravity center of the triangle and gl is the gravity line.

In order to get the coordinates of the gravity center of a polygon the gravity center coordinates of each triangle in that polygon are multiplied with the area of that triangle. Then all of these products are summed and the sum is divided by the area of the polygon. The area of the polygon is calculated as the sum of areas of all the triangles.

$$G_x = \frac{\sum_i gx_i \, B_i - \sum_i gx_i \, C_i}{B - C}$$

$$G_y = \frac{\sum_i gy_i \, B_i - \sum_i gy_i \, C_i}{B - C} \qquad (5)$$

The amount of mismatch is expressed through the area encountered with the intersection points and the vertices M of the one of the tested polygons.

Both polygons that are being compared have the same area, according to the proposed shape recognition algorithm. Suppose there are two polygons whose areas are equal.

$$A_1 = A_2 \qquad (6)$$

The mismatch area M is equal to:

$$
\begin{aligned}
A_1 &= A_2 \quad \text{and} \quad A_i = A_i \\
A_1 - A_i &= A_2 - A_i \\
M &= A_1 - A_i = A_2 - A_i
\end{aligned}
\quad , \quad A_i = A_1 \cap A_2 \,(7)
$$

3. ALGORITHM OVERVIEW

3.1 Similarity Measure Function $M\left(p_1, p_2\right)$ and Its Proprieties

A metric function that measures distances between polygons is needed. The proposed function is defined as:

$$M\left(p_1, p_2\right) \overset{def.}{=} \min_{f \in ISO\left(\Re^2\right)} \left(A\left(p_1 \setminus f\left(p_2\right)\right)\right),$$

$$p_1, p_2 \in poly_1\left(\Re^2\right)$$

(8)

where ISO($\mathbf{R}^2$) is a set of isometric transformations of the $\mathbf{R}^2$ plain and p_1 and p_2 are arbitrary unit-area polygons. Obviously it is a metric for classes of identical unit-area polygons. Thus:

$$M\left(p, p\right) = 0$$

$$M\left(p_1, p_2\right) = 0 \implies p_1 \cong p_2$$

since we are dealing with normalized-area polygons.

$$M\left(p_1, p_2\right) = M\left(p_2, p_1\right)$$

Symmetry propriety, the order of comparison does not matter. Normalized-area polygons are being used here.

$$M\left(p_1, p_3\right) \leq M\left(p_1, p_2\right) + M\left(p_2, p_3\right)$$

is apparent. Triangle inequality propriety.

The triangle inequality propriety is important for shape recognition methods and visual recognition applications because if shape p_1 is similar to shape p_2 and shape p_2 is similar to p_3, then p_1 and p_3 should be similar as well.

Other similarity measure function proprieties:

1. It is invariant under translation, rotation and scale change, which means that only the shape of the polygon is measured.
2. It is simple from a computational point of view, so that it can be easily implemented in practical purposes.

3. This function is noise-resistant. The area of the noise is small compared to the area of the whole polygon. The noise is compensated with the total area of the polygon. It matches the intuitive notions of shape resemblance, which means that it gives similar answers to human ones. This also means that this metric should be insensitive to added noise, small perturbations and errors in the data.

The proposed technique successfully recognizes similar shapes with displaced gravity centers by translation of a polygon along x and y axes. Translation of one of the polygons along two dimensional axes compensates possible deformations of the shape of one of the polygons along axes.

3.2 Theorems Proving Maximization of Intersection Area

Translation Theorem: Given two polygons, one polygon p_1, held stationary and the other polygon p_2 variable in translation position, there exist at least one translation position for p_2, for which the intersection area between these two polygons $p_1 \cap p_2$ is maximum.

Proof: Every translation is a sum of translations in both basis vector directions x and y. Every polygon can be decomposed into triangles. The intersection area of any triangle from polygon p_2 and any triangle contained in polygon p_1 is a differentiable function of translation position regarding x and y directions. When the sum of the derivatives of all triangles equals zero there is either a maximum or a minimum intersection area. It is proved that in any direction there is a position of maximum intersection area. Let one triangle from polygon p_2 be cut and positioned to move so that one of its vertices is outside polygon p_1.

Figure 4. Translation theorem

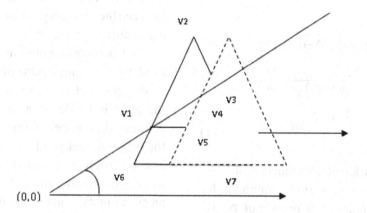

Let triangle $\triangle_{V_2 V_6 V_7}$ have area T. As triangle $\triangle_{V_2 V_6 V_7}$ moves into x direction, side $V_1 V_2$ changes by the amount $V_4 V_5$ on the side of the triangle $\triangle_{V_2 V_4 V_5}$. By the law of sines:

$$\frac{\Delta V}{\sin \varepsilon} = \frac{\Delta x}{\sin(\Theta - \varepsilon)}, \; \Theta = \angle\left(V_2 V_6 V_7\right)$$

(9)

Since triangle $\triangle_{V_1 V_2 V_3}$ has constant angles and one side changes in proportion to the Δx, its area changes in proportion to $(\Delta x)^2$. The area is a differentiable function with respect to x:

$$A \propto (\Delta V)^2$$
$$A \propto (\text{const} \cdot \Delta x)^2 = (\text{const})^2 (\Delta x)^2 = \text{const} \cdot (\Delta x)^2$$
$$A \propto (\Delta x)^2$$

(10)

The intersection area of the two polygons is equal to the area of the sum of all triangles constituting the translated polygon from which are subtracted triangles outside of the stationary polygon. This area has a derivative respect to x position of the displaced polygon that can be set to zero. By the mean value theorem there exist, in the interval of x where $p_1 \cap p_2 \neq \text{null set}$, at least one maximum area for some value of x.

The same proof is valid and applicable for any direction.

Rotation Theorem: Given two polygons, one polygon p_1, held stationary and the other polygon p_2 variable in rotational position, there exist at least one rotational position for p_2, for which the intersection area between these two polygons $p_1 \cap p_2$ is maximum.

Proof: Let triangle $\triangle_{V_1 V_2 V_3}$ be one of the triangles of polygon p_2 such that p_2 rotates about V_1. Triangle $\triangle_{V_1 V_2 V_5}$ is determined by angle

$$\angle\left(V_2 V_4 V_5\right) = \angle\left(V_4 V_1 V_3\right) + \Delta\Theta$$

$$V_4 V_2 = V_1 V_2 - \frac{Y}{\sin\left(\angle\left(V_2 V_1 V_3\right) + \Delta\Theta\right)},$$

and angle

$$\angle\left(V_4 V_2 V_5\right) = \text{const}$$

$\Delta\Theta$ is a rotational increment. The area of triangle $\triangle_{V_1 V_2 V_5}$ is:

$$A_{\triangle_{V_2 V_4 V_5}} =$$

$$\frac{1}{2}\left[V_1 V_2 - \frac{Y}{\sin\left(\angle\left(V_2 V_1 V_3\right) + \Delta\Theta\right)}\right] \cdot$$

$$\frac{\sin(\angle\left(V_4 V_2 V_5\right))}{\sin(\pi - \angle\left(V_4 V_2 V_5\right) - \angle\left(V_2 V_1 V_5\right) - \Delta\Theta)} \cdot$$

$$\left[V_1 V_2 \sin(\angle\left(V_4 V_1 V_3\right) + \Delta\Theta) - Y\right]$$

$$(11)$$

This area is a differentiable function of $\Delta\Theta$ which can be set to zero to find a minimum for the sum of the triangles of p_2 outside of p_1. By the mean value theorem and the cycling propriety of $\Delta\Theta$ through 2π radians there must be at least one value of $\Delta\Theta$ for which the area of summation of external triangles of p_2 is minimum and therefore the intersection area of the two polygons $p_1 \cap p_2$ is maximum.

The polygons are scaled in size so that they have the same area. Then they are positioned so that one polygon's center of gravity is fixed and the other polygon's gravity center is translated along axes. One polygon is rotated one degree at the time and translated throughout whole image while the other one remains stationary. After each one degree rotation and arbitrary translation all points, where a side of one polygon intersects a side of the other, are calculated. All these techniques are performed in vector graphics.

This having been done the area of intersection between the two polygons is computed as follows, using bitmap graphics:

Each polygon is represented in a 200x200 pixel mask by assigning a value of one to pixels inside of polygon and zero to those outside. Whether the pixel is inside or outside is determined by counting the number of times a line segment from the origin to that pixel crosses a polygon's side. The line segment is tested for all sides. An odd number of crossings indicates an inside pixel and an even number, an outside pixel. Every pixel in a mask is tested.

Those pixels, that are in both polygons, are identified by applying the logical AND operation to two binary images, that represent tested polygons. If the pixel has the value of one for both polygons it is an intersection area pixel. These intersection pixels are counted. This yields the intersection area which is compared to the area of one of the polygons (both polygons have the same area).

All these bitmap graphic operations are repeated for each angular position till the whole circle (360 degrees) is circumscribed and for each x-y position in the image. The choice of angular increment size as well as increment along x and y axes is arbitrary and can be adjusted according to the application requirements.

The angular and x-y position which yields the closest match, i.e. the biggest intersection area,

Figure 5. Rotation theorem

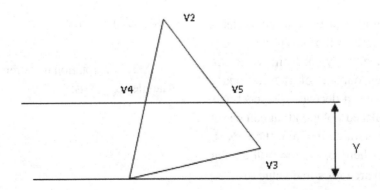

and the quality of that match are recorded. The quality of that match is defined as the ratio of the intersection area to the area of the one of the polygons. The similarity between two polygons is proportional to the match quality. The bigger the match quality the more similar the polygons are.

3.3 Alternative Approaches to Get an Optimal Solution

There are other ways to find the optimal match for rotational or translation position of one polygon over another. As each position is tested and the intersection area is measured for each of these positions, one could take from a small number of evenly spaced positions enough data points to produce a polynomial approximation of intersection area as a function of position. For instance one can, while evaluating the intersection area as the function of rotational position, take ten measurements, one every 36 degrees. A polynomial approximation is made, the derivative of the polynomial is set to zero, and the value of rotational position for which the derivative is zero, is tested by comparing intersection area values on either side of extremal to establish whether it is a maximum or a minimum. This can be refined by taking an interval on either side of each maximum, and measuring the intersection area for every degree of rotation, making a new polynomial approximation for the interval that surrounds the first maximum and use the same method to find a more accurate angular position for the maximum.

However two things can go wrong in this approach.

First, making polynomial approximations from data points, taking a derivative, finding extremals where derivative is equal to zero and testing the derivative for whether or not it is a maximum, requires many more operations then simply, directly taking the largest intersection area from all those measured as a polygon is rotated one degree at a time.

Second, a sampling of only a few data points could miss significant match positions and polynomial approximation generated by too few sample points will not detect this failure. A maximum could have a neighborhood between two minima that surround it and this neighborhood could be so small that it will hide between two data points and no polynomial approximation from the data points will detect it. This reliability shortcoming is regarded as reason to measure intersection area for every degree of rotation and the largest intersection area is taken directly from all possible rotational positions.

Finding the maximum intersection area from different translation positions will suffer the same disadvantages, as did finding the maximum intersection area as a function of rotational position. For translation, the need for reliability requires us to take the maximum intersection area directly from all translation positions.

Alternative ways of taking the maximum would be less reliable and would consume at least as much computational time as taking the maximum directly from all translation and rotational positions. The obtained results show that the tool that best fits the job, in this case, simply taking the maximum intersection area from the array of intersection areas for every different position, works best because it gives the optimal solution at pixel level precision and that is the best precision that can be gotten. The sub-pixel precision would not be real.

It was found by testing different shapes that placing the center of gravity of one polygon over that of the other and rotating it one degree at a time, it took only couple of seconds to obtain a measure of match and give sub-optimal solution for finding maximal intersection area. When the polygon is translated to each pixel and rotated it one degree at a time, it takes more time. This approach gives optimal solution considering that all possible translation and rotational positions are tested and the maximum intersection area is recorded. No better solution can be obtained considering the fact that calculations on sub-pixel or fractional pixel level cannot be performed.

If polynomial approximations are used to fit data points and derivatives taken and tested to find a maximum, the algorithm would be much more time consuming, it would be more complicated from computational point of view and it would be systematically less reliable.

The proposed algorithm is designed in such a way that it includes translation and rotational displacements and gives optimal maximal intersection area, for such applications as surveillance video signals or x-ray pictures. For such use, this algorithm must execute in a reasonable amount of time. Also the resolution of shape identification needs only to be of the order of 90%. It can make economical use of time and be more than precise enough. For this purpose, if necessary, it could be more precise, for example 99% or more. The precision of the algorithm is limited by pixel resolution.

3.4 Optimal vs. Sub-Optimal Solution

Let us define the closest match achieved by rotation of one polygon over the other polygon with concurrent centers of gravity as a sub-optimal match. Let us define the closest match achieved by rotation and translation of one of the polygons as an optimal match. It must be considered whether the use of the latter, which multiples the execution time by the number of different gravity center positions along x and y axes in the image O(num_x*num_y), as the former is justified. This is especially the case when a much faster program is almost certain to be demanded by a user.

If the polygons are perfectly matched, it is obvious that the sub-optimal match will equal the optimal match because both will have the gravity center at the same coordinates. Suppose a small perturbation of area from one side of one of these polygons is removed, than the area of that polygon has to be rescaled. This will be done by reintroducing it as a band of constant width circumscribing

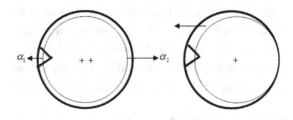

Figure 6. Gravity centers

the perimeter of that polygon. This will shift the gravity center by a small monotonic function of the perturbation area.

The approximation is made that the maximum distance across the perturbation area is much less than the width of the reintroduced band. As the perturbed polygon is shifted to bring the gravity centers closer together some of the perturbation area that was excluded from the intersection area diminishes. Let us call this diminution area α_1. But this diminution is much smaller than the area changes of the band as some of the band enters the intersection area and some intersection area adjacent to the band exits the intersection area. As a polygon shifts, part of the band opposite the perturbation enters the intersection area. The resulting increase in intersection area is α_2.

On the side of the polygon where the perturbation is, a nearly equal amount of area exits the intersection area. This area is α_3.

$$\alpha_2 \approx \alpha_3 \qquad (12)$$

As the shift continues α_1 and α_2 are increasing and α_3 is decreasing, and due to the following equation

$$\alpha_1 + \alpha_2 > \alpha_3 \qquad (13)$$

the intersection area increases with the shift position until the centers of gravity meet. After the gravity centers meet, any further shift causes α_2 to be a decrease in the intersection area. The area

α_3 continues to decrease the intersection area. Since $\alpha_2 + \alpha_3 >> \alpha_1$ we now have an intersection area decreasing with further shifting of the polygon. Thus, there is maximum intersection area where the gravity centers meet and the perturbation is small.

If the two polygons must be closely match, the deviation from that match, taken as a perturbation, calls for the execution time economical, sub-optimal solution. If the match need not be so close, the requirement for the greater precision offered by an optimal solution, will usually be irrelevant unless there is a very unusual special type of application, like character recognition, and in which execution time is not important. Therefore the sub-optimal solution is recommended that gives high result precision, almost as good, as the one obtained by optimal solution, and is very efficient in time. This is confirmed with the testing different polygonal shapes and from various experimental results. The first two testing groups of polygonal shapes mostly gave the same result for optimal and sub-optimal solution. Only character shapes demand optimal solution algorithm because there is a difference about 8 % between optimal and sub-optimal solutions.

3.5 Elapsed Time Calculation

Considering that compared polygons have m and n vertices, where num_deg is number of rotations and num_x and num_y are different gravity center positions along x and y axes in the image. The time necessary to calculate the best match between these two polygons is the following:

1. **Area Calculation:** $O(n) + O(m) = O(\max(m, n))$
2. **Gravity Center Calculation:** $O(n) + O(m) = O(\max(m, n))$
3. **Translation Calculation:** $O(n) + O(m) = O(\max(m, n))$
4. **Rotation Calculation:** $O(n) + O(m) = O(\max(m, n))$
5. **Intersection Marking:** $O(n^2) + O(m^2) = O(\max(m^2, n^2))$
6. **Intersection Area Calculation:** $O(n^2) + O(m^2) = O(\max(m^2, n^2))$

The whole time is:

$$T = O(\max(m,n)) + O(\max(m,n)) + O(\max(m,n)) + O(num\_x) * O(num\_y) * O(num\_deg) * (O(\max(m, n)) + O(\max(m^2, n^2)) + O(\max(m^2, n^2)))$$

$$T = O(\max(m,n)) + O(num\_x * num\_y * num\_degrees) * O(\max(m^2,n^2)) = O(\max(m,n)) + O(num\_x * num\_y * num\_deg * \max(m^2, n^2))$$

The total calculation of elapsed time for the optimal solution algorithm is:

$$T = O(num\_x * num\_y * num\_deg * \max(m^2, n^2)).$$

The total calculation of elapsed time for the sub-optimal solution algorithm is:

$$T = O(num\_deg * \max(m^2, n^2)).$$

It is obvious that the sub-optimal solution algorithm is $O(num\_x * num\_y)$ times more executive that optimal solution algorithm and gives as precise results as optimal solution algorithm which will be shown in the experimental results.

4. EXPERIMENTAL RESULTS

The testing of the optimal solution algorithm and the sub- optimal solution algorithm on different polygonal shapes is performed. The optimal solution algorithm performs changes in rotational and translation positions determining the best match and the sub- optimal solution algorithm does only rotational changes while keeping the concurrent gravity centers of both polygons at the position x axis 100 and y axis100, in order to find the best match.

The performance of these two algorithms is realized by testing three different groups of shapes. The first test group contains typical polygonal shapes and the same shapes with added noise. The second and the third testing groups have real life shapes and their noisy counterparts. The second group contains some car and truck shapes that could usually be detected with moving object detection algorithms in some real applications. The third group has letter forms for character recognition applications.

The choice of the similarity threshold in the proposed algorithm depends upon the application. The conclusions were made, after variety of different examples and testing that the complexity of the examined shapes influences the threshold level. It is concluded that the best similarity threshold level for all three groups of examples should be 80%.

Several examples of different convex and concave polygons of complex shapes are presented here and compared them with the algorithm described in (Arkin, 1991). The threshold that the mentioned authors use is 0.5 which means that all values below 0.5 indicate resemblance and all values beyond 0.5 indicate two different shapes.

According to the obtained results the proposed algorithms in this chapter have shown themselves to be efficient and able to tolerate severe noise and shape deformation. They have the ability to identify the close match between the noisy polygon that has a significantly greater number of sides and the assigned polygon. The sub-optimal solution algorithm shows to be more speedy and efficient then the optimal solution algorithm, as expected. For the first two testing polygon shapes groups both of the proposed algorithms give the same similarity results. Only for character shape testing group the optimal solution algorithm gives

Figure 7. Typical polygonal shapes

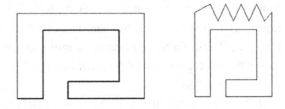

Table 1. Typical polygonal shapes (See Figure 7)

Algorithm	Similarity Percentage
The proposed algorithm Optimal solution	94.000000 % for angle 2 degrees X=100 and Y=100
The proposed algorithm Sub-optimal solution	94.000000 % for angle 2 degrees X=100 and Y=100
Algorithm in (Arkin, 1991)	0.722187

for about 8% more precise results than the sub-optimal solution algorithm.

4.1 Typical Polygonal Shapes

Observing above results, it can be seen that the proposed algorithms give the same result and in spite of severe noise show high similarity between two polygons while the technique from (Arkin, 1991) indicates two different shapes.

In this case, the proposed algorithms give again the same result and detect two similar shapes, while (Arkin, 1991) indicates limit similarity. This means that the result can be interpreted as two different or similar shapes.

Under sever distortions of the examined polygon the proposed algorithms still show high similarity between two polygons and give the same result, while the technique from (Arkin, 1991) indicates two different shapes.

In the case of two circle shapes where one of them has a tail added to one of its sides, the proposed algorithms are not seriously affected by a long thin appendage and still indicates relatively

Figure 8. Typical polygonal shapes

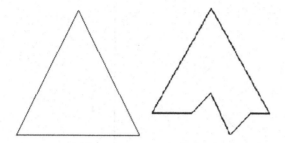

Table 2. Typical polygonal shapes (See Figure 8)

Algorithm	Similarity Percentage
The proposed algorithm Optimal solution	96.000000 % for angle 239 degrees X=100 and Y=100
The proposed algorithm Sub-optimal solution	96.000000 % for angle 239 degrees X=100 and Y=100
Algorithm in (Arkin, 1991)	0.485575

Figure 9. Typical polygonal shapes

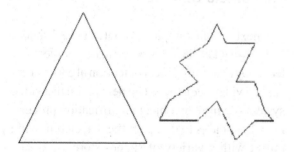

Table 3. Typical polygonal shapes (See Figure 9)

Algorithm	Similarity Percentage
The proposed algorithm Optimal solution	88.000000 % for angle 243 degrees X=100 and Y=100
The proposed algorithm Sub-optimal solution	88.000000 % for angle 243 degrees X=100 and Y=100
Algorithm in (Arkin, 1991)	0.572476

Figure 10. Typical polygonal shapes

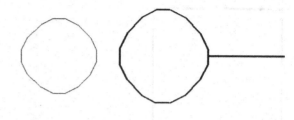

Table 4. Typical polygonal shapes (See Figure 10)

Algorithm	Similarity Percentage
The proposed algorithm Optimal solution	92.000000 % for angle 6 degrees X=100 and Y=100
The proposed algorithm Sub-optimal solution	92.000000 % for angle 6 degrees X=100 and Y=100
Algorithm in (Arkin, 1991)	0.589517

high similarity between two polygons while the technique from (Arkin, 1991) indicates two different shapes. Both proposed algorithms have again the same result.

The proposed algorithms successfully interpret the polygon with saw tooth noise present all of its sides as a shape similar to polygon without noise. They give again the same result. The technique from (Arkin, 1991) fails to detect this match.

In this case all three algorithms show similarity between two shapes in spite of different size, rotational position and translation. This proves the properties of insensitivity to range scale, rotation and translation of the proposed metric. Again optimal and sub-optimal solution algorithms give the same result.

When the noise is introduced to one of the shapes the proposed algorithms still identify the same shape while the method in (Arkin, 1991) indicates two different shapes. They give again the same result.

It can be concluded that for the first group of polygonal shapes, the proposed optimal solution algorithm gives as the best solution the one obtained by sub-optimal solution algorithm.

Figure 11. Typical polygonal shapes

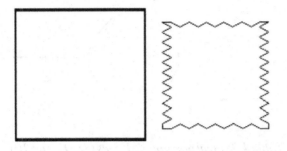

Table 5. Typical polygonal shapes (See Figure 11)

Algorithm	Similarity Percentage
The proposed algorithm Optimal solution	87.000000 % for angle 5 degrees X=100 and Y=100
The proposed algorithm Sub-optimal solution	87.000000 % for angle 5 degrees X=100 and Y=100
Algorithm in (Arkin, 1991)	0.915269

Figure 12. Typical polygonal shapes

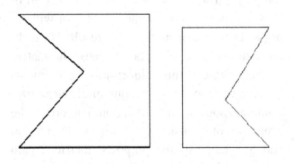

Table 6. Typical polygonal shapes (See Figure 12)

Algorithm	Similarity Percentage
The proposed algorithm Optimal solution	87.000000 % for angle 188 degrees X=100 and Y=100
The proposed algorithm Sub-optimal solution	87.000000 % for angle 188 degrees X=100 and Y=100
Algorithm in (Arkin, 1991)	0.332056

Figure 13. Typical polygonal shapes

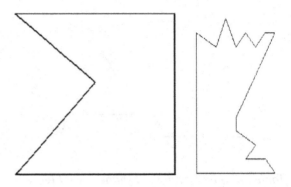

Table 7. Typical polygonal shapes (See Figure 13)

Algorithm	Similarity Percentage
The proposed algorithm Optimal solution	85.000000 % for angle 190 degrees X=100 and Y=100
The proposed algorithm Sub-optimal solution	85.000000 % for angle 190 degrees X=100 and Y=100
Algorithm in (Arkin, 1991)	0.516919

4.2 Vehicle Shapes

The next set of examples is related to real shapes from everyday life. Suppose that the object detected by a moving object detection algorithm is a car in a video sequence. The next phase in a video system is a moving object identification process. Now the goal is to compare the detected moving object with a variety of shapes stored in a data base. When the detected car shape is compared to some car shape from data base the following results are obtained. The performed testing, with this type of shapes, suggests the same threshold level as before, 80%.

In the ideal case of a noise and distortion free detected moving object all three algorithms successfully identify the object's shape. The optimal solution algorithm gives the same solution as the sub-optimal solution algorithm.

Figure 14. Vehicle shapes

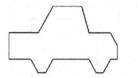

Table 8. Vehicle shapes (See Figure 14)

Algorithm	Similarity Percentage
The proposed algorithm Optimal solution	98.000000 % for angle 0 degrees X=100 and Y=100
The proposed algorithm Sub-optimal solution	98.000000 % for angle 0 degrees X=100 and Y=100
Algorithm in (Arkin, 1991)	0.373186

Figure 15. Vehicle shapes

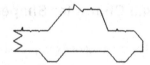

Table 9. Vehicle shapes (See Figure 15)

Algorithm	Similarity Percentage
The proposed algorithm Optimal solution	96.000000 % for angle 0 degrees X=100 and Y=100
The proposed algorithm Sub-optimal solution	96.000000 % for angle 0 degrees X=100 and Y=100
Algorithm in (Arkin, 1991)	0.367044

Figure 16. Vehicle shapes

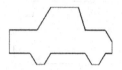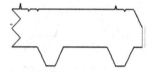

Table 10. Vehicle shapes (See Figure 16)

Algorithm	Similarity Percentage
The proposed algorithm Optimal solution	96.000000 % for angle 0 degrees X = 100 and Y = 99
The proposed algorithm Sub-optimal solution	88.000000 % for angle 0 degrees X=100 and Y=100
Algorithm in (Arkin, 1991)	0.520216

Figure 17. Vehicle shapes

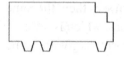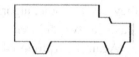

Table 11. Vehicle shapes (See Figure 17)

Algorithm	Similarity Percentage
The proposed algorithm Optimal solution	89.000000 % for angle 0 degrees X = 100 and Y = 100
The proposed algorithm Sub-optimal solution	89.000000 % for angle 0 degrees X = 100 and Y = 100
Algorithm in (Arkin, 1991)	0.530306

When a minor noise is introduced, which is more likely real situation, all three algorithms successfully identify the object's shape. Again, in spite the noise the optimal solution algorithm solution coincides with the sub-optimal solution algorithm.

Under real life conditions, because of numerous distortion causes such as weather conditions, where moving object detection methods usually extract distorted and noisy shapes the proposed object identification algorithms successfully identify the object's shape while the algorithm in (Arkin, 1991) fails to do so.

In this case, because of the serious shape deformations the optimal solution algorithm gives 8% more precise similarity between two shapes than the sub-optimal solution algorithm, due to the gravity center shift of the deformed shape, for one pixel along y axis. Both algorithms give the correct answer.

In the ideal case of a noise and distortion free detected moving object The proposed algorithms

Figure 18. Vehicle shapes

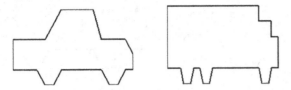

Table 12. Vehicle shapes (See Figure 18)

Algorithm	Similarity Percentage
The proposed algorithm Optimal solution	77.000000 % for angle 0 degrees X = 100 and Y = 100
The proposed algorithm Sub-optimal solution	77.000000 % for angle 0 degrees X = 100 and Y = 100
Algorithm in (Arkin, 1991)	0.521760

Figure 19. Character shapes

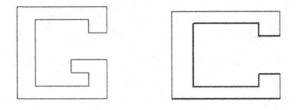

Table 13. Character shapes (See Figure 19)

Algorithm	Similarity Percentage
The proposed algorithm Optimal solution	79.000000 % for angle 358 degrees X = 99 and Y = 100
The proposed algorithm Sub-optimal solution	78.000000 % for angle 2 degrees X = 100 and Y = 100
Algorithm in (Arkin, 1991)	0.561497

successfully identify a trailer truck shape and a panel truck shape as two similar shapes, which they are. The other algorithm sees them for some reason as two different shapes, which is false.

Again, both proposed algorithms give the same result.

If a car shape is compared to a trailer truck shape and similarity threshold of 80% is used, according to tests performed on these types of polygons and shapes, the result is obtained that indicates two different shapes for all three shape recognition algorithms. The optimal solution algorithm result coincides with the sub-optimal solution algorithm, again.

It is obvious that the proposed optimal solution algorithm gives in majority of cases the same solution as the one obtained by sub-optimal solution algorithm, for the second group of polygonal shapes. Only under the conditions of the serious shape distortions of one of the shapes, the optimal solution algorithm gives the result of 8 % higher precision due to gravity center displacement but at the same time requesting longer executive time. The sub-optimal solution algorithm still gave the correct answer about the similarity between the two compared shapes, except that optimal solution algorithm gave the result with higher certainty.

4.3 Character Shapes

The next set of examples shows completely different shape types from the previous one. It is again related to real shapes from everyday life. These processed shapes represent different characters. This is very important in character recognition applications. That is why the proposed algorithms are tested on ideally shaped characters and on noisy and distorted ones. After character extraction the detected character shape is compared to some character shape from the data base. The performed testing, with this type of shapes, suggests the same threshold level, 80%.

In the ideal case of noise and distortion free two very similar characters like C and G, all three algorithms successfully identify the object's shape and indicate high similarity level. The result difference between the two proposed algorithms is only 1%.

But if a severe noise distortion is introduced to one letter and now try to identify distorted C character with the normal one from data base, which is more likely real life situation, the proposed algorithms successfully identify high similarity

Figure 20. Character shapes

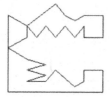 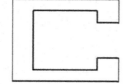

Figure 21. Character shapes

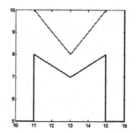 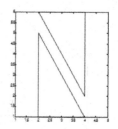

Table 14. Character shapes (See Figure 20)

Algorithm	Similarity Percentage
The proposed algorithm Optimal solution	87.000000 % for angle 359 degrees X = 100 and Y = 101
The proposed algorithm Sub-optimal solution	80.000000 % for angle 2 degrees X = 100 and Y = 100
Their algorithm	0.857566

Table 15. Character shapes (See Figure 21)

Algorithm	Similarity Percentage
The proposed algorithm Optimal solution	57.000000 % for angle 90 degrees X = 100 and Y = 98
The proposed algorithm Sub-optimal solution	53.000000 % for angle 21 degrees X = 100 and Y = 100
Algorithm in (Arkin, 1991)	0.882812

between these two characters. Algorithm in (Arkin, 1991) reports a false result.

In this case the result difference between the two proposed algorithms is higher and is 7%. But still both algorithms give truthful results.

Now again, if two different, but at the same time two very similar characters like M and N are compared, under ideal conditions, that are both noise and distortion free, all three algorithms successfully identify the object's shape and indicate high similarity level. In this case the result difference between the two proposed algorithms is 4% and both algorithms give truthful results.

But under severe noise distortions added to one letter, when the distorted M character is being identified with the normal one from data base, which is more likely real life situation, the proposed algorithm reports very high similarity between these two characters, unlike the algorithm in (Arkin, 1991) which fails and gives false result. In this case the two proposed algorithms give the same result.

In the case of two very similar characters like capital M and W, where one rotated for 180 degrees

Figure 22. Character shapes

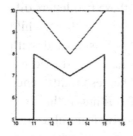 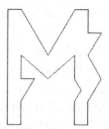

Table 16. Character shapes (See Figure 22)

Algorithm	Similarity Percentage
The proposed algorithm Optimal solution	90.000000 % for angle 0 degrees X = 100 and Y = 100
The proposed algorithm Sub-optimal solution	90.000000 % for angle 0 degrees X = 100 and Y = 100
Algorithm in (Arkin, 1991)	0.548648

Figure 23. Character shapes

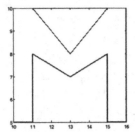 

Table 17. Character shapes (See Figure 23)

Algorithm	Similarity Percentage
The proposed algorithm Optimal solution	75.000000 % for angle 180 degrees X=100 and Y=98
The proposed algorithm Sub-optimal solution	50.000000 % for angle 4 degrees X=100 and Y=100
Algorithm in (Arkin, 1991)	0.483166

Figure 24. Character shapes

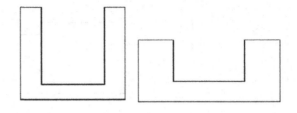

Table 18. Character shapes (See Figure 24)

Algorithm	Similarity Percentage
The proposed algorithm Optimal solution	63.000000 % for angle 90 degrees X=103 and Y=102
The proposed algorithm Sub-optimal solution	45.000000 % for angle 42 degrees X=100 and Y=100
Algorithm in (Arkin, 1991)	0.606414

looks a lot like the other one, the proposed algorithms report two different characters, unlike the algorithm in (Arkin, 1991) which fails and gives false result. The proposed technique turned out to be successful in finding these two letters different even though they have similar shape, while algorithm in (Arkin, 1991) was misled with similar shapes of these characters and reported the false interpretation. The result difference between the two proposed algorithms in this case, is 25% and both algorithms give truthful results.

All these performed experiments with different polygonal shapes and the obtained results lead to a conclusion stated above, that the described algorithms have shown high tolerance to severe noise and shape deformations and distortions that are very much likely in real image processing analysis. The proposed methods have the ability to identify the close match between the noisy polygon that has a significantly greater number of sides and the assigned polygon, but at the same time they are capable to differentiate two different characters with very similar shapes.

They show to be efficient and easy for real time implementations. The sub-optimal solution algorithm shows to be more speedy and efficient then the optimal solution algorithm giving at the same time as truthful and reliable results as the optimal solution algorithm.

The next two examples show similar shapes. These processed shapes represent actually two identical characters written in different ways. One of them is deformed along one of the axes and has thicker edges than the other one. These cases are often and very important in character recognition applications. That is why the proposed algorithms are tested on ideally shaped characters and on distorted ones. After character extraction the detected character shape is compared to some character shape from the data base. The threshold level is 80%.

In the case of huge deformation of the character shape where one of them represents U and the other one looks more like rotated letter C, both algorithms equally report two different shapes which is close to the truth. Extracted character is slightly shorter along y axis and is strongly stretched along x axis, while having thicker edges

Figure 25. Character shapes

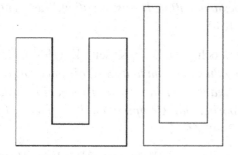

Table 19. Character shapes (See Figure 25)

Algorithm	Similarity Percentage
The proposed algorithm Optimal solution	80.000000 % for angle 356 degrees X=100 and Y=99
The proposed algorithm Sub-optimal solution	73.000000 % for angle 4 degrees X=100 and Y=100
Algorithm in (Arkin, 1991)	0.424163

then the letter in the data base. That is why all three algorithms report two different characters.

But under slight distortions along both x and y axes and in the case of thicker edges of one of the letters when distorted U character is being identified with the normal one from data base, which is more likely real life situation, the optimal solution algorithm and the algorithm proposed in (Arkin, 1991) report truthfully similarity between these two characters. The sub-optimal solution algorithm gives 7% less similarity percentage between two shapes and considering that we are in threshold zone this is interpreted as wrong answer.

It is obvious that the proposed optimal solution algorithm gives in majority of cases the different solution as the one obtained by sub-optimal solution algorithm, for the character group of polygonal shapes. The optimal solution algorithm gives the result with higher precision due to gravity center displacement but at the same time requesting longer executive time. The sub-optimal solution algorithm still gives the correct answers about

the similarity between the two compared shapes, except for the last example where there was edge case. The optimal solution algorithm gives results with higher certainty and demands more execution time.

5. CONCLUSION

The novel metric for measuring shapes resemblance is presented in this chapter. The suggested methods for shape recognition and shape comparison have several advantages:

1. This is metric for polygonal shapes.
2. It is equally applicable on convex and concave polygons.
3. It works well for very complex polygonal shapes as well for simple ones.
4. It is invariant under translation, rotation and scale change, which means that only the shape of the polygon is being measured.
5. It is simple from a computational point of view, so that it can be easily implemented in practical purposes.
6. The optimal solution algorithm takes $O(num\_x*num\_y*num\_deg* \max(m^2,n^2))$ time to compare an m vertex polygon with an n vertex polygon.
7. The sub-optimal solution algorithm takes $O(num\_deg* \max(m^2,n^2))$ time to compare an m vertex polygon with an n vertex polygon.
8. This function is noise-resistant. The area of the noise is small compared to the area of the whole polygon so it gets compensated with the total area of the polygon. It matches our intuitive notions of shape resemblance, which means that it gives similar answers to human ones. This also means that this metric should be insensitive to added noise, small perturbations and errors in the data.
9. The proposed optimal solution technique successfully recognizes similar shapes with displaced gravity centers by translation of a

polygon along x and y axes. Translation of one of the polygons along two dimensional axes compensates possible deformations of the shape of one of the polygons along axes. This characteristic makes this metric insensitive to possible shape deformations and distortions.

Vector graphics is combined with the bitmap graphics, which slightly increased the time necessary for algorithm execution.

The optimal solution algorithm gives the result with higher precision due to gravity center displacement but at the same time requesting longer executive time and the sub-optimal solution algorithm gives results of less certainty and demands much less execution time. The application of one of two proposed techniques depends of the examined polygonal shapes and the time necessary for results obtaining because the compromise has to be made between precision and execution time. The optimal solution method gives higher result precision and demands more execution time and the sub-optimal solution method provides less precise results but is more speedy and executive.

REFERENCES

Arkin, E. M., Chew, L. P., Huttenlocher, D. P., Kedem, K., & Mitchel, J. S. B. (1991). An efficiently computable metric for comparing polygonal shapes. *IEEE Transactions on Pattern Analysis and Machine Intelligence, 13*(3). doi:10.1109/34.75509

Avis, D., & ElGindy, H. (1983). A combinatorial approach to polygon similarity. *IEEE Transactions on Information Theory, 29.*

Cox, P., Maitre, H., Minoux, M., & Ribeiro, C. (1989). Optimal matching of convex polygons. *Pattern Recognition Letters,* (9): 327–334. doi:10.1016/0167-8655(89)90061-5

Hong, J., & Tan, X. (1988). *The similarity between shapes under affined transformation.* Washington, DC: IEEE.

Huttenlocher, D. P., & Kedem, K. (1990). *Computing the minimum hausdorff distance for point sets under translation.* In *Proceedings ACM Symposium for Computational Geometry,* (pp. 340-349). ACM.

O'Rourke, J., & Washington, R. (1985). Curve similarity via signatures. *Computational Geometry,* 295–318.

Schwartz, J. T., & Sharir, M. (1984). *Some remarks on robot vision.* New York: New York University.

Schwartz, J. T., & Sharir, M. (1987). Identification of objects in two and three dimensions by matching noisy characteristics curves. *The International Journal of Robotics Research, 6*(2), 29–44. doi:10.1177/027836498700600203

Shapiro, L. G., & Haralick, R. M. (1982). Organization of relational models for scene analysis. *IEEE Transactions on Pattern Analysis and Machine Intelligence, 4*(6), 595–602. doi:10.1109/TPAMI.1982.4767312 PMID:22499633

Vincelette, R. B., Tameze, C., Savic, M., & Zeljkovic, V. (2007). Efficient shape recognition method using novel metric for complex polygonal shapes. In *Advances in Applied and Computational Mathematics* (Vol. 2). New York: Nova Science Publishers.

Wolson, H. (1987). *On curve matching.* Miami Beach, FL: IEEE.

Zeljkovic, V., Vincelette, R. B., & Savic, M. (2006). *Novel object identification algorithm.* Paper presented at the 6th Conference Digital Speech and Image Processing DOGS. New York, NY.

Zeljkovic, V., Vincelette, R. B., & Savic, M. (2006). *Efficient shape recognition method using novel metric for complex polygonal shapes.* MOBIMEDIA. doi:10.1145/1374296.1374321

Chapter 9
Nonlinear Diffusion Filters Combined with Triangle Method Used for Noise Removal from Polygonal Shapes

ABSTRACT

A two-step process for removing noise from polygonal shapes is presented in this chapter. A polygonal shape is represented as its turning function and then a nonlinear diffusion filter and triangle method is applied. In the first step, several different nonlinear diffusion filters are applied to the turning function that identify dominant vertices in a polygon and remove those vertices that are identified as noise or irrelevant features. The vertices in the turning function which diffuse until the sides that immediately surround them approach the same turning function are identified as noise and removed. The vertices that are enhanced are preserved without changing their coordinates, and they are identified as dominant ones. In the second step, the vertices that form the smallest area triangles are removed. Obtained experimental results demonstrate that the proposed two-step process successfully removes vertices that should be dismissed as noise while preserving dominant vertices that can be accepted as relevant features and give a faithful description of the shape of the polygon. In experimental tests of this procedure successful removal of noise and excellent preservation of shape is demonstrated thanks to appropriate emphasis of dominant vertices.

1. INTRODUCTION

The comparison of two different shapes has always had significant theoretical and practical importance in computer vision (Arkin, 1991), (Floriani, 2007), (Kimmel, 2004). Model-based recognition is concerned with comparing a shape, stored as a model in the database, with a shape found to exist in an image. If these two shapes are close to being the same, then a vision system should report a match and return a measure of how good that match is. The focus of this chapter is on the pre-processing stage of shape comparison which deals with extraction of dominant vertices and noise removal. When a polygon is found in an image it should be identified. First, found polygon is simplified, the dominant vertices are extracted and it is de-noised. This procedure will significantly accelerate the comparison phase and make it more efficient. The idea is to find a polygon's equivalent

DOI: 10.4018/978-1-4666-4896-8.ch009

representation in its turning function space based on coordinates of its vertices. Then in the turning function space de-noising is applied through the application of a nonlinear diffusion filter and it is converted back to vertex coordinate space with extracted and identified dominant vertices of the original polygon without any loss of its shape.

Standard representation of a polygon is done by describing its boundary with a circular list of vertices where each vertex is given as a pair of its coordinates. Instead of applying de-noising method and dominant vertices identification in this domain an alternative space is used to represent the analyzed polygon. Each polygon is represented by its turning function $\Theta_A(s)$ that measures the angle of the counterclockwise tangent as a function of arclength s. $\Theta_A(0)$ is the angle that the tangent at the reference point makes with some reference orientation associated with the polygon (such as the x-axis) and keeps track of the turning that takes place, increasing with left-hand turns and decreasing with right-hand turns. The curvature function for a curve which represents the first derivative of the turning function is frequently used as a shape signature which can be found in the literature (Hong and Tan, 1988), (Hong, 1988), (Schwartz, 1984), (Wolfson, 1987), (O'Rourke, 1985). The definition, in which $\Theta_A(0)$ is the angle of the tangent line at the reference point (Hong and Tan, 1988), leads to a simple correspondence between a shift of $\Theta_A(s)$ about the origin and a rotation of the polygon. Representation of planar curves and particularly polygons as the function of arc length has been used by a number of other researchers in computational geometry (Schwartz, 1984), (Wolfson, 1987), (O'Rourke, 1985) and computer vision (Ballard, 1982).

Multi scale description of images is a very important part of computer vision (Rosenfeld, 1971). It is achieved through scale-space filtering introduced by Witkin (Witkin, 1983) and further developed by Koenderink (Koenderink, 1984), Babaud, Duda, and Witkin, (Babaud, 1986), Yuille and Poggio, (Yuille, 1986), and Hummel (Hummel, 1987), (Hummel, 1986). Perona and Malik, (Perona, 1990), introduced an anisotropic diffusion method of removing noise and sharpening the edges of objects all in one process. The essential idea of multi scale description of images is quite simple. It suggests embedding the original image in a family of derived images obtained by convolving the original image with a Gaussian kernel of variance t. Larger values of the scale-space parameter correspond to images at coarser resolutions. According to Koenderink (Koenderink, 1984) and Hummel (Hummel, 1986), a parameter family of derived images may equivalently be viewed as the solution of heat conduction, or diffusion. Koenderink (Koenderink, 1984) uses the diffusion equation formulation by stating two criteria: 1) Causality: Any feature at a coarse level of resolution is required to possess a "cause" at a finer level of resolution although the reverse need not be true, i.e. no spurious detail should be generated when the resolution is diminished; 2) Homogeneity and Isotropy: The blurring is required to be space invariant. These criteria lead naturally to the diffusion equation formulation proposed by Perona and Malik in (Perona, 1990).

Nonlinear diffusion equations found in the literature (Perona, 1990), are used here adapted to the one dimensional case in which pixel intensity is replaced with the turning functions of the sides of polygons. Some modifications were made that improve upon the speed of the conduction coefficient functions they offer as examples and a simpler to use value of the parameter K is used. Dominant vertices are enhanced and therefore identified as vertices that will survive application of the nonlinear diffusion equation. Those vertices that are noise diffuse and are eliminated. The vertices that survive retain their original coordinates so that any changes due to vertex enhancement are ignored and the enhancement will not introduce any distortion to the shape of the polygon. The diffusion of noise vertices continues as far as it can go before shape distortion sets in due to approximation errors of the exact locations of noise vertices. At this point it is switched to the triangle method to further simplify the polygon.

This method contributes a combination of two different methods for removing noise and for preserving dominant points in the turning function (Arkin, 1991), of the discrete polygon. First the nonlinear diffusion filter (Perona, 1990) is applied and then the triangle method is implemented in order to remove noise. An explanation that is similar to the triangle method is given in (Latecki, 1999). In the years since Perona and Malik published their work in (Perona, 1990), their filter equations have been applied to two dimensional images. Here their filter equation principles are applied in a new way, specifically in one dimension, to turning functions in a way that prevents instabilities. By applying nonlinear diffusion filters proposed in (Perona, 1990), noise diffusion and dominant vertex preservation is achieved, which introduces no diverging shape distorting changes in turning functions or positions of dominant vertices. That way only those vertices that have their turning function gradients enhanced the way a Perona-Malik filter enhances edges in a two dimensional image are identified. The positions of the dominant vertices are not changed but extracted and in this way instability problems are circumvented. This is how the noise is removed and the stability of dominant vertices is preserved. This is the motivation for the new way to diffuse noise vertices from polygons by applying nonlinear diffusion filters to their turning functions. No one else has used a diffusion filter in this way before. To enhance objectivity in evaluating the performance of the proposed method, the Hausdorff metric is used to make a meaningful quantitative measure of how well the method performs on figures to which noise has been added.

2. THE TURNING FUNCTION

Any polygon A can be represented through the turning function $\Theta_A(s)$ presented in (Arkin, 1991). The turning function describes the rotational orientation of each side of a polygon. It is defined as follows. Let a horizontal ray extend horizontally to the right from any point on the line segment, but between the end points of that line segment, that forms a side of a polygon. The turning function is the measure of the angle Θ taken from the upper side of the horizontal ray counterclockwise all the way around till it meets the polygon side from the exterior of the polygon. The turning function can begin at any point on the perimeter of the polygon. It is plotted as the horizontal ray that extends to the right has its origin move along the perimeter of the polygon in the counterclockwise direction until it circumscribes the polygon thereupon returning to the starting point on the perimeter. This circumscription brings the value of the turning function, Θ, from its starting turning function Θ_0, to $\Theta_0 + 2\pi$. Because each side of a polygon is a line segment of constant turning function, those values of s that correspond to each side plot as horizontal line segments shown in Figure 1. Each vertex is represented by a step function; if the vertex is convex, the step function increases and if it is concave the step function decreases. The absolute value of the range can exceed 2π for polygons that have a spiral shape but the domain is [0, 1].

Without loss of generality, it is assumed that each polygon is rescaled so that the total perimeter length is 1. $\Theta_A(0)$ is a monotone function, starting at some value $\Theta_A(0)$ and increasing to value $\Theta_A(1) = \Theta_A(0) + 2\pi$. For a non-convex polygon, $\Theta_A(s)$ may become arbitrarily large, since it accumulates the total amount of turn, which can grow as a polygon "spirals" inward. Although $\Theta_A(s)$ may become very large over the interval [0,1], in order for the function to represent

Figure 1. The turning function $\Theta_A(s)$

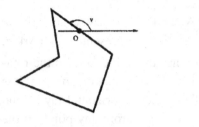

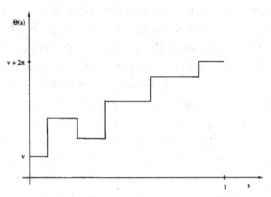

a simple closed curve, there must be $\Theta_A(1) = \Theta_A(0) + 2\pi$. The range of $\Theta_A(s)$ can be extended to the entire real line by allowing angles to continue to accumulate as we continue around the perimeter of the polygon. For a simple closed polygon, the value of $\Theta_A(s+1) = \Theta_A(s) + 2\pi$ for all s. The function $\Theta_A(s)$ is well-defined even for an arbitrary not necessarily simple or closed polygonal path A in the plane. The turning function of a polygonal path is piecewise-constant, with jump points corresponding to the vertices of A. It is customary to plot $\Theta_A(s)$ as a function of the summation of the sides s around the polygon and to scale the perimeter of the polygon to unity.

The analyzed polygon is converted from its coordinate space to turning function space (Arkin, 1991) and then a nonlinear diffusion filter (Perona, 1990) is applied to the turning function (Arkin, 1991) of polygonal shapes in order to remove noise.

3. IMPROVED NONLINEAR DIFFUSION FILTERS

The paper by Perona and Malik (Perona, 1990) gives us an anisotropic diffusion process that diffuses noise and sharpens edges simultaneously through appropriate choice of a conduction coefficient function in a heat transfer process. Their work regards each pixel as a particle that contains a quantity of heat that corresponds to the intensity of that pixel. Each pixel is connected to its four nearest neighbors by heat conduction paths through which conduction is a function of the gradient as temperature difference between the pixels on either side of the heat conduction path. If a pixel deviates from its neighbors because it is a bright or hot "salt" dot or because it is a dark or cold "pepper" dot, the temperature difference between itself and its surroundings will cause that deviation to diffuse towards the temperature of its surrounding pixels. The process is no different from "salt" dots as hot sparks that are placed on a conducting sheet which conducts the heat away from the sparks and cools them down to the temperature of the environment or little pellets of dry ice that heat up to the temperature of the environment. However, heat must conduct from hot to cold in a way that causes the gradient of temperature in a region containing a large edge to increase so that the edge will sharpen. As found in the literature (Perona, 1990) a properly designed conduction coefficient function of temperature gradient, ∇I, where I is the intensity of the pixel, will do this. The mathematical formulation of the nonlinear diffusion filter suggested is:

$$I_{ij}^{t+1} = I_{ij}^{t+1} + \lambda \begin{bmatrix} c_N * \nabla_N I + c_S * \nabla_S I + \\ c_E * \nabla_E I + c_W * \nabla_W I \end{bmatrix} \quad (1)$$

where suffix N S E W represent pixels up, down, right and left, respectively, of the analyzed pixel. The operator ∇ represents the nearest neighbor difference. The conduction coefficients are upgraded in every iteration applying the gradient operator expressed with the following equations:

$$c_i = g(\nabla I) = \frac{1}{1 + \left(\frac{|\nabla I|}{K}\right)^2}, i = N, S, W, E \quad (2)$$

$$c_i = g(\nabla I) = \frac{1}{1 + \left(\frac{|\nabla I|}{K}\right)^4}, i = N, S, W, E \quad (3)$$

$$c_i = g(\nabla I) = e^{-\left(\frac{|\nabla I|}{K}\right)^2}, i = N, S, W, E \quad (4)$$

$$c_i = g(\nabla I) = e^{-\left(\frac{|\nabla I|}{K}\right)^4}, i = N, S, W, E \quad (5)$$

$$c_i = g(\nabla I) = \sec h \left(\frac{|\nabla I|}{K}\right)^2 =$$

$$\left(\frac{e^{\left(\frac{|\nabla I|}{K}\right)^2} + e^{-\left(\frac{|\nabla I|}{K}\right)^2}}{2}\right)^{-1} \quad (6)$$

$$i = N, S, W, E$$

Equations (2) and (4) are proposed in (Perona, 1990). The proposed Equations (3), (5) and (6) meet the required differential properties in order to enhance gradients and to diffuse noise as derived in literature. The new equations are proposed with the goal to improve the overall performance of the algorithm.

In (Perona, 1990), the coefficient K was computed by setting it to 90% of the histogram of the absolute values of the gradients throughout the image. The algorithm is modified, simplifying it by making K equal to the standard deviation of the gradients of the current image pixel intensity as per following equation:

$$K = {}^!\sigma_i = \sqrt{\frac{1}{card\{I\}} \sum_i (I_i - mean\{I\})^2} \quad (7)$$

The results obtained with this slight improvement to the nonlinear diffusion filter were as good as the results obtained using the algorithm by Perona and Malik (Perona, 1990).

A one dimensional version of the nonlinear diffusion filter is applied on the turning function of the analyzed polygon which is a modified version of a two dimensional nonlinear diffusion filter suggested in literature. The idea was to use the advantages of Perona and Malik's diffusion filter that enhances edges that are in this case dominant vertices and diffuses noise and irrelevant texture, which represent irrelevant and noisy vertices.

If $\Theta_{n+1} - \Theta_n$ and $\Theta_n - \Theta_{n-1}$ have the same sign then Θ_n represents a local maximum or minimum, and if, for instance, Equation (2) is used the new calculated value of the angle is calculated by:

$$\dot{\Theta}_n = \frac{1}{1 + \left(\frac{|\Theta_{n+1} - \Theta_n|}{K}\right)^2} * (\Theta_{n+1} - \Theta_n) -$$

$$\frac{1}{1 + \left(\frac{|\Theta_n - \Theta_{n-1}|}{K}\right)^2} * (\Theta_n - \Theta_{n-1}) \quad (8)$$

Whenever the difference in angles between two adjacent sides becomes 0, $\Theta_{n+1} - \Theta_n = 0$, these sides are joined together and the turning function is recalculated. Equation (8) is an example of one dimensional nonlinear diffusion filter derived from Equation (2).

An important matter must be considered about the nonlinear diffusion process: the nonlinear diffusion filter can only approximate which vertices were most dominant before the polygon was corrupted with noise spike vertices. When a nonlinear diffusion filter reduces the number of vertices the approximation error increases shape distortion. Just before this happens it is switched to the triangle method.

4. THE TRIANGLE METHOD

The nonlinear diffusion filter closely approximates which vertices are least dominant and removes them. As many vertices as possible are removed by means of a nonlinear diffusion filter before inaccuracies of approximation cause significant shape distortion. Then it is switched to another method, the triangle method, similar to the one described in (Witkin, 1983), for identification and removal of least dominant vertices.

The triangle method takes over after nonlinear diffusion has been carried as far as it will go before approximation errors become significant.

In this method the triangle of each vertex v_n is taken and the triangle from vertices v_{n-1}, v_n, and v_{n+1} within the analyzed polygon is formed. The lengths of the sides are computed from the coordinates of these vertices and find the area of the triangle from the well known formula:

$$AREA = \sqrt{s\,(s-a)\,(s-b)\,(s-c)} \qquad (9)$$

where a, b, and c are the sides of the triangle and they are computed from the Euclidean distances between the coordinates of the vertices v_{n-1}, v_n and v_{n+1}.

$$s = \frac{a+b+c}{2} \qquad (10)$$

The dominance of each vertex v_n is defined as the area of triangle v_{n-1}, v_n, v_{n+1} and the least dominant vertex corresponding to the triangle with the smallest area is removed in each iteration. The polygon is simplified to as few sides as chosen in advance.

The area of each triangle is the measure of the dominance of vertex v_n. Because the square root in Equation (9) increases monotonically with $s(s-a)(s-b)(s-c)$, the step of taking the square root can be skipped for a faster working measure of dominance. Once a measure of dominance for each vertex is determined, the vertex that has the smallest measure of dominance is eliminated. If more than one vertex has the same measure of dominance and that is the smallest measure all vertices that tie for least dominance are eliminated. If the triangle method is carried out far enough, it could eventually result in a regular polygon in which every vertex has the same dominance. This could, for instance, be a rectangle or an equilateral triangle. It is unlikely that a shape would be recognizable after carrying out the triangle method this far.

One possible objection to the triangle method is that we could encounter a triangle that is very flat but very wide, that is, the distance between vertex v_{n-1} and vertex v_{n+1} is very large and the distance between vertex v_n to the chord v_{n-1}, v_{n+1} is very small. This results in a triangle that is so flat that it should be considered less dominant than a triangle of the same area that is not nearly so flat and therefore represents a more prominent vertex. Fortunately, when a polygon is processed several times by a nonlinear diffusion filter, the filter will remove those vertices that are surrounded by sides that have nearly the same turning function. This eliminates any excessively flat triangles before the triangle method is applied. This is why the triangle method works so well after a polygon is processed by nonlinear diffusion.

A decision has to be made as to how far to diminish the number of sides when the triangle method is being used. It is found in the experimental results that the polygons can be taken down to the original number of vertices using the triangle method and a shape that closely matched that of the unprocessed polygon is still being preserved. Hausdorff metric is calculated for comparison of original and recovered shapes.

5. EXPERIMENTAL RESULTS

The described algorithms for edge enhancement and highlighting are applied on various polygonal shapes. The proposed combined methods of the different nonlinear diffusion filters with the triangle technique is tested on polygons with many vertices, depicted in Figures 2 and 3. The shapes in Figure 2 are uncorrupted and noise is introduced that makes them resemble figures that are likely to be extracted from video images. The polygon shapes in Figures 2(a)-(d) contain 769, 47, 918 and 77 vertices, respectively. The polygon shapes in Figures 3(a)-(c) contain 791, 685 and 1074 vertices, respectively.

After applying the proposed methods, the Hausdorff metric is used and filtered shapes are compared to the original shapes to produce quan-titative measures of how well the recovered shapes approximated the uncorrupted shapes. The ratio between the Hausdorff distance and the maximum of the width or height of the shapes, Hausdorff distance/max{height, width}, is also used in order to measure the similarity between the recovered and the original shape. Let X and Y be two non-empty subsets of a metric space (M,d). Their Hausdorff distance $d_H(X,Y)$ is defined by:

$$d_H(X,Y) = \max\{ \sup_{x \in X} \inf_{y \in Y} d(c,y),$$
$$\sup_{y \in Y} \inf_{x \in X} d(c,y)\}. \tag{11}$$

where sup represents the supremum and inf the infimum. The locus of all points in the sides of polygons and their vertices as the sets (X,Y) are used.

Figure 2. (a) Noisy shape with 769 vertices; (b) Original shape with 47 vertices; (c) Noisy shape with 918 vertices; (d) Original shape with 77 vertices

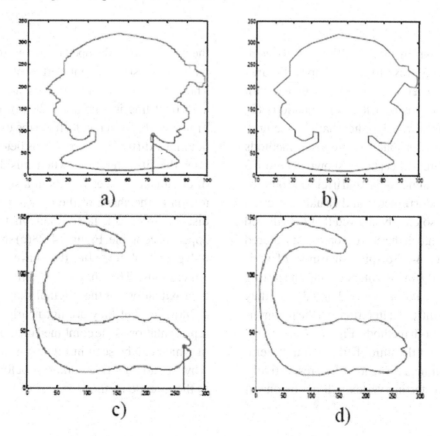

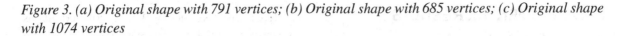

Figure 3. (a) Original shape with 791 vertices; (b) Original shape with 685 vertices; (c) Original shape with 1074 vertices

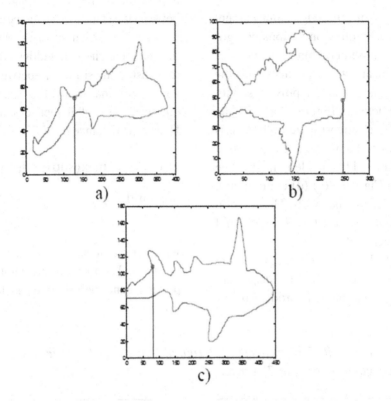

Shapes shown in Figures 2(b) and (d) were tested by adding noise to these shapes, Figures 2(a) and (c). Then they were processed with the nonlinear diffusion filters of Equations (2) through (6) followed by the triangle method, Figures 4-13. After that, the proposed methods are tested on three other shapes shown in Figure 3 that already contained noise and irrelevant details. Here, the Hausdorff metric and visual inspection is used which so clearly showed that the filtered shapes nearly match the corresponding unfiltered shapes. Figures 4-28 display snapshots of various nonlinear diffusion filters evolution starting with the noisy data in Figure 2 and 3, i.e., they correspond to different iterations on the polygons after applying both methods. Figures 4-28 (a), (b) and (c) represent the third, fifth and ninth iteration of the nonlinear diffusion filter, respectively. In order that a starting vertex will not be one of the vertices to be dropped each iteration is begun with the most dominant vertex of the polygon. These most dominant vertices are marked by a vertical line in Figures 4-28 (a), (b) and (c). From the obtained results from the use of various nonlinear diffusion filters it was determined that after the fifth iteration, when misidentification of dominant vertices results in a significant distortion to the shape of the polygon, these shape distortions became larger than what is judged to appear acceptable. Figures 4-28(c) show what the polygons look like after they have been through 9 iterations. The shapes are still recognizable approximations of the original shapes in Figures 4-28(a)-(c), but they are not nearly as precise a representation as the combined method the results of which can be seen in Figures 4-28(d). This is why we did only five iterations before switching to the triangle method.

Figure 4. a)-c) 3ʳᵈ, 5ᵗʰ and 9ᵗʰ iteration of the nonlinear diffusion filter from Equation (2); d) triangle method applied after the 5ᵗʰ iteration of the nonlinear diffusion filter; e) comparison of Figure 2 a) & Figure 3 d); f) comparison of Figure 2 b) & Figure 4 d)

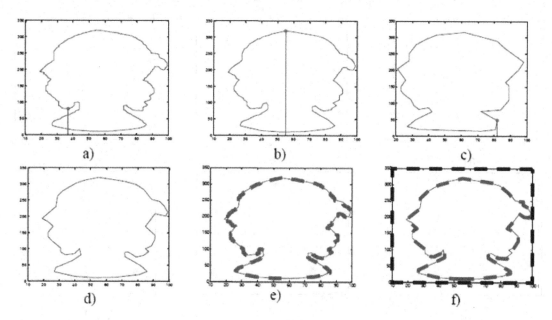

a)   b)   c)

d)   e)   f)

Figures 4-5 and 14-16 represent the results obtained after the application of the nonlinear diffusion filter expressed with Equation (2). Figures 6-7 and 17-19 represent the results obtained after the application of the nonlinear diffusion filter expressed with Equation (3). Figures 8-9 and 20-22 represent the results obtained after the application of the nonlinear diffusion filter expressed with Equation (4). Figures 10-11 and 23-25 represent the results obtained after the application of the nonlinear diffusion filter expressed with Equation (5). Figures 12-13 and 26-28 represent the results obtained after the application of the nonlinear diffusion filter expressed with Equation (6).

Tables 1-2 give the number of dominant vertices remaining in each polygon after 3, 5 and 9 iterations obtained by the application of five different proposed nonlinear diffusion filters on shapes in Figures 2 and 3, respectively. It is shown in Tables 1 and 2 that the number of pixel widths of the Hausdorff metric and that distance is com-

pared to the maximum of the height or the width of the shape. In Table 1 Equation (5) gave the best result; the shape in Figure 2(b) had a Hausdorff distance of only 1.5 pixel widths or 0.48% of the height of the shape, the shape in Figure 2(d) had a Hausdorff distance of 1.54 pixel widths or 0.6% of the width of the shape. This demonstrates the precision with which the recovered shape approximates the shape that existed before it was noise corrupted, since the Hausdorff distance is largest deviation of a vertex of one polygon to the nearest point on another polygon.

The comparisons are made from the number of vertices left after various iterations and the Hausdorff distance is measured between the shapes from Figure 3 and the recovered shapes after our method in Figures 14-24(d).

Table 2 shows that the nonlinear diffusion filter expressed with Equation (3) left the most vertices and therefore should be considered the poorest performer and the nonlinear diffusion filters expressed with Equations (4) and (5) left the fewest

Figure 5. (a)-(c) 3rd, 5th and 9th iteration of the nonlinear diffusion filter from Equation (2); (d) triangle method applied after the 5th iteration of the nonlinear diffusion filter; (e) comparison of Figure 2 (c) & Figure 3 (d); (f) comparison of Figure 2 (d) & Figure 5 (d)

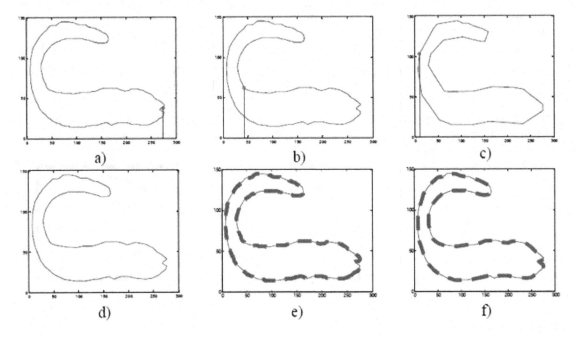

Figure 6. (a)-(c) 3rd, 5th and 9th iteration of the nonlinear diffusion filter from Equation (3); (d) triangle method applied after the 5th iteration of the nonlinear diffusion filter; (e) comparison of Figure 2 (a) & Figure 3 (d); (f) comparison of Figure 2 (b) & Figure 6 (d)

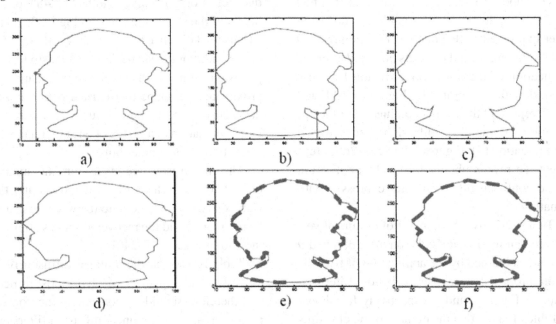

Figure 7. (a)-(c) 3ʳᵈ, 5ᵗʰ and 9ᵗʰ iteration of the nonlinear diffusion filter from Equation (3); (d) triangle method applied after the 5ᵗʰ iteration of the nonlinear diffusion filter; (e) comparison of Figure 2 (c) & Figure 3 (d); (f) comparison of Figure 2 (d) & Figure 7 (d)

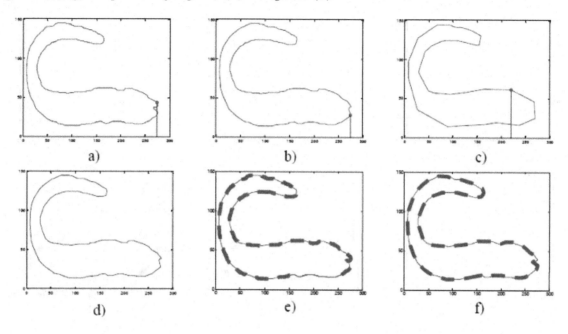

Figure 8. (a)-(c) 3ʳᵈ, 5ᵗʰ and 9ᵗʰ iteration of the nonlinear diffusion filter from Equation (4); (d) triangle method applied after the 5ᵗʰ iteration of the nonlinear diffusion filter; (e) comparison of Figure 2 (a) & Figure 3 (d); (f) comparison of Figure 2 (b) & Figure 8 (d)

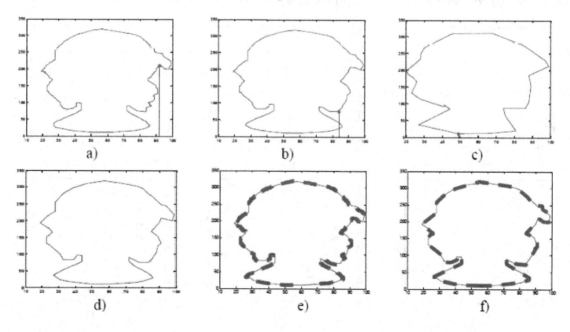

Figure 9. (a)-(c) 3rd, 5th and 9th iteration of the nonlinear diffusion filter from Equation (4); (d) triangle method applied after the 5th iteration of the nonlinear diffusion filter; (e) comparison of Figure 2 (c) & Figure 3 (d); (f) comparison of Figure 2 (d) & Figure 9 (d)

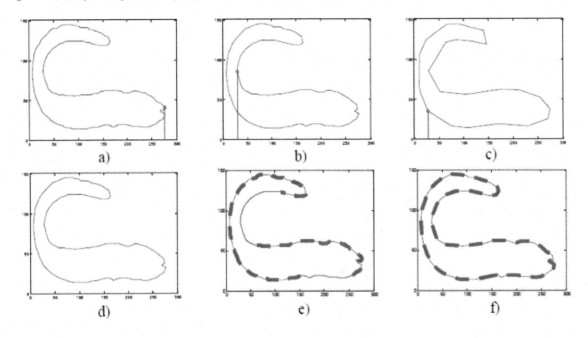

Figure 10. (a)-(c) 3rd, 5th and 9th iteration of the nonlinear diffusion filter from Equation (5); (d) triangle method applied after the 5th iteration of the nonlinear diffusion filter; (e) comparison of Figure 2 (a) & Figure 3 (d); (f) comparison of Figure 2 (b) & Figure 10 (d)

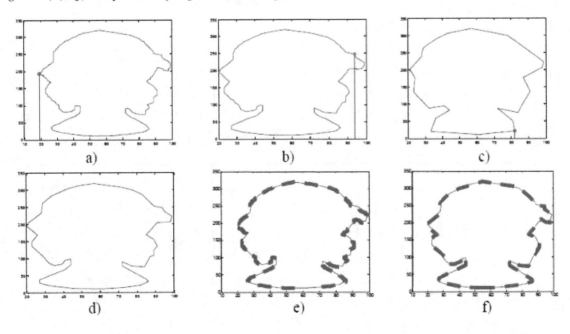

Figure 11. (a)-(c) 3ʳᵈ, 5ᵗʰ and 9ᵗʰ iteration of the nonlinear diffusion filter from Equation (5); (d) triangle method applied after the 5ᵗʰ iteration of the nonlinear diffusion filter; (e) comparison of Figure 2 (c) & Figure 3 (d); (f) comparison of Figure 2 (d) & Figure 11 (d)

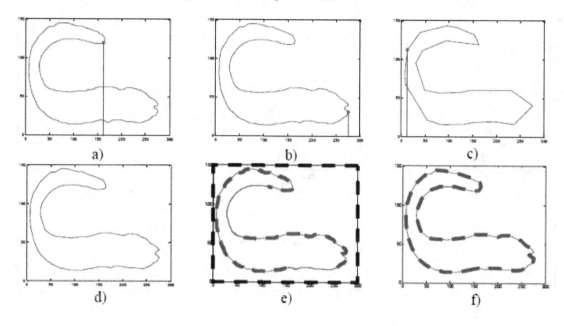

Figure 12. (a)-(c) 3ʳᵈ, 5ᵗʰ and 9ᵗʰ iteration of the nonlinear diffusion filter from Equation (6); (d) triangle method applied after the 5ᵗʰ iteration of the nonlinear diffusion filter; (e) comparison of Figure 2 (a) & Figure 3 (d); (f) comparison of Figure 2 (b) & Figure 12 (d)

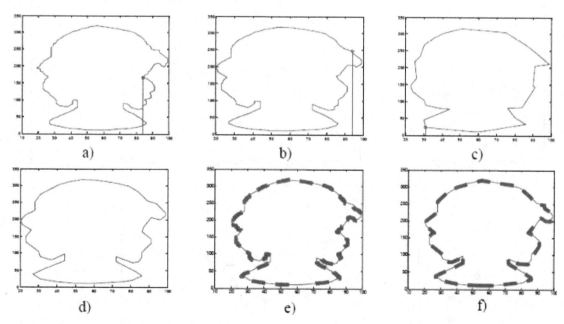

Figure 13. (a)-(c) 3rd, 5th and 9th iteration of the nonlinear diffusion filter from Equation (6); (d) triangle method applied after the 5th iteration of the nonlinear diffusion filter; (e) comparison of Figure 2 (c) & Figure 3 (d); (f) comparison of Figure 2 (d) & Figure 13 (d)

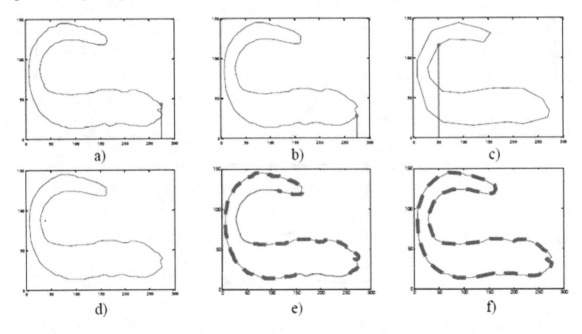

Figure 14. (a)-(c) 3rd, 5th and 9th iteration of the nonlinear diffusion filter from Equation (2); (d) triangle method applied after the 5th iteration of the nonlinear diffusion filter; (e) comparison of Figure 2 (a) & Figure 14 (d)

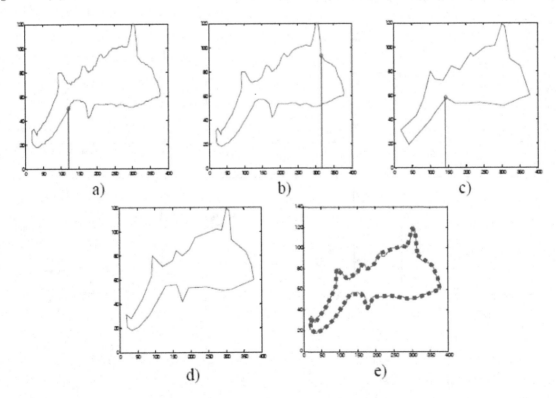

Figure 15. (a)-(c) 3ʳᵈ, 5ᵗʰ and 9ᵗʰ iteration of the nonlinear diffusion filter from Equation. (2); (d) triangle method applied after the 5ᵗʰ iteration of the nonlinear diffusion filter; (e) comparison of Figure 2 (a) & Figure 15 (d)

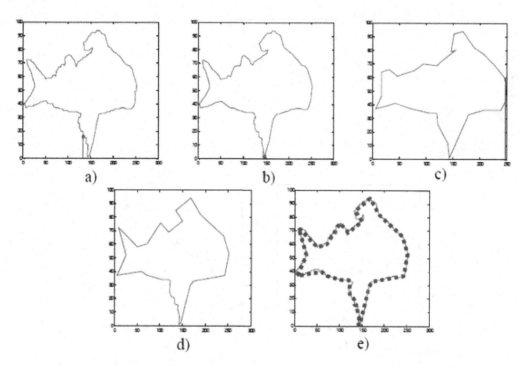

Figure 16. (a)-(c) 3ʳᵈ, 5ᵗʰ and 9ᵗʰ iteration of the nonlinear diffusion filter from Equation (2); (d) triangle method applied after the 5ᵗʰ iteration of the nonlinear diffusion filter; (e) comparison of Figure 2 (a) & Figure 16 (d)

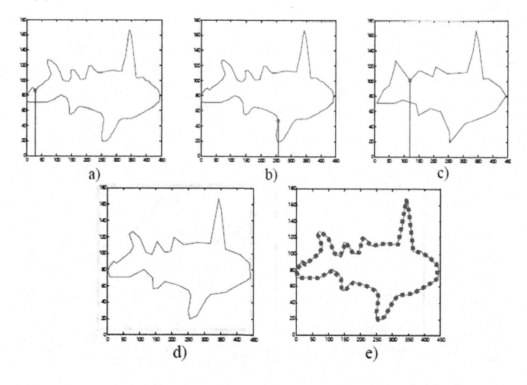

Figure 17. (a)-(c) 3rd, 5th and 9th iteration of the nonlinear diffusion filter from Equation (3); (d) triangle method applied after the 5th iteration of the nonlinear diffusion filter; (e) comparison of Figure 2 (a) & Figure 17 (d)

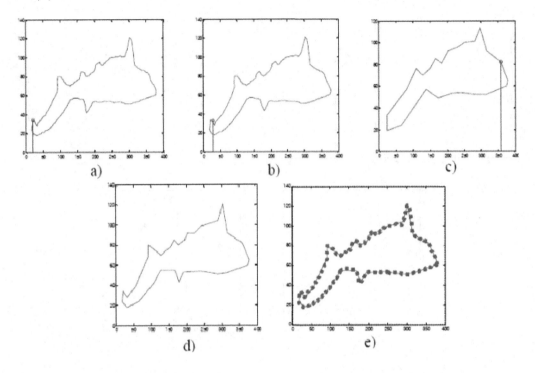

Figure 18. (a)-(c) 3rd, 5th and 9th iteration of the nonlinear diffusion filter from Equation (3); (d) triangle method applied after the 5th iteration of the nonlinear diffusion filter; (e) comparison of Figure 2 (a) & Figure 18 (d)

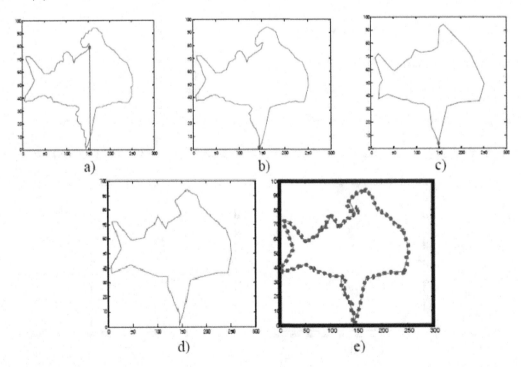

Figure 19. (a)-(c) 3ʳᵈ, 5ᵗʰ and 9ᵗʰ iteration of the nonlinear diffusion filter from Equation (3); (d) triangle method applied after the 5ᵗʰ iteration of the nonlinear diffusion filter; (e) comparison of Figure 2 (a) & Figure 19 (d)

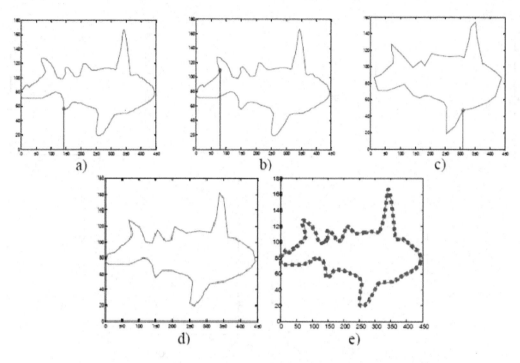

Figure 20. (a)-(c) 3ʳᵈ, 5ᵗʰ and 9ᵗʰ iteration of the nonlinear diffusion filter from Equation (4); (d) triangle method applied after the 5ᵗʰ iteration of the nonlinear diffusion filter; (e) comparison of Figure 2 (a) & Figure 20 (d)

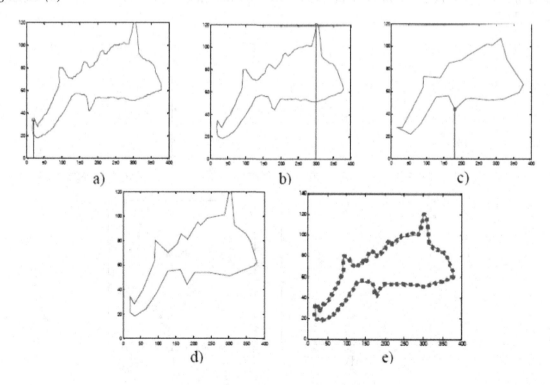

Figure 21. (a)-(c) 3ʳᵈ, 5ᵗʰ and 9ᵗʰ iteration of the nonlinear diffusion filter from Equation (4); (d) triangle method applied after the 5ᵗʰ iteration of the nonlinear diffusion filter; (e) comparison of Figure 2 (a) & Figure 21 (d)

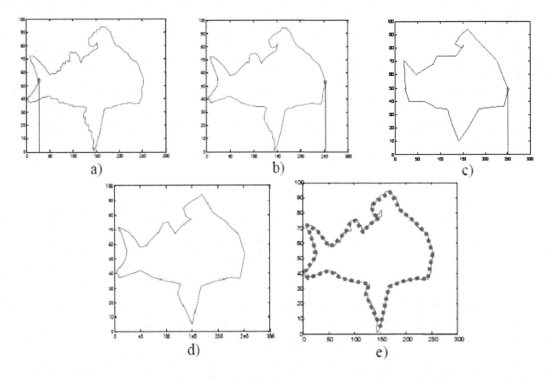

Figure 22. (a)-(c) 3ʳᵈ, 5ᵗʰ and 9ᵗʰ iteration of the nonlinear diffusion filter from Equation (4); (d) triangle method applied after the 5ᵗʰ iteration of the nonlinear diffusion filter; (e) comparison of Figure 2 (a) & Figure 22 (d)

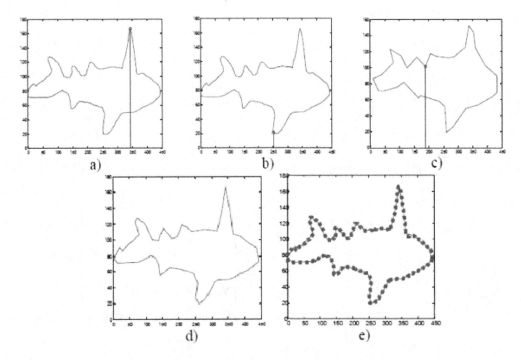

Figure 23. (a)-(c) 3rd, 5th and 9th iteration of the nonlinear diffusion filter from Equation (5); (d) triangle method applied after the 5th iteration of the nonlinear diffusion filter; (e) comparison of Figure 2(a) & Figure 23 (d)

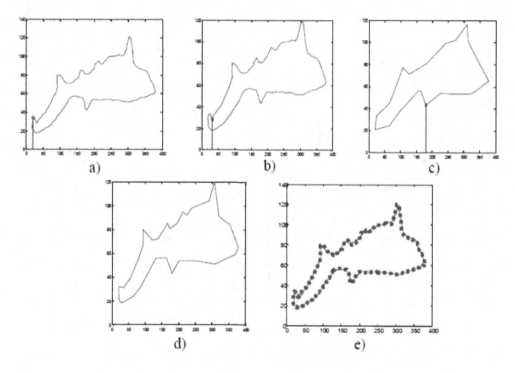

Figure 24. (a)-(c) 3rd, 5th and 9th iteration of the nonlinear diffusion filter from Equation (5); (d) triangle method applied after the 5th iteration of the nonlinear diffusion filter; (e) comparison of Figure 2 (a) & Figure 24 (d)

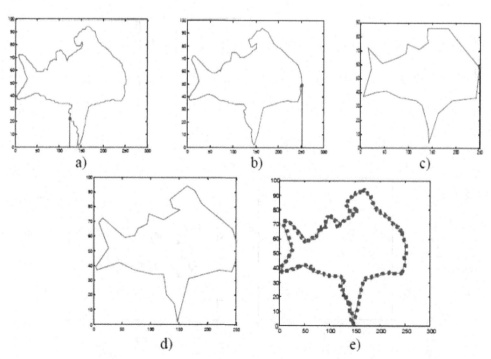

Figure 25. (a)-(c) 3rd, 5th and 9th iteration of the nonlinear diffusion filter from Equation (5); (d) triangle method applied after the 5th iteration of the nonlinear diffusion filter; (e) comparison of Figure 2 (a) & Figure 25 (d)

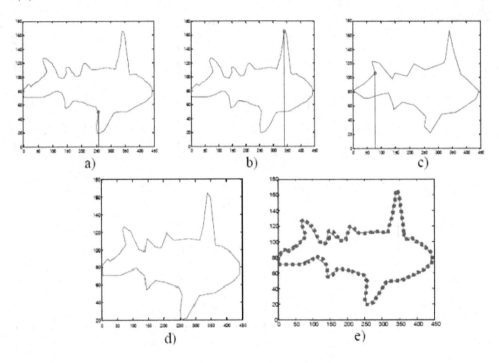

Figure 26. (a)-(c) 3rd, 5th and 9th iteration of the nonlinear diffusion filter from Equation (6); (d) triangle method applied after the 5th iteration of the nonlinear diffusion filter; (e) comparison of Figure 2 (a) & Figure 26 (d)

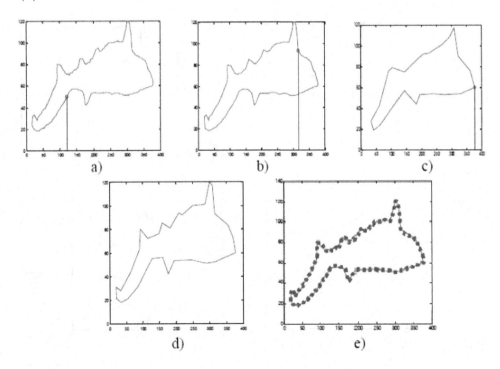

Figure 27. (a)-(c) 3rd, 5th and 9th iteration of the nonlinear diffusion filter from Equation (6); (d) triangle method applied after the 5th iteration of the nonlinear diffusion filter; (e) comparison of Figure 2(a) & Figure 27(d)

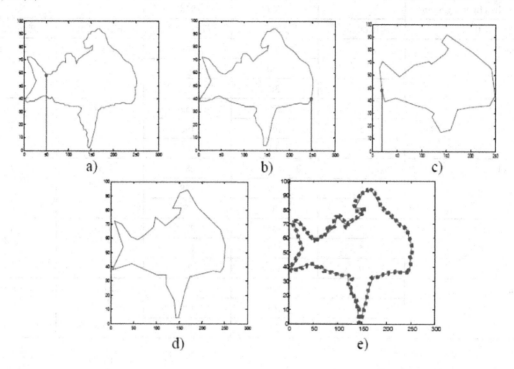

Figure 28. (a)-(c) 3rd, 5th and 9th iteration of the nonlinear diffusion filter from Equation (6); (d) triangle method applied after the 5th iteration of the nonlinear diffusion filter; (e) comparison of Figure 2 (a) & Figure 28 (d)

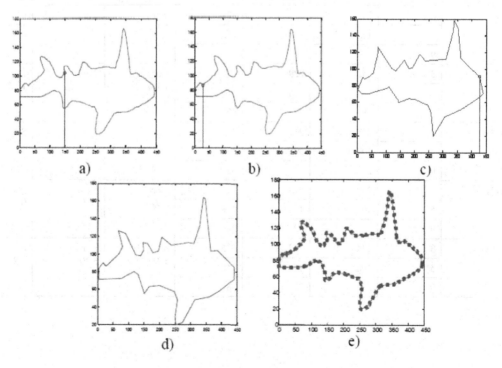

Table 1.

# of Vertices in Original Shape		**47**	**77**	**Hausdorff Distance**	
# of Vertices in Noisy Shape		**769**	**918**		
Method	Iteration	Figure 2 b)	Figure 2 d)	Figure 2 b)	Figure 2 d)
Equation (2)	3	262	306	2.35 or 0.76%	2.12 or 0.8%
	5	130	146		
	9	36	31		
Equation (3)	3	279	357	2.6 or 0.84%	5.1 or 2%
	5	161	198		
	9	40	42		
Equation (4)	3	252	281	1.6 or 0.52%	2.24 or 0.87%
	5	122	128		
	9	30	27		
Equation (5)	3	245	277	1.5 or 0.48%	1.54 or 0.6%
	5	117	126		
	9	28	27		
Equation (6)	3	256	282	2.83 or 0.92%	5.1 or 2%
	5	161	129		
	9	33	28		

Table 2.

# of Vertices in Original Shape		**791**	**685**	**1074**	**Hausdorff Distance**		
Method	**Iteration**	Figure 3 a)	Figure 3 b)	Figure 3 c)	Figure 3a)	Figure 3 b)	Figure 3 c)
Equation (2)	3	247	227	325	4 or 1.1%	6 or 2.4%	6 or 1.7%
	5	115	114	152			
	9	28	30	33			
Equation (3)	3	242	229	374	4 or 1.1%	7 or 2.7%	7 or 1.6%
	5	126	126	170			
	9	28	33	42			
Equation (4)	3	238	212	322	8 or 2.2%	8 or 3.2%	8 or 1.8%
	5	107	99	148			
	9	23	25	32			
Equation (5)	3	239	218	324	7 or 1.9%	6.5 or 2.6%	3.5 or 0.8%
	5	108	104	148			
	9	23	28	34			
Equation (6)	3	239	223	325	5 or 1.1%	8 or 3.2%	8 or 1.8%
	5	108	106	150			
	9	24	27	38			

vertices in all shapes and at the same time gave the same visual quality, shown in Figures 14-28 a)-c). Considering these results, the nonlinear diffusion filters expressed with Equations (4) and (5) have the best performances while it is as efficient as the other nonlinear diffusion filters.

The obtained results show that the performance of various nonlinear diffusion filters does not depend upon the shape of the polygon being filtered. Figures 4-13 and 14-28 d) show the polygons after the triangle method applied on the fifth iteration of the nonlinear diffusion filter, shown in Figures 4-13 and 14-28 b), has simplified them down to 47, 77, 30, 30, and 40 vertices respectively. The combined method of nonlinear filter and triangle method diminishes the number of vertices of the original polygon by a factor of approximately 24 to 27 in the case of the shapes in Figure 3. The noise and insignificant detail have been removed while the dominant vertices that convey the shape information have been preserved with a precision visibly far superior to the results observed in Figures 4-13 and 14-28 c). After this remarkable simplification, it is shown how closely each simplified polygon resembles its original one. In Figures 4-13 e)-f) and 4-28 e) the original polygons from Figures 2 and 3 are overlaid upon their processed simplified selves from Figures 4-13 and 14-28 d) respectively. In Figures 4-13 e)-f) and 14-28 e) it can be seen that the simplified shapes are almost indistinguishable from their originals which is obvious from calculated Hausdorff distances between original and recovered shapes, shown in Tables 1 and 2.

6. CONCLUSION

According to the experimental results, it can be concluded that all proposed nonlinear diffusion filters are very effective in selecting for removal those vertices that are most likely to be noise or irrelevant details. They efficiently give satisfactory results according to Hausdorff distance and visual inspection.

The nonlinear diffusion filters expressed with Equation (4) and (5) removed the highest number of noisy vertices, but differences in the performances of all proposed nonlinear diffusion filters indicate that all of the tested nonlinear diffusion equations produced shape preservation with good precision while being equally efficient from a necessary time of performance point of view.

The dominant vertices to be preserved are closely but not always exactly identified. When there are many closely spaced vertices, the effect of a near-miss identification is very slight but when the tested figures were simplified down to approximately one hundred sides, misidentification errors resulted in noticeable shape distortion. During nonlinear diffusion, the vertices to be preserved as most dominant are closely but not always exactly identified. For example, if vertex v_n is locally a most dominant vertex, noise corruption could cause vertex v_{n+1} or vertex v_{n-1} to be identified as the vertex that was most locally dominant before v_{n-1} through v_{n+1} were obscured by the noise. When there are many vertices close together, such an error is inconsequential, but as the polygon is simplified the vertices are spaced further apart. Then such a misidentification results in a larger and therefore noticeable distortion to the shape of the figure. When the tested figures were simplified down to approximately one hundred sides it is switched from nonlinear diffusion to the triangle method for continued removal of vertices that are treated as noise.

The triangle method is tested in place of nonlinear diffusion for smoothing noise from polygons that have on the order of several hundred sides and it was discovered that it cannot preserve the shape as accurately as the nonlinear diffusion filters. But it worked very well when it was applied to polygons that had been simplified down to about one hundred sides by the nonlinear diffusion filter. Also, nonlinear diffusion filters, applied prior to the triangle method, solved the problem of flat triangles that might appear dominant to the triangle method which computes triangle area as a measure of vertex dominance.

Nonlinear diffusion filters, where the triangle method does not work well, followed by the triangle method, where nonlinear diffusion filters do not work well, allow us to use the advantages of both methods while circumventing their disadvantages. This resulted in a simplification and precision far superior to what could be achieved by either method used by itself.

Two different novel algorithms are described in the next chapter that can identify aircraft categories from Inverse Synthetic Aperture Radar (ISAR) images that use both the radar reflection pulse shape, which includes the duration or size of the radar pulse that is reflected, and the Doppler shifts of different parts of the aircraft caused by rotational motions of the aircraft as it maneuvers. The first method forms numerical equivalents to shape, size and other aircraft features as critical criteria to constitute the algorithm for their correct classification. The second method compares each ISAR image to unions of images of the different aircraft categories. Automatic body detection and identification of a person is one of the most recent research topics that have gained a lot of attention from researchers. Automated systems that will store the human biometrics along with the personal information can be of a significant assistance in investigations and security issues. This is why one such a concept is illustrated in the next chapter. Another topic in the fourth chapter is a comparative study of ability of two novel image retrieval algorithms to provide automated touch-free identification of persons by iris recognition. Numerical experiments on a real biometric database indicate feasibility of the presented approach as automated iris recognition tool without special image pre-processing.

REFERENCES

Babaud, J., Witkin, A., Baudin, M., & Duda, R. (1986). Uniqueness of the Gaussian kernel for scale-space filtering. *IEEE Transactions on Pattern Analysis and Machine Intelligence*, 8. PMID:21869320

Ballard, D. H., & Brown, C. M. (1982). *Computer vision*. Englewood Cliffs, NJ: Prentice-Hall.

Barnsley, M. (1993). *Fractals everywhere*. San Francisco, CA: Morgan Kaufmann.

Cao, F., Lisani, J. L., Morel, J. M., Muse, P., & Sur, F. (2006). *A theory of shape identification*. Berlin: Springer.

De Floriani, L., & Spagnuol, M. (2007). *Shape analysis and structuring*. Berlin: Springer.

Hong, J., & Tan, X. (1988). *The similarity between shapes under affine transformation*. Washington, DC: IEEE.

Hong, J., & Wolfson, H. J. (1988). *An improved model-based matching method using footprints*. Rome, Italy: Pattern Recognition.

Hummel, A. (1986). *Representations based on zero-crossings in scale-space*. In *Proceedings of IEEE Computer Vision and Pattern Recognition Conf.*, (pp. 204-209). IEEE.

Hummel, A. (1987). *The scale-space formulation of pyramid data structures in parallel computer vision*. New York: Academic Press.

Kimmel, R. (2004). *Numerical geometry of images: Theory, algorithms, and applications*. Berlin: Springer. doi:10.1007/978-0-387-21637-9

Koenderink, J. (1984). The structure of images. In *Biological Cybernetics*. Springer-Verlag.

Krim, H., & Yezzi, A. Jr. (2006). *Statistics and analysis of shapes (modeling and simulation in science, engineering and technology).* Boston: Birkhauser. doi:10.1007/0-8176-4481-4

Latecki, L. J., & Lakamper, R. (1999). Convexity rule for shape decomposition based on discrete contour evolution. *Computer Vision and Image Understanding*, 73(3), 441–454. doi:10.1006/cviu.1998.0738

Munkres, J. (1999). *Topology* (2nd ed.). Upper Saddle River, NJ: Prentice Hall.

O'Rourke, J., & Washington, R. (1985). Curve similarity via signatures. *Computational Geometry*, 295–318.

Perona, P., & Malik, J. (1990). Scale-space and edge detection using anisotropic diffusion. *IEEE Transactions on Pattern Analysis and Machine Intelligence*, 12(7), 629–630. doi:10.1109/34.56205

Rosenfeld, A., & Thurston, M. (1971). Edge and curve detection for visual scene analysis. *IEEE Trans. Compu.*, (C-20), 562-569.

Schwartz, J. T., & Sharir, M. (1984). *Some remarks on robot vision.* New York: New York University.

Tameze, C., Vincelette, R. B., Melikechi, N., Zeljković, V., & Izquierdo, E. (2007). *Empirical analysis of LIBS images for ovarian cancer detection.* WIAMIS. doi:10.1109/WIAMIS.2007.40

Vincelette, R.B., Tameze, C., Zeljković, V., & Izquierdo, E. (2008). *Noise removal from polygonal shapes using combined inverse diffusion filter and triangle method.* London: CBMI.

Witkin, A. (1983). *Scale-space filtering.* Karlsruhe, Germany: IEEE.

Wolfson, H. (1987). *On curve matching.* Miami Beach, FL: IEEE.

Yuille, A., & Poggio, T. (1986). Scaling theorems for zero crossings. *IEEE Transactions on Pattern Analysis and Machine Intelligence*, 8. PMID:21869319

Zeljković, V., Tameze, C., Vincelette, R. B., & Izquierdo, E. (2008). *Nonlinear diffusion filter and triangle method used for noise removal from polygonal shapes.* Xi'an, China: VIE. doi:10.1049/cp:20080306

Zeljković, V., Tameze, C., Vincelette, R. B., & Izquierdo, E. (2009). *Different nonlinear diffusion filters combined with triangle method used for noise removal from polygonal shapes.* IET Image Processing.

Zeljković, V., Vincelette, R. B., Tameze, C., & Izquierdo, E. (2008). *Combined nonlinear inverse diffusion filter and triangle method used for noise removal from polygonal shapes.* ICIP.

Section 4
Object Identification Algorithms and their Applications

Two different novel algorithms are offered that can identify aircraft categories from Inverse Synthetic Aperture Radar images that use both the radar reflection pulse shape and the Doppler shifts of different parts of the aircraft. The first method forms numerical equivalents to shape, size, and other aircraft features as critical criteria to constitute the algorithm for their correct classification. The second method compares each ISAR image to unions of images of the different aircraft categories. The obtained results indicate that in most parts of the holding pattern the category of the aircraft can be successfully identified with both proposed methods.

Automatic body detection and identification of a person is one of the most recent research topics that has gained a lot of attention from researchers. Automated systems that will store human biometrics along with personal information can be of a significant assistance in investigations and security issues.

Another topic in this section is a comparative study of the ability of two novel image retrieval algorithms to provide automated touch-free identification of persons by iris recognition. Numerical experiments on a real biometric database indicate feasibility of the presented approach as automated iris recognition tool without special image pre-processing.

Chapter 10
Algorithms for ISAR Image Recognition and Classification

ABSTRACT

Two different novel methods for classification of aircraft categories of Inverse Synthetic Aperture Radar (ISAR) images are presented. The first method forms numerical equivalents to shape, size, and other aircraft features as critical criteria to constitute the algorithm for their correct classification. The second method compares each ISAR image to unions of images of the different aircraft categories. ISAR images are constructed based on the Doppler shifts of various parts, caused by the rotation of the aircraft and the radar reflection pulse shape, which includes the size or duration of the radar pulse. The proposed classification algorithms were tested on seven aircraft categories. All seven different aircraft models are flying a holding pattern. The aim of both algorithms is to quickly match and determine the similarity of the captured aircraft to the seven different categories where the aircraft is in any position of a prescribed holding pattern. Experimental results clearly indicate that in most parts of the holding pattern the category of the aircraft can be successfully identified with both proposed methods. The union method shows more successful identification results and is superior to the results we obtained in the first proposed method.

1. INTRODUCTION

Inverse Synthetic Aperture Radar (ISAR) acquires both range and Doppler shifts to form an image of a target. It offers more information about the target than a one dimensional range profile obtained from timing and duration of a radar echo return alone. Any rotation of the target introduces Doppler shifts in frequency from different parts of the target. Together with pulse return shape, these Doppler shifts reveal information about the shape and the size of the target. Some methods test only for features that are extracted from the ISAR image to identify what kind of target has been detected, as described in (Saidi, 2008), (Maskall,

2002), (Vespe, 2006), (Manikandan, 2007). This is more efficient than evaluating the whole target. Some methods use optimal classifiers, presented in (Kim, 2005), (Martorella, 2008), (Hu, 2007), to determine what kind of target is responsible for the image. In military applications, it is desirable to be able to automatically identify the aircraft model from as little radar information as possible. It is likely that the combat crews of attacking aircraft will do everything they can to deprive their target of the use of radar information about their attack. Usually, automatic electronic countermeasure avionics on the attacking aircraft or an electronic warfare officer in the flight crew will jam the radar as soon as the radar is detected. The target

DOI: 10.4018/978-1-4666-4896-8.ch010

of the attack will have only the first radar pulses to try to identify what categories of aircraft are making the attack. It would be a great advantage to know from as little as one returned radar pulse what kind of aircraft are involved.

Many schemes of ISAR target recognition have been developed that test only the features taken from the ISAR images with high efficiency. This saves the time exhausted while trying to compare the whole target aircraft. Some methods use optimal classifiers to determine what kind of target is responsible for the image.

Algorithms for automatic classification of various aircraft models are proposed in this chapter. Just as in direct human observation of a target such as an aircraft there are limits of what an observer, in this case the proposed automatic software can see and this will make it difficult to identify what classification of aircraft is observed. There are situations in which there are limits of what is possible to determine from an ISAR image. These limits will be discussed and possible ways to get more information out of the ISAR images will be suggested.

2. PRINCIPLE OF ISAR IMAGING

2.1. ISAR Imaging Technique

ISAR imaging is implemented by coherently processing echoes from a moving target and exploiting information that can be gleaned from Doppler frequency shifts caused by rotation of the target relative to the radar station. Of course, overall Doppler frequency shift must be compensated for when the target has a velocity component towards or away from the radar station.

There is a geometric relationship between a radar station and a target that is shown in Figure 1.

The target is rotating about an origin O, of an X-Y Cartesian coordinate system. The origin is a distance r_a from the radar. Any point, P, on the target has coordinates, r_o, θ_o from O. The target

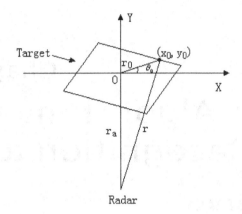

Figure 1. Variant cross-range scale

is rotating about O with an angular velocity of ω. The distance from the radar to point $P(r_o, \theta_o)$ at time t is:

$$r(t) = \left[r_0^2 + r_a^2 + 2r_0 r_a \sin\left(\theta_0 + \omega t\right)\right]^{1/2} \quad (1)$$

But radar and targets are far away from each other so this far field condition will be considered $(r_a \gg r_0)$. Under this condition equation (1) can be approximated by the following equation:

$$r(t) \approx r_a + x_0 \sin \omega t + y_0 \cos \omega t \quad (2)$$

Rotation will introduce a Doppler shift and Doppler frequency of echoes will be:

$$f_d = \frac{2}{\lambda} \frac{dr(t)}{dt} = \frac{2x_0 \omega}{\lambda} \cos \omega t - \frac{2y_0 \omega}{\lambda} \sin \omega t \quad (3)$$

where λ is the wavelength of the radar. Under the assumption that it is dealt with a short period of time when $t \to 0$, equations (3) and (4) can be approximated

$$r = r_a + y_0 \quad (4)$$

$$f_d = 2x_0 \omega / \lambda \quad (5)$$

It is now possible to determine the coordinates of $P(x_o,y_o)$ from the Doppler shift and the echo delay time and to construct an image of the aircraft from all positions $P(x_o,y_o)$ that constitute the observed aircraft.

Because $P(x_o,y_o)$ can be solved from Doppler shift and echo delay, the image of the aircraft can be constructed from all points $P(x_o,y_o)$.

Overall Doppler shift is taken into account when the target has a translational velocity component in the r direction in radial coordinates from the radar. This image gives us useful information about the shape of the aircraft, (Prickett, 1980), (Li, 2007).

ISAR imaging forms target image from range and Doppler shifts caused by rotation of the aircraft. Sufficient Doppler shift sampling frequency and observation window enable the image to be easily recognized by ISAR or human perception. However, there are visual limits due to Doppler induced distortion and reflection characteristics and shadows.

The direction and speed of the rotation vector ω influence Doppler frequency shifts variation. The radar return changes with the rotational position, θ. Doppler modulations are introduced by rotating parts on aircraft, such as propeller blades or rotating compressor blades of jet engines.

When the incident radar pulse encounters an aircraft it is subjected to the laws of optics. It can be scattered by passage through boundaries between media of different dielectric constants, it can be reflected, or it can be absorbed. The reflections are influenced, among other things, by the cross sectional area the aircraft presents to the radar receiver antenna. A long thin aircraft with a heading parallel to the Pointing vector of the radar will make a smaller echo than an aircraft illuminated broadside because the former orientation offers a smaller cross sectional area than the latter. The shape of the reflecting surface has a great effect on how much radar is reflected back to the radar receiving antenna. Edge diffraction is significant at radar frequencies. Also, parts of the aircraft will cast shadows that will make other parts of the aircraft invisible to the radar receiver.

2.2. Difficulties in Target Recognition from ISAR Images

ISAR imaging techniques can provide an image of a target from range and Doppler shifts caused by rotation of the target. Given a sufficient Doppler shift sampling frequency and observation window, the image is easily recognized by human perception or by an automatic target recognition and classification system. However, there are limits of what they can do. These limits are outlined as follows:

2.2.1. Doppler Induced Distortion

Doppler frequency shifts vary with the direction and speed of the rotation vector ω. The radar reflection also changes with the rotational position, θ. Figure 2 gives two ISAR images from the same target in different observing directions and rotation

Figure 2. Variant cross-range scale

A   B

speeds. Obviously, target image A is distorted so that it is difficult to recognize while target image B shows the unmistakable shape of an airplane. The cross-range varies because Doppler frequency changes with rotation speed.

Also, moving parts of an aircraft will introduce Doppler modulations. Propellers are an obvious example. So are the turbine blades in the compressor sections of jet engines that are illuminated by radar. Figure 3 gives an ISAR image from aircraft with rotating jet engine compressor blades. The cross-range noise is an extended Doppler spectrum modulated by rotating jet engine compressor blades.

Ships at sea present an interesting problem. They experience roll, yaw and pitch. Whether the top of a ship is moving towards the radar or away can cause a radical difference in the shape of the ISAR image. A positive Doppler shift when the top of the ship is moving towards the radar station is shown in image A of Figure 4 and a negative Doppler shift when the top of the ship is moving away is shown in image B.

2.2.2. Reflection Characteristics and Shadows

Radar reflection is a form of scattering of incident electromagnetic radiation either by passage of radiation from a medium of one dielectric

Figure 3. Variant cross-range scale

constant into one of another, as per Snell's law, or by reflection off a conducting surface. Since most aircraft are constructed with a sheet aluminum skin, (typically 2024 T3 alloy), which is a very efficient reflector at radar frequencies, radar reflection is very interesting. Of course, in the future, composite plastic airframe parts may change that.

There are several things of interest that will explain what kind of radar reflection an airframe will return:

1. The first is the cross section of the airframe presented to the incident radiation. A long thin airframe heading directly into or away from incident radiation will present much less surface area to reflect that beam than it will when the incident radiation strikes it broadside.
2. Second of these is the way a conducting surface scatters its incident radiation. A convex surface will scatter the radar radiation widely so that it will be visible to the radar receiver.
3. A flat reflecting surface must be oriented precisely so that the reflection will be properly directed to the radar receiver. The finite size of the reflecting flat surface will cause some edge scattering by diffraction.
4. Parts of an airframe cast a shadow on other parts of an airframe thereupon preventing the shadowed parts from reflecting any radiation.

All of these things are affected by features of the shape of the aircraft in addition to its size and they are greatly affected by the orientation of the airframe relative to the direction of the radiation illuminating it. This orientation depends upon the heading of the aircraft relative to direction of the radiation and on how much the aircraft is banked when it is making a turn.

The above explained reflection characteristics and shadows can make it difficult to get shape

Figure 4. Doppler reversal

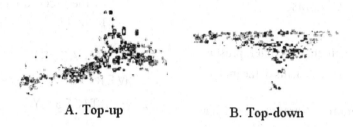

A. Top-up   B. Top-down

information of a target by analyzing its ISAR image, which is visually shown and obvious from Figure 5.

3. ISAR IMAGES CLASSIFICATION ALGORITHMS

3.1 Automated Classification Algorithm

Various criteria for radar object recognition are developed. The set of these criteria gives us the final answer about the shape of the detected radar object. The procedure of the developed automatic ISAR image classification algorithm, (Zeljković, 2009), (Zeljković, 2009), is the following:

1.   The acquired image is resized without changing the size of the airplane within it so that the acquired image is of the same dimensions as the images in database in order that the

classification algorithm in Step 4 b)-f) below is applied appropriately.

2.   The resized image is de-noised by setting all the pixels that are equal to or smaller than predetermined threshold 15 to black and the rest of the pixels whose intensities are higher than 15 remain the same.

$$\hat{I}_m(x,y) = \begin{cases} I_m(x,y) & \text{if } I_m(x,y) > 15 \\ 0 & \text{if } I_m(x,y) \le 15 \end{cases} \quad (6)$$

where $\hat{I}_m(x,y)$ are pixel intensities that represent the two dimensional matrix elements of the image.

3.   The de-noised image is turned into a gray scale image and binarized by setting all the pixels that are different from black to 255 gray level, obtaining a black and white image where white denotes the object and black the background.

Figure 5. Reflection characteristics and shadows in an ISAR image

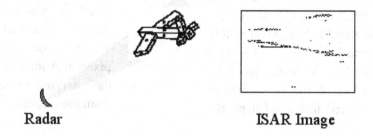

Radar   ISAR Image

$$\hat{I}_m(x,y) = \begin{cases} 255 & \text{if } I_m(x,y) \neq 0 \\ 0 & \text{otherwise} \end{cases} \qquad (7)$$

where $\hat{I}_m(x,y)$ are pixel intensities that represent the two dimensional matrix elements of the image.

4. The following parameters are calculated that are later used for shape recognition:

   a. Number of pixels contained in the object, BR.

   b. Average value of x-coordinate of pixels forming the object, MIX.

   c. Average value of y-coordinate of pixels forming the object, MIY.

   d. Size of the object along x-coordinate, SIZEX, by subtracting the lowest x-coordinate of the pixel forming the object that is positioned most to the left in the image from the largest x-coordinate of the pixel forming the object that is positioned most to the right in the image.

   e. Size of the object along y-coordinate, SIZEY, by subtracting the lowest y-coordinate of the pixel forming the object that is positioned most towards the bottom in the image from the largest y-coordinate of the pixel forming the object that is positioned most towards the top in the image.

   f. Size of the object along x and y coordinates, SIZE, by adding size of the object along x-coordinate and size of the object along y-coordinate.

   g. Stored in a vector x and y coordinates of all the pixels forming the object, VERTICES_X and VERTICES_Y.

   h. Shape measure, SHAPE_MEASURE, as the summation of squared distances of all pixels' x-coordinates from the average value of the x-coordinates added to squared distance of all pixels'

y-coordinates from the average value of the y-coordinates according to the formula:

$$\begin{aligned} SHAPE\_MEASURE = \\ \sum_{i \in Object} [(VERTICES\_X[i] - MIX)^2 + \\ (VERTICES\_Y[i] - MIY)^2] \end{aligned} \qquad (8)$$

5. The criteria for shape recognition are calculated according to the following rules:

   a. The similarity coefficients between two inspected images are calculated based on the following formula:

$$sim = 1 - arccos\left[\frac{I_1^T * I_2}{norm(I_1) * norm(I_2)}\right] \qquad (9)$$

   where $I_1(x,y)$ and $I_2(x,y)$ are corresponding pixel intensities, transformed into vectors, in two compared images, the analyzed object and each shape from the database.

   b. The percentage of the same pixels are calculated that form the objects in both compared images, the analyzed object and the shapes from the database.

   c. The difference between shape measures of the analyzed object and the shapes from the database is calculated.

   d. The difference between sizes of the object along x-coordinate of the analyzed object and the shapes from the database are calculated.

   e. The difference between sizes of the object along y-coordinate of the analyzed object and the shapes from the database are calculated.

   f. The difference in the number of the pixels that form the objects between the analyzed object and the shapes from the database are calculated.

6. The analyzed object is compared with the shapes from the database and calculate the above mentioned criteria:

    a. Two top shapes are found from the database that have the maximal similarity coefficient with the analyzed object.

    b. Two top shapes are found from the database that have the maximal percent of same pixels with the analyzed object.

    c. Two top shapes are found from the database that have the minimal shape measure difference from the analyzed object.

    d. Two top shapes are found from the database that have the minimal size difference with the analyzed object along x-coordinate.

    e. Two top shapes are found from the database that have the minimal size difference with the analyzed object along y-coordinate.

    f. Two top shapes are found from the database that have the minimal number of pixels difference from the analyzed object.

7. Based on the above six criteria and twelve potentially extracted shapes from the database that satisfy the majority of the described conditions the two are extracted that appear most frequently.

8. It is said that the shape recognition method that has defined the analyzed object resembles most the extracted shape from the database that satisfies the majority of the described conditions most frequently.

The resemblance between the analyzed object and the aircraft image from the database is measured by the highest number of appearances of the same shape category in satisfying the conditions listed in Step 6. The total number of the resemblance conditions is six but for each condition two top shapes are taken from the database which makes it twelve.

3.2 Unions of ISAR Images Classification Algorithm

The proposed algorithm for ISAR image classification, (Zeljković, 2009), is very simple. It makes a single comparison of one ISAR image to the union of images of all positions of the aircraft category in a holding pattern. This new method produced results that are superior to the results obtained by applying previously described method. There are in memory 360 different ISAR images of aircraft categories 1 through 5, 180 different ISAR images for category 6 and 60 images for category 7. These ISAR images represent different positions of aircraft in their holding patterns. The procedure of the ISAR image classification algorithm is the following:

1. For each category, the center of gravity is taken of each ISAR image. This is done because when one image is compared to another, they are placed one over the other and it is found how many pixels of one image intersect those of the other image. This is usually a maximum number when the images are positioned with their centers of gravity concurrent.

2. ISAR images union is formed in which all centers of gravity are concurrent.

$$R(x,y) = \bigcup_{i=1}^{N} I_i(x,y) \qquad (10)$$

where N is the number of ISAR images in the holding pattern and R(x,y) is the pixel in the formed union image. $I_i(x,y)$ is the set of pixels of each ISAR image that belongs to the airplane in the data base for each aircraft category.

3. The analyzed object is compared with the shapes from the database by placing it over each of the seven category unions, R(x, y).
4. The similarity coefficient between the ISAR return and each of the category unions is calculated based on the following formula:

$$sim = 1 - arccos\left[\frac{I_1^T * I_2}{norm(I_1) * norm(I_2)}\right] \quad (11)$$

5. The category that gives the largest similarity coefficient with the analyzed object is considered the most likely match.

4. EXPERIMENTAL RESULTS

4.1 ISAR Imaging Simulation

The radar transmits Linear Modulated Frequency (LMF) signals, central frequency 35GHz, pulse recurrent frequency 460 pulses per second, bandwidth 400MHz which gives a resolution of 0.375 meters.

To simulate ISAR images there are each of five different models of aircraft flying a left hand holding pattern with no wind, a true airspeed of 250m/s, banking 30 degrees during the turning part of the holding pattern for a radius of turn of 11046 meters, an altitude of 17000 meters or flight level 560, P1 in Figures 7 and 8 is 30,000 meters from the radar with an azimuth of 50 degrees. A holding pattern consists of flight along a race track shaped path. 180 degree turns are alternated between periods of straight and level flight to make this flight path. The azimuth angle of 50 degrees between a straight and level part of the flight path and the line of sight to the radar gives great variety of front and rear angled views of the aircraft in the straight and level parts of the maneuver. The varying range varies the elevation angle from approximately 30 to 64 degrees.

Five scattering point plane models are created. Each of them consists of scatter points with a 0.33m interval. All the scatter points have uniform scattering coefficients. In the far field condition, scatter points behind the radar illumination are not considered. The EM scattering model is the point scatter model described in (Haywood, 1997). Table 1 and Figure 6 give the size parameters and shapes of 5 model planes respectively. The positions of the simulated flight in the holding pattern consist of evenly spaced positions in the holding pattern that correspond to aircraft heading. The other two categories are taken from Internet.

There are in memory 360 different ISAR images of aircraft categories 1 through 5, 180 different ISAR images for category 6 and 60 images for category 7.

This pattern as a whole presents the utmost variety of different viewing angles of the aircraft in both straight and level flight and in turning flight. It also captures different banking angles as the aircraft varies bank angle while entering and exiting each turn, see Figures 7 and 8. Between P315 and P45 the aircraft is seen in straight and level flight from a varying rear view that becomes more to the rear as it approaches P45. Between P135 and P225 a front view is presented. The two turning portions of the holding pattern present more radical changes in orientation due to bank angle and changes in heading.

The positions of the simulated flight in the holding pattern do not always correspond to aircraft heading but rather to evenly spaced positions in the holding pattern. At P315 through P45 the heading of the aircraft is constant at 360 degrees and between P135 and P225, the heading is constant at 180 degrees.

Six different artificially simulated categories of airplanes and one real aircraft category that has a lot of noise present in the ISAR images are being compared. The seven tested aircraft categories are presented in Figure 9.

Figure 6. Shapes of five different generated airplane models

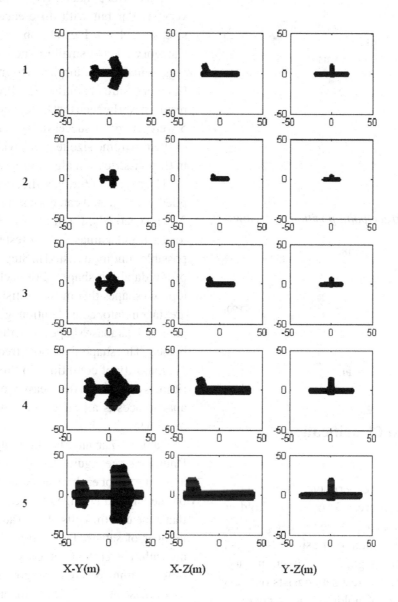

Table 1. Size parameters of five different generated airplane models

Model	1	2	3	4	5
Body length [m]	46	22	34	69	85
Wing Span [m]	33	15	38	73	88
Body Height [m]	10	6	11	21	24

Figure 7. Geometrical relationship

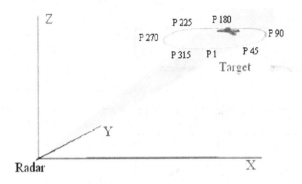

Figure 8. Target trace point position (top view)

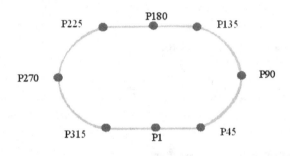

4.2 Automated Classification Algorithm

The database in our experiments is the set of images that contains every 3rd of the 360 holding pattern positions for each of the five categories of aircraft. The specifications of the sizes and shapes of each of aircraft categories are given in Table 1 and in Figure 6. The test set consists of every 10th position of the 360 holding pattern positions for each of the five categories of aircraft. The test set contains one third of the images contained in the database and two thirds of tested images are not contained in the database.

The test set is tested against the database set in order to identify matches. It is interesting to conclude in testing at what parts of the holding pattern it is possible to automatically identify what kind of aircraft corresponds to the tested ISAR image.

It is obvious that all five airplane models are very similar but with differences in shape and size, see Table 1. It can be observed that airplane Category 2 is the smallest and Category 5 is the biggest in size. The airplanes from Category 1 and Category 3 are of similar size. From the obtained results it can be seen that Category 2 and Category 5 were the most successfully classified because of their extreme size features which are inherent in the classification algorithm, see Tables 2-7.

The results of the classification algorithm applied to five tested categories are given in Tables 2-7, respectively. From Step 7 of the algorithm, for each radar image being tested, there are six possible conditions listed in Step 6 that match one of the database shapes. For each condition, the top two shapes that mostly satisfy that condition are taken into consideration giving us twelve potential database shapes with the highest resemblance. The shape that most frequently satisfies the majority of conditions in Step 6 of the algorithm is considered the measure of match. Twelve appearances is a perfect score which is defined in Step 9.

Tables 2-7 arrange holding pattern positions or P numbers, see Figures 7 and 8, every 10 "degrees" along the top of each table. Aircraft categories are on the left and arranged vertically. The numbers that appear in the cells of the Tables represent the number of satisfied conditions in Step 6 of the algorithm of certain category shapes on the left most column. Where a category scores the highest of these numbers that number is given. If that number is not 12, the score of the second place category is given. Where the correct category has the highest number or score we have a match. Where an incorrect category has the highest score we have a mismatch. The P numbers that suffer a mismatch are shaded.

The obtained results show similar behavior of the proposed algorithm for all five airplane categories, i.e. models. As a matter of fact, the algorithm fails to correctly classify the observed airplane mostly on the curved parts of the airplane

Table 2. Category 1

	10	20	30	40	50	60	70	80	90	100	110	120	130	140	150	160	170	180
1	9	12	10	8	12	10	11	9	12	9	11	8	7	5	6	10	8	10
2	1				2		3		3	1	3				4	2		
3			2										5	4			3	1
4			1				1											
5																		

	190	200	210	220	230	240	250	260	270	280	290	300	310	320	330	340	350	360
1	5	9	9	8	7	6	5	5	5	4							5	5
2		2		2		2		3						3		2		2
3	5		2													4		
4					4		4		3	3	3	4	3	5	3			
5											5	4	6		5		4	

Table 3. Category 2

	10	20	30	40	50	60	70	80	90	100	110	120	130	140	150	160	170	180
1	1		1				1											
2	10	10	10	9	10	12	10	12	12	12	12	12	12	7	12	11	11	11
3		2		2	2									5		1	1	1
4																		
5																		

	190	200	210	220	230	240	250	260	270	280	290	300	310	320	330	340	350	360
1	1		1					4		3	3	2	3	6	4	4		
2	11	10	10	10	7	10	5	6	4	7	5	5	6	5	4	7	6	9
3		2		2	5	2	5	6		3								2
4																		
5																		

paths in the positions from 110° to 180° and from 220° to 360°. The images of the positions that are incorrectly classified by the algorithm are marked in blue in the Tables 2-6. These positions seem to be the most critical ones for the recognition even visually. Figures 10-16 show the images of the critical positions for all five airplane models that are even visually difficult to distinguish.

With the exception of the mentioned obscured positions, it was possible to successfully identify aircraft categories. In the radar images, there were orientations in certain intervals of heading during which parts of the airframe seemed to disappear.

Table 4. Category 3

	10	20	30	40	50	60	70	80	90	100	110	120	130	140	150	160	170	180
1	3														1			3
2		2	1	4	3	5	2	4	2	6	6	8	9	11	10	10	5	7
3	9	8	11	7	8	7	10	7	9	6	5	4	2	1		2	7	
4																		
5																		

	190	200	210	220	230	240	250	260	270	280	290	300	310	320	330	340	350	360
1							9	8										4
2	4	2	4	7	3	3						4	4	5	4	5	3	
3	7	9	6	4	6	8	3	3	4	5	3						4	5
4									4	4	5	4	6	5	5	3		
5																		

Table 5. Category 4

	10	20	30	40	50	60	70	80	90	100	110	120	130	140	150	160	170	180
1			1		2	2	2	3		2	2		6	7		8	6	4
2				2								2				2		
3															4		2	
4	10	8	11	9	8	8	10	7	12	8	9	8	6	3	5			6
5	2	2																

	190	200	210	220	230	240	250	260	270	280	290	300	310	320	330	340	350	360
1	4	3							4	2	5		4		4			5
2			3		1													
3			2										2	4	2			
4	6	6	7	6	5	8	6	5	5								4	3
5					5		4	4	7	6	10	6	7		10	5	6	

Targets 3, 4, and 5 had intervals of 110 and 150 degrees in Category 3, 140, 160 and 170 degrees in Category 4 and 130, 140 and 160 degrees in Category 5, in which large parts of the radar image were invisible, see Figures 14-16. This took place during the part of the holding pattern when the aircraft was flying towards the radar mostly in straight and level flight. In the case of Target 5, between P130 and P135, the aircraft was rolling out of a left turn. All targets except number 5 had the wings become nearly invisible about the heading of 270 degrees where the wings and the nose of the airframe presents a small radar cross section area because the aircraft is heading almost directly towards the radar station. This could be affected by such things as the thickness and size

Table 6. Category 5

	10	20	30	40	50	60	70	80	90	100	110	120	130	140	150	160	170	180
1				2		2								3	5	6		
2																		
3		1						1										
4							2		2	3	2	4	6	4			1	5
5	12	10	12	10	12	10	9	10	10	5	10	6	4		6	3	11	6

	190	200	210	220	230	240	250	260	270	280	290	300	310	320	330	340	350	360
1								1					2	3	2	2		
2						2												
3			3						2									
4	5	3	2		2		1			2	2					3	3	
5	7	5	10	7	8	7	10	7	12	10	10	7	9	6	10	8	9	8

Table 7. Comparison of the classification results for images without noise and with noise of various SNR

Airplane Category		1	2	3	4	5
Number of Images in the Holding Pattern		360	360	360	360	360
No noise	A	290-340	330	110-180, 220, 250, 260, 290-340	140, 160, 170, 270-360	130, 140, 160
	B	6	1	17	13	3
6 dB	A	140, 260-340	270-290	110-200, 260-340	140-170, 260-350	130-150
	B	10	3	19	14	3
10 dB	A	140, 260-340	290-310	130-200, 250, 260, 290-340	140-170, 200, 260-350	130, 140, 160
	B	10	3	16	15	3
13 dB	A	140, 280-340	290-310	110-200, 250, 260, 290-340	140-170, 260-350	140, 160, 320
	B	8	3	18	14	3
20 dB	A	140, 260-340	280-300	100-220, 260-340	140-170, 260-360	140, 160, 320
	B	10	3	22	15	3

of the wings and how airfoil curvature scatters the incident radiation.

To test the effect of the noise presence and the robustness to noise of the proposed classification algorithm Gaussian noise is added to the proposed model. Gaussian noise is introduced in the receiver channel with different Signal to Noise Ratios SNR = 6, 10, 13 and 20 dB. Suppose the

Figure 9. Classified airplane models: a) Category 1; b) Category 2; c) Category 3; d) Category 4; e) Category 5; f) Category 6; g) Category 7

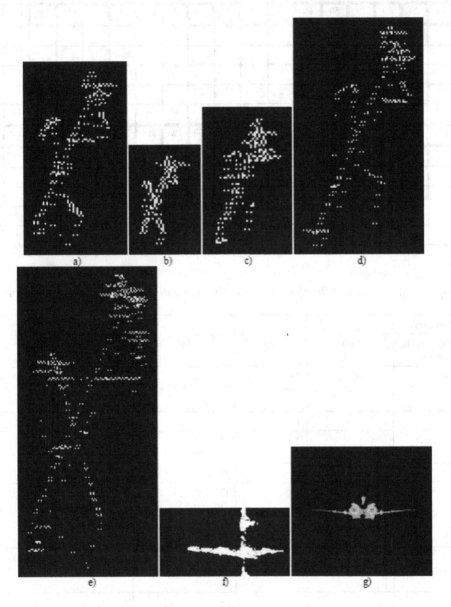

number of ISAR coherent processing periods is $N = 256$ radar pulses at $f_r = 460$ pulses per second at $v = 250$ meters per second true air speed or the target traveled distance

$$D = vN / f_r = 139.13m$$

If the target has a tangential motion to the radar, the azimuth angle

$$\theta_a = D / R = 4.6 \times 10^{-3}$$

radians where $R = 30000$ meters from the radar to the target. Under these conditions the cross-range resolution is:

Figure 10. Category 1 and its ISAR Image at different positions

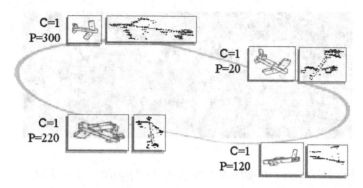

Figure 11. Category 1 ISAR images at various misclassified positions: a) 290; b) 300; c) 330; d) 340

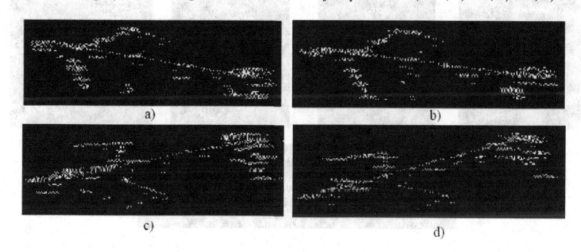

Figure 12. Category 2 and its ISAR image at different positions

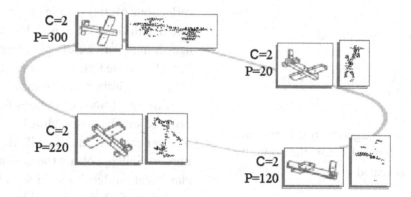

Figure 13. Category 2 ISAR images at different misclassified position 330

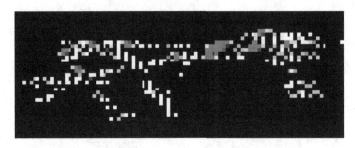

Figure 14. Category 3 ISAR images at various misclassified positions: a) 110; b) 150; c) 220; d) 250; e) 300

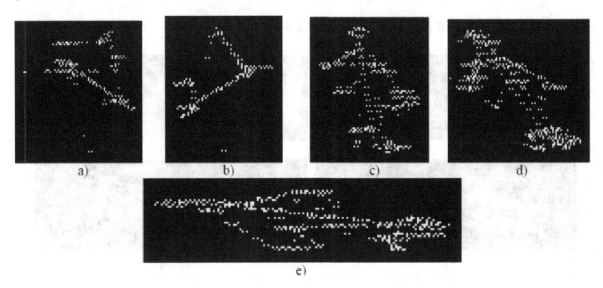

$$\Delta x = \lambda \, / \, 2\theta_a \approx 0.93m$$

so the scaling in azimuth should be:

$$f_d = \frac{2x\omega}{\lambda} = \frac{2x\theta_a}{\lambda \cdot \Delta T} = \frac{2x\theta_a f_r}{\lambda \cdot N} \approx 1.93x \,.$$

For a maneuvering target, the rotational velocity ω needs to be estimated, before the azimuth of the ISAR image is scaled.

- Misclassified positions.
- Number of misclassifications.

Because radar receives noise in addition to reflections off targets, the proposed method was tested with Gaussian noise added to the radar images. Simulations were implemented with different Signal to Noise Ratios SNR to test the robustness of the classification method to the presented noise. Four different SNR conditions 6, 10, 13 and 20 dB were simulated by adding Gaussian noise into receiver channel. Although ISAR techniques can improve SNR by coherent processing, the proposed classification algorithm was still tested for a worst condition of SNR = 6 dB. Figure 17 shows the images of airplane Category 5 at position 3 that have been corrupted with noise of various SNR including the original image without the noise.

Figure 15. Category 4 ISAR images at various misclassified positions: a) 140; b) 160; c) 170; d) 300; e) 360

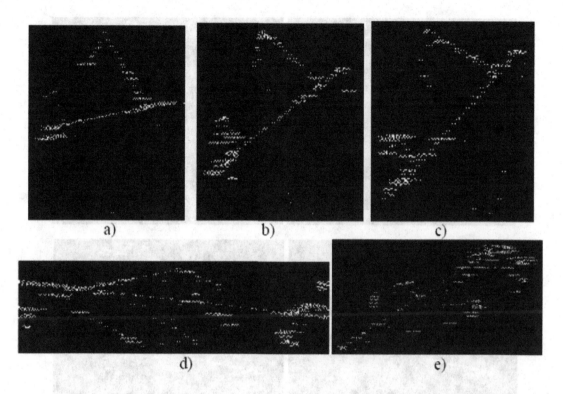

Figure 16. Category 5 ISAR images at various misclassified positions: a) 130; b) 140; c) 160

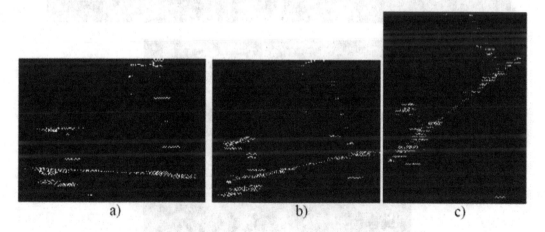

Figure 18 gives us images from Figure 17 after the de-noising method was applied to them, described in Step 2 of the classification algorithm. It is obvious that removing of the noise makes all these images very close to, visually indistinguishable, from the original noise free images.

The summed results of classification performed on images with and without noise added are shown in Table 7. Comparison shows that noise produced only slight differences, which could be considered insignificant, in classification performance. Category 5 showed no difference in classification

Figure 17. Gray level images of Airplane Category 5 at position 3 corrupted with noise of SNR: a) 6 dB; b) 10 dB; c) 13 dB; d) 20 dB; e) no noise

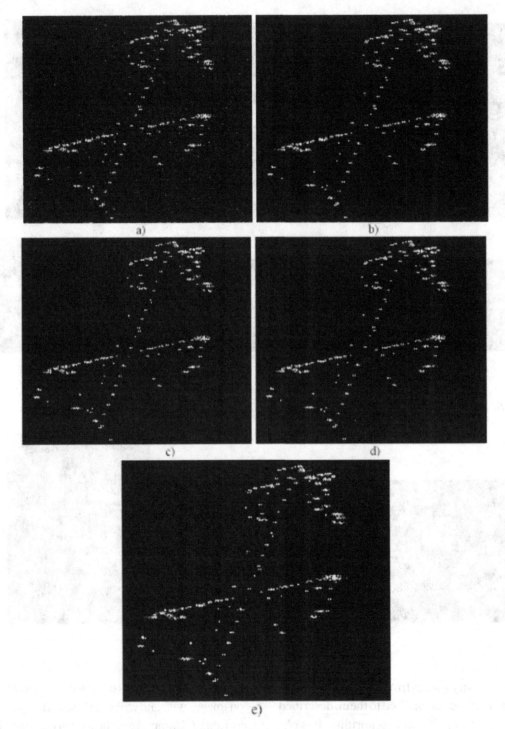

Figure 18. ISAR images of Airplane Category 5 at position 3 after de-noising the images in Step 2 of classification algorithm. De-noised images with SNR: a) 6 dB; b) 10 dB; c) 13 dB; d) 20 dB; e) no noise

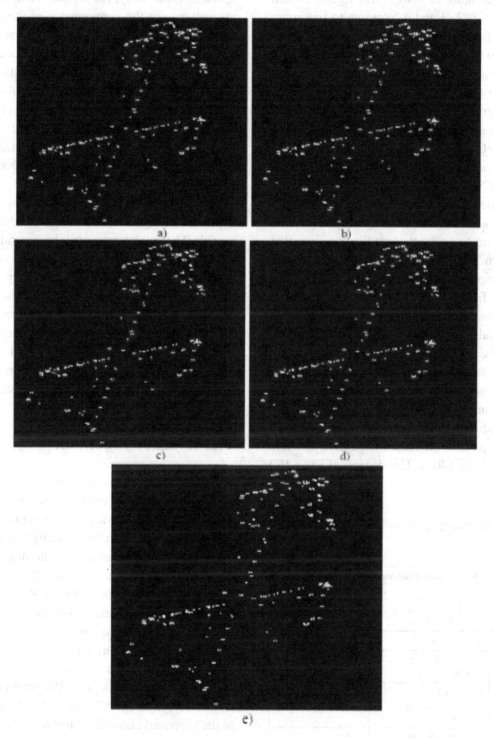

results for images without noise and for images with added noise of SNR 6, 10, 13 and 20 dB. Categories 1, 2, 3 and 4 have one to five more misclassifications for images with noise in comparison to images without noise.

The misidentification rate in our algorithm is one out of 45 which gives a correct identification rate of approximately 97.78%. This compares well with the method presented in the literature, Vespe M., Baker C.J., Griffiths H.D., "Outline Structural Representation for Radar Target Classification Based on Non-Radar Templates", that has lower correct identification rate in comparison to the proposed identification technique. The algorithm in literature has correct identification rates that vary from 77.06% to 99.30% depending on the multi perspective classifiers they tested.

In the first proposed classification algorithm it is automatically identify what kind of aircraft corresponds the most to one of the ISAR image categories.

The obtained results for all seven tested video ISAR sequences are presented in Table 8. The positions in which parts of the airframe seemed to disappear for category 6 are presented in Figure 19.

Large parts of the radar image were invisible in intervals of 140 to 150 degrees, 130 to 180

degrees, and 130 to 140 degrees for categories 1, 3, and 5, respectively. These positions in the holding pattern are the consequence of the aircraft flying towards the radar mostly in straight and level flight. The aircraft is rolling out of a left turn in the case of category 5, between positions 130 and 135. The wings become nearly invisible about the heading of 270 degrees for all categories except category 5. In that case the wings and the nose of the airframe present a small radar cross section area because the aircraft is heading almost directly towards the radar station.

The obtained results show similar behavior of the proposed algorithm for all six tested airplane models. The seventh category is successfully classified without any misclassifications. For other six categories the algorithm fails to correctly classify the observed airplane mostly on the curved parts of the airplane paths in the positions from 110° to 180° and from 220° to 360°. These positions seem to be the most critical ones for the recognition even visually based on the above Figures considering that they are even visually difficult to distinguish.

4.3 Unions of ISAR Images Classification Algorithm

Every picture from the database is taken for the comparison which consists of the images that represent all 360, 180 and 60 different positions in the paths of all seven different airplane models. It is tested for what parts of the holding pattern it is possible to automatically identify what kind of aircraft corresponds to the ISAR image. The unknown model is compared with the union images of every aircraft category present in the database that are shown in Figure 20.

Each individual image is taken, all 360 of them from categories 1 through 5, 180 from category 6 and 60 from category 7, and tested it according to the proposed classification algorithm.

The category that yielded the highest similarity coefficient was considered a match. Table 9 shows

Table 8. Summary of the obtained results for all seven categories

Airplane Category	Misclassified Positions	Percent of Misclassifications
1	100, 120, 140, 180280, 300, 320, 340	26.67%
2	280, 300, 340	10%
3	80, 120, 280, 300, 320, 340, 360	23.33%
4	100, 120, 180, 200 260, 280, 300, 320 340, 360	33.33%
5	100, 120, 140, 160	13.33%
6	60, 180	22.22%
7	-	0%

Figure 19. Category 6 ISAR images at misclassified positions: a) 60; b) 180

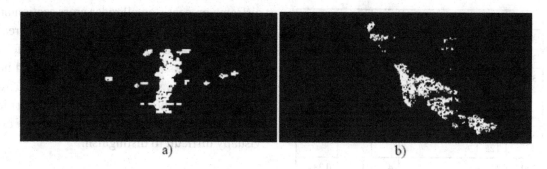

Figure 20. Union image of airplane models: a) Category 1; b) Category 2; c) Category 3; d) Category 4; e) Category 5; f) Category 6; g) Category 7

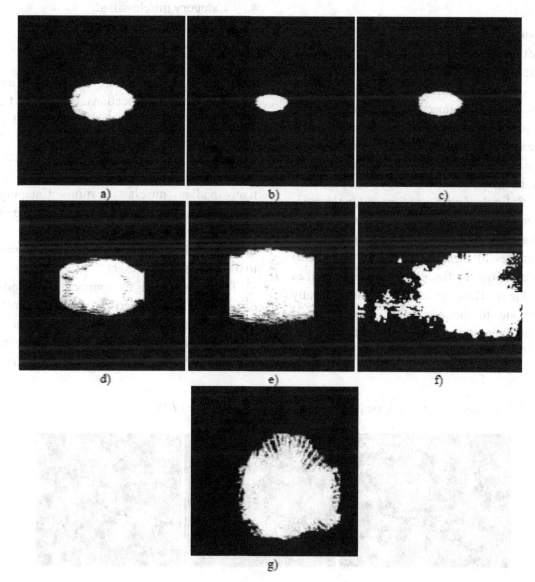

Table 9. Summary of the obtained results

A	B	C	D	E	F
1	360	112, 125, 128	3	3	0.83%
2	360	-	-	0	0%
3	360	101, 103, 105, 116-122, 125-129, 131-136, 141,142, 145-147, 151, 153, 155	2	28	7.78%
4	360	117-122, 125, 126	1	8	2.22%
5	360	115	4	1	0.28%
6	180	-	-	0	0%
7	60	-	-	0	0%

the results of the proposed method for automated aircraft model classification.

The obtained results show that the algorithm fails to correctly classify the observed airplane mostly on the right upper curved part of the airplane paths which means in the positions 112°, 125° and 128° for the first airplane category, in the positions from 101° to 155° for the third category, in the positions from 117° to 122°, 125° and 126° for the fourth category and in the position from 115° for the fifth category. In these positions the aircraft was rolling into a left turn. The images of these positions that are incorrectly classified by the algorithm are marked in the Table 9. These positions are even visually critical ones for the recognition. This is the part of the holding pattern when the aircraft fly towards the radar. In these positions the wings become nearly invisible and the wings and the nose of the airframe present a small radar cross section area because the aircraft is heading almost directly towards the radar station. This could be affected by the thickness and size of the wings and how airfoil curvature scatters the incident radiation. Figures 21-24 show the images of the critical positions for all airplane models that are even visually difficult to distinguish.

1. Airplane Category
2. Number of images in holding pattern
3. Misclassified positions
4. Category misclassified
5. Number of misclassifications
6. Percent of misclassifications

As Table 9 summarizes, category 2, 6 and 7 suffered no misclassifications. Categories 1 and 5 have less than 1% misclassifications and only one as high as 7.78%. What is surprising is that categories 6 and 7, which have less information because they have only 180 and 60 images respectively had no misclassifications. Category 6 contains significant noise which makes the classification more difficult. The proposed automated algorithm has shown itself to be resistant to the severe noise present.

The ISAR imaging environment varies and it is difficult to make comparison of different airplane identification methods on various aircraft models. The results obtained with the proposed classification method are compared to the results shown in

Figure 21. Category 1 at misclassified positions: a) 112; b) 125; c) 128

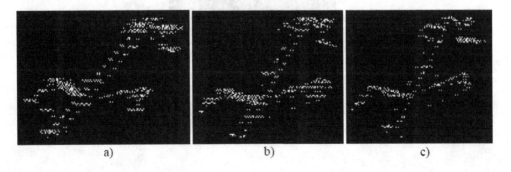

a)   b)   c)

Figure 22. Category 3 at misclassified positions: a) 105; b) 120; c) 125; d) 135; e) 155

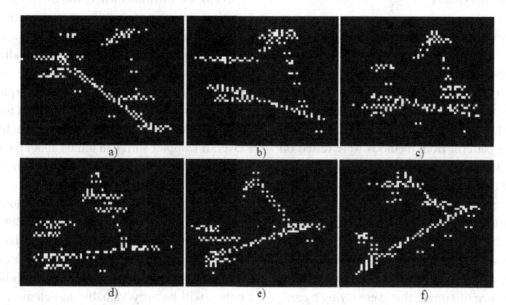

Figure 23. Category 4 at misclassified positions: a) 120; b) 125; c) 126

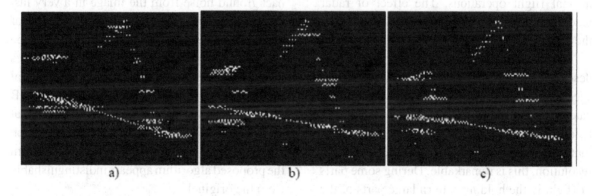

Figure 24. Category 5 at misclassified position 115

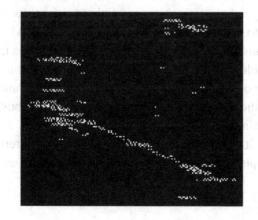

Table 8 obtained using the method described in section 3.1 on the same aircraft model sets. This method shows itself to be much more successful in correct and efficient classification than the one described in previous section. The percent of correctly classified images with the proposed method is three to thirty times higher than with the method proposed in section 3.1.

5. CONCLUSION

Two novel algorithms have been developed. One proposed method combines several matching features between simulated ISAR radar images. The other proposed algorithm makes a single comparison of one ISAR image to the union of images of all positions of the aircraft category in a holding pattern. Both methods were tested on simulated ISAR radar images stored in the database and the ones taken from Internet. This way there were the advantages of several different but computationally efficient measures of similarity with which to compare and to identify aircraft categories. The proposed algorithms were tested on ISAR images generated by simulations and real sequence of aircraft that were flying a carefully prescribed holding pattern that presented the aircraft to the radar from as many airframe orientations as are likely to be encountered in normal flight operations. The effect of radar receiver noise was tested on the performance of the proposed algorithms.

During most parts of the holding pattern, the described classification algorithms were able to successfully identify to which of seven aircraft categories, i.e. models, each tested ISAR image belonged. Considering the limits of what information radar can convey, for example, its limited resolution, this is remarkable. During some parts of flight in the holding pattern large parts of the aircraft became invisible in the ISAR image and here the first algorithm suffered misidentification in Categories 3, 4 and 5. As can be seen in Figures 14-16, it is most difficult to tell by human visual inspection to which category the images belong because large parts of the aircraft were missing from the image. Most of such losses are due to radar shadowing.

The proposed classification algorithms successfully identify the tested aircraft models for most of the holding pattern failing only in small parts for the positions where the ISAR images of airplane are even visually unrecognizable.

ISAR images can tell us many things about an aircraft from very little information. In addition to giving us some measure of both size and shape of the aircraft, it can use Doppler modulation patterns such as can be seen in Figure 3 to detect rotating propeller blades of jet engine compressor blades. Overall Doppler shift can tell us about the speed of the aircraft. It may also be possible to track any maneuvers the aircraft is making.

If aircraft are engaged in an invasion, it is likely that ISAR radar will be able to illuminate the aircraft with several pulses before the flight crews can apply electronic countermeasures. The information that can be gleaned from those few pulses will be very valuable in defense against such an invasion.

ISAR by itself is quite robust against noise. But Step 2 of the first proposed algorithm removes background noise from the image in a very fast and simple way that can better insure resistance of the proposed classification algorithm to noise. The first algorithm was additionally tested on images to which Gaussian noise was added with signal to noise ratios of 6 dB, 10 dB, 13 dB and 20 dB as can be seen in Figure 17. Figure 18 shows that even with a SNR of 6 dB the image from which Gaussian noise had been removed by Step 2 from the proposed algorithm appears indistinguishable from the original.

Table 7 shows the summarized results of the performance of the first classification algorithm applied to original images without noise as well as to images corrupted by various levels of added Gaussian noise. The comparison of the results in Table 7 shows very little difference in the number of misclassifications for the images with and without the noise. Thus the algorithm is robust against the noise.

It is difficult to make comparison of different airplane identification methods on various aircraft models considering the fact that the ISAR imaging environment varies. The results obtained with the both proposed classification methods are compared testing the same aircraft model sets. The second proposed union algorithm shows itself to be much more successful in correct and efficient classification than the first described algorithm. The percent of correctly classified images with the union method is three to thirty times higher than with the first method proposed.

It is obvious by analyzing and comparing Tables 8 and 9 that during most part of the holding pattern, the second proposed method that uses unions of images successfully identified the category of tested ISAR images. Categories 2, 6, and 7 had no errors and Category 3 showed the largest identification error of less than 8%. Category 4 had approximately 2.2% error, Category 1 had less than 1% error and Category 5 had less than 1/3% error.

The union algorithm is far superior not only in accuracy but also in speed to the results obtained with the first described classification method.

Considering the limits of information that radar can convey in the reflection off an aircraft the obtained results for both proposed algorithms are remarkable. During the parts of the flights, when the program failed to identify aircraft category, large portions of the aircraft disappear from the ISAR images which is normal in the holding pattern. The ISAR images in these critical positions in the holding pattern are even visually difficult to distinguish by human interaction.

REFERENCES

Haywood, B., Anderson, W. C., Morris, J. T., & Kyprianou, R. (1997). Generation of point scatterer models for simulating ISAR images of ships. *Radar*, *97*, 700–704.

Kershner, W.K. (1998). *The instrument flight manuel* (5th ed.). ASA Publishers.

Kim, K.-T., Seo, D.-K., & Kim, H.-T. (2005). Efficient classification of ISAR images. *IEEE Transactions on Antennas and Propagation*, *53*(5), 1611–1621. doi:10.1109/TAP.2005.846780

Li, Q. (2007). *Study of monopulse radar target three dimensional imaging and recognition.* (Ph.D dissertation). Xidian University.

Manikandan, J., Venkataramani, B., & Jayachandran, M. (2007). Evaluation of edge detection techniques towards implementation of automatic target recognition. In *Proceedings of Conference on Computational Intelligence and Multimedia Applications*, (vol. 2, pp. 441-445). IEEE.

Martorella, M., & Giusti, E. et al. (2008). Automatic target recognition by means of polarimetric ISAR images: A model matching based algorithm. [RADAR.]. *Proceedings of Radar*, *2008*, 27–31.

Maskall, G. T. (2002). An application of nonlinear feature extraction to the classification of ISAR images. *RADAR*, *15*(17), 405–408.

Prickett, M. J., & Chen, C. C. (1980). *Principles of inverse synthetic aperture radar imaging.* Arlington, VA: Electronics and Aerospace Systems.

Saidi, M.N., Hoeltzener, B., et al. (2008). Recognition of ISAR images: Target shapes features extraction. In *Proceedings of ICTTA 2008 3rd International Conference*. ICTTA.

Vespe, M., Baker, C. J., & Griffiths, H. D. (2006). *Outline structural representation for radar target classification based on non-radar templates.* Paper presented at the CIE 2006 International Conference. New York, NY.

Yuankui, H., & Yiming, Y. (2007). Automatic target recognition of ISAR images based on Hausdorff distance. In *Proceedings of APSAR 2007 1st Asian and Pacific Conference*, (pp. 477-479). IEEE.

Zeljković, V., Li, Q., Vincelette, R. B., Tameze, C., & Liu, F. (2009). *Automatic algorithm for ISAR images recognition and classification.* IET Radar, Sonar, and Navigation.

Zeljković, V., Li, Q., Vincelette, R. B., Tameze, C., & Liu, F. (2009). *Aircraft identification by unions of ISAR images.* MOBIMEDIA. doi:10.4108/ICST.MOBIMEDIA2009.7904

Zeljković, V., Li, Q., Vincelette, R. B., Tameze, C., & Liu, F. (2009). Noise resistant algorithm for radar images recognition and classification. *Signal and Data Processing of Small Targets.*

Zeljković, V., Tameze, C., & Vincelette, R. B. (2010). *Algorithms for radar image identification and classification.* Paper presented at the High Performance Computing & Simulation Conference: Workshop on Pattern Analysis and Recognition. New York, NY.

Chapter 11

Anthropometric Algorithm Used for Automatic Body Dimensions and Skin Color Detection Aimed for Homeland Security Systems

ABSTRACT

Automatic body detection and identification of a person is one of the most recent research topics that has gained a lot of attention from researchers. Automated systems that will store human biometrics along with the personal information can be of significant assistance in investigations and security issues. Biometrics represents unique aspects of the body that are measurable, robust, distinctive, physical characteristic, or personal traits of an individual by which a person can be identified. Biometric surveillance systems measure and analyze human physical and behavioral characteristics for identification purposes. A method of body measurement can be used for human identification, with the means of using a static camera. Body measurement calculation based on similar triangles is proposed. The focal length of the camera is a very important aspect of the method. This process can provide the means for obtained image segmentation, measurement of the body parts of the subject, and finally, these measurements can be used for identification of the person.

1. INTRODUCTION

The measurement related to human body with an intention of understanding his or her physical variations is referred to as anthropometry. This technique is today widely used in cloth designing, (Lu, 2008), (Meunier, 2000), (Petrak, 2006), industrial designing, ergonomics, architecture and homeland security, (Abdelkader, 2010), (Bracewell, 2001), (Gittoes, 2009), (Lv, 2006), (Rao, 2006), (Stancic, 2009), (Yeadon, 1990). In these fields, statistical data about the variation and

distribution of body measurements in the targeted population are used to customize and optimize the products. Several factors lead to changes in body measurements. This may include changes in lifestyles, ethnic and nutrition. For example, obesity epidemics may change the body measurement of the individuals affected thus making the anthropometric data updating necessary.

A method of body measurement can be used for human identification, with the means of using a static camera. There are certain methods that can enable obtainment of the body measurements. It

DOI: 10.4018/978-1-4666-4896-8.ch011

is proposed in this chapter body measurements calculation based on similar triangles. The focal length of the camera is a very important aspect of the method. This process can provide the means how obtained image should be segmented, how the body parts of the subject can be measured and finally these measurements can be used for identification of the person.

But before starting the process some very important facts have to be assumed. The scene where the action is taking place has to be a constant one and the ground on which the subject is standing or positioning himself or herself has to be flat for the purpose of correctness of the later calculations. The cameraman has to know the distance between the person and the camera, and other information about the focal length can be obtained from the camera itself. Also, an object of a known height should be placed in the scene for the purpose of proportion calculations.

The process of the measurements of the proposed algorithm is fast and simple, and a practitioner can execute the process successfully. In recent times the introduction of the digital camera and computer has greatly reduced the physical stress of the examiner. And the most important part of this is that the lesser physical strain has resulted in lower human error in the process. The computer also validates the results automatically and compares with the estimated values from the models.

Automatic body detection and identification of a person is one of the most recent research topics that have gained a lot of attention from researchers. Automated systems that will store the human biometrics along with the personal information can be of a significant assistance in investigations and security issues.

The applications of these programs can be wide; it can be used for the purpose of monitoring criminals and terrorists, cards and supermarkets among other things. Sometimes additional measurements apart from the three basic measurements can be used to read the body measurements of the person. These developments will be immensely beneficial in the aspects of security as they will definitely improve the process of tracking the person. It should be noted out that these processes are quite complicated and time consuming as a whole.

In modern times, anthropometric studies are conducted for a variety of purposes. But the primary most demand of the anthropometrics is in the field of forensics and physical anthropology. Anthropologists, in their academic endeavors investigate the evolutionary changes in body measurements of groups of people whose forefathers lived in different environmental setups. It has been proved that human beings exhibit body measurement variations depending on the different climatic conditions of the environmental settings they dwell. For example, scientists have identified that individuals living in cold climates will tend to have greater body measurements compared to people who dwell in warm climatic conditions.

Outside academics, anthropometry study is conducted to determine the range of cloth sizes which need to be manufactured for a specific group of people. As the demand of personalized clothing is growing with every passing day these processes are used by the manufactures only to get the more accurate measurements for their customers. It lowers the price of the product and also ensures faster delivery, which saves both the efforts of the maker and the time of the buyer. Foot measurements are used in the manufacture of footwear. The above explained issues depict the importance of anthropometric studies in the modern world. Body measurements are important in manufacturing companies because they get to understand the nature of their customers thus manufacturing goods exactly to the preference of their customers.

In today's world, there is a growing demand from consumers to purchase customized products which are needed at lower prices and delivered in time. The advanced technology has given globalization a new dimension of conducting business. The customers are able to place their orders online to suppliers who deliver the goods to their premises or even ship to them. The procedure is simple in the transactions involving standardized goods where no great deal of specifications is required.

Anthropology is also very useful in the identification of individuals. For example, the US military conducted the anthropometric survey of 1988 to specifically identify the army personnel with their body measurements. Anthropometric studies have developed greatly today. People are performing the study using the three dimensional scanners. The scan is taken on the individual body and the measurements are taken from the scan rather than the individual himself. This is important in the sense that the person measured does not have to wait for all the measurements to be taken separately.

The national defense systems are faced with overwhelming tasks of image identification in their operations. There are several reported cases of the criminals bypassing this screening systems because the system recognizes the information published in its databases and the systems have a "weakness" or inability to detect inconsistency between any two images of the same person. This loophole has been manipulated by criminals to secure their freedom. The installation of closed circuit television cameras commonly referred to as CCTVs was thought to be a solution. Nonetheless, the human is being creative enough to beat this security measure in institutions. Therefore, there is a need to develop a way to overcome this threat to the world's security systems.

The image processing system gives hints on how the application of anthropometrics can be used to come up with a technique of image identification. This will speed the manufacturers to accelerate the processing of their online customer orders. The intelligence systems will be able to detect and obtain the true information of criminal with some credible degree of precision. In order to be in a position to develop a workable prototype of a code, thorough understanding and analysis of image processing metrics becomes vital.

There are several metrics that can be used in image processing. These approaches depend on the nature of the image in question. These include: image based approach to obtaining anthropometric measurement for inertia modeling (statistical modeling applies in this concept), image calibration, and using computer vision system for human anthropometric parameters estimation. The parameters used to process images size include head size, facial configuration, waist size and frame stature among others.

Automating a manual process can improve consistency of the workflow. By creating an automated system of identification the search for information about one person becomes easier. The lack of a complete database that contains all information and biometrics of each individual within the population can cause weak homeland security system and it may increase the potential of identity theft within society.

Original identification system based on automatic body dimensions and skin color detection (Zeljkovic, 2011) is proposed in this chapter that can significantly improve and help homeland security system.

2. AUTOMATIC ANTHROPOMETRIC MEASUREMENTS ALGORITHM

Biometrics represents unique aspects of the body that is measurable, robust, distinctive, physical characteristic or personal trait of an individual by which a person can be identified. Biometric surveillance systems measure and analyze human physical and behavioral characteristics for identification purposes. Biometric identifiers include fingerprints, hand prints, vein dimensions, iris signatures, the pattern of blood vessels in the retina, body odors, characteristic and unique movements, individual voices, facial features and DNA. Applications of biometrics systems are numerous: transportation mass points like airports, seaports and railways; law enforcement in court and other law institutions, security and counter-terrorism, immigration, correctional institutions, schools and day care, missing children, residential security, internet e-commerce, healthcare, benefit payments, voter verification, banking. Countries all around the world apply various biometric surveillance systems.

Biometric surveillance systems encompass two phases: collecting biometric samples and comparing the acquired sample with the data that represent the enrollee's biometric located in a database. The example is facial recognition technology that reads the information or sample provided and compares it to many templates in the database and then reports or estimates who the person is from its database.

Face recognition is one of the most relevant biometric identifiers and one of the most important applications of image processing. It exploits unique configuration of a person's facial features in order to accurately identify them. According to many authorities from the biometrics industry it is the most appropriate technique for busy transport terminals as it seems more acceptable to the general public. This type of biometric verification systems can control access to computers, secured areas and verify passport information or citizenship status. Despite human ability to successfully identify known faces, it is difficult to deal with a large amount of unknown faces. The automated intelligent algorithms for face recognition applied on powerful computers with huge memory and computational speed, should overcome human limitations. However, the possibility to build an intelligent automated system which performs equivalent function to human ability to recognize faces remains a true challenge still nowadays. The position of the face in the image is one of many factors that make facial recognition technology not completely successful in its applications. Face recognition represents an unsolved problem and a demanded technology.

Face recognition is a relevant subject in computer vision research, pattern recognition, neural networks, computer graphics, image processing and psychology as it has wide application in many different industry areas like video surveillance, human-machine interaction, photo cameras, virtual reality, law enforcement, etc. The earliest research in face recognition problem began in the 1950's in psychology and in the 1960's in engineering. It was shown that there is a special process in human brain that is dedicated to recognize human faces. Based on this many scientists used this human face recognition ability to develop a non-human face recognition algorithms while the other methods just used mathematical tools. Some methods use the most obvious facial features like mouth, eyes, cheeks and their geometric measures like between-eye distance, width-length ratio, etc. paying attention to which facial features contribute to a good recognition rate. Other face recognition techniques apply abstract mathematical tools leaving out human-relevant features and anthropocentric approach. The best approach to address this problem is to apply the algorithms that use the knowledge that psychology, neurology or simple observation provide and at the same time to perform abstractions and implement pure mathematical and computational aspect.

Skin color cue is an important feature for face detection. The fact that color cue is irrelevant when a person tries to recognize chromatically similar objects and at the same time it is very important in distinguishing degraded shapes could be extrapolated to face recognition systems.

One of the face recognition methods is detecting faces in color images with complex backgrounds by fitting a Gaussian model on the transformed image from the RGB color space to the chrominance space in order to calculate a likelihood image which is thresholded to segment skin pixels and to form a binary skin map, that contains the candidate face regions.

Ear recognition represents another promising biometric technique as the morphology of the outer ear, in Latin pinna, is simple compared to the rich texture of the iris or the random distribution of minutiae in fingerprints. The structure of the ear is fairly stable, and robust to change in facial expressions. The detailed structure of the ear is unique. It appears to degrade little over the course of a human life and it does not suffer from some problems associated with other non-contact biometrics, such as face recognition. Ear has relatively uniform distribution of color in comparison to face. Other ear recognition advantages are faster matching, subject exclusion and forensic analysis.

Ear recognition method used as human identification and biometric tool was discovered by the French criminologist Bertillon, and further refined by the American police officer Iannarelli, who proposed ear recognition system based on seven features. Ear recognition methods are used as a component of smart surveillance systems and forensic image analysis and can be even more successfully applied in combination with the face recognition methods in the context of multi-pose face recognition as well as when the face is occluded.

The ear recognition methods' challenges and limitations are imposed by controlled indoor conditions, variation in illumination, hair occlusion, ear print forensics, ear symmetry, ear classification, ear individuality.

One of the methods for human identification using ear biometrics extracts the features from an ear image by measuring geometric relations like lengths and angles between predetermined points. Ear recognition and consequently human identification is based on these geometrical structures observed from pixel value distances.

Another approach implemented in human recognition is gate recognition used as one more biometric tool in a variety of applications, such as access control, surveillance, etc. People naturally on a daily basis distinguish different persons by the manner they walk. Movement features and various articulated moving body parts' shape characteristics constitute gate signatures. According to psychological studies gait signatures obtained from video can be used as a biometric tool in order to perform human identification. This inspired researchers in the field of computer vision to build mathematical algorithms capable of automatically extracting potential gait signatures from sequence of images to identify individuals.

Most gait recognition methods extract gate recognition features from silhouette images and are invariant to factors like color, texture, or type of clothing. Even though gate features are invariant to texture and color, static human shape intertwines with movement features. Gait recognition comprises of two important steps: reliable extraction of gait features and their recognition.

The proposed project is a part of the Anthropometric Measurement System aimed at person identification. It calculates the following:

1. The body dimensions (Height, Width, Chest, Waist, Hips) based on an image.
2. Locates the shoulders and chest positions in the image.
3. The size based on the body dimensions.
4. Extracts the RGB (R:Red, G:Green, B:Blue) codes for the purpose of skin tone determination.

Skin color detection plays a major role in face recognition and identification of skin areas in images or surveillance videos. It could help in identifying different people present in a picture or video. Therefore the previous algorithm was modified to detect skin color and it was tested on male subjects.

To reduce error the images are taken under the exact same conditions in the same environment. It is also necessary to take an image of an object with a known height which is placed in the scene. The distance from the camera should be known.

The proposed system automatically extracts body dimensions and skin color. It has the following features as shown in Figure 1:

1. Biometrics (Fingerprint, Iris recognition, and Dental record.)
2. Personal information.
3. Body dimensions extraction.
4. Skin tone and facial features extraction.
5. Storing the data in the database.
6. Issuing the ID card.

The following condition should apply to the room where the image is taken:

1. A plain background. Shiny walls or Sunlight on the background should be avoided.
2. The same camera with the same focal length should be used. There should be no difference in the zoom or focus between the images.
3. The camera should be placed at a certain known distance from the background or scene where the images are taken. This distance should not change because it would produce calculation errors. Also, the height level where the camera is set should not be changed.
4. An object of a known height should be in the scene. The distance between the camera and

Figure 1. Proposed system database

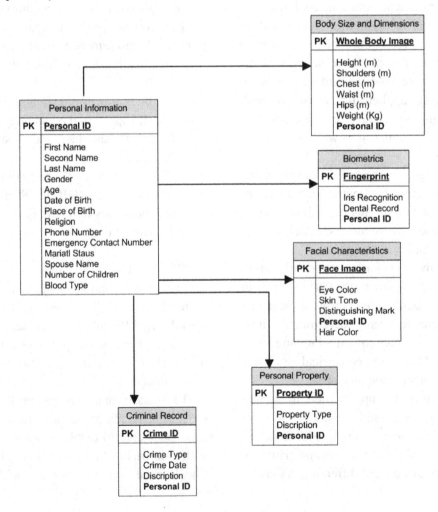

146

Figure 2. Proposed system

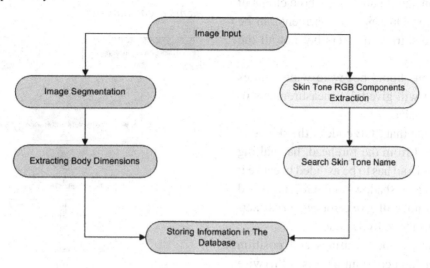

Figure 3. Image environment

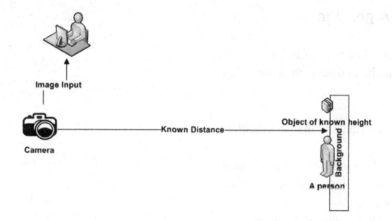

the object is important. If the camera is too close to the object, it should be placed in a high place, but if the camera is far from the object, it should be placed at a lower height.

2.1 Taking Images Procedure

The camera should be set at a known distance from the scene and at a certain height. Camera focal length has to be known. The focus is set at a certain level and it is kept constant for all the taken pictures. These conditions remain unchanged for all the taken images because otherwise calculations errors are produced.

The following pictures are shot:

1. A picture of the background.
2. A picture of the testing object with the background.
3. A picture of the person in the same background setting. Pictures of different people are taken under the same conditions.

The following precautions are taken:

1. The person should not ware clothes of the same or similar color as the background color is. If for example the background is white

the person should not ware whole cloths in white color. One piece of garment can be white like shirt or trousers but not all the clothes.

2. The person should not ware wide clothes because it will give false measurements of one's body size.

3. Considering that RGB code of the skin tone is extracted from the forehead, hair falling on the forehead has to be avoided because it could produce shadow on the forehead and the algorithm will give errors when extracting the skin tone RGB code.

4. Image size, camera settings and position have to be kept constant because otherwise calculations errors will be produced.

2.2 Proposed Algorithm

The following algorithm, shown in Figure 4, is used to measure the body dimensions and calculate its size:

1. Load person's image and the background's image.

2. Convert loaded images into one plane grayscale images since there is no need for the three RGB planes.

3. Take the absolute difference between the background and each person's image. This will identify the object or the person in the scene.

4. Binarize the absolute difference images obtained in step 3 by setting the adequate threshold. Different image environments will impose different threshold values therefore the threshold is obtained empirically. Every pixel with intensity gray level higher than 90 is set to 255 or white color and every pixel whose intensity gray level is lower than 90 is set 0 or black color. The obtained binary image has two color levels: black color which represents the background and white which

Figure 4. Automatic anthropometric measurements algorithm steps

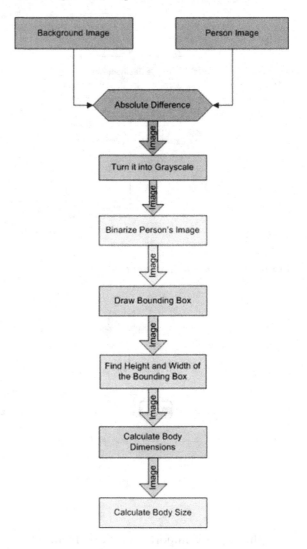

shows the object or a person. This precisely identifies the object in the scene.

5. Identify the top, the bottom, the most left and the most right pixels of the object or person in the scene. This marks the area which is occupied by the object or person in the image.

6. Draw the bounding box around the object or body. This creates the boundary of the area occupied by the body.

7. Calculate the dimensions of the body according to the following formulas:

Figure 5. Measurement based on the principle of similar triangles

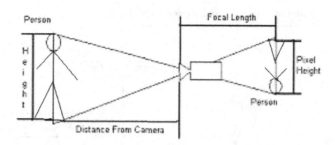

a. **Body Height in Pixels:** Top Pixel of the Bounding Box – Bottom Pixel of the Bounding Box.

b. **Body Width in Pixels:** The Most Left Pixel of the Bounding Box – The Most Right Pixel of the Bounding Box.

Using similar triangles, the following formulas for height and width can be obtained as found in the literature by Bracewell, Lobo, & Shah.

a. **Height in Meters:** (Height in Pixels * Known Object Height in meters)/ Known Object Height in pixels

b. **Width in Meters:** (Width in Pixels * Known Object Height in meters)/ Known Object Height in pixels

c. **Hips:** 0.9 * Width

d. **Waist:** 0.7 * Width

e. **Chest:** (2/3) * Width

f. **Shoulders Position in the Image:** Top of the Bounding Box + (Top of the Bounding Box – Bottom of the Bounding Box)/5

g. **Chest Position in the Image:** Top of the Bounding Box + (Top of the Bounding Box – Bottom of the Bounding Box)/3.8

8. Skin color detection plays a major role in face recognition and identification of skin areas in images or surveillance videos. It could help in identifying different people present in a picture or video. Therefore it is important to detect skin color as well, see Figure 6. Extracting Skin Tone RGB Code:

a. Locating the forehead:

    i. **Head Height=** Height of Person in Pixels/7. Head represents about one seventh of the body height

    ii. **Forehead = 1/3 Head Height**

    iii. **Central Pixel of Forehead =** Top Box + 1/3 Head and Left Box + Width/2

b. Create a of 5*5 pixels box around the determined central pixel in the forehead

c. Take the average value of the pixels in the three different RGB planes (R:Red, G:Green, B:Blue) .

3. EXPERIMENTAL RESULTS

The generated results of the proposed algorithm are shown. A step by step image results are presented along with a table of the calculated dimensions. Load the person's image and the background's image.

9. Turn loaded colored images into one plane grayscale images since there is no need for the three RGB planes.

10. Take the absolute difference between the background image shown in Figure 8 and each person's image shown in Figures 9-12.

11. Binarize the obatiend absolute difference images by setting a threshold to intensity

Figure 6. Anthropometric measurements and skin color algorithm

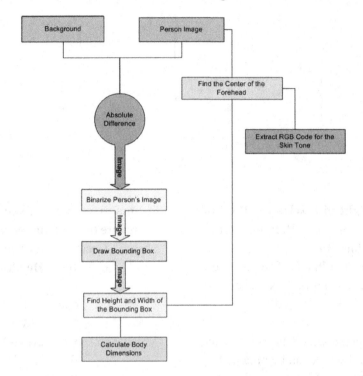

value 90 so every pixel which intensity value us higher than 90 will be set to white or 255 grayscale value and every pixel which intensity value is lower than 90 will be set to black, 0 grayscale value. These binarezed images are shown in Figures 17-20.

12. Extract the top pixel, the bottom pixel, the most left pixel and the most right pixel of the body.

13. Draw the bounding box around the body. The images with marked boxes around the extracted objects are shown in Figures 21-24.

The automatically obtained results for body dimension determination using the proposed algorithm are presented in Table 1. The real dimensions of the tested individuals are shown in parallel with the generated results. The errors obtained by the proposed method are presented for each

Figure 7. Object with a known height

Figure 8. Background

Figure 9. Person No. 1

Figure 10. Person No. 2

Figure 11. Person No. 3

Figure 12. Person No. 4

Figure 13. Absolute difference image between background image in Figure 8 and Person No. 1

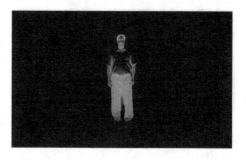

Figure 14. Absolute difference image between background image in Figure 8 and Person No. 2

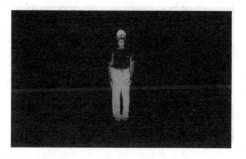

Figure 15. Absolute difference image between background image in Figure 8 and Person No. 3

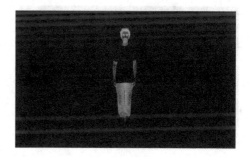

Figure 16. Absolute difference image between background image in Figure 8 and Person No. 4

Figure 17. Binarized image of the absolute difference image in Figure 13 of Person No. 1

Figure 21. Bounding box drawn around Person No. 1 in Figure 17

Figure 18. Binarized image of the absolute difference image in Figure 14 of Person No. 2

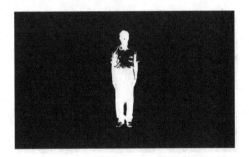

Figure 22. Bounding box drawn around Person No. 2 in Figure 18

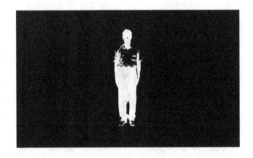

Figure 19. Binarized image of the absolute difference image in Figure 15 of Person No. 3

Figure 23. Bounding box drawn around Person No. 3 in Figure 19

Figure 20. Binarized image of the absolute difference image in Figure 16 of Person No. 4

Figure 24. Bounding box drawn around Person No. 4 in Figure 20

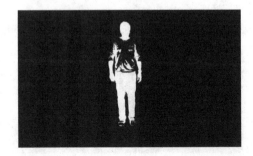

Table 1. Body dimensions results

Person	Height [m]	Width [m]	Hip [m]	Waist [m]	Chest [m]	Chest Position [pixels]	Shoulder Position [pixels]
No.1 Results	1.5485	0.6011	0.5410	0.4208	0.4007	1626	1527
Actual Dimensions	1.5240	0.5842	0.5070	0.4445	0.4371		
Error	2.45%	1.69%	3.4%	2.37%	3.64%		
No.2 Results	1.6381	0.5529	0.4976	0.3870	0.3686	1576	1471
Actual Dimensions	1.6002	0.5334	0.4750	0.4318	0.3941		
Error	3.79%	1.95%	2.26%	4.48%	2.55%		
No.3 Results	1.6469	0.4516	0.4064	0.3161	0.3010	1545	1436
Actual Dimensions	1.6376	0.4206	0.3784	0.3424	0.3290		
Error	1.14%	3.1%	2.8%	2.63%	2.8%		
No.4 Results	1.7669	0.6011	0.5410	0.4208	0.4007	1485	1368
Actual Dimensions	1.7272	0.5750	0.5250	0.4550	0.4413		
Error	3.97%	2.61%	1.6%	3.42%	4.06%		

person in red rows in Table 1. These errors represent the difference between automatically calculated each person's body dimensions by the proposed algorithm from the real person's dimensions.

The results from Table 1 clearly show that the error of the proposed algorithm is the most around 5% which makes the proposed method applicable in real security system.

The automatically obtained results for skin tone determination using the proposed algorithm are presented in Table 2. The extracted colors are represented in the RGB domain.

Skin tones color charts are shown in Figures 25 and 26. They can be used for automatic skin tone color detection and expression and verbalization in the exact name of the extracted skin tone.

Skin Tone RGB rates are within the following range:

Table 2. Skin tone results

Person No	Red	Green	Blue
Person No.1	101	79	57
Person No.2	28	22	17
Person No.3	83	63	47
Person No.4	23	19	15

- 110 <= R <= 255
- 48 <= G <= 207
- 26 <= B <= 192

4. CONCLUSION

The algorithm generates the results that show errors of at most 4.48% which makes the algorithm applicable in real systems. Height errors might be

Figure 25. Skin tones color chart

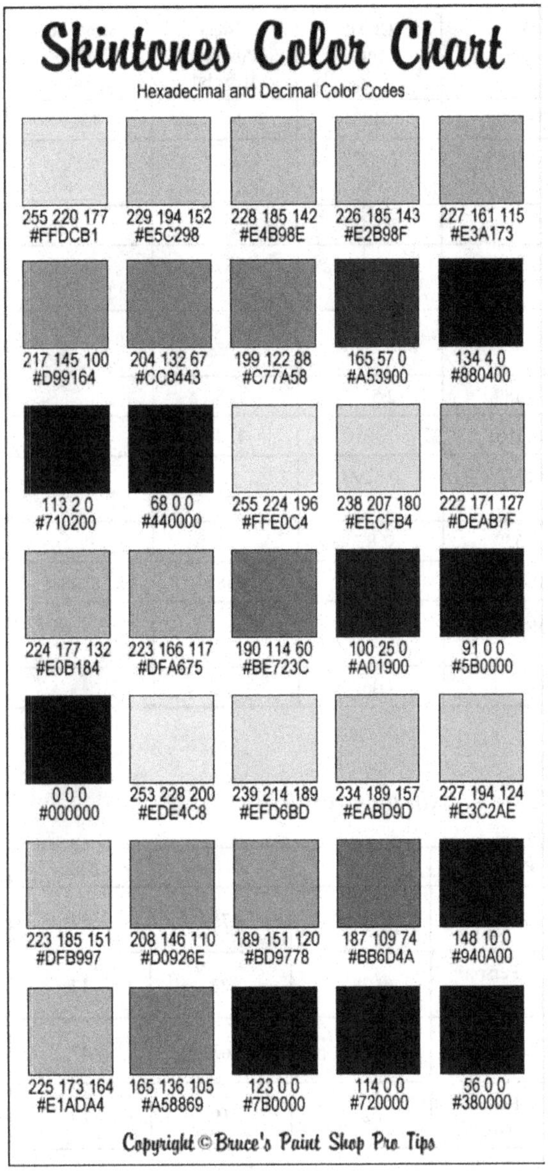

Figure 26. RGB codes for different skin tones

NAME OF SKIN	TONE	RGB
Adam & Eve	Persephone	168-108-077
Baiastice	Porcelain	230-156-123
Baiastice	Sun	197-127-092
Baiastice	Dark	150-073-040
Beauty Avatar	Dark	177-100-067
Beauty Avatar	Light	190-137-101
Beauty Avatar	Light (Delia)	195-142-099
Beauty Avatar	Natural	172-110-072
Beauty Avatar	Bronze	181-112-070
Belleza	Tan	152-090-066
LionSkins	Forbidden	206-192-192
LionSkins	Noir	215-173-151
LionSkins	Zulu	168-092-054
Redgrave	Porcelain	255-207-162
Redgrave	Pale	237-179-140
Redgrave	Tan	171-111-077
Redgrave	Tan	136-089-067
Redgrave	Tan	160-105-074
Redgrave	Tan	164-093-059
Redgrave	DeepTan	206-135-097
Redgrave	Bronze	164-083-055
Redgrave	Bronze	148-071-036
Redgrave	Bronze	188-114-074
Redgrave	Bronze (Hana)	204-127-082
Redgrave	Deep Bronze	183-109-074
Redgrave	Dark	110-053-034
Redgrave	Dark	147-075-049
Rockberry Uma	Tan	171-104-069
Soul	Dark	111-064-042
Soul	Dark	095-048-026
Staged	Tan	180-111-075

produced because of the footwear. Each person is wearing a shoe in the image while removing it when the manual measurements are taken. It is advised to take off footwear before taking the pictures. The errors generated in the body dimensions calculations could be caused by the difference in body shape of each individual or because of the difference in clothing (like having a wide sleeve or wide clothes). These errors could be reduced

if a side image of each person was taken, since it would give a better realization of the body shape and contour. The percentages of the errors for each image is within an acceptable range, which makes this project promising.

Table 2, which contains the results of the RGB code for the skin tone, shows that some of the numerical values extracted from the images do not fall in the range of skin tone RGB rates. The area in which the results were extracted is in the center of the forehead, therefore the error in extracting the RGB code might be caused by the difference in hair styles which could create a shadow on the area.

REFERENCES

Abaza, A., Ross, A., Hebert, C., Harrison, M. A. F., & Nixon, M. S. (2013). A survey on ear biometrics. *ACM Computing Surveys*, *45*(2). doi:10.1145/2431211.2431221

Abdelkader, B., & Chiraz, Y. Y. (2010). Statistical estimation of human anthropometry from a single uncalibrated image. Abu Dhabi, UAE: New York Institute of Technology.

Adler, F.H. (n.d.). *Physiology of the eye, clinical applications*. London: C. V. Mosby.

Ballan, L., Bertini, M., Del Bimbo, A., Dini, F., Lisanti, G., Seidenari, L., & Serra, G. (n.d.). *Recent research activities in video surveillance*. Florence, Italy: University of Florence, Multimedia Integration and Communication Center.

Bracewell, D. B., Lobo, D. V. N., & Shah, M. (2001). *Obtaining body measurements for human identification*. Pennsylvania: The Pennsylvania State University CiteSeer Archives.

Canny, J. (1986). A computational approach to edge detection. *IEEE Transactions on Pattern Analysis and Machine Intelligence*, 679–698. doi:10.1109/TPAMI.1986.4767851 PMID:21869365

Daugman, J. G. (1993). High confidence visual recognition of persons by a test of statistical independence. *IEEE Transactions on Pattern Analysis and Machine Intelligence*, *15*(11), 1148–1161. doi:10.1109/34.244676

Daugman, J. G. (1994). *Biometric personal identification system based on iris analysis* (U.S. Patent No. 5, 291,560). Washington, DC: US Patent Office.

Daugman, J. G. (2001). Statistical richness of visual phase information: Update on recognizing persons by iris patterns. *International Journal of Computer Vision*, *45*(1), 25–38. doi:10.1023/A:1012365806338

Daugman, J. G. (2003). The importance of being random: statistical principles of iris recognition. *Pattern Recognition*, *36*(2), 279–291. doi:10.1016/S0031-3203(02)00030-4

Frank, T. (2007). Face recognition next in terror fight. *USA Today*.

Gittoes, M., Bezodis, I., & Wilson, N. C. (2009). An image-based approach to obtaining anthropometric measurements for inertia modeling. *Journal of Applied Biomechanics*, (25): 265–270. PMID:19827477

Gohringer, C. (n.d.). Advances in face recognition technology and its application in airports. *Allevate Limited*.

Heseltine, T., & Whitehead, N. (n.d.). Facial recognition – Finding a reliable system that works in all conditions. *Ingenia, 48*.

Kovesi, P. (n.d.). *Video surveillance: Legally blind*. Crawley, Australia: School of Computer Science & Software Engineering, The University of Western Australia.

Lai, W.-H., & Li, C.-T. (2006). *Skin colour-based face detection in color images*. Sydney, Australia: IEEE.

Lu, J.-M., & Wang, M. J. (2008). An intelligent system for customized clothing making. In *Proceedings of Conf. On Computational Intelligence, Man-Machine Systems and Cybernetics*, (pp. 171-174). IEEE.

Lv, F. T., & Zhao, N. R. (2006). Camera calibration from video of a walking Human. *Journal of Biomechanics*, 1513–1518. PMID:16929736

Marques, I., & Grana, M. (2010). *Face recognition algorithms*. Proyecto Fin de Carrera.

Meunier, P., & Yin, S. (2000). Performance of a 2D image-based anthropometric measurement and clothing sizing system. *Applied Ergonomics*, 445–451. doi:10.1016/S0003-6870(00)00023-5 PMID:11059458

Nieto, M., Johnston-Dodds, K., & Wear Simmons, C. (n.d.). *Public and private applications of video surveillance and biometric technologies*. Berkeley, CA: California Research Bureau, California State Library.

Petrak, S., & Rogale, D. (2006). Systematic representation and application of a 3D computer-aided garment construction method. *International Journal of Clothing Science and Technology*, 179-187.

Pflug, A., & Busch, C. (2012). Ear biometrics: A survey of detection, feature extraction and recognition methods. *IET Biometrics*, *1*(2), 114–129. doi:10.1049/iet-bmt.2011.0003

Rao, G., Amarantini, D., Berton, E., & Favier, D. (2006). Influence of body segments' parameters estimation models on inverse dynamics solutions during gait. *Journal of Biomechanics*, 1531–1536. doi:10.1016/j.jbiomech.2005.04.014 PMID:15970198

Ross, A., & Byrd, R.C. (n.d.). *Advances in ear biometrics*. Academic Press.

Scin Colors. (n.d.). Retrieved from http://www.stilettomoody.com/faq/how-do-i-match-my-skin-color/how-do-i-find-the-numerical-value-rgb-for-my-skin-color.html

Stancic, I., Supuk, T., & Cecic, M. (2009). Computer vision system for human anthropometric parameters estimation. *WSEAS Transactions on Systems*, 430-443.

Wang, P., & Xu, C. (n.d.). *Robust face recognition via sparse representation*. Academic Press.

Williams, M. (2007). *Better face-recognition software*. Academic Press.

Woodward, J., & Horn, C. (2003). *Biometrics a look at facial recognition*. Academic Press.

Wright, J., Yang, A., Ganesh, A., Sastry, S., & Ma, Y. (2009). Robust face recognition via sparse representation. *IEEE Transactions on PAMI*, *31*(2), 210–227. doi:10.1109/TPAMI.2008.79 PMID:19110489

Yeadon, M. R. (1990). The simulation of aerial movement-II: A mathematical inertia model of the human-body. *Journal of Biomechanics*, 67–74. doi:10.1016/0021-9290(90)90370-I PMID:2307693

Zeljkovic, V., Abu-Khamis, N., & Al Qahtani, H. (2011). *Algorithm for automatic body dimensions and skin colour detection used in homeland security systems*. Jeddah, Saudi Arabia: Ministry of Higher Education Second Scientific Conference.

Chapter 12
Algorithm for Automated Iris Recognition Using Biorthogonal Wavelets

ABSTRACT

A comparative study of ability of two novel image retrieval algorithms to provide automated touch-free identification of persons by iris recognition is presented. Namely, applied biorthogonal wavelet methods and the SVD-Free Latent Semantic method are analyzed. Moreover, in case of the applied biorthogonal wavelet method, two approaches were tested and compared: the processing of the whole image and the processing of the image converted to a vector. The point is that different methods for getting rid of the noise were successfully applied in both cases. Numerical experiments on a real biometric database indicate feasibility of the presented approach as an automated iris recognition tool without special image pre-processing.

1. INTRODUCTION

Methods of human identification using biometric features like fingerprint, hand geometry, face, voice and iris are widely studied. A human eye iris has a unique structure given by pigmentation spots, furrows and other tiny features that are stable throughout life (Adler, 1965). It is possible to scan iris without physical contact in spite of wearing eyeglasses or contact lens. The iris can be hardly forged, e.g. replaced or copied. This makes the iris a suitable object for the identification of a person. Iris recognition seems to be more reliable than other biometric techniques like face recognition (Daugman, 2001). Iris biometric systems for public and personal use have been designed and deployed commercially by British Telecom, US

Sandia Labs, UK National Physical Laboratory, NCR, Oki, IriScan, and others. The applications of these systems are expected in personal identification, access control, computer and Internet security, etc. Studies about iris recognition are discussed in (Daugman, 1993), (Daugman, 1994), (Daugman, 2001), (Daugman, 2003), (Dobeš, 2007), (Praks, 2007).

Alternative approach to the recognition of the human iris images is presented in this chapter. The aim is to show the ability of using the biorthogonal wavelets to recognize iris images. The proposed algorithm is described by Matlab language. The main reason is that Matlab by Mathworks is popular language for description of matrix-oriented computations (Grossman, 2000), (Praks, 2007). The proposed methods are tested using the real iris database.

DOI: 10.4018/978-1-4666-4896-8.ch012

2. IMAGE DATABASE

The iris is scanned by TOPCON optical device connected to the CCD Sony camera (Dobeš, 2007). The acquired digitized image is RGB of size 576×768 pixels. Only the red (R) component of the RGB image participates in recognition. The reason is that the recognition based on the red component appears to be more reliable than recognition based on green (G) or blue (B) components or grayscale images. It is in accord with the study of Daugman (Daugman, 2003), where near-infrared wavelengths are used.

3. BIORTHOGONAL WAVELETS

The biorthogonal wavelets are used in this study (Gonzales, 2004), (Prasad, 1997) as a tool for iris recognition problem. Two techniques are applied. Two-dimensional and one dimensional biorthogonal wavelet filters are used.

The first technique (Xu, 1994), (Chang, 2000) implies procedure with an image converted to gray image. Even though the processing of Red component of images has shown the best results, in this case the procedure of gray images appeared to give superior results. Every image is processed as a two-dimensional $m \times n$ matrix image. The two-dimensional biorthogonal wavelets are applied to gray images.

In the second approach (IEEE Transactions on Information Theory, 1992), (IEEE Transactions on Signal Processing, 1993), only Red component of the image is extracted and processed. Every image is then represented and processed as a sequence of pixels. A converted image is observed as a $p \times 1$-dimensional vector, where p denotes the number of pixels. A two-dimensional $m \times n$ matrix image is converted to related to $p \times 1 = m*n$ vector. After that the one-dimensional biorthogonal wavelet is applied to vector converted image.

As it can be observed that both techniques apply image de-noising and pre-processing by wavelet filter application. The obtained numerical results pointed out, that the application of de-noising methods increases the ability of the algorithm to perform the successful iris recognition.

After the application of different wavelet functions for both methods it can be concluded, based on the obtained results that mostly different wavelet families gave similar results and the biorthogonal wavelets have shown the slightly better result. It is observed that the results obtained by the application of the lower order of the applied wavelet family filter are better. This is concluded based on calculations conducted for all applied wavelet families.

The obtained results have driven to the conclusion to apply biorthogonal wavelets of the first order.

In the current computer implementation of the proposed iris recognition procedures, no pre-processing of images is assumed. The presented numerical experiments indicate optimistic application of the proposed techniques for iris recognition.

The colors of images are coded in Matlab (tm) as non-negative integral numbers and no scaling was used. The application of the proposed procedures can be written in Matlab as follows.

```
% Input:
% A ... the m × n document matrix
% Output:
% sim ... the vector of similarity
coefficients
 [m,n] = size(Image);
```

- Extract the red component of the Image, calculate the gray image presentation and reshape the red component of the Image to the vector in the case when the first proposed technique is applied:

```
RedImage=Image(:,:,1);
Gray=rgb2gray(Image);
Vector=reshape(RedImage,m*n,1);
```

- Apply one-dimensional biorthogonal wavelet on reshaped red component of the Image.

```
ImageWavelet1 = wden(Vector,'minimaxi
','s','mln',7,wavelet);
```

- Apply two-dimensional biorthogonal wavelet on gray two-dimensional Image.

```
[thr,sorh,keepapp] =
ddencmp('den','wv',RedImage);
% de-noise image using global thresh-
olding option
ImageWavelet2 = wdencmp('gbl', RedIma
ge,wavelet,1,thr,sorh,keepapp);
```

- Compute the similarity coefficients between two inspected images.

```
xx= ImageWavelet2 '*ImageWavelet20;
xx= xx/(norm(ImageWavelet20)*norm(Ima
geWavelet2));
sim(i) = 1-acos(xx)
```

The proposed two algorithms give at the output the similarity coefficients *sim*. The absolute value of *i*-th element of *sim* coefficient is a measure of the similarity between two compared images.

Both algorithms give acceptable and competitive results. They are efficient, easy for implementation and fast enough for real application.

4. EXPERIMENTAL RESULTS

The collection of six color iris images was analyzed, see Figure 1. The width of images is 768 pixels and the height of images is 576 pixels. So the each picture is characterized by 442 368 attributes. For example, the name "001L_3.png" implies that the left iris of Person No.1, the series 3 is assumed.

The images were open using the Matlab (tm) command *imread*. Only the last component of RGB matrix is assumed for iris recognition. The queries were represented as images from the collection.

Figure 1. The collection of analyzed iris images

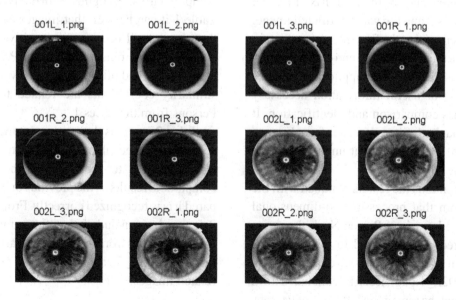

Figure 2. Borthogonal wavelet applied on: (a) the left iris of Person No.1, the series 2 and (b) the right iris of Person No.1, the series 2

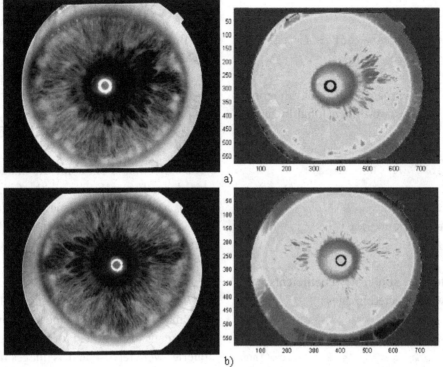

The Figure 2 represents: (a) the left iris of Person No.1, the series 2 and the same image after applied wavelets and (b) the right iris of Person No.1, the series 2 and the wavelet filtered image. It can be observed that the filtered images contain emphasized a unique structure and elements present in the iris. The wavelet application enables the extraction of useful information necessary for further iris comparison and identification. It is obvious that both filtered images form Figures 2(a) and 2(b) extract different unique elements present in the iris.

Table 1 contains the results obtained with the first algorithm that processes two-dimensional images. If the left iris of Person No.1, the series 2 is compared, with the goal to determine the identification of the person whose left iris is on the image (002L_1.png), it can be concluded form the Table 1 that the remaining left irises of Persons

No.2 and NO.3, images 002L_2.png and 002L_3. png are selected as the most related images. The compared iris is recognized correctly. Analyzing Table 1 it can be seen that images are sorted in the way that all images with positive similarity coefficients are related to irises of Persons from the series 2, and all other images with negative similarity coefficients are related to irises of Persons from the series 1.

Table 2 contains the results obtained with the second proposed algorithm that processes images converted to vectors. This method gives comparable results as the previous one. The compared iris is recognized correctly. From the Table 2 it can be concluded that the remaining left irises of Persons from the series 2, images 002L_2. png and 002L_3.png are selected as the most related images.

Table 1. Iris recognition problem using query image 002L_1.png and two-dimensional algorithm

Image	Similarity	Image	Similarity
002L_1	1	001R_3	-0,541
002L_2	0,9026	001L_3	-0,541
002L_3	0,8183	001L_1	-0,5829
002R_3	0,8041	001R_1	-0,5829
002R_2	0,7979	001R_2	-0,6018
002R_1	0,7433	001L_2	-0,6018

Table 2. Iris recognition problem using query image 002L_1.png and one-dimensional algorithm

Image	Similarity	Image	Similarity
002L_1	1	001L_3	-0,5814
002L_2	0,9227	001R_2	-0,5852
002L_3	0,8562	001R_1	-0,6167
002R_3	0,8613	001L_2	-0,6274
002R_2	0,8612	001L_1	-0,6344
002R_1	0,8192	001R_3	-0,6433

Table 3. Iris recognition problem using query image 002R_1.png and two-dimensional algorithm

Image	Similarity	Image	Similarity
002R_1	1	001R_1	-0,5393
002R_2	0,8258	001R_2	-0,5419
002R_3	0,7931	001L_1	-0,5747
002L_2	0,7555	001R_3	-0,5977
002L_1	0,7433	001L_2	-0,6588
002L_3	0,7324	001L_3	-0,6608

Table 4. Iris recognition problem using query image 002R_1.png and one-dimensional algorithm

Image	Similarity	Image	Similarity
002R_1	1	001R_2	-0,5576
002R_2	0,8863	001R_1	-0,5731
002R_3	0,8533	001R_3	-0,6176
002L_2	0,8297	001L_1	-0,6244
002L_1	0,8192	001L_3	-0,6555
002L_3	0,8137	001L_2	-0,6712

In the case of comparison of the right iris of Person No.1, the series 2, assumed as the compared image (002R_1.png), the remaining right irises of Persons No.2 and No.3, images 002R_2.png and 002R_3.png, are selected by both proposed algorithms as the most related images. The compared iris is recognized in both cases correctly and all images with positive similarity coefficients are related to irises of Persons from the series 2.

Table 3 and Table 4 present the obtained results by processing the images with two-dimensional biorthogonal wavelet and by converting the image to a vector and applying one-dimensional biorthogonal wavelet, respectively.

In all performed experiments both algorithms have shown compatible, accurate and comparable results. The advantage of one of the proposed methods can be only in their speed and practical implementation and realization.

5. CONCLUSION

Two approaches to the recognition of real iris images are presented. The results of the recognition test are promising and they show the ability of presented algorithms to recognize real iris images.

Two different biorthogonal wavelet methods are applied to get proper iris comparison and identification. The two following algorithms were tested and compared: the processing of the whole image and the processing of the image converted to a vector. Both applied techniques perform de-noising and pre-processing by wavelet filter application. As it can be observed from presented numerical results, the application of de-noising methods increases the ability of the algorithm to perform the successful iris recognition, indicating optimistic application possibilities of the proposed techniques. Both algorithms have shown compatible, accurate and comparable results. The advantage of one of the proposed methods can be only in their speed and practical implementation and realization.

Application of video surveillance applied in industry and problem of automatic pattern classification of real metallographic images from the steel plant ArcelorMittal Ostrava is addressed in the next chapter. The automatic software capable to analyze the homogeneity of the surface and characterize features of the molten steel level such as presence of slag clusters is developed as well. A new heuristic algorithm for porosity segmentation for the colored petro-graphic images is also proposed in the fifth chapter. The algorithm automatically detects the porosities that represent the presence of oil, gas or even water in the analyzed thin section rock segment based on the color of the porosity area filled with dies in the analyzed sample.

A comparative study of ability of the proposed novel image retrieval algorithms is performed in the fifth chapter to provide automated object classification invariant of rotation, translation and scaling. Simple cosine similarity coefficient methods are analyzed. Numerical experiments on a real database sets indicate feasibility of the presented approach as automated object classification tool without special image pre-processing.

REFERENCES

Abaza, A., Ross, A., Hebert, C., Harrison, M. A. F., & Nixon, M. S. (2013). A survey on ear biometrics. *ACM Computing Surveys*, *45*(2). doi:10.1145/2431211.2431221

Adler, F.H. (n.d.). *Physiology of the eye: Clinical applications.* London: C. V. Mosby.

Ballan, L., Bertini, M., Del Bimbo, A., Dini, F., Lisanti, G., Seidenari, L., & Serra, G. (n.d.). *Recent research activities in video surveillance.* Florence, Italy: University of Florence, Multimedia Integration and Communication Center.

Canny, J. (1986). A computational approach to edge detection. *IEEE Transactions on Pattern Analysis and Machine Intelligence*, 679–698. doi:10.1109/TPAMI.1986.4767851 PMID:21869365

Chang, S. G., Yu, B., & Vetterli, M. (2000). Spatially adaptive wavelet thresholding with context modeling for image denoising. *IEEE Transactions on Image Processing*, *9*(9), 1522–1531. doi:10.1109/83.862630 PMID:18262990

Daugman, J. G. (1993). High confidence visual recognition of persons by a test of statistical independence. *IEEE Transactions on Pattern Analysis and Machine Intelligence*, *15*(11), 1148–1161. doi:10.1109/34.244676

Daugman, J. G. (1994). *Biometric personal identification system based on iris analysis* (U.S. Patent No. 5, 291,560). Washington, DC: US Patent Office.

Daugman, J. G. (2001). Statistical richness of visual phase information: Update on recognizing persons by iris patterns. *International Journal of Computer Vision*, *45*(1), 25–38. doi:10.1023/A:1012365806338

Daugman, J. G. (2003). The importance of being random: Statistical principles of iris recognition. *Pattern Recognition*, *36*(2), 279–291. doi:10.1016/S0031-3203(02)00030-4

Dobeš, M., & Machala, L. (n.d.). *Iris database.* Retrieved from http://phoenix.inf.upol.cz/iris/

Gohringer, C. (n.d.). Advances in face recognition technology and its application in airports. *Allevate Limited.*

Gonzales, R. C., Woods, R. E., & Eddins, S. L. (2004). *Digital image processing using MATLAB.* Pearson Education, Prentice Hall.

Grossman, D. A., & Frieder, O. (2000). *Information retrieval: Algorithms and heuristics.* Kluwer Academic Publishers.

Heseltine, T., & Whitehead, N. (n.d.). Facial recognition – Finding a reliable system that works in all conditions. *Ingenia, 48*.

Kovesi, P. (n.d.). *Video surveillance: Legally blind*. Crawley, Australia: School of Computer Science & Software Engineering, The University of Western Australia.

Labský, M., Svátek, V., Praks, P., & Šváb, O. (2005). *Information extraction from HTML product catalogues: Coupling quantitative and knowledge-based approaches*. Wadern, Germany: Semantic Web. Retrieved from http://www.smi. ucd.ie/Dagstuhl-MLSW/proceedings/labsky-svatek-praks-svab.pdf

Lai, W.-H., & Li, C.-T. (2006). *Skin colour-based face detection in color images*. Sydney, Australia: IEEE.

Machala, L., & Pospíšil, J. (2001). Proposal and verification of two methods for evaluation of the human iris video-camera images. *Optik (Stuttgart), 112*(8), 335–340. doi:10.1078/0030-4026-00066

Machala, L., Praks, P., & Snášel, V. (2004). *Two methods for iris recognition using mutual information*. Brno, Czech Republic: Znalosti.

Marques, I., & Grana, M. (2010). *Face recognition algorithms*. Proyecto Fin de Carrera.

Nieto, M., Johnston-Dodds, K., & Wear Simmons, C. (n.d.). *Public and private applications of video surveillance and biometric technologies*. Berkeley, CA: California Research Bureau, California State Library.

Pflug, A., & Busch, C. (2012). Ear biometrics: A survey of detection, feature extraction and recognition methods. *IET Biometrics, 1*(2), 114–129. doi:10.1049/iet-bmt.2011.0003

Praks, P., Černohorský, J., & Briš, R. (n.d.). *Human expert modelling using numerical linear algebra: A heavy industry case study*. IOS Press.

Praks, P., Dvorský, J., & Snášel, V. (2003). *Latent semantic indexing for image retrieval systems*. Williamsburg, VA: SIAM. Retrieved from http://www.siam.org/meetings/la03/proceedings/Dvorsky.pdf

Praks, P., Machala, L., & Snášel, V. (n.d.). On SVD-free latent semantic indexing for iris recognition of large databases. In V. A. Petrushin, & L. Khan (Eds.), *Multimedia data mining and knowledge discovery*. Berlin: Springer Verlag.

Prasad, L., & Iyengar, S. S. (2007). *Wavelet analysis with applications to image processing*. Boca Raton, FL: CRC Press.

Praus, P., & Praks, P. (2007). Information retrieval in hydrochemical data using the latent semantic indexing approach. *Journal of Hydroinformatics*.

Ross, A., & Byrd, R.C. (n.d.). *Advances in ear biometrics*. Academic Press.

Wang, P., & Xu, C. (n.d.). *Robust face recognition via sparse representation*. Academic Press.

Williams, M. (2007). *Better face-recognition software*. Academic Press.

Woodward, J., & Horn, C. (2003). *Biometrics a look at facial recognition*. Academic Press. Frank, T. (2007). Face recognition next in terror fight. *USA Today*.

Wright, J., Yang, A., Ganesh, A., Sastry, S., & Ma, Y. (2009). Robust face recognition via sparse representation. *IEEE Transactions on PAMI, 31*(2), 210–227. doi:10.1109/TPAMI.2008.79 PMID:19110489

Xu, Y., Weaver, J. B., Healy, D. M. Jr, & Lu, J. (1994). Wavelet transform domain filters: A spatially selective noise filtration technique. *IEEE Transactions on Image Processing, 3*(6), 747–758. doi:10.1109/83.336245 PMID:18296244

Zeljković, V., & Praks, P. (2007). *A comparative study of automated iris recognition using the biorthogonal wavelets and the SVD-free latent semantic methods*. Ostrava, Czech Republic: VSB-Technical University of Ostrava.

Section 5

Video Surveillance Applied in Industry and Quality Control

The goal of automatic pattern classification of real metallographic images from the steel plant Arcelor-Mittal Ostrava is to monitor the quality process in the steel plant. The number and sizes of dark dots produced by the production procedure imperfections are automatically determined; that represents a measure of how imperfect each plate is.

Steel Companies use a ladle furnace refining process that refines under a non-oxidizing atmosphere and supports slag-metal reaction through stirring by Ar gas injection. The automatic software capable to analyze the homogeneity of the surface and characterize features of the molten steel level such as presence of slag clusters is developed.

A new heuristic algorithm for porosity segmentation for the colored petro-graphic images is proposed as well. The algorithm automatically detects the porosities that represent the presence of oil, gas, or even water in the analyzed thin section rock segment based on the color of the porosity area filled with dies in the analyzed sample.

A comparative study of the ability of the proposed novel image retrieval algorithms is performed to provide automated object classification invariant of rotation, translation, and scaling. Simple cosine similarity coefficient methods are analyzed. Numerical experiments on real database sets indicate the feasibility of the presented approach.

Chapter 13
Algorithm for Automatic Pattern Classification Designed for Real Metallographic Images

ABSTRACT

The problem of automatic pattern classification in real metallographic images from the steel plant ArcelorMittal Ostrava is addressed. The goal is to monitor the process quality in the steel plant. In the images of metal, there are dark dots that are produced by imperfections along the central axis of each plate. It is necessary to determine automatically the number and sizes of these dots. The number and sizes of the dots is a measure of how imperfect each plate is. The process is presented that segments the area of plates that contains segregation, identifies those rows of pixels along which the dots lie, and counts the pixels that are marked as dots by evaluating all the vertical columns of pixels that intersect the rows that contain the dots. The threshold value is set to be 95% of the mean value of grey scale for each column of pixels and makes the dots white. White dots that are most likely noise are removed to identify dots that are smaller than 4 connected pixels across. The explanations related to the obtained results are firmly related to the information provided by human experts.

1. INTRODUCTION

Every industrial technology seeks to replace human labor with some automatic operation. Labor saving devices are a cardinal feature of improvement in the quality of lives experienced by humans who are set free thereby from the limitations imposed by life's burdens of drudgery. In the case of human perception, in particular for the application of this method, vision, a video image is examined and evaluated for defects that manifest themselves as dark dots in metal plates. Slab samples taken from the slab caster are analyzed. The material is used for the production of thermo-rolled strips

intended for the manufacture of high pressure pipes according to EN or API standards. Rather than have the dots counted and their sizes measured manually by a human operator, or having the human operator make a subjective judgment on how badly the dots indicate how defective the plate is, an algorithm is being developed and automated software is derived to perform this activity with far superior efficiency, precision, reliability, and objectivity.

The problem of automatic pattern classification in real metallographic images from the steel plant ArcelorMittal Ostrava plc (Ostrava, Czech Republic) is addressed in this chapter. The goal of

DOI: 10.4018/978-1-4666-4896-8.ch013

this research is to monitor the process quality in the steel plant. The image classification algorithm is developed for this purpose to automatically identify the segregations i.e. dots in the analyzed images and to determine their sizes, i.e. counts the number of pixels contained in the detected segregated areas. The proposed method for image classification first segments the area in the plate that contains dots, detects the rows of pixels along which the dots lie and counts the pixels that are marked as dots.

In this case, the human labor saved is perception, i.e. vision. Sensory impressions must be interpreted and evaluated. However, when human perception is substituted with machine perception one cannot realistically expect to copy the machine language of the human brain, but fortunately this is not necessary so long as the computer simulation of the human perception produces the desired results (Niemann, 1990), (Webb, 2002), (Praks, 2008). Research on mathematical aspects of perception is the field of pattern recognition. More specifically, when the pattern recognition simulates vision, images are analyzed. In the case of this chapter, known patterns in an image are recognized, interpreted and evaluated (Berry, 1999), (Berry, 1995).

The photographing of analyzed metal plates, i.e. the acquisition of their digital images, is a very time consuming, complicated and risky procedure. The originally produced metal plates are completely dark and image analysis and dots detection is impossible without prior pre-processing. The pre-processing procedure requires a very complicated chemical process many details of which are classified. During chemical processing the metal plates are exposed to an acid solution which makes the dots visible. The process is time demanding and must be performed under strict safety requirements. Consequently, the number of samples available to us for image analysis is limited.

Two applied techniques that perform automatic image segmentation (Wolfson, 1987), (Grady, 2004), are presented as well as the detailed explanations of the proposed intelligent algorithm for automatic segregation identification and the determination of size of the detected segregations in each plate. Experimental results obtained with the proposed algorithm for image classification are given below.

2. AUTOMATIC PATTERN CLASSIFICATION ALGORITHM-IMAGE SEGMENTATION

The metal plate image segmentation was done using the methods provided by the Leo Grady Graph Analysis Toolbox found in the literature (Wolfson, 1987), (Grady, 2004).

Grady and Schwartz have described (Wolfson, 1987) a MATLAB package which they call the Graph Analysis Toolbox. The purpose of this toolbox is to facilitate computer vision by providing algorithms and data structures so that arbitrary vision sampling arrangements that even exclude space-variant sensors can be used. Its theoretical principle draws upon space-variant computer vision that is, in their words, "biologically inspired".

Grady estimates the isoperimetric content of an image graph in (Grady, 2004). Rather than partitioning the graph by means of spectral methods, the proposed method segments and clusters spectral methods with improved speed and stability. Four reasons are given for what are called graph theoretic approaches to image segmentation:

1. The relationship between the part and the whole is important in both biological and machine image processing. Graph theoretical algorithms are well suited for expressing local-global interactions.

2. There are many well-explored algorithms from which to create new ones for image processing.

3. Image processing on sensor architectures that have space-variant visual sampling require what Grady calls a connectivity graph. Space-variant architectures offer great data compression. Consequently, they have been thoroughly studied during the past few decades.

4. New architectures for image processing can be built to generalize the Cartesian design. Vision sensing devices usually are space-invariant, that is, the pixels are fixed in number, and they operate at a fixed rate that is synchronized by a clock. This is very inefficient and the efficiency can be greatly improved by using a spatially adaptive sensor and/or an adaptive system for temporal sampling.

Both methods the spectral segmentation (Wolfson, 1987) and isoparametric segmentation (Grady, 2004) are applied on metallographic plate images. The obtained results, shown in Figure 1, were equally efficient and good for both used methods: the spectral segmentation and isoparametric segmentation.

3. AUTOMATIC PATTERN CLASSIFICATION ALGORITHM – SEGREGATION IDENTIFICATION AND ITS SIZE DETERMINATION

The steel plant of ArcelorMittal Ostrava plc (Ostrava, Czech Republic) has provided images of metal plates. Each plate has a thickness of 150 mm (+/- 1 mm, but more likely – 1 mm). The idea is to develop an efficient, automatic intelligent algorithm capable of supplying a measure of defectiveness along the central axis of the plates. The dots represent segregation in the sample and can be observed as "failures" in the metal plates that decrease their quality of production.

The failures are generated as consequence of the technological process – a coldness process. The material is hot initially and the temperature de-

Figure 1. (a) Original plate image; (b) spectral segmentation; (c) isoparametric segmentation

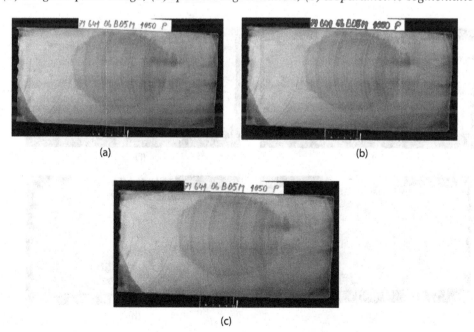

(a)

(b)

(c)

creases from the border to the centre of the sample. These dots are situated in the centre because of a non-homogenity of the technological process.

The defectiveness of each plate is to be measured by counting the number of dots in the image of the plate along the central axis. The number and the size of dots influence the quality of the produced metallographic plates. The sizes of the dots, which vary, are to be measured as to whether they are 1-3 mm across, 3-5 mm across, or more than 5 mm across. These dots, i.e. segregations, are the manifestation of defects that are caused by the manner in which the plates, which begin at a higher temperature, are cooled from the borders

Figure 2. Metal samples (a) 70528_06_B05M_C; (b) 71638_06_B05M_L; (c) 72635_03_B04M_L; (d) 72635_06_B04M_P; (e) 72914_06_B06M_P; (f) 73305_03_B05M_L_CLASS3; (g) 73314_03_B05M_P; (h) 71644_09_B05M_840_L

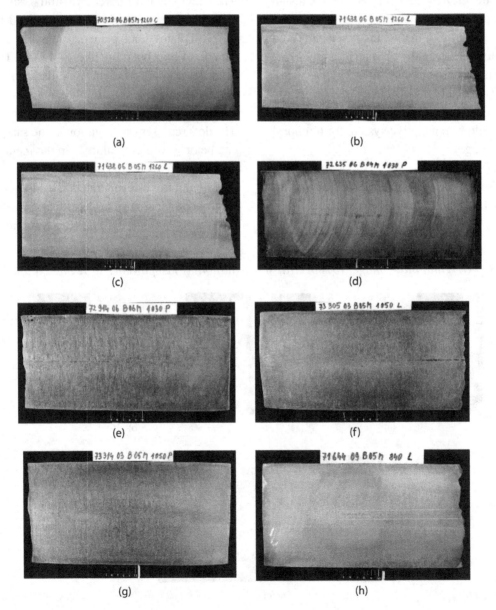

to the central axis. Because the cooling process is non-uniform, defects are caused along the central axis. The other sources of defects include also inappropriate conditions of the chemical composition, secondary cooling, casting speed, the non-uniform cooling process and so on. Because of these imperfections, defects are caused along the central axis. The goal is to measure the defect of each plate by detecting the dots and measuring their sizes.

The proposed algorithm (Zeljkovic, 2009) should replace human labor in this tedious and time consuming procedure of plate classification by microscope analysis.

Figure 2 represents images of metal plates provided by the steel plant ArcelorMittal Ostrava plc (Ostrava, Czech Republic). The numerical code of the image includes the heat number. The symbol B05M denotes the internal steel grade.

The segmentation can automatically recognize the border of the metal sample - the segmentation works without difficulties because the background is very nearly homogenous. The dots are small spots that are mostly of darker grey scale than their surroundings.

The justification for the proposed method comes from observing the analyzed images that all give a minimum in the central part of the image which indicates the presence of the dots with the lowest intensity. Figure 3 represents mean values of each row in analyzed images from Figure 2. It can be observed in Figure 3 that for each row, there is a local pixel mean value of grey scale minimum in the near centre rows of pixels that contain the dots and this justifies the assumption that the dots that are of interest are in the centre group of rows of pixels. This can be seen for all sample plates in Figure 3.

The proposed algorithm for automatic classification of real metallographic images contains the following steps:

Figure 3. Mean values of each row in analyzed images from Figure 2

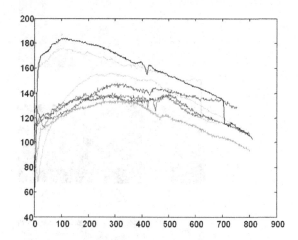

1. The analyzed image is converted to a grey level image
2. Based on segmented images shown in Figure 1 the segmentation process is further refined by selecting the region of interest using simple geometrical calculations. Figure 4 shows the segmented regions of interest.
3. The contrast stretching transformation is applied on the analyzed images, shown in Figure 5, in order to further emphasis the dark dots using the following formula from [6]:

$$\hat{I}(x,y) = \frac{255}{1 + \dfrac{123}{(I(x,y)+1)^{20}}} \tag{1}$$

4. The average intensity value is found in each row of the analyzed image and place it in the vector of a length that is equal to number of rows in the image, shown in Figure 6.
5. A minimization filter applied to the average intensity row vector of Figure 6 while attempting to emphasize the rows that contain the targeted dots which are darker than their background, Figure 7.

Figure 4. Segmented region of interest from analyzed images from Figure 2

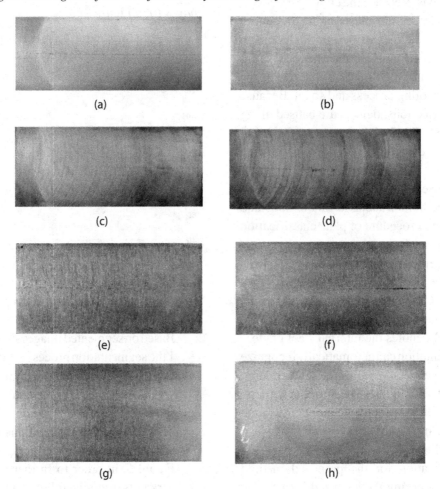

6. An averaging filter is applied to the average intensity row vector while attempting to smooth the consequences of the minimizing filter but the indications of the presence of dots are still preserved. Figure 8 contains the obtained results of averaging.

7. The local minima is determined in the average intensity row vector using the 8-connected neighborhood principle because the goal is to identify the rows with the lowest intensity value, i.e. the darkest ones that contain the dots, presented in Figure 9.

8. The local minimum is identified that has a width that extends from its centre above and below by the predicted dimensions of the dots.

9. The minima is localized that has the greatest dip in amplitude thereby identifying the central line or band in the analyzed image that contains the greatest concentration of the darkest dots, shown in Figure 10.

10. The pixels are examined in each column (contained in the analyzed rows containing the dots) and the darkest dot in each column in the extracted band is found.

11. The binarized image is formed that contains white pixels in the area that coincides with the dots by thresholding each column with the threshold that is equal to 95% of the intensity mean value of the pixels in that column.

Figure 5. Stretching transformation shown in (1) applied on Figure 2

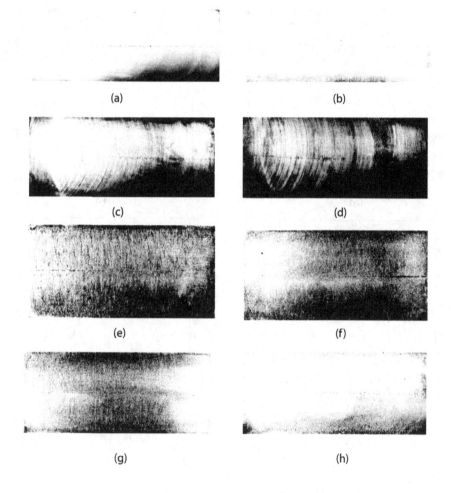

(a)

(b)

(c)

(d)

(e)

(f)

(g)

(h)

12. The formed binarized image is de-noised by deleting detected white dots that are smaller than 4 connected pixels. This is achieved by using the 8-connected neighborhood principle. The obtained results are presented in Figure 11.

13. The size of identified dots region is determined by counting the number of white pixels that belong to the detected dots in the analyzed images.

The proposed automatic pattern classification algorithm that performs dots identification and its size determination is applied on the metallographic plate images shown in Figure 2.

4. EXPERIMENTAL RESULTS

Based on segmented images shown in Figure 1 the segmentation is further refined by selecting the region of interest using simple geometrical calculations. Figure 4 shows the segmented regions of interest.

In the Step 3 of the proposed algorithm the contrast stretching transformation is applied on the analyzed images applying Equation (1) in order to further emphasis the dark dots. The results are shown in Figure 5.

In Step 4 the average intensity value is found in each row of the analyzed image and it is placed in the vector whose length is equal to number of

Figure 6. Mean values of each row in analyzed images from Figure 2

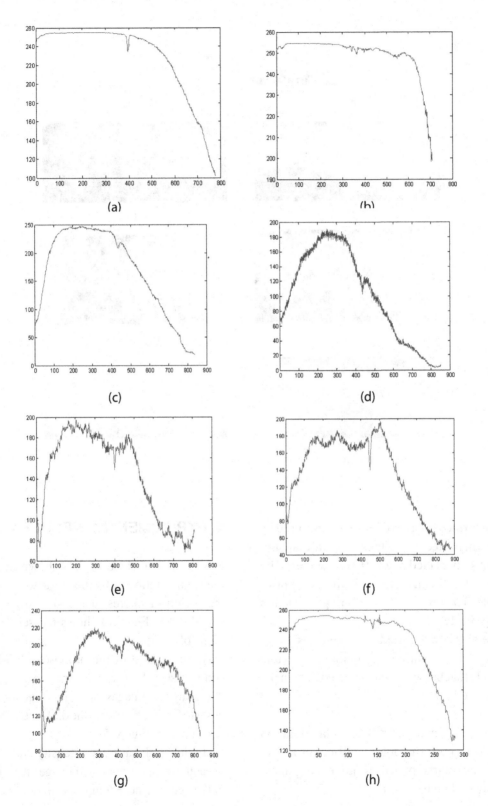

Figure 7. Minimization filter applied on Figure 6

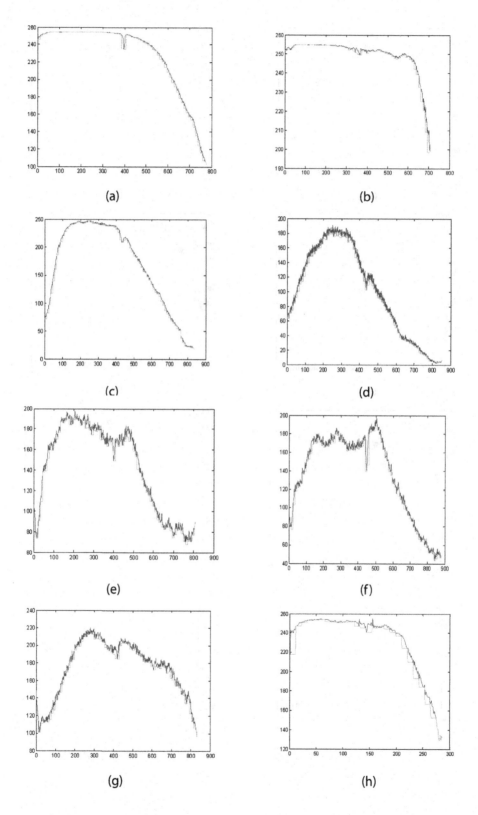

Figure 8. Averaging filter applied on Figure 7

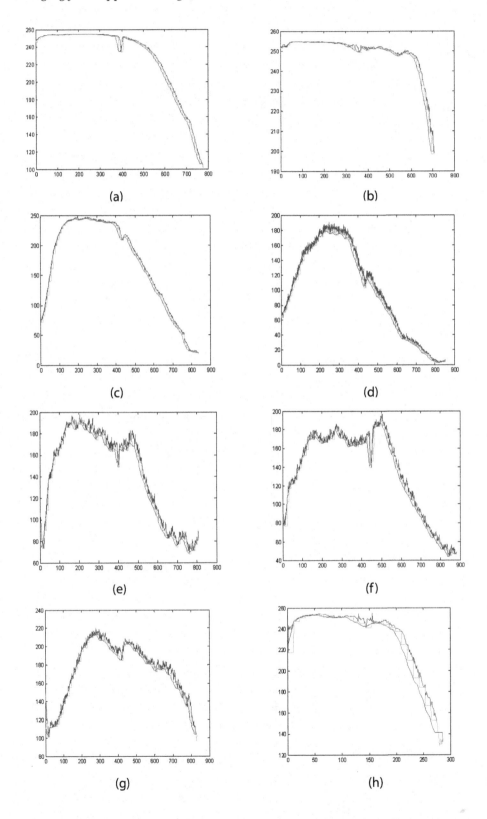

(a)

(b)

(c)

(d)

(e)

(f)

(g)

(h)

Figure 9. Extracted minima present in Figure 8

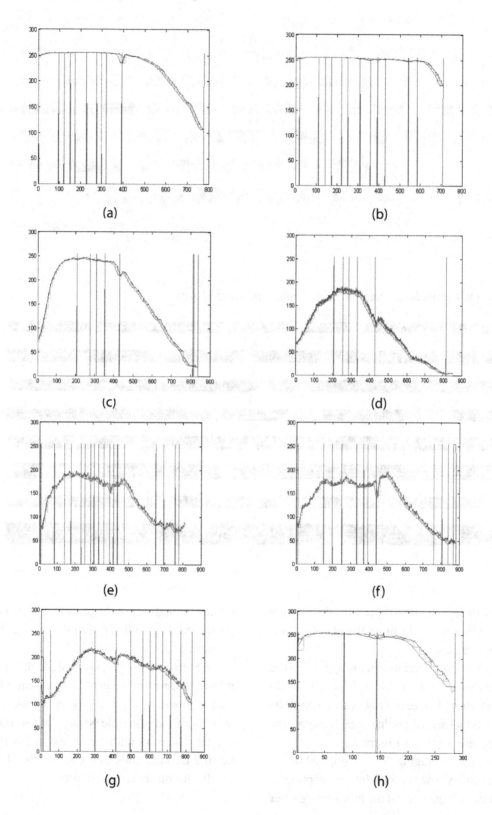

Figure 10. Extracted region containing the minima intensity pixels

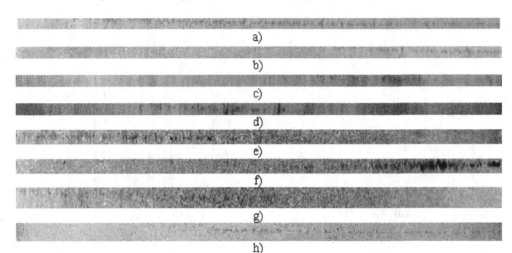

Figure 11. De-noised binarized image with marked detected dots

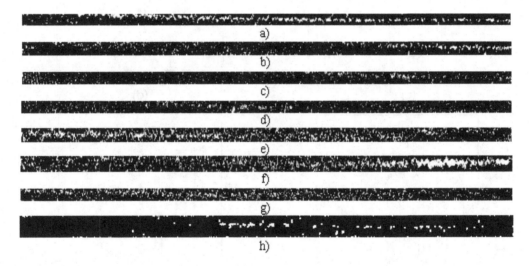

rows in the image. Figure 6 represents the average intensity values of each row of the analyzed images from Figure 2.

In step 5 a minimization filter is applied to the average intensity row vector in Figure 6 while attempting to emphasize the rows that contain the targeted dots that are darker than their background. The results are shown in Figure 7.

In Step 6 an averaging filter is applied to the average intensity row vector while attempting to smooth the consequences of the minimizing filter but the indications of the presence of dots are still preserved. Figure 8 contains the obtained results of averaging.

In Step 7 of the proposed algorithm the local minima is determined in the average intensity row vector shown in Figure 8 using the 8-connected neighborhood principle because it is important to identify the rows with the lowest intensity value, i.e. the darkest ones that contain the dots. The results are presented in Figure 9.

Step 9 provides localization of the minima that have the greatest dip in amplitude thereby identifying the central line or band in the analyzed image that contains the greatest concentration of the darkest dots, shown in Figure 10.

Finally the formed binarized image band is de-noised by deleting detected white dots that are smaller than 4 connected pixels. This is achieved this by using the 8-connected neighborhood principle. The obtained results are presented in Figure 11.

Figure 12 contains the final metal plates images with detected segregations marked as white pixels.

Table 1 shows the counted number of pixels that belong to the detected dots in the analyzed images.

Table 1 gives the number of pixels that were considered part of the dark dots after Step 11 thresholded and binarized them. However, there is some noise in all the images so those pixels that were noise rather than dots are eliminated from consideration. This is done by dismissing as noise those dots that the 8-connected neighborhoods principle showed to be smaller than 4 connected pixels. The first image retained 94% of its pixels. This is significantly more than the others. Images 2, 3, and 5 through 7 retained between 77% and 86%. Images 4 and 8 retained significantly fewer pixels, 64% and 51% respectively. The explanations related to the obtained results are firmly related to the information provided by ArcelorMittal Ostrava company by whose courtesy the analyzed images are obtained.

Figure 12. Segmented plate images from Figure 2 with detected dots marked with white

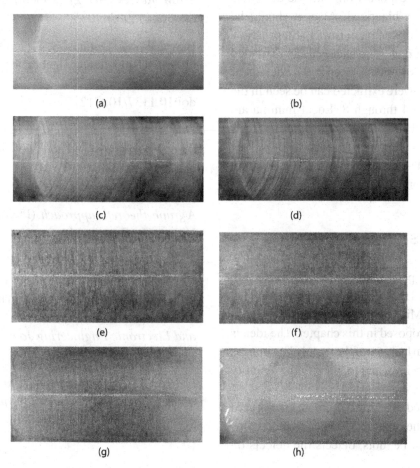

(a)

(b)

(c)

(d)

(e)

(f)

(g)

(h)

Table 1.

Number of Plate Image	Number of Detected Pixels	De-noised Detected Pixels
70528_06_B05M_C	6817	6400
71638_06_B05M_L	4743	3643
72635_03_B04M_L	4308	3359
72635_06_B04M_P	6588	4292
72914_06_B06M_P	9805	8448
73305_03_B05M_L_CLASS3	9967	8586
73314_03_B05M_P	8607	6900
71644_09_B05M_840_L	938	477

Step 9 shows the segment of rows that contain the dots in each of the images. It can be seen that by comparing them to the binarized and de-noised rows in Step 12, the white dots from which pixels are counted, correspond well with the dark dots before they were binarized. Also, it should be noted that the strips of pixel rows in Step 9 show that the rows of dots were successfully extracted from the images shown in Step 2. The details of how these rows were extracted can be seen in the graphs in Steps 4 through 8. Local minima are easily identified and sectioned off into the strips of rows in Steps 9 through 13. Step 13 shows the binarized and de-noised images without isolating the rows that contain the dots.

5. CONCLUSION

An automatic pattern classification algorithm designed for real metallographic images provided by the ArcelorMittal Ostrava plc (Ostrava, Czech Republic) is proposed in this chapter. The idea is to measure from features of the metal plate images an imperfection level and to classify the quantity of defects that were reported.

The proposed algorithm segments the region of interest of the analyzed images that contains the segregation, i.e. dots, detects the defects on

the plates and counts the size of the identified defects. This is the effort to replace human inspection, which can be subjective and given to human error, with a machine analysis of images that measures with more than sufficient precision, the degree to which the central axis of a plate suffers from manufacturing imperfections. In examining the images after they have been processed with the proposed algorithm shown in Figure 12 and comparing them to the original images shown in Figure 2, it can be easily seen that the areas of white pixels cover the dark dots in a reasonably accurate way.

REFERENCES

Berry, W. M., Drmac, Z., & Jessup, J. R. (1999). Matrices, vector spaces, and information retrieval. *SIAM Review*, *41*(2), 336–362. doi:10.1137/S0036144598347035

Berry, W. M., Dumais, S. T., & O'Brien, G. W. (1995). Using linear algebra for intelligent information retrieval. *SIAM Review*, *37*, 573–595. doi:10.1137/1037127

Gonzales, R. C., & Woods, R. E. (2002). *Digital image processing* (2nd ed.). Upper Saddle River, NJ: Prentice Hall.

Grady, L. (2004). *Space-variant computer vision: A graph-theoretic approach.* (PhD thesis). Boston University, Boston, MA.

Kotas, P., Praks, P., Válek, L., Zeljković, V., & Vondrak, V. (2012). Automated region of interest retrieval of metallographic images for quality classification in industry. *Advances in Electrical and Electronic Engineering Journal, 10*(1).

Kotas, P., Praks, P., Zeljković, V., & Válek, L. (2010). *Automated region of interest retrieval of metallographic images for quality scoring estimation.* Houston, TX: IEEE. doi:10.1109/IAS.2010.5615510

Niemann, H. (1990). *Pattern analysis and understanding*. Berlin: Springer-Verlag. doi:10.1007/978-3-642-74899-8

Praks, P., Grzegorzek, M., Moravec, R., Válek, L., & Izquierdo, E. (2008). Wavelet and Eigen-space feature extraction for classification of metallography images. In *Information Modelling and Knowledge Bases XIX*. IOS Press.

Webb, A. R. (2002). *Statistical pattern recognition*. Chichester, UK: John Wiley & Sons Ltd. doi:10.1002/0470854774

Wolfson, H. (1987). *On curve matching*. Miami Beach, FL: IEEE.

Zeljković, V., Praks, P., Vincelette, R. B., Tameze, C., & Válek, L. (2009). *Automatic pattern classification of real metallographic images*. Houston, TX: IEEE. doi:10.1109/IAS.2009.5324864

Chapter 14

Algorithm for Monitoring Impact of Intensity of Inert Gas Blowing to Visual Character of Molten Steel Surface

ABSTRACT

Steel companies use a ladle furnace refining process. The main feature of this ladle technology exists in refining under non-oxidizing atmosphere and support of slag-metal reaction through stirring by Ar gas injection for a desired long time due to the temperature compensation by arc heating. A CCD camera, placed above the ladle, monitors the slag formation (so called eyes) that has a different temperature and therefore a different color than the metal. The automatic software capable of analyzing the homogeneity of the surface and characterizing features of the molten steel level such us presence of slag clusters is developed and presented in this chapter. The method for visual monitoring and automated retrieval of slag clusters taken from the CCD camera are described.

1. INTRODUCTION

Ladle furnaces, that possesses electrode heating system is one of the secondary steelmaking process that has an important position in steelmaking because of its flexible and versatile applicability.

The ladle furnace technology adopts slag refining for the principal refining method instead of vacuum treatment which is applied in other ladle furnace processes (Yuasa, 1984). It is present in all steel industry companies because it is known to be convenient and widely available in steelmaking, for all the products' grades (Yuasa, 1984).

The ladle furnace refining is a secondary steelmaking process which promotes all of reduction

refining stages under ideal conditions (Yuasa, 1984). Reduction refining is a special metallurgical field (Yuasa, 1984).

The initial purpose of ladle furnace development was in transferring reduction refining to the ladle (Yuasa, 1984).

Unlike other secondary steelmaking processes ladle furnace does not depend on vacuum degassing but employs basic white slag as a means of refining (Yuasa, 1984).

Most of the metal-melting operations use ladles to transfer molten metal from melting furnaces to refining or pouring stations. Ladle refining furnaces are ladles with a heating source and lid. Ladle refining furnaces are used to reheat or

DOI: 10.4018/978-1-4666-4896-8.ch014

maintain steel tapped from a steel-making furnace to a precise temperature and or refine it to exact chemical specifications. Refining procedure is performed by adding chemicals to remove impurities, adding ingredients which enhance strength, and homogenizing the molten steel to achieve uniform characteristics.

2. LADLE FURNACE REFINING PROCEDURE

Ladle Furnace Refining process covers all functions in reduction period: deoxidation (Conejo, 2006), desulfurization, inclusion removal, temperature and molten steel chemistry adjustment, reduction of metal oxide in the slag, large quantity alloy addition and slag off (Yuasa, 1984). All of these operations can be achieved with easier handling, higher quality and better reproducibility than in usual melting (Yuasa, 1984).

The ladle furnace refining consists of a ladle with a porous brick at the bottom for Ar gas injection to induce molten steel stirring and accelerate slag-metal reaction, a lid for sealing the vessel chamber to keep the non-oxidizing atmosphere, and an electrode heating system in the upper part (Yuasa, 1984). The arc heating is usually applied in the form of slag submerged arc because it provides a better heating efficiency and a favorable protection of lining refractory, due to the absence of arc radiation.

Ladle refining furnace provide an ideal refining station with precise temperature control, stirring action for homogeneity, and ports for alloy addition and slag removal. Reheating steel in a ladle refining furnace is typically accomplished by electric arc heating.

Molten steel for high quality or specialty applications is subjected to further refining in a number of alternative processes collectively known as ladle metallurgy, ladle refining or secondary steelmaking (Zarandi, 2009). There are four refining functions which are unique to the ladle furnace process (Yuasa, 1984):

1. Non-oxidizing atmosphere or deoxidization procedure for Oxygen removal.
2. Ar gas stirring.
3. Arc heating.
4. Existence of basic white slag.

At the beginning of the ladle process deoxidation additions (Oikawa, 1999) are added into the steel ladle (Fruehan, 1998).

The consequence of the steel pouring is the slag creation. The metal is casting from the furnace to the ladle, depicted in Figures 1 and 2, where it is further processed.

The electric arc is used for the ladle heating which is powered by three electrodes situated above the ladle. The slag during blowing of argon from the bottom of the ladle forms an eye on the molten steel level. The steel is colder, thus darker, than the slag, as can be seen in Figure 1. Many studies have considered surface eye analysis in detail in (Kang, 2007), (Krishnapisharody, 2008), (Iguchi, 2004), (Mazumdar, 2003), (Subagyo, 2003).

During the procedure of adding additions to the steel, usually they are added directly into the metal by filling profile. If there is an eye on the

Figure 1. Indication of the region of interest by a human expert (red curve). Inside of the region is a steel segment.

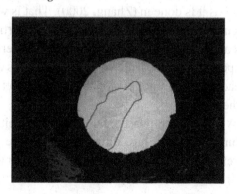

Figure 2. Description of the technological process: Ladle with admitted inert gas. The CCD camera above monitors the surface.

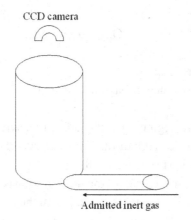

CCD camera

Admitted inert gas

surface, there is a danger that the outside air will be sucked into the steel. In order to avoid contact of the metal with the outside air, the aim is to have uniform cover of the slag on the surface.

The slag has multiple functions during the technological process, which are subject to its sufficient flow properties. On the other hand, too much fluidity of the slag would cause too much dissolution of the gas in the steel.

The metal is already relatively clean at this stage of the process. The slag can take impurities from the metal. Ideally, the slag would be liquid on the molten surface, but not too much liquid on the top. The slag is also suitable for preservation of the metal against external influences.

An admitted inert gas (for example argon or nitrogen) is not catalyzing the metal, but only bubbling through the metal, so it homogenizes the metal as it is done in (Zhang, 2000). That is why it is important to analyze the bubbles properties. It is also important to avoid zones with different temperatures in the ladle volume because, as it is already known, argon is blowing from the bottom of the ladle.

A CCD camera, placed above the ladle monitors its surface. The slag has a different temperature and therefore a different color than the metal. For this

reason, it is possible to analyze the homogeneity of the surface and/or characterize features of the molten steel level such us presence of clusters of slag deficiency (so called eyes) during time. Better understanding of the technological process can reduce power consumption and increase the quality of the production (Zeljkovic, 2009). In this chapter, the approaches for visual monitoring and automated retrieval of slag clusters using a CCD camera will be described.

3. APPLIED SEGMENTATION TECHNIQUES

The spectral segmentation (Wolfson, 1987) and isoparametric segmentation (Grady, 2003) methods were applied to metallographic plate images.

MATLAB package called the Graph Analysis Toolbox contains the description of Grady and Schwartz methods (Grady, 2003). This toolbox facilitates computer vision by providing algorithms and data structures so that arbitrary vision sampling arrangements can be used even if space-variant sensors are excluded. Its theoretical principle is based on space-variant computer vision that is, in their words, "biologically inspired".

Grady (Grady, 2003) estimates the isoperimetric content of an image graph. Instead of partitioning the graph by means of spectral methods the proposed method segments and clusters spectral methods with improved speed and stability.

Results of spectral and isoparametric segmentation methods are presented in Figure 3. Both isoparametric and spectral methods provides interesting segmentation results, shown in Figure 4. The Matlab toolbox successfully detects the boundaries of the ladle. But, the eye is not retrieved by the Matlab toolbox. For this reason, an alternative segmentation method is proposed.

Figure 3. (a) Original image; (b) Isoperimetric segmentation; (c) Spectral segmentation; (d) Ncuts segmentation

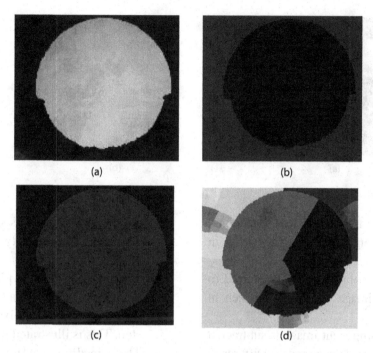

(a) (b)

(c) (d)

Figure 4. (a) Red component of color Metallographic image; (b) Green component of color Metallographic image; (c) Blue component of color Metallographic image.

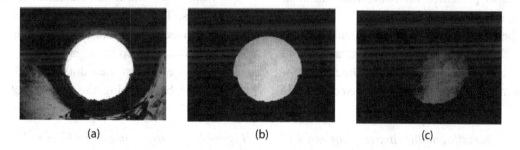

(a) (b) (c)

4. EXPERIMENTAL RESULTS

The metallographic image shown in Figure 1 was analyzed with the goal to automatically detect and identify the bordered region.

The proposed algorithm for automatic detection of imperfections in real metallographic images contains the following steps:

Figure 5. Gray level Metallographic image

Figure 6. (a) Difference image between the Green component image and the Grey level image; (b) Inverted image of (a).

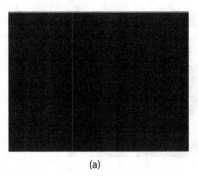

(a)   (b)

1. Image is decomposed into Red, Green and Blue component images as illustrated in Figure 4.
2. The analyzed color image is converted to a Grey level image which can be seen in Figure 5.
3. The Green component image is subtracted from the Grey level image and the Difference image shown in Figure 6 a) is composed. The inverted version of the Difference image is also presented for better illustration in Figure 6 b).
4. The pixels that have certain intensity range in the Difference image are localized and certain intensity range in the Green component image is determined. The detected pixels are marked with red as shown in Figure 7. The identified intensity range is obtained empirically.
5. The binarized image is formed that contains white pixels in the area that coincides with the dots and marked pixels in the previous step. This is illustrated in Figure 8.
6. The formed binarized image and color image with marked segregated dots are de-noised by deleting detected white and red dots, respectfully that are smaller than 4 connected pixels. This is achieved this by using the 8-connected neighborhood principle. Figure 9 shows this step in the algorithm.
7. The size of identified dots region is determined by counting the number of white

Figure 7. Metallographic image with marked segregation pixels in red

Figure 8. Binarized image in Figure 7 with red segregation pixels marked in white

Figure 9. (a) De-noised Figure 8; (b) De-noised Figure 7

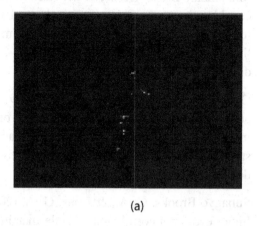

(a)

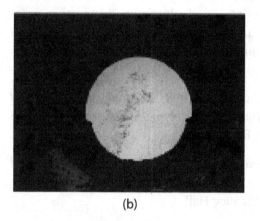

(b)

pixels that belong to the detected dots in the analyzed images as marked in Figure 10.

The proposed automatic pattern classification algorithm that performs dots identification and its size determination is applied on the metallographic plate image shown in Figure 1. The number of segregations determined in the analyzed image is 61166 and the number of segregations in the de-noised image is 22872. The proposed algorithm successfully identifies the slag areas on the molten metal surface that coincides with the one manually detected.

Figure 10. Metallographic image with the marked region of interest

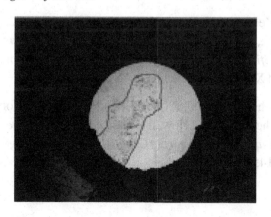

5. CONCLUSION

Results of experiments presented in this chapter prove a very high performance of the proposed algorithm in a real world environment. The automatically extracted slag segments are consistent with ones detected by the industry human expert.

For the future research, it could be interesting to repeat experiments contained in this contribution and also to provide time-dependent analysis of the video-sequence taken from the CCD camera.

Also the objective of the future research will be testing of influence of the blowing gas tension to conduct the slag surface. At high tension, the slag can reach walls of the ladle. The lower tension of the blowing gas is suitable. But it is necessary to determine the minimum tension of the gas, which over-press the hydrostatic tension given by the steel height.

The CCD camera can also monitor how argon influences the slag formation. By analyzing the visual characteristics of the surface, it can be deduced whether the argon tension is large enough for passing through the ladle height.

REFERENCES

Bovik, A. (2005). *Handbook of image & video processing* (2nd ed.). London: Elsevier.

Conejo, A. N., & Hernandez, D. E. (2006). Optimization of aluminum deoxidation practice in the ladle furnace. *Materials and Manufacturing Processes*, *21*(8), 796–803. doi:10.1080/10426910600837764

Fruehan, R. J. (1998). *The making, shaping and treating of steel (steel making and refining)*. AISE Steel Foundation.

Gonzalez, R. C., & Woods, R. E. (2002). *Digital image processing* (2nd ed.). Upper Saddle River, NJ: Prentice Hall.

Gonzalez, R. C., Woods, R. E., & Eddins, S. L. (2004). *Digital image processing using MATLAB*. Upper Saddle River, NJ: Pearson Education, Prentice Hall.

Grady, L., & Schwartz, E. L. (2003). *The graph analysis toolbox: Image processing on arbitrary graphs*. Boston: Boston University.

Hatfield, K., & Garnham, J. (2001). The application of image analysis to improve permeability prediction. *Petrophysics*, *42*(5), 457–467.

Iguchi, M. et al. (2004). Spout eye area in ladle refining process. *ISIJ International*, *44*(3), 636–638. doi:10.2355/isijinternational.44.636

Kang, Y. J., Yu, L., & Sichen, D. (2007). Study of inclusion removal mechanism around open eye in ladle treatment. *Ironmaking & Steelmaking*, (34): 253–261. doi:10.1179/174328107X168101

Kotas, P., Praks, P., Zeljković, V., & Válek, L. (2010). *Automated region of interest retrieval of metallographic images for quality scoring estimation*. Houston, TX: IEEE. doi:10.1109/IAS.2010.5615510

Krishnapisharody, K., & Irons, G. A. (2008). An extended model for slag eye size in ladle metallurgy. *ISIJ International*, *48*(12), 1807. doi:10.2355/isijinternational.48.1807

Mazumdar, D., & Evans, J. W. (2003). Some considerations concerning empirical correlations for plume (spout) eye area in slag covered metallic melts. *ISIJ International*, *43*(12), 2076–2078. doi:10.2355/isijinternational.43.2076

Oikawa, K., Sumi, S.-I., & Ishida, K. (1999). The effects of addition of deoxidation elements on the morphology of (Mn, Cr)S inclusions in stainless steel. *Journal of Phase Equilibria*, *20*(3), 215–223. doi:10.1361/105497199770335749

Subagyo Brooks, G. A., & Irons, G. A. (2003). Spout eyes area correlation in ladle metallurgy. *ISIJ International*, *43*(2), 262–263. doi:10.2355/isijinternational.43.262

Wolfson, H. (1987). *On curve matching*. Miami Beach, FL: IEEE.

Yuasa, G., Yajima, T., Ukai, A., & Ozawa, M. (1984). Refining practice and application of the ladle furnace (LF) process in Japan. *Transactions of the Iron and Steel Institute of Japan*, *24*(5), 412–418. doi:10.2355/isijinternational1966.24.412

Zarandi, M. H., & Ahmadpour, P. (2009). *Fuzzy agent-based expert system for steel making process. expert systems with applications*. Elsevier.

Zeljković, V., Praks, P., & Husar, I. (2010). *Monitoring the impact of the intensity of blowing of an inert gas to the visual character of the molten steel surface*. Paper presented at the IEEE International Energy Conference and Exhibition. Washington, DC.

Zeljković, V., Praks, P., Vincelette, R. B., Tameze, C., & Válek, L. (2009). *Automatic pattern classification of real metallographic images*. Houston, TX: IEEE. doi:10.1109/IAS.2009.5324864

Zhang, L., et al. (2000). Effect of bubble size on the liquid steel flow in air-stirred ladles. *Selected Papers of Engineering Chemistry and Metallurgy*, 145-157.

Chapter 15
Algorithm for Petro–Graphic Color Image Segmentation Used in Oil Exploration

ABSTRACT

A new heuristic algorithm for porosity segmentation for the colored petro-graphic images is proposed. The proposed algorithm automatically detects the porosities that represent the presence of oil, gas, or even water in the analyzed thin section rock segment based on the colour of the porosity area filled with dies in the analyzed sample. For the purpose of the oil exploration, the thin section fragments are died in order to emphasize the porosities that are analyzed under the microscope. The percentage of the porosity is directly proportional to the probability of the oil, gas, or even water presence in the area where the drilling is performed (i.e. the increased porosity indicates the higher probability of oil existence in the region). The proposed automatic algorithm shows better results than the existing K-means segmentation method.

1. INTRODUCTION

Geological and petrophysical domains are becoming more appreciative of the use of digital image processing in many of their applications. One example is the extraction of porosity and different components of solid fraction information (grains, matrix, and cement) from the microscopic digital images of their thin sections (Hatfield, 2001). This appreciation came as a trivial result of the increased demand in oil production, especially from non-conventional reservoirs, e.g., within carbonate structures, which requires more in-depth analysis of logs, seismic, and cores where thin sections can be obtained.

Some petrologists can easily estimate macro porosities using microscope images since the porous media possess a very distinct color such as the light blue and pink as shown in Figure 1. However, the process is time consuming and may have a certain degree of error in the final results (Hatfield, 2001).

Moreover, generally quite a large number of thin sections are made for every cored well. Therefore, an automatic and efficient technique is required for extracting and quantifying different components of rocks from their thin sections. Hence, this requires a successful technique for dividing petrographic images of thin sections into different regions where each region is nearly

DOI: 10.4018/978-1-4666-4896-8.ch015

Figure 1. Samples of colour microscopic images of rock segments

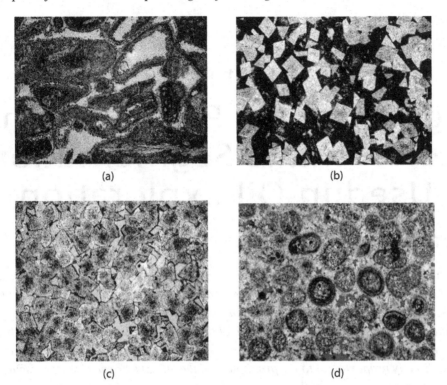

(a)

(b)

(c)

(d)

homogenous and the union of any two regions is not. This division process is known as digital image segmentation (Gonzalez, 2002), (Bovik, 2005).

Such application of digital image segmentation for carbonate thin section images is getting more attention from researchers.

The proposed method for automatic porosity detection and segmentation was tested on four different real world color microscope images. The color microscopic images with died porosities in blue and one with died porosities in pink are shown in Figure 1. The Figure represents four different thin section images of different rock types, namely, grainstone, dolomitic grainstone, and dolostone.

The colour images belong to the Red-Green-Blue (RGB) domain. Samples 1-3 have resolution of 1550 x 2087 x 3 in JPEG format and Sample 4 has resolution of 774 x 1183 x 3 in JPEG format.

Samples of microscopic images contain different level of porosity which indicates the presence of oil, gas or even water in the particular area.

The proposed novel heuristic algorithm is described and the experimental results show a promising advance of the addressed method in comparison to the known k-means technique.

2. COLOR BASED POROSITY SEGMENTATION ALGORITHM COMBINED WITH WAVELET DE-NOISING ANALYSIS

The research leading to this study has been focused on implementing a robust algorithm that is capable of porosity detection in petro-graphic color images. The proposed novel automatic algorithm combines a de-noising method realized with wavelets analysis and the porosity detection based on color analysis. The color based heuristical model is derived taking advantage of the color of the dyed targeted porosities. Instead of developing a complex mathematical model and algorithm that would be detecting the unpredictable contours of the porosities, here the color is used as the parameter for the porosities detection and recognition providing a simpler and efficient technique.

2.1. Wavelet Analysis and De-Noising

One of the most successful methods for noise suppression is wavelet transformation analysis and application (Gonzalez, 2002), (Hubbard, 1998), (Mallat, 1989), (Chang, 2000). This method returns a de-noised version of a given two dimensional input signal obtained by thresholding the wavelet coefficients up to a certain level. From the signal analyst's point of view, wavelet analysis is a decomposition of the signal on a family of analyzing signals, which is usually an "orthogonal function method". From an algorithmic point of view, wavelet analysis offers a harmonious compromise between decomposition and smoothing techniques. The de-noising objective is to suppress the noise part of the signal and to recover de-noised signal. The wavelet de-noising procedure proceeds in three steps: decomposition of the signal at a level N, detail coefficients thresholding at each level and wavelet reconstruction based on the original approximation coefficients of the level N and the modified detail coefficients of levels from 1 to N.

The symlet wavelets (Gonzalez, 2002), (Gonzalez, 2004) are applied up to the second level of the decomposition on each red, green and blue component of the color images separately. Then all three color components are combined back to the color RGB image. The wavelet analysis enabled clearer image with more distinct color differences which is illustrated in the Figure 2. It shows smoothed noise presence and more obvious color distinction which is important for the next

algorithm phase which is color based segmentation that successfully extracts the targeted porosity regions. The algorithm is applied in RGB space because the results in HIS space were not as close to ground truth as results obtained in RGB space.

2.2 Color Based Porosity Segmentation

After the de-noising procedure, the empirically obtained color based porosity detection algorithm is applied that successfully extracts blue died porosity areas in the sample petro-graphic images. The segmentation procedure is application motivated considering that all analyzed images are died with the same color which imposes certain empirical scientific approach. The following equation represents the mathematical model of the applied algorithm which constitutes the general form that encompasses all colors:

$$I_{new}(i,j) = \begin{cases} 1 & \text{if}((\text{Blue}(i,j) < \max_{BLUE}) \text{ \&} \\ & (\text{Blue}(i,j) < \min_{BLUE}) \text{ \&} \\ & (\text{Red}(i,j) < \max_{RED}) \text{ \&} \\ & (\text{Red}(i,j) < \min_{RED}) \text{ \&} \\ & (\text{Green}(i,j) < \max_{GREEN}) \text{ \&} \\ & (\text{Green}(i,j) < \min_{GREEN}) \\ 0 & \text{Otherwise} \end{cases}$$

(1)

I_{new} represents the new value of the pixel intensity in the generated binary image. The values Blue(i, j), Red(i, j) and Green(i, j), represent the intensity pixel value in the blue, red and green color planes, respectively. Parameters $\max_{BLUE}$, $\min_{BLUE}$, $\max_{RED}$, $\min_{RED}$, $\max_{GREEN}$ and $\min_{GREEN}$ represent the range of the pixel intensity in blue, red and green color plane, respectively. They are varying variables that change according to the color of the porosities in analyzed sample. White pixels denote the detected porosity regions and the black pixels represent the background. After the

Figure 2. Applied wavelet de-noising analysis on samples of colour microscopic images of rock segments

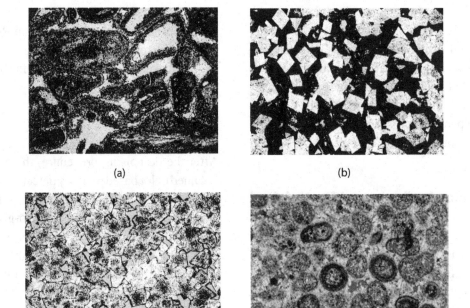

(a)

(b)

(c)

(d)

porosity detection post processing filling procedure is applied with a 3x3 mask that additionally improves the obtained results.

The proposed colour based segmentation procedure is applied on the samples shown in Figure 2 after they have been exposed to the de-noising wavelet technique. Considering that analyzed Samples 1-3 are died with the same blue colour, the following equation represents the mathematical model of the applied algorithm:

$$
{}^{I}new(i, j) = \begin{cases} 1 \text{ if}((Blue(i, j) < 255) \ \& \\ \quad (Blue(i, j) > 150) \ \& \\ \quad (Red(i, j) < 150) \ \& \\ \quad (Red(i, j) > 0) \ \& \\ \quad (Green(i, j) < 250) \ \& \\ \quad (Green(i, j) > 0) \\ 0 \qquad\qquad \text{Otherwise} \end{cases} \quad (2)
$$

Samples a) and c) contain only two different color regions and sample b) contains three color regions. That is why another empirical color model is derived which extracts the dolomite whitish region that is later in Figure 4 marked in green. The following equation is used as the mathematical model of the colour based applied algorithm that extracts whitish dolomite areas:

$$
{}^{I}new(i, j) = \begin{cases} 1 \text{ if}((Blue(i, j) < 255) \ \& \\ \quad (Blue(i, j) > 150) \ \& \\ \quad (Red(i, j) < 255) \ \& \\ \quad (Red(i, j) > 150) \ \& \\ \quad (Green(i, j) < 255) \ \& \\ \quad (Green(i, j) > 150) \\ 0 \qquad\qquad \text{Otherwise} \end{cases} \quad (3)
$$

Figure 3 illustrates the binary images generated after application of the color based porosity segmentation algorithm expressed with equations (2) and (3) on the images, shown in Figure 2.

For the illustration purpose and truthful presentation of the proposed color based shape segmentation method it is applied on the Sample 4 with porosities dyed in different colour. Sample 4's porosities are in pink colour. The modified pink colour based mathematical model used for the sample with the marked porosities in pink, which represents the version of the general mathematical model expressed in the equation (1), is the following:

$$I_{new}(i, j) = \begin{cases} 1 & \text{if}((Blue(i, j) < 150)\ \& \\ & (Blue(i, j) > 100)\ \& \\ & (Red(i, j) < 200)\ \& \\ & (Red(i, j) > 150)\ \& \\ & (Green(i, j) < 100)\ \& \\ & (Green(i, j) > 0) \\ 0 & \text{Otherwise} \end{cases} \quad (4)$$

Figure 3. Applied proposed colour based porosity segmentation method on samples of colour microscopic images of rock segments de-noised with the wavelet analysis

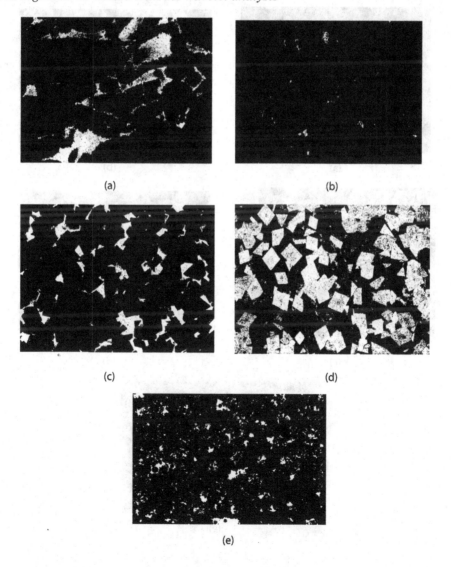

(a)

(b)

(c)

(d)

(e)

The detected porosity regions are marked with red colour on the original Sample image in Figure 4.

3. EXPERIMENTAL RESULTS

For the comparison purpose K-means clustering method is used which partitions the observations in the data into K mutually exclusive clusters. The K-means method is more suitable for clustering large amounts of data. It treats each observation in the data as an object having a location in space (Gonzalez, 2002), (Gonzalez, 2004).

Figure 5 contains the results obtained by the segmentation with K-means method clustering Sample 1 with two clusters, Sample 2 with three clusters, Sample 3 with two clusters and Sample 4 with three clusters. The porosity area in the Sample 1 is marked with green color, in the Sample 2 is marked with green color, in the Sample 3

Figure 4. Applied proposed colour based porosity segmentation method on samples of colour micro-scopic images of rock segments de-noised with the wavelet analysis illustrated on the original Samples

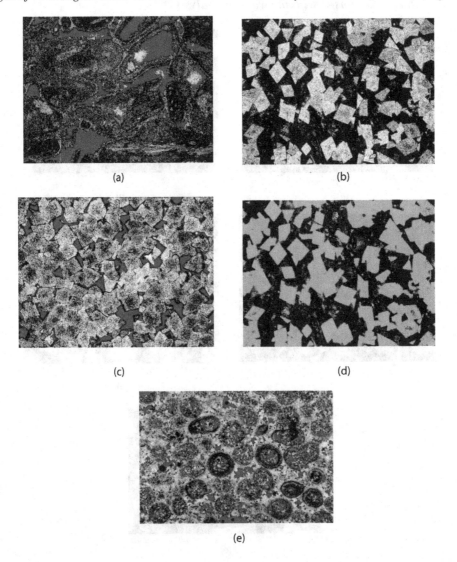

Figure 5. Applied K-means clustering method on samples of colour microscopic images of rock segments

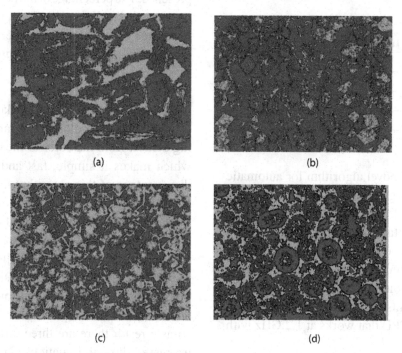

is marked with red color and in the Sample 4 is marked with green color.

It is obvious from the obtained results that the segmentation is not clear enough and does not give precise information about the porosity presence. Table 1 contains the comparison between the ground truth percentage of the porosity and the percentage calculated by the K-means segmentation method.

The results in Table 1 show the obvious discrepancy between the ground truth results and the ones generated by the segmentation method.

The proposed color based model method for porosity detection that contains three stages:

Table 1. K-means segmentation technique

Sample	Ground Truth [%]		K-Means [%]	
1	15.69		32.59	
2	0.58	45.28	21.93	31.69
3	8.72		55.69	
4	15.69		24.16	

1. De-noising with wavelets.
2. Color based porosity detection.
3. Filling procedure is applied on the Sample images in Figure 1.

The obtained results are shown in Figure 4 for all tested four different samples, where the marked detected porosity areas are directly indicated on the original images. Sample 2 contains porosity with the dolomite background area.

The detected porosity regions are marked with red colour on the original Sample images. Considering that the Sample 2 has three regions the detected porosity pixels are marked with red and dolomite background pixels with green color.

Table 2 contains the ground truth percentage of the porosity and the percentage calculated by the proposed novel segmentation method.

The results in Table 2 show that the proposed algorithm very successfully detects the porosity regions. The obtained results are very close to the ground truth results.

Table 2. Color model based segmentation technique

Sample	Ground Truth [%]		Proposed Algorithm [%]	
1	15.69		13.30	
2	0.58	45.28	0.55	43.36
3	8.72		10.68	
4	15.69		14.36	

The proposed novel algorithm for automatic porosity detection gives very faithful results close to the real ground truth ones unlike the known K-means segmentation method. The proposed algorithm shows to be superior to the known segmentation technique in the automatic porosity detection in the color microscopic images.

The experiments were performed in Matlab on Intel Core Duo CPU that works at 1.2 GHz with 1.99 GB of RAM.

Table 3 shows the execution time for both proposed color model segmentation algorithm and K-means method.

Table 3 shows obvious superiority of the proposed algorithm from execution time point of view. K-means method takes approximately twice as much time as the proposed method.

4. CONCLUSION

A novel heuristic algorithm for porosity detection in the colored petro-graphic thin section geological images is presented in this chapter. The proposed algorithm automatically detects the porosities

Table 3. Execution time of novel proposed algorithm and K-means method

Sample	Proposed Algorithm [sec]	K-Means [sec]
1	364.000	577.203
2	279.032	693.531
3	327.937	602.484
4	83.375	165.875

presence. The percentage of the porosity is directly proportional to the probability of the oil presence in the area where the drilling is performed, i.e. the increased porosity indicates the higher probability of oil existence in the region.

The advantage of the proposed method is that it is not iterative method but it takes just one span over the analyzed color petro-graphic image taking benefit from the color of the dyed porosities which makes it simple, fast and efficient. The disadvantage of this algorithm is that it is color based which means that the color mathematical model ranges and limits depend on the color in which the targeted porosities are dyed so it has to be changed accordingly. The illustration to this are the four samples whose porosities are dyed in blue, Sample 2 whose dolomite areas are whitish and Sample 4 whose porosities are dyed in pink so as a result there are three different versions, expressed through Equations (2), (3) and (4), of general colour mathematical model shown in Equation (1).

The proposed automatic algorithm shows better results to the existing segmentation method and takes half less execution time. K-means segmentation technique gives visually as well as numerically very poor results where different porosity and the background regions are poorly segmented. The numerical results show the deviation in the porosity detection from real ground truth results is not acceptable for the oil exploration purpose.

The proposed novel color model algorithm consists of three stages: de-noising method realized with wavelets analysis, the porosity detection based on the color analysis and filling procedure.

It appears that the proposed algorithm is well suited for removing noise and successfully detecting porosity regions in the colored microscopic images. The obtained results show precise porosity detection with the variation of up to maximum 20% of the real ground truth results. Visual results analysis gives even higher subjective porosity detection efficiency of the proposed method. The obtained results represent the proof of the effectiveness of the proposed novel method.

REFERENCES

Bovik, A. (2005). *Handbook of image & video processing* (2nd ed.). London: Elsevier.

Chang, S. G., Yu, B., & Vetterli, M. (2000). Spatially adaptive wavelet thresholding with context modeling for image denoising. *IEEE Transactions on Image Processing, 9*(9), 1522–1531. doi:10.1109/83.862630 PMID:18262990

Gonzalez, R. C., & Woods, R. E. (2002). *Digital image processing* (2nd ed.). Upper Saddle River, NJ: Prentice Hall.

Gonzalez, R. C., Woods, R. E., & Eddins, S. L. (2004). *Digital image processing using MATLAB*. Upper Saddle River, NJ: Pearson Education, Prentice Hall.

Hatfield, K., & Garnham, J. (2001). The application of image analysis to improve permeability prediction. *Petrophysics, 42*(5), 457–467.

Hubbard, B. B. (1998). *The world according to wavelets-The story of a mathematical technique in the making* (2nd ed.). Wellesley, MA: A. K. Peters, Ltd.

Mallat, S. G. (1989). A theory for multiresolution signal decomposition: The wavelet representation. *IEEE Transactions on Pattern Analysis and Machine Intelligence, 11*(7), 674–693. doi:10.1109/34.192463

Niemann, H. (1990). *Pattern analysis and understanding*. Berlin: Springer-Verlag. doi:10.1007/978-3-642-74899-8

Webb, A. R. (2002). *Statistical pattern recognition*. Chichester, UK: John Wiley & Sons Ltd. doi:10.1002/0470854774

Zeljković, V., & Mousa, W. (2011). *An algorithm for petro-graphic colour image segmentation used for oil exploration*. Paper presented at the High Performance Computing & Simulation Conference: Workshop on Pattern Analysis and Recognition. New York, NY.

Chapter 16
Automatic Object Classification and Image Retrieval by Sobel Edge Detection

ABSTRACT

A comparative study of ability of the proposed novel image retrieval algorithms is performed to provide automated object classification invariant of rotation, translation, and scaling. Simple cosine similarity coefficient methods are analyzed. Considering applied cosine similarity coefficient methods, the two following approaches were tested and compared: the processing of the whole image and the processing of the image that contains edges extracted by the application of the Sobel edge detector. Numerical experiments on a real database sets indicate feasibility of the presented approach as an automated object classification tool without special image pre-processing.

1. INTRODUCTION

Automatic object recognition and classification is very important and has numerous applications, such as image retrieval and robot navigation.

Rapid development of information technologies provides users an easy access to a large amount of multimedia data, for instance images and videos. Unfortunately, wide popular text retrieval techniques, which are based on keyword matching, are not efficient for describing rich multimedia context. Recently, wavelets and various methods of numerical linear algebra are successfully used for automated information retrieval and identification tasks (Tan, 2005), (Zeljković, 2007), (Berry, 1995), (Praks, 2008). Moreover, genetic programming is used as a tool for image feature synthesis and recognition (Krawiec,

2007), (Watchareeruetai, 2011). In this chapter, a comparison of modified Sobel edge detection for automatic object classification and retrieval is presented.

2. PROPOSED METHODS FOR AUTOMATIC OBJECT CLASSIFICATION

Three different methods are proposed in this chapter invariant of rotation, translation or scaling of the classified objects. They successfully perform object classification on set of three different groups of objects Dinosaurs, Mummies and Sculls represented by images taken under various rotational, scaling and zooming conditions.

Two techniques for automatic object classification are applied. Sobel edge filtered images are

DOI: 10.4018/978-1-4666-4896-8.ch016

used for similarity computation in the first method and in the second method simple cosine similarity coefficient is applied on plain gray images with the goal to classify them.

The first technique implies procedure with an image converted to gray image with the extracted edges using Sobel edge detection method (Engel, 2006), (Jähne, 1999), (Farid, 2004), (Kroon, 2009), (Scharr, 2007), (Gonzalez, 2001). The idea behind this method is to significantly reduce the amount of data and filter out useless information, while preserving the important structural properties of an image and the targeted object.

Every image is processed as a two-dimensional $m \times n$ matrix image. The two-dimensional Sobel masks are applied to gray images. The Sobel operator performs a 2-D spatial gradient measurement on an image. It is used to find the approximate absolute gradient magnitude at each point in an input grayscale image. The Sobel edge detector uses a pair of 3×3 convolution masks, one estimating the gradient in the x-direction (columns) and the other estimating the gradient in the y-direction (rows). After that the magnitude of the gradient is calculated. In the next step cosine similarity coefficient (Singhal), (Garcia, 2005), (Tan, 2005), (Zeljković, 2007) is applied in order to extract the image containing the most similar object in the database.

In the second approach, color images are converted to gray scale images and processed. Then simple cosine similarity coefficient (Singhal), (Garcia, 2005), (Tan, 2005), (Zeljković, 2007) is applied as in the first method.

In the initial study, image de-noising and pre-processing by wavelet filter application is applied for both techniques. The obtained numerical results pointed out, that the application of de-noising methods does not have any influence of the proposed algorithms to perform more successful object recognition. This additionally slowed down the algorithm so it is concluded that it is the best to omit that pre-processing stage.

Different edge detection functions are applied and it is concluded, based on the obtained results that the Sobel edge detector gave the most clear and emphasized edge extracted results for the first proposed method.

In the current computer implementation of the proposed object recognition procedures, no pre-processing of images is assumed. The presented numerical experiments indicate optimistic application of the proposed techniques for object recognition and classification.

The colors of images are coded in Matlab (tm) as non-negative integral numbers and no scaling was used. The application of the proposed procedures can be written in Matlab as follows.

```
% Input:
% A … the m × n document matrix
% Output:
% sim … the vector of similarity co-
efficients
[m,n] = size(Image);
```

1. Calculate the gray image presentation for both proposed techniques:

```
Gray = rgb2gray(Image);
```

2. Apply Sobel edge detector on gray scale Image.

```
ImageSobel = edge(Gray,'sobel');
```

3. Compute the similarity coefficients between two inspected images.

```
xx = ImageSobel '*ImageSobel0;
%for the first method
%or
xx = Gray '*Gray0;
%for the second method
xx= xx/(norm(ImageSobel0)*norm(Sob
el));
sim(i) = 1-acos(xx);
```

The proposed two algorithms give at the output the similarity coefficients *sim*. The absolute value of *i*-th element of *sim* coefficient is a measure of the similarity between two compared images.

Both algorithms give acceptable and competitive results. They are efficient, easy for implementation and fast enough for real application.

3. EXPERIMENTAL RESULTS

The collection of three different groups, each containing 24 images, in total 24×3=72 color images was analyzed. The sample images representing versatility in scale, rotation and distance from the camera for all three groups is presented in Figure 1. The dimensions of images varied so all of them were set to the same width of 2000 pixels and the height of 2000 pixels. So the each picture is characterized by 4,000,000 attributes. For example, the name "D_3.jpg" implies that the third image from Dinosaurs group of images is considered. The analyzed image database is available for research purposes under an e-mail request.

The queries were represented as images from the collection.

Figure 2 represents: a) Gray scale converted and rescaled Dinosaur image No.1 and the same image after Sobel edge detector, b) Gray scale converted and rescaled Mummy image No.1, and the same image after Sobel edge detector and c) Gray scale converted and rescaled Scull image No.1, and the same image after Sobel edge detector. It can be observed that the filtered im-

ages contain an emphasized unique structure and edge elements present in the classified object. The Sobel edge extraction application enables us to extract useful information necessary for further object comparison and identification. It is obvious that all three filtered images also contain the background edges that could be drawback in object classification due to introduction of emphasized non useful information.

Table 1 contains the results obtained for the Dinosaur group of images used as query with both proposed algorithms.

The first column in Table 1 represents the query image, second column represents the most similar image retrieved by each method and the third column is the maximum similarity coefficient determined by the applied technique.

Analyzing Table 1 it can be concluded that there are 100% correct classification results obtained with the second method. The compared objects are recognized correctly. There are seven misclassifications obtained by the first method. Dinosaur images 2, 5, 10, 16, 17, 18 and 21 are wrongly classified as Mummy images 11, 16, 11, 21, 3, 16 and 21. The first method gave 70.83% correct classifications for the Dinosaurs group.

Table 2 contains the results obtained for the Mummy group of images used as query with both proposed algorithms.

Even better results are obtained for both methods for the Mummy group of images used as query images. The compared Mummy images are recognized correctly. Analyzing Table 2 it can be concluded that there is 100% correct classification

Figure 1. Image database examples

   (a)   (b)   (c)

Figure 2. Gray scale images and Sobel edge detector applied on database images

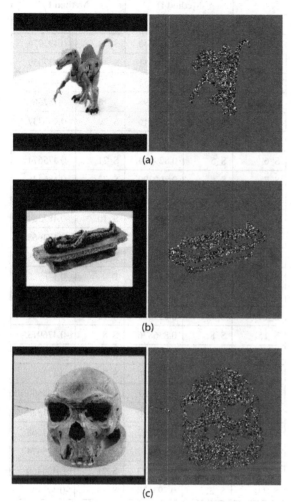

(a)

(b)

(c)

Table 1. Dinosaur image retrieval result

Image	Method II		Method I	
	Similar	Similarity	Similar	Similarity
D_0	D_1	0.792098	D_22	-0.477922
D_1	D_2	0.825600	D_9	-0.462840
D_2	D_6	0.827910	M_11	-0.452429
D_3	D_2	0.793506	D_11	-0.467122
D_4	D_3	0.781580	D_13	-0.467995
D_5	D_2	0.818380	M_16	-0.468481
D_6	D_2	0.827910	D_20	-0.462955
D_7	D_0	0.781627	D_15	-0.480580
D_8	D_9	0.794382	D_7	-0.483005
D_9	D_10	0.801764	D_1	-0.462840
D_10	D_14	0.844410	M_11	-0.462095
D_11	D_10	0.809539	D_3	-0.467122
D_12	D_11	0.783882	D_3	-0.478209
D_13	D_11	0.791611	D_4	-0.467995
D_14	D_10	0.844410	D_10	-0.467348
D_15	D_14	0.795961	D_6	-0.463719
D_16	D_20	0.846660	M_21	-0.467024
D_17	D_16	0.839282	M_3	-0.479152
D_18	D_17	0.835905	M_16	-0.481522
D_19	D_16	0.834931	D_5	-0.480134
D_20	D_16	0.846660	D_6	-0.462955
D_21	D_20	0.840781	M_21	-0.488171
D 22	D_21	0.829590	D_0	-0.477922
D_23	D_16	0.838982	D_1	-0.473084

results obtained with both proposed methods for the Mummy query group.

Table 3 contains the results obtained for the Scull group of images used as query with both proposed algorithms.

The first column in Table 3 represents the query image, second column represents the most similar image retrieved by each method and the third column is the maximum similarity coefficient determined by the applied technique.

Analyzing Table 3 it can be concluded that we have 100% correct classification results obtained with the second method as for the previous two query groups Dinosaur and Mummy. The com-

pared objects are recognized correctly. There are only two misclassification obtained by the first method. Scull images 11 and 12 are wrongly classified as Mummy image 17 and Dinosaur image 1, respectively. The first method gave 91.67% correct classifications for the Scull group.

4. CONCLUSION

Two approaches to the recognition and classification of different objects in various images are presented in this chapter. The results of the recognition test are promising and they show the

Table 2. Mummy image retrieval result

Image	Method II		Method I	
	Similar	Similarity	Similar	Similarity
M_0	M_4	0.809849	M_22	-0.473274
M_1	M_5	0.817501	M_23	-0.473435
M_2	M_6	0.863856	M_6	-0.456423
M_3	M_7	0.846556	M_7	-0.449088
M_4	M_0	0.809849	M_18	-0.475947
M_5	M_1	0.817501	M_23	-0.474928
M_6	M_2	0.863856	M_2	-0.456423
M_7	M_3	0.846556	M_21	-0.448823
M_8	M_12	0.821392	M_22	-0.464342
M_9	M_13	0.794741	M_0	-0.485602
M_10	M_14	0.848961	M_14	-0.469516
M_11	M_15	0.863644	M_15	-0.448240
M_12	M_8	0.821392	M_18	-0.466055
M_13	M_9	0.794741	M_4	-0.486284
M_14	M_10	0.848961	M_10	-0.469516
M_15	M_11	0.863644	M_11	-0.448240
M_16	M_20	0.879378	M_20	-0.451026
M_17	M_21	0.874138	M_21	-0.444759
M_18	M_22	0.866241	M_22	-0.448271
M_19	M_23	0.866393	M_23	-0.454096
M_20	M_16	0.879378	M_16	-0.451026
M_21	M_17	0.874138	M_17	-0.444759
M_22	M_18	0.866241	M_18	-0.448271
M_23	M_19	0.866393	M_19	-0.454096

Table 3. Scull image retrieval result

Image	Method II		Method I	
	Similar	Similarity	Similar	Similarity
S_0	S_7	0.786640	S_14	-0.492076
S_1	S_2	0.786951	S_16	-0.477059
S_2	S_1	0.786951	S_17	-0.477816
S_3	S_4	0.785398	S_18	-0.487566
S_4	S_5	0.798016	S_20	-0.480737
S_5	S_6	0.829434	S_20	-0.478156
S_6	S_5	0.829434	S_21	-0.475674
S_7	S_6	0.800299	S_22	-0.486436
S_8	S_15	0.836876	S_15	-0.476013
S_9	S_10	0.848330	S_10	-0.482384
S_10	S_11	0.860406	S_20	-0.474668
S_11	S_10	0.860406	M_17	-0.478968
S_12	S_11	0.847018	D_1	-0.478980
S_13	S_12	0.836781	S_21	-0.483276
S_14	S_15	0.819025	S_15	-0.478761
S_15	S_8	0.836876	S_8	-0.476013
S_16	S_17	0.793790	S_1	-0.477059
S_17	S_16	0.793790	S_2	-0.477816
S_18	S_19	0.793851	S_3	-0.487566
S_19	S_20	0.801040	S_4	-0.481828
S_20	S_21	0.825262	S_10	-0.474668
S_21	S_20	0.825262	S_6	-0.475674
S_22	S_21	0.804423	S_21	-0.484460
S_23	S_22	0.793238	S_16	-0.491731

ability of presented algorithms to successfully recognize various objects in real images. Of course, the quality of images and proper localization can influence the resulting errors by inaccurate localization.

The proposed methods also show to be rotation, translation and scale invariant which open their potential application in wide range of areas.

Two different methods are applied in order to get proper object comparison and identification. The two following algorithms were tested and compared: the processing of the image with extracted edges and the processing of the whole image.

As it can be observed from presented numerical results, both algorithms have shown compatible, accurate and comparable results. The advantage of the second proposed method is its simplicity, effectiveness, 100% correct classification results and practical implementation and realization.

The following chapter offers descriptions related to how to: Capture an image; Transform the image to the video signal format; Transmit this signal to a remote location's receiver; Display the image on a monitor; and Save the image and print it for preservation.

The sixth chapter outlines technologies that are currently in their infancy but are expected to be integrated into security systems in the near future. A video surveillance system design requires making decisions that demand knowledge of basic options and the rationale for selecting from different ones available on the market. One needs to face making the key decisions. High definition television is becoming ever more popular, opening up the market to new high-definition technologies. High quality network cameras are a good choice for surveillance video quality as they confirm that high definition television standards can show good performance in high frame rate, resolution, and color fidelity.

REFERENCES

Berry, W. M., Dumais, S. T., & O'Brien, G. W. (1995). Using linear algebra for intelligent information retrieval. *SIAM Review*, (37): 573–595. doi:10.1137/1037127

Duda, R., & Hart, P. (n.d.). *Pattern classification and scene analysis*. Hoboken, NJ: John Wiley and Sons.

Engel, K., Hadwiger, M., Kniss, J., & Rezk-Salama, C. (2006). *Real-time volume graphics*. AK Peters, Ltd.

Farid, H., & Simoncelli, E. P. (2004). Differentiation of discrete multi-dimensional signals. *IEEE Transactions on Image Processing*, *13*(4), 496–508. doi:10.1109/TIP.2004.823819 PMID:15376584

Garcia, E. (2005). *Patents on duplicated content and re-ranking methods*. San Jose, CA: SES.

Jähne, B., Scharr, H., & Körkel, S. (1999). *Principles of filter design. Handbook of Computer Vision and Applications*. Academic Press.

Krawiec, K., & Bhanu, B. (2007). Visual learning by evolutionary and coevolutionary feature synthesis. *IEEE Transactions on Evolutionary Computation*, *11*(5), 635–650. doi:10.1109/TEVC.2006.887351

Kroon, D. (2009). *Numerical optimization of kernel based image derivatives*. Eschedne, The Netherlands: University Twente.

Praks, P., Dvorský, J., Snášel, V., & Černohorský, J. (2003). *On SVD-free latent semantic indexing for image retrieval for application in a hard industrial environment*. ICIT. doi:10.1109/ICIT.2003.1290365

Praks, P., Kučera, R., & Izquierdo, E. (2008). *The sparse image representation for automated image retrieval*. ICIP. doi:10.1109/ICIP.2008.4711682

Praus, P., & Praks, P. (2010). Hierarchical clustering of RGB surface water images based on MIA-LSI approach. *Water S.A.*, *36*(1), 143–150. doi:10.4314/wsa.v36i1.50922

Scharr, H. (2007). *Optimal second order derivative filter families for transparent motion estimation*. Poznan, Poland: IEEE.

Singhal, A., Buckley, C., & Mitra, M. (n.d.). *Pivoted document length normalization*. Ithaca, NY: Cornell University.

Tan, P. N., Steinbach, M., & Kumar, V. (2005). *Introduction to data mining*. Reading, MA: Addison-Wesley.

Watchareeruetai, U., Takeuchi, Y., Matsumoto, T., Kudo, H., & Ohnishi, N. (2011). Redundancies in linear GP, canonical transformation, and its exploitation: A demonstration on image feature synthesis. *Genet Program Evolvable*, *12*, 49–77. doi:10.1007/s10710-010-9118-x

Zeljković, V., & Praks, P. (2011). *Automatic object classification and image retrieval by Sobel edge detection and latent semantic methods*. MOBIMEDIA.

Section 6
Video Technology Overview

The first chapter in the following section is a description of the technology with which we can: capture an image, transform the image to the video signal format, transmit this signal to a remote location's receiver, display the image on a monitor, and save the image and print it for preservation.

High definition television is becoming ever more popular, opening up the market to new high-definition technologies. Image quality and color fidelity have experienced improvements faster than ever. The video surveillance market has been affected by high definition television demand. Since video surveillance calls for large amounts of image data, high-quality video frame rates are generally compromised. However, a network camera that conforms to high definition television standards shows good performance in high frame rate, resolution, and color fidelity. High quality network cameras are a good choice for surveillance video quality.

Industry experts are predicting that the advancement of video security technology will lead to a general increase in demand for surveillance systems. Over the next ten years these technological advances will continue, improving existing equipment and generating new methods. The next chapter outlines technologies that are currently in their infancy but are expected to be integrated into security systems in the near future.

A video surveillance system design requires making decisions that demand knowledge of basic options and the rationale for selecting from different ones available on the market. One needs to face making the following key decisions:

1. *Choosing the best video surveillance companies.*
2. *Camera types.*
3. *Camera connection to video management system.*
4. *Video management system types.*
5. *Storage type.*
6. *Video analytics type.*
7. *Surveillance video display.*
8. *Integrating video with other systems.*

Chapter 17
Video System Overview

ABSTRACT

This chapter is a description of the technology with which we can: capture an image, transform the image to the video signal format, transmit this signal to a remote location's receiver, display the image on a monitor, and save the image and print it for preservation.

1. ONE-CAMERA ANALOG VIDEO SECURITY SYSTEM

Video surveillance technology improved by leaps and bounds in the last half of the 1990s. Video components, including digital cameras, multiplexers, and DVRs developed rapidly. Also, security systems have become more prevalent; they have been integrated into wide area networks (WANs), computer-based local area networks LANs, wireless networks, intranets, and World Wide Web communications systems.

Today's video surveillance system hardware is so advanced thanks to the great progress made on the following technologies: digital processing, wireless and wired signal transmission, microprocessor computing power, and solid-state and magnetic memory. Of course, the video system utilizes a lens, camera, means of transmission, monitor, recorder, and other basic equipment.

Video surveillance systems exist in order to assist security forces either centrally or remotely. The camera, lens, transmission method, and of course a light source and setting are the vital aspects of such a system. Secondary equipment often includes switchers, multiplexers, VMDs (video motion detectors), combiners and splitters, housings, and character generators. The following chapter is a description of the technology with which we can:

- Capture an image.
- Transform the image to the video signal format.
- Transmit this signal to a remote location's receiver.
- Display the image on a monitor.
- Save the image and print it for preservation.

Figure 1 shows the simplest configuration; it calls for one video camera and one monitor.

The above one-camera configuration requires the following (Kruegle, 2007):

- **Lens:** The light source emits rays that reflect the image of the monitored area onto the camera's sensor.
- **Camera:** After the lens captures the scene, the camera's sensor transforms it into a transmittable electrical signal.

DOI: 10.4018/978-1-4666-4896-8.ch017

Figure 1. The simplest configuration: one video camera and one monitor

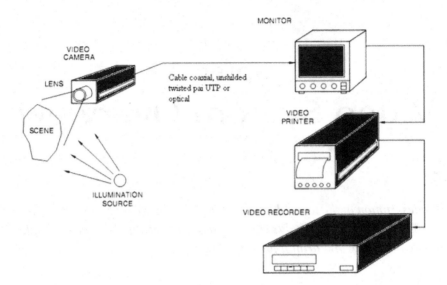

- **Transmission Link:** The electrical video signal is then transferred from the camera to the remote monitor via a transmission medium. These include (a) coaxial, (b) two-wire unshielded twisted-pair (UTP), (c) fiber-optic cable, (d) Local area network LAN, (e) Wide area network WAN, (f) intranet, and (g) Internet network. Wirelessly, one can transmit via (a) radio frequency (RF), (b) microwave, or (c) optical infrared (IR). Transmitted signals can be digital or analog.

- **Monitor:** In order to display the image, the monitor (which can be a liquid crystal display [LCD], plasma, or cathode ray tube [CRT]) converts the video signal back to a visible image format.

- **Recorder:** The scene can be recorded onto either a magnetic tape cassette using a VCR or onto a magnetic disk hard drive using a DVR.

- **Printer:** To produce a hard-copy printout of a scene, a video printer is necessary. It functions using a lens that collects light from the image and prints using printing technology like inkjet, laser, and thermal printing.

2. MULTI-CAMERA ANALOG VIDEO SECURITY SYSTEM

Block diagrams in Figures 2 and 3 depict a multi-camera analog video security system that uses the previously mentioned modules along with extra options and hardware to increase functionality and complexity. These additions can include: camera switchers, quads, multiplexers, environmental camera housings, camera pan/tilt mechanisms, image combiners and splitters, and scene annotators.

- **Camera Switchers, Quads, and Multiplexers:** A camera switcher, a quad, or a multiplexer can be utilized to switch between multiple cameras either manually or automatically in a closed-circuit television (CCTV) security system. These switchers can also be used to display the scenes on more than one monitor, showing either one or more than one scene. Quads combine four cameras while a multiplexer works with 4, 9, 16, and 32 cameras.

- **Housings:** Indoor camera housings are generally made of lightweight material and function as a shield for the camera and lens, preventing tampering. Protection

Figure 2. Multi-camera analog video security system

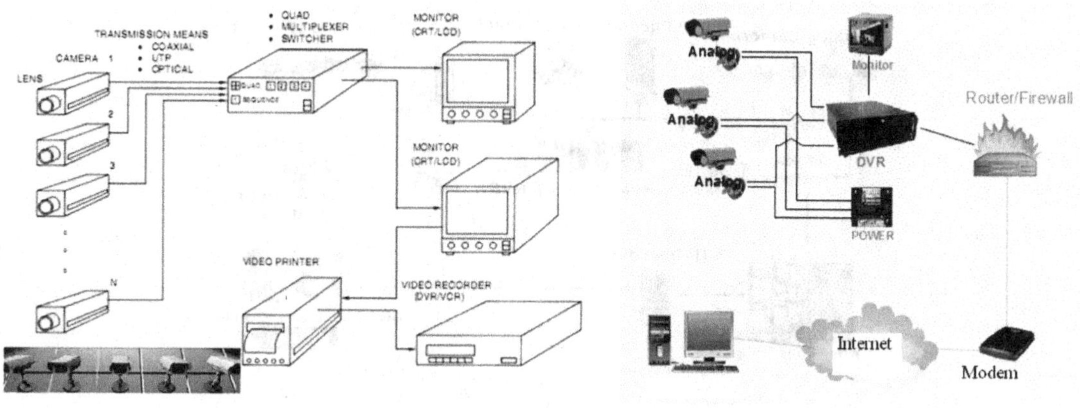

(a)

(b)

from environmental factors such as extreme temperatures, dirt, and precipitation is provided by heavier-duty outdoor housings. Some housing assemblies offer both indoor and outdoor protection.

- **Dome housing:** Both fixed cameras and cameras with pan/tilt and zoom functionality can be protected by a hemispherical plastic dome.
- **Plug-and-Play Camera/Housing Combination:** Some manufacturers offer a ready-to-use set including the camera, the lens, and the housing. This simplifies the installation of surveillance systems. They are ready to mount on a ceiling or wall and plug in to the necessary inputs and outputs.
- **Pan/Tilt Mechanism:** In order to cover large areas, a pan/tilt mechanism (mount) is utilized to rotate the camera horizontally and vertically.
- **Splitter/Combiner/Inserter:** To display more than one scene on a single monitor, an electronic or optical image combiner/splitter is used.
- **Annotator"** An annotator is used to display text on the output screen. This includes a time and date generator (for chronological information) and a camera identifier (for

spatial identification of the scene [for example, BASEMENT or CAMERA 2]).

3. NETWORKED DIGITAL VIDEO SECURITY SYSTEM

Most devices in an analog video system are utilized in a digital video surveillance system as well. The differences lie within the video devices themselves, which operate with digital electronics and processing as opposed to analog. These components use digital signal processing (DSP); they also compress, transmit, record, and view digitally. The block diagrams of the entire digital video system, shown in Figure 3, illustrate these devices and the paths of their signals.

See Figure 4 for an overview of a CCTV camera setting. The scene observed by the camera and lens with the help of an illumination source is called the camera-lens combined field of view (FOV).

4. THE ROLE OF LIGHT AND REFLECTION

Illumination sources can be natural or artificial. Sunlight, moonlight, and starlight are natural sources, while man-made sources are numerous:

Figure 3. Networked digital video system (Google, 2013)

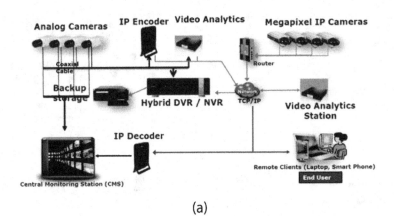

(a)

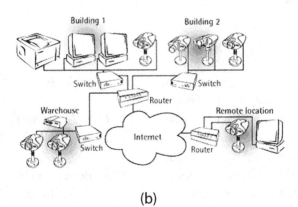

(b)

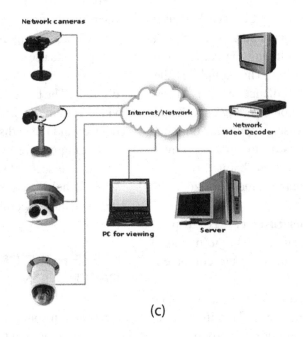

(c)

Figure 4. The video system

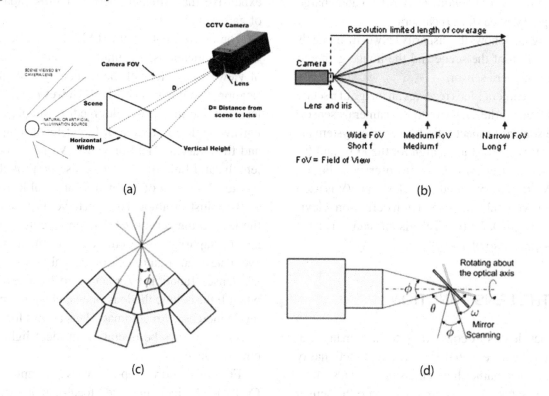

(a)

(b)

(c)

(d)

infrared, mercury, fluorescent, metal arc, incandescent, and sodium.

Light from the scene is directly reflected onto the camera lens.

From 5% to 90% of the light reflected from objects reaches the camera lens depending on the scene and the light quality.

Standard panoramas like streets, business personnel, cars and transport, and foliage tend to have values from 25% to 65%, whereas areas covered in snow can reach up to 90%.

Three factors affect the lens' reception of light: the strength of the light source, the scene's reflectivity, and atmospheric factors affecting transmission.

Outdoor scenes are characterized by a long optical path from the light source to the scene to the camera, so the interference of environmental factors must be taken into account.

Ideally, atmospheric conditions are clear so that light reflection can occur without interruption. Interruption occurs when there is precipitation and in smoky, dusty, or sandy environments. Extreme heat can cause distortion and disruption of the reflection of light.

No image can be formed in situations of zero visibility.

Solid-state cameras can only see the scene if it is visible to the human eye, as well. This is because such cameras operate in the same wavelength region as human sight, the near-infrared region.

If a scene is rendered invisible to the human eye by environmental factors, increasing the lighting will be useless. Filtering out visible light and isolating infrared (IR) light on the scene might increase visibility. Thermal IR imaging cameras function outside of humans' wavelength region and thus are one solution to a scene's lack of visibility.

The disadvantages of a thermal IR imaging camera are its reduced image quality and increased price. Its images are monochrome and the technology costs more than complimentary metal oxide semiconductor (CMOS) and charge coupled device (CCD) cameras.

Figure 5 shows the disparity between a human's perception of the scene and the image gathered by the camera sensor.

The camera's lens receives an image of a scene and focuses the image onto the camera's sensor. The standard aspect ratio for security systems is 4 units wide by 3 units high for the FOV and for the sensor itself, which can be observed in Figure 5. Width is represented by h/H, while v/V is used for the vertical parameter. High definition television (High Definition Television) cameras have an aspect ratio of 16-by-9.

5. THE LENS FUNCTION

Camera lenses are comparable to the human eye in shape as can be seen in Figure 6 and functionality in that they gather light emission from a scene.

Lenses then focus the image onto the sensor of a CCTV camera with the help of natural and/or artificial light. In general, a larger lens will gather more light and produce a brighter, higher-quality final image. Such lenses are thus more

expensive than smaller-aperture lenses capable of gathering less light.

The fixed-focal-length (FFL) lens, used for video applications, maintains a constant field of view like the lens of the human eye. Magnification also remains constant. However, CCTV lenses come in wide-angle, medium-angle, and narrow-angle to provide different focal lengths and thus varying field of views. Variable focal lengths and field of views can also be provided by the adjustment of zoom and varifocal lenses.

To adjust the amount of light traveling through the lens to the censor, CCTV lenses come with an iris diaphragm to resemble that of the human eye. These can be automatic or manual. Automatic iris lenses function by reacting to light levels: when light is low, the lens opens, closing when levels increase. An automatic lens allows for the sensor to always be operating in ideal lighting circumstances.

Figure 7 shows representative samples of CCTV lenses, including fixed-focal-length, varifocal, zoom, pinhole, and a large catadioptric lens for long range outdoor use (which combines both mirror and glass optical elements).

Figure 5. The disparity between a human's perception of the scene and the image gathered by the camera sensor

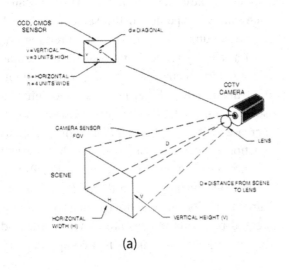

(a)

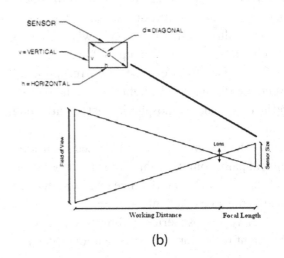

(b)

Figure 6. Analogy between camera lens and eye scene view

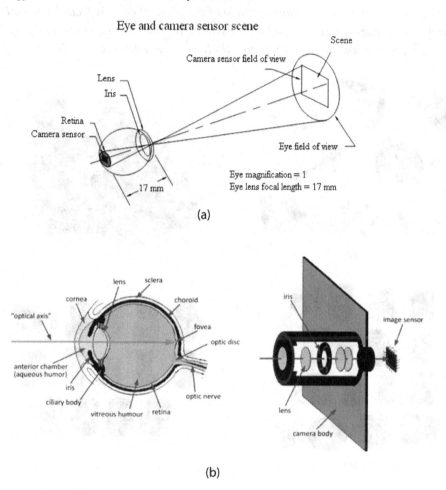

(a)

(b)

Figure 8 illustrates various camera lens models' dimensions and parameters.

Figure 9 shows the correlation between various camera lens models' size and its achievable distance to the object and field of view. As it is expected, the larger camera lenses more successfully take pictures of objects at larger distances from the camera.

6. THE CAMERA FUNCTION

The video camera's image sensor functions like an eye's retina or a photographic camera's film. The electronic parts of a video camera convert the image projected onto the censor into an electrical signal that can be transmitted to a monitor. The basics of a typical CCTV camera are diagrammed in Figure 10.

The lens creates an optical image that is, in turn, converted by the camera into an electric signal that responds to the scene's light distribution and variance through modulation.

In order to make up for the variable nature of the recorded scene, other electronic circuits in the camera emit pulses to synchronize time. This allows the material to be displayed on monitors, recorders, and in printed form.

The scanning process remains static for almost all cameras irrespective of their sizes and

Figure 7. Various video lenses (a) motorized zoom, catadioptric long ffl, flexible fiber optic, wide field of view fixed focal lens, rigid fiber optic, narrow field of view (telephoto) fix focal lens, mini-lens, straight and right-angle, pinhole lenses; (b) manual CCTV lenses; (c) Auto iris and manual iris C/Cs mount lens for special CCTV applications; (d) CCTV auto IRIS lenses; (e) and (f) CCTV lenses.

(a)

(b)

(c)

(d)

(e)

(f)

shapes. Surveillance cameras necessarily scan on a point-by-point basis, changing position at predetermined intervals, except when an image intensifier is involved.

A majority of surveillance systems utilize solid-state CMOS or CCD monochrome or color cameras. CCD cameras equipped with IR illuminators are used in low-light situations. Intensified

Figure 8. Various camera lens models' parameters

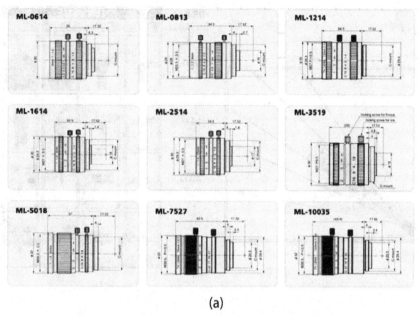

(a)

CCTV specifications

Model / item	Focal distance	Focus (F No.)	Field of view (VxH)	Closest distance	Filter screw	Weight (g)	Maximum compatible camera size	Mount
ML-0614	6mm	F1.4~close	42.3° × 54.6°	0.2m	M27 P0.5	60	1/2"	C-mount
ML-0813	8mm	F1.3~close	45.0° × 57.8°	0.2m	M25.5 P0.5	60	2/3"	C-mount
ML-1214	12mm	F1.4~close	21.9° × 29.0°	0.3m	M27 P0.5	60	1/2"	C-mount
ML-1614	16mm	F1.4~close	23.0° × 30.4°	0.4m	M27 P0.5	60	2/3"	C-mount
ML-2514	25mm	F1.4~close	21.6° × 28.5°	0.5m	M27 P0.5	45	1"	C-mount
ML-3519	35mm	F1.9~close	10.8° × 14.4°	0.5m	M27 P0.5	50	2/3"	C-mount
ML-5018	50mm	F1.8~close	7.9° × 10.5°	1m	M30.5 P0.5	60	2/3"	C-mount
ML-7527	75mm	F2.7~close	4.9° × 6.5°	1m	M30.5 P0.5	65	2/3"	C-mount
ML-10035	100mm	F3.5~close	3.8° × 5.1°	1m	M30.5 P0.5	65	2/3"	C-mount

(b)

CCD (ICCD) cameras are used in extremely low-light, covert situations. The cost and complexity of these cameras is prohibitive.

Figure 11 is a block diagram of an analog camera that is equipped with DSP and the all-digital Internet protocol (IP) video camera.

Security cameras, specifically the non-broadcast variety, were not sufficiently stable, sensitive, or high-resolution up until the early 1990s.

Advances in solid-state color sensor technology were driven by an increased demand for consumer CCD cameras like camcorders in the mid 1990s. Before these advances, security outfits were unlikely to use color cameras. Today, color cameras are the standard for CCTV security operations.

Figure 12 shows a block diagram of the all digital internet protocol (IP) video camera.

Figure 13 shows CCTV cameras, including monochrome, CCD, and CMOS cameras, plus a small single board camera and a miniature remote head camera.

Figure 9. Correlation between camera lens size and distance to the object

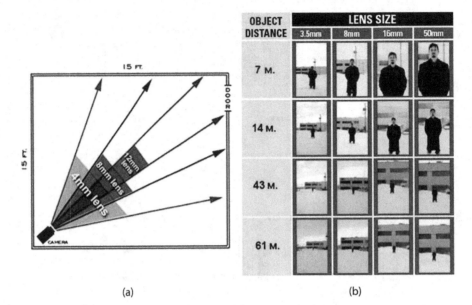

(a)   (b)

Figure 10. The basics of a typical CCTV camera

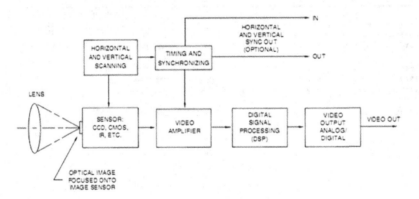

7. THE TRANSMISSION FUNCTION

After the camera translates the scene's image to an electrical video signal, one of many possible transmitters conduct the signal to a security monitoring site. Transmission apparatuses can be coaxial cables, two-wire twisted-pair apparatuses, local area network LAN, wide area network WAN, intranet, Internet, fiber optic cable, or various wireless methods. The decision of which apparatus to use depends on factors such as distance, environment, and spatial layout.

Short distances of 10 and 500 feet between the camera and the monitor call for the following transmitters: coaxial cable, UTP, fiber optic, and wireless.

Fiber optic cables and UTP are optimal for distances of 500 to several thousand feet, or in places with electrical disruptions.

Fiber optics is the only choice for extremely long distances, severe environments, and in situations in which electrical grounding is lacking.

Sometimes security operations must span over roadways, separating camera and monitor. In these

Figure 11. (a) the analog camera with digital signal processing and (b) the all digital internet protocol (IP) video camera

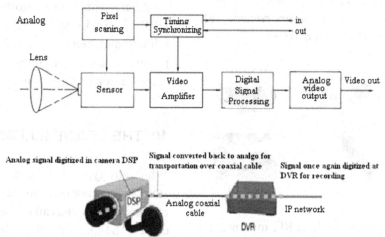

There are many conversions when done in analog way

(a)

(b)

Figure 12. IP network digital video system

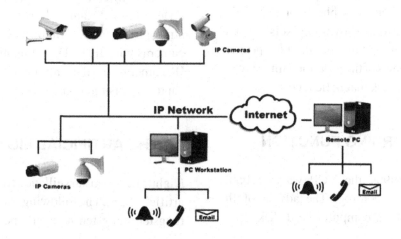

Figure 13. Various camera models (a) intensified CCD camera ICCD; (b) 1/3" format CS mountcolor camera; (c) 1/2" format CS mount monochrome camera; (d) miniature camera; (e) remote head camera; and (f) thermal.

cases, wireless systems such as RF, microwave, and optical transmitters are used.

For long distance operations, surveillance should be done with digital or Internet IP cameras. Compression techniques must optimize signals traveling long distances. These signals cannot be real-time, but often are only slightly delayed.

8. THE MONITOR FUNCTION

After transmission to the monitoring site, a monitor must convert the signal back to an image. CRT, LCD, and plasma monitors are suitable for this task. The conversion process is done via an electronic path inverse to that of a camera.

A scanning electron beam in the monitor's CRT creates the final image. It is displayed on the face of the monitor by activating phosphor in the CRT. The image can also be shown in pixels on LCD and plasma screens. At this point, video printers can print hard copies of the monitor's images onto cassettes or hard disk magnetic recorders.

9. THE RECORDING FUNCTION

Until the mid-1990s, the VCR was a reliable means of video recording. The advent of the DVR, which uses a computer hard disk drive,

allows larger quantities of data to be stored and thus more detailed security capabilities.

Along with greater storage capabilities, the DVR is superior to the VCR because it is more reliable and more easily searchable. Also, it is possible to make many copies of the video without deterioration of the original.

10. THE SCENE ILLUMINATION

While any type of light, natural or artificial, is suitable for a monochrome camera, color cameras require light that has all of the visible spectrum's colors. The spectral distribution of colors must be even in order to produce a representative image. Direct sunlight is optimal because it allows for the highest contrast of images, whereas cloudy and low-light days make it harder to distinguish between objects. Since light varies throughout the days and seasons, equipping the camera with an automatic iris is necessary.

The unit of measurement for a scene's illumination is called a foot-candle (Fc). Its range is from 10,000 to 1, which is larger than most camera sensors need to reproduce a high quality image.

Light reflected by the moon is detectable only with a very sensitive monochrome camera, which is required for nighttime surveillance.

In an extremely dark scene in which the moon is not visible, there are only three potential sources of light: artificial local sources, "night glow" (the reflection of distant light off of particles in the atmosphere), and starlight. ICCD, monochrome cameras with IR LED illumination, and thermal IR cameras are the only technology capable of capturing visible images in these conditions.

11. THE ARTIFICIAL LIGHT

Nighttime video surveillance frequently requires artificial light. The following sources can be used: tungsten, tungsten-halogen, metal-arc, mercury, sodium, xenon, IR lamps, and light-emitting diode (LED) IR arrays.

Figure 14 shows several examples of artificial light sources.

Architectural obstacles and circumstances determine which type of light is chosen. Engineers tend to take into account not only the quality of the video camera's image, but also visibility for personnel working at the scene.

Indoor illumination varies slightly. Fluorescent lighting is most frequently used in addition to high-pressure sodium, metal arc, and mercury lamps. Consistent indoor conditions render artificial irises unnecessary. However, if a surveillance area is subject to daily changes in light, an artificial iris or a camera with an electronic shutter is essential.

Indoor lighting is usually 100 to 1,000 times less intense than outdoor lighting.

12. THE SCENE CHARACTERISTICS

Other factors besides lighting affect the video image. These variables are the level of contrast between objects in the scene and the background, the amount of action in a scene, and objects' state of motion. Surveillance systems' effectiveness in identifying objects depends on these factors.

12.1 Target Size

Light, contrast, and apparent size (as depicted through a camera's angular FOV) determine the accuracy of a person's object detection within an image.

Within a scene, security personnel attempt to detect an object, determine its position, recognize the object, and identify it. This task depends on

Figure 14. Various artificial light sources (a) tungsten halogen; (b) fluorescent straight shape and fluorescent u shape; (c) high pressure sodium; (d) tungsten par spot and tungsten par flood; (e) xenon long arc; (f) high intensity discharge metalarc; (g) tungsten lamps; (h) tungsten halogen lamps (Google, 2013).

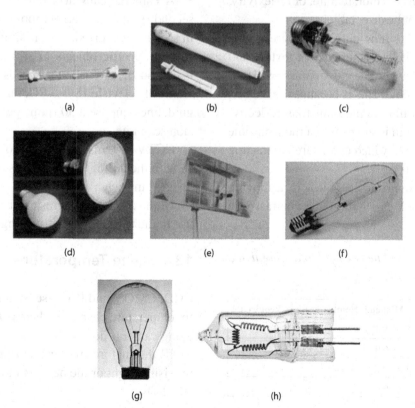

system resolution, contrast, and signal/noise ratio (S/N).

Most observers can pinpoint a target at an angle of about .01 degrees.

Standard video images are comprised of 525 horizontal lines (NTSC), and have a resolution of 350 vertical TV lines and 500 horizontal TV lines.

Table 1 shows how many lines are needed to distinguish a target in a television image.

When there is bad lighting, background commotion, little contrast, or fast movement, the amount of TV lines needed increases.

12.2 Reflectivity

Objects have a huge range of reflectivity, or the amount of light reflected from the physical scene to the camera sensor; reflectivity changes based on the objects' textures and structures.

The brightest images are those that depict highly reflective objects.

If one object is inside of another, it has to be different in terms of color, texture, or reflexivity, or else it will not be detectable.

If a red box is sitting in front of a green wall and they share the characteristics of texture and reflexivity, a monochrome video camera will render the box invisible. This is because the red box and the green wall have the same total reflectivity. A color camera is superior to a monochrome camera in a case in which colors are contrasting and reflectivity is equal.

When searching for an object in a moving image, it is much easier to notice contrast in a color scene than to notice a change in gray scale in a monochromatic scene. The minimum size a target needs to be in order to be identified is smaller in color images than in monochromatic images, as well.

12.3 Effects of Motion

Assuming the proper usage of security cameras, moving targets are generally more difficult to recognize but easier to detect than motionless ones.

The downside of a low-light-level camera is that moving targets become smeared. This phenomenon is called "smear" and "lag."

CCD, CMOS, and ICCD sensors, which are all solid-state, are capable of producing sharp images of both motionless and moving objects at average light levels.

Image intensifiers are susceptible to the smear phenomenon either when the scene moves quickly or when the FOV of the lens is obstructed by a bright light.

A camera scans at a rate of 30 frames per second. Images of targets moving very quickly in scenes are blurred. This is similar to the blurring of specific objects in still photographs; it is caused by slow shutter speeds. However, the National Television System Committee (NTSC)'s guidelines impose a 30 frame per second television scan rate.

CCTV systems are immune to this regulation, so with the use of CCD cameras blurring can be avoided in such a system.

High scan rate cameras can be purchased for use in the tracking of fast-moving targets.

12.4 Scene Temperature

CCD, CMOS, and ICCD sensors do not respond to temperature changes, whereas IR thermal imaging cameras do.

IR thermal imaging cameras are not affected by visible light or the near-IR radiation found in IR LEDs.

Table 1. Number of lines needed to distinguish a target in a television image

Capability	Minimum Number of Lines Required
Detection	1 +/- 0.25
Orientation	1.4 +/- 0.35
Recognition	4 +/- 0.8
Identification	6.4 +/- 1.5

Thermal imagers measure temperature, so the sensitivity of the camera is measured by the smallest possible variation in temperature that registers a change in the camera's detection.

REFERENCES

3D The World Seen Through Multiple Cameras. *(n.d.). Retrieved from* http://www.upc.edu/saladepremsa/informacio/monografics/3d-el-mundo-visto-desde-multiples-camaras?set_language=en

Analog to IP Network. (n.d.). Retrieved from http://r3.cygnuspub.com/files/cygnus/image/SIW/2005/DEC/600x400/1135031175643_10560636.jpg

Bradski, G., & Kaehler, A. (2009). *Learning OpenCV*. Sebastopol, CA: O'Reilly Media, Inc.

Bulb. (n.d.). Retrieved from http://i00.i.aliimg.com/wsphoto/v0/638768082/-font-b-Tungsten-b-font-font-b-Halogen-b-font-font-b-Bulb-b-font.jpg

Camera Field of View. (n.d.). Retrieved from http://www.customs.gov.au/webdata/resources/images/fov-vs-focus.gif

Camera. (n.d.). Retrieved from http://mtxglobal.com/wp-content/themes/mtxglobal/images/fov.jpg

Camera View. *(n.d.). Retrieved from* http://www.google.com.hk/imgres?q=Multi-Camera+Three+Dimensions&um=1&hl=en&newwindow=1&safe=strict&sa=N&biw=1360&bih=673&tbm=isch&tbnid=rrqwfuUhbiaUwM:&imgrefurl=http://projects.washingtonpost.com/top-secret-america/galleries/gallery-technology/&docid=rhifFwxgaJRU-M&imgurl=http://media.washingtonpost.com/media/images/2010/07/15/07152010-63v_606x404.jpg&w=606&h=404&ei=ZRkuUe7wMInukgX98oDADA&zoom=1&iact=rc&dur=644&sig=117471693243402725643&page=1&tbnh=171&tbnw=266&start=0&ndsp=18&ved=1t:429,r:10,s:0&tx=1168&ty=366

Canon CX-1 Camera. (n.d.). Retrieved from http://www.canon-europe.com/Medical/Eye_Care/CX-1/

Caputo, A. C. (2010). *Digital video surveillance and security*. London: Elsevier.

CCTV Lens. (n.d.). Retrieved from http://ganpati-infosys.com/?page_id=108

CCTV Lenses. (n.d.a). Retrieved from http://www.goyooptical.com/products/cctv/manual.html

CCTV Lenses. (n.d.b). Retrieved from http://www.goyooptical.com/products/cctv/airis.html

CCTV Lenses. (n.d.c). Retrieved from http://img.directindustry.com/pdf/repository_di/29083/cctv-lenses-10334_1b.jpg

CCTV Lenses. (n.d.d). Retrieved from http://www.si-cube.com/Products/Lensassembly/7/

Damjanovski, V. (2005). *CCTV networking and digital technology*. London: Elsevier.

Eye Structure and Camera Structure. (n.d.). Retrieved from http://electronicimaging.spiedigitallibrary.org/data/Journals/ELECTIM/23509/033009_1_1.png

Field of View. (n.d.). Retrieved from http://ars.els-cdn.com/content/image/1-s2.0-S1077314211002384-gr10.jpg

Foresman, C. (n.d.). *Lytro's new light field camera lets you focus* after *you take a picture*. Retrieved from http://arstechnica.com/gadgets/2011/10/lytros-new-light-field-camera-lets-you-focus-after-you-take-a-picture/

Image Tracking System. (n.d.). Retrieved from http://www.tracab.com/technology.aspx

IP (Network) Digital Video Recording System. (n.d.). Retrieved from http://www.dynapost.com/index.php?page_no=33

Kruegle, H. (2007). *CCTV surveillance analog and digital video practices and technology* (2nd ed.). London: Elsevier.

Lens Field of View. (n.d.a). Retrieved from http://www.image-tmart.com/info_images/CCTV-Cameras-2.jpg

Lens Field of View. (n.d.b). Retrieved from http://www.videosurveillance.co.in/images/cctv%20view.jpg

Lens Geometry. (n.d.). Retrieved from http://ars.els-cdn.com/content/image/1-s2.0-S0926580511002251-gr2.jpg

Lens Size. (n.d.). Retrieved from http://www.elplanbg.com/EN/wordpress/wp-content/uploads/2012/10/CCTV_lens.jpg

Network System. (n.d.). Retrieved from http://embedded.communities.intel.com/servlet/JiveServlet/showImage/38-5444-3988/DSS+diagram.JPG

Network Video. (n.d.). Retrieved from www.axis.com

Network Video System. (n.d.). Retrieved from http://www.axis.com/products/video/camera/about_cameras/img/video_system.gif

Nilsson, F. (2009). *Intelligent network video - Understanding modern video surveillance systems.* Boca Raton, FL: CRC Press Taylor & Francis Group.

Rapid Eye Hybrid, H. D. *(n.d.). Retrieved from* http://www.honeywellvideo.com/products/recorders/pc/306064.html

Switched Digital Video. (n.d.). Retrieved from http://static.ddmcdn.com/gif/switched-digital-video-3.gif

Video Network. (n.d.). Retrieved from http://www.axis.com/products/cam_292/img/ipsurvnw.jpg

Chapter 18
High Definition Television (HDTV) and Video Surveillance

ABSTRACT

High definition television is becoming ever more popular, opening up the market to new high-definition technologies. Image quality and color fidelity have experienced improvements faster than ever. The video surveillance market has been affected by high definition television demand. Since video surveillance calls for large amounts of image data, high-quality video frame rates are generally compromised. However, a network camera that conforms to high definition television standards shows good performance in high frame rate, resolution, and color fidelity. High quality network cameras are a good choice for surveillance video quality.

1. INTRODUCTION

High definition television is becoming ever more popular, opening up the market to new high-definition technologies. Image quality and color fidelity have experienced improvements faster than ever.

High definition television resolution can be up to five times higher than analog TV resolution, and contains twice the amount of linear resolution. In addition, HDTV has DVD-quality audio capabilities and widescreen formatting. Thanks to all of these advantages, high definition television market growth has been huge.

35% of all U.S. households had an High Definition Television in 2007, and it was projected that by 2012, that number would rise to 85%. A huge amount of television products and accessories are already High Definition.

There are two important High Definition Television standards in existence today:

1. The SMPTE 296M.
2. The SMPTE 274M.

Where SMPTE stands for the Society of Motion Picture and Television Engineers, the organization who defines standards.

2. HIGH DEFINITION TELEVISION IMPACT ON THE VIDEO SURVEILLANCE MARKET

Since customers are becoming accustomed to high-quality video, even the video surveillance market has been affected by high definition television demand.

DOI: 10.4018/978-1-4666-4896-8.ch018

"Megapixel" standards, which overall represent the video surveillance industry's top products, refer to the amount of image sensors a digital camera contains. Megapixel cameras can theoretically perform the same quality job as high definition television cameras.

However, since surveillance calls for large amounts of image data, high-quality data would be taxing for surveillance systems. Thus, frame rates are generally compromised.

So high image quality in a surveillance system cannot be achieved by a megapixel camera alone.

However, a network camera that conforms to high definition television standards can perform much in the same way: high frame rate, resolution, and color fidelity. High quality network cameras are a good choice for surveillance video quality.

3. DEVELOPMENT OF HIGH DEFINITION TELEVISION

The number of pixels in the image information is the main difference between analog TV and high definition television.

The first high-resolution TV was developed in 1958.

The Soviet Military created a TV system that produced good quality, crisp, clear images. This system was called Transformator, and it could create an image that had 1,125 lines of resolution. Its intention was to organize teleconferences.

In the late 1960s NHK, the Japanese broadcasting association developed this technology into a commercially usable system.

At this time, high definition television piqued the interests of manufacturers, as they could see a rising global trend. However, proper compression techniques were not available at the time for the transmission of such large amounts of data. Because of this, experimental high definition television systems never gained ground because their bandwidth requirements were too high.

These early high definition television broadcast systems called for about two to four times the amount of bandwidth of a regular broadcast system. Those using high definition television had to transmit data via satellite.

It was soon obvious that high definition television must be more efficient to be introduced into the consumer market. Even then, engineers realized that digital methods were the only possible way to transmit so much data at once, but these digital methods had not been developed yet.

The first step to high definition television transmission was the development of the MPEG compression standards in the early 1990s. Soon after, in 1993, came MPEG-2.

The Video Coding Experts Group of the International Telecom Union joined with MPEG to develop the ITU into H.264, which is also called MPEG-4 Part 10/AVC compression.

H.264 was a breakthrough; it made high definition television not just possible logistically but also economically.

4. HOW HIGH DEFINITION TELEVISION WORKS

High definition television represents huge progress in the world of TV transmission since its resolution is almost 5 times higher than analog TVs. This manifests itself as:

1. A 16:9 widescreen ration.
2. Improved color fidelity.
3. Much sharper images.

There are three major factors that constitute the high definition television system:

1. Frame size.
2. Scanning system.
3. Frame rate.

4.1 Frame Size

The number of horizontal pixels multiplied by the number of vertical pixels gives you the frame rate, for example, 1280x720 or 1920x1080. Often you will see the number of horizontal pixels listed by itself because the vertical pixels can then be calculated.

Figure 1 shows different aspect ratios of regular television National Television System Committee NTSC which represents analog television system that is used in most of North America and high definition television.

The most common systems are 720 and 1080, followed by either i or p, representing interlaced or progressive scanning.

Traditional TV broadcasts are 704x576i and 704x480i, so high definition television is generally two to five times more resolute and contains two to five times more data.

4.2 Scanning

Interlaced (i) and progressive (p) are the two available types of scanning. The original purpose of interlaced scanning was to avoid bandwidth consumption while still increasing the quality of video signals.

Now it can be said that interlaced video scanning provides a bandwidth reduction of a factor of two, which enables an increased refresh rate, allowing for flicker reduction and improved depiction of motion.

However, interlaced scanning has some disadvantages:

1. **Motion Artifacts:** At high speeds, the location of an object will change in the time in which it takes to switch from scanning one field to the next, creating a stilted picture. Usually this is not visible but can be seen if video is displayed at a slow speed.
2. **Interline Twitter:** When a frame contains intricate vertical details it can almost reach the video format's horizontal resolution, leading to a visible interline twitter effect.

Progressive scanning makes up for these limitations since it captures, transfers, and shows each line in the image in one frame, not splitting the frame into two fields.

Progressive scanning is done from top to bottom, line by line. It avoids interlaced scanning's "flickering" effect since the images are not split into two fields.

This type of scanning is most useful in a surveillance application when viewing a moving image

Figure 1. Different aspect ratios of NTSC (analog television system that is used in most of North America) and high definition television

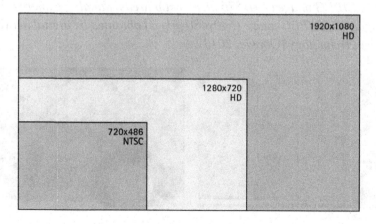

and trying to pinpoint details. Unlike interlaced scanning, progressive scanning provides single frames that can be substituted for still photographs. This is especially beneficial when using video evidence in a court. However, progressive scanning requires more bandwidth.

Figure 2 picturesquely illustrates the advantage of using digital network camera which is using progressive scan technique in comparison to analog camera which is using interlaced scanning. Figure 2 a) is a full sized JPEG image of size 704x576 pixels captured by analog camera which is using interlaced scanning. Figure 2 b) represents a full sized JPEG image of size 640x480 pixels obtained by digital network camera that is using progressive scan technology. The speed of the car is the same in both images and is 20 km/h or 15 mph. Both cameras digital network camera and analog camera use the same type of lens. It can be observed that the background is clear in both images in Figure 2. However, the driver is clearly visible and possible to identify for surveillance purposes only in the image obtained by using progressive scan technology.

4.3 Frame Rate

The amount of image frames per second is the frame rate, abbreviated as fps.

Interlaced systems' frame rate is usually twice as high as progressive systems' since each frame has two fields.

Globally, countries split into two sides, using either 25/50 fps or 30/60 fps. This depended on the electricity supplies' frequency because this frequency affected the stability of the image.

Both 25/50 fps and 30/60 fps are compatible with high definition television and therefore can be used in video surveillance.

5. HIGH DEFINITION TELEVISION STANDARDIZATION

MPEG-1 compression was the first step towards digital TV; it encouraged modern TV development all across the globe.

The Society of Motion Picture and Television Engineers is the most prominent organization in charge of high definition television standards. They are considered the international managers of standard development and practices in television, film, video, and multimedia. They finalized the two most prevalent standards in use today: SMPTE 296M and SMPTE 274M.

While SMPTE 296M has a resolution of 1280x720 under progressive scanning, SMPTE 274M's resolution is 1920x1080 in either progressive or interlaced scanning.

Figure 2. (a) Full sized JPEG image (704x576 pixels) captured by analog camera which is using interlaced scanning; (b) full sized JPEG image (640x480 pixels) obtained by digital network camera that is using progressive scan technology (Google, 2013).

The introduction of MPEG-2 and H.264 meant that even a single analog TV channel's bandwidth is enough to carry either five digital TV signals or two high definition television channels, with the use of progressive scanning.

6. HIGH DEFINITION TELEVISION FORMATS

Since high definition television usually has an aspect ratio of 16:9 and a progressive scanning horizontal resolution of 1920, it can be calculated that the frame resolution is 2,073,600 pixels, or 1920x1080. However, this frame rate is variable; these variations go after the letter "p" in their designations. For example, 1080p30 and 1080p50 are possibilities. 1080i and 720p are other possibilities.

All formats have a 16:9 aspect ratio. 1080i uses interlaced scanning for 1920x1080 lines, whereas 720p uses progressive scanning for a resolution of 1280x720 pixels.

7. BENEFITS OF HIGH DEFINITION TELEVISION IN VIDEO SURVEILLANCE

Network cameras using progressive scanning techniques and equipped with high definition television capabilities can produce an extremely clear image despite the speed and complexity of the scene. As a result, high definition television is very beneficial in most surveillance situations such as in airports, stores, passport control stations, highways, casinos, and other places that require great attention to detail. While these technologies have long been desired, they could only be realized recently upon the advancement of video compression technology.

H.264 compression is both open and licensed, making it an easily adaptable technology. Without reducing image quality, it can compress a file up to 80% more than Motion JPEG compression

and up to 50% more than MPEG-4 Part 2. Given its convenience, flexibility, power, and storage economy, H.264 is emerging as the most adaptable and popular compression standard. H.264 was definitely a necessary development in the trajectory of high definition television systems. It is efficient in that it allows for high resolution, increased frame rates, and an aspect ratio of 16:9.

High definition television monitors have square pixels like computer screens, so the same network video input can be shown on both high definition television and standard screens and monitors. However, high definition television video has an advantage in that it does not need to be converted or deinterlaced before processing and display for the screen.

High-definition television has brought rapid advances in both the technology and expectations of the consumer video market. The surveillance market has followed suit. High definition television is a great solution in surveillance installations thanks to its resolution, 16:9 aspect ratio, color fidelity, and frame rate, all of which comply with international standards.

REFERENCES

Bradski, G., & Kaehler, A. (2009). *Learning OpenCV*. Sebastopol, CA: O'Reilly Media, Inc.

Caputo, A. C. (2010). *Digital video surveillance and security*. London: Elsevier.

Damjanovski, V. (2005). *CCTV networking and digital technology*. London: Elsevier.

Kruegle, H. (2007). *CCTV surveillance analog and digital video practices and technology* (2nd ed.). London: Elsevier.

Nilsson, F. (2009). *Intelligent network video - Understanding modern video surveillance systems*. Boca Raton, FL: CRC Press Taylor & Francis Group.

Chapter 19
New Video Technologies

ABSTRACT

Industry experts are predicting that the advancement of video security technology will lead to a general increase in demand for surveillance systems. Over the next ten years these technological advances will continue, improving existing equipment and generating new methods. This chapter outlines technologies that are currently in their infancy but are expected to be integrated into security systems in the near future.

1. OVERVIEW

The last decade has seen extraordinary growth and improvements in the industry of video technology. Components have been refined, analog systems improved, and multiplexers, large-scale switchers, and digital video equipment have been introduced into the market of security surveillance.

Industry experts are predicting that the advancement of video security technology will lead to a general increase in demand for surveillance systems, and they will become more widespread.

The new functions of digital technology include:

1. Very high-resolution pictures that can be digitally manipulated. For example, one can add graphics and digital data.
2. Video can be transmitted, viewed, and stored literally anywhere around the world.

Digital technology will soon take over analog in all security installations (Kruegle, 2007). Two-way Local Area Network LAN, Wide Area Network WAN, Metropolitan Area Network MAN, and wireless WiFi networks are used to send information. They require data encryption in all security uses.

Rapid growth has occurred largely thanks to improvements in electronic circuits. They have gotten smaller and denser with time, which has led to smaller, more capable equipment. More specifically, solid-state cameras, digital signal processing (DSP) cameras, Digital Video Recorders DVR, and hard drives have benefited from electronic circuit advances. Hard drives are now smaller and can store much more.

Over the next ten years these technological advances will continue, improving existing equipment and generating new methods.

The following chapter will outline technologies that are currently in their infancy but are expected to be integrated into security systems in the near future.

2. CAMERA TECHNOLOGY

Lenses have sufficiently developed to adapt to advances in video camera installations. However, there are other ways to get even more information from the scene at hand, including 3D

DOI: 10.4018/978-1-4666-4896-8.ch019

(three-dimensional) displays and optics-sensor combinations that mirror the human eye ("human eye" setups). Solid-state sensors like those used in thermal and visual IR cameras will benefit from continual improvement.

The consumer market, which is driven by standard color cameras, will encourage the development of better resolution and sensitivity in consumer products.

Eventually automatic iris lenses will be replaced by advanced camera-sensor dynamic range technology. However, the greatest improvements will come for thermal IR cameras: their sensitivity and resolution will increase by leaps and bounds.

As soon as manufacturing technology catches up with engineered improvements, monochrome IR cameras that are capable of seeing through fog will emerge on the market at a competitive price.

3. SMART CAMERAS

It is predicted that smart cameras' intelligence will continue increasing. They will be able to "make decisions" like humans in addition to "learning" and being able to respond to changes in their environment.

Pattern recognition and predetermined software algorithms will assist smart cameras in making automatic decisions, based on stored information in their intelligence systems.

4. INFRARED CAMERAS

Infrared IR imaging cameras that are equipped with IR sensors that are cooled mechanically cost anywhere from 50,000 to 100,000 dollars.

These types of cameras are generally used in the military for their high sensitivity and high resolution.

More reasonably priced IR cameras that range from 5,000 to 10,000 dollars use IR sensors at room temperature and have decent resolution and sensitivity.

The next years will see the evolution of room temperature thermal IR cameras into combined visual and infrared IP camera.

Although thermal imaging cameras are currently prohibitively expensive, a new technology will drastically reduce the price to around $1000. This technology is thermal light valve, or TLV. It converts thermal IR radiation, which is difficult to image, into light radiation. This radiation can then be translated by regular CMOS cameras.

The camera's conversion chip was developed based on technology used in large-scale communications networks.

IR cameras work by focusing an 8-14 micron image on a TTF, or temperature tunable filter, stack in addition to a reference light beam of 850 nm. The temperature tunable filter TTF then outputs an 850 nm copy of the original IR image. After that the CCD or CMOS sensor reads the 850 nm image and outputs a camera image representative of the original IR image.

5. MILLIMETER WAVE TECHNOLOGY

Something more than infrared technology and metal detection is necessary to screen items and people going through buildings' entrances and exits. This need is met by the blend of video and passive millimeter wave technology. The mentioned combination makes it possible to scan both crowds and individuals at very close and far-off distances. This technology has a reach of up to 40 feet.

Millimeter wave cameras will soon come with on-screen graphics windows that can be focused on the specific part of a person's clothing that is concealing an item. They can also analyze the contents of a closed container. Guns, knives, and other concealed items will be able to be detected.

While this millimeter sensor will not be able to recreate distinguishable images of objects and people, it will be able to distinguish between familiar and foreign objects, such as weapons.

The millimeter wave sensor and infrared operate similarly, but the millimeter wave sensor functions in a longer wavelength region. Since every object emits a varied radiation signature, millimeter sensors are used to perceive the variance.

6. TWO CAMERA THREE DIMENSIONS

Three dimensional 3D video systems are available in a few varieties.

Intelligence of video surveillance systems can be increased by three dimensional technology which allows guards to make more informed judgments about a situation. Two dimensional 2D flat-screen monitors do not offer as much information as three dimensional images.

Three dimensional systems output two images in the form of one three dimensional image using two video channels and two cameras. Bi-split lenses and dual-lens/camera combinations can be used to display a three dimensional image on a three dimensional monitor.

In the future, security systems will utilize 3D for specific functions.

7. MULTI-CAMERA THREE DIMENSIONS

In order to gather images from more than one camera viewing the same room, one can utilize three dimensional volumetric imaging technology. It also can digitize and store the images, and after taking the camera's position and viewing angle into account, can incorporate individual images into one three dimensional image. Figure 1 illustrates multiple cameras and three dimensional volumetric imaging.

The application of multi camera three dimensional volumetric imaging technology is various.

Figure 2 a) shows the system that is based on stereo vision technology. Every inch of the sur-

Figure 1. Multiple cameras and 3D volumetric imaging

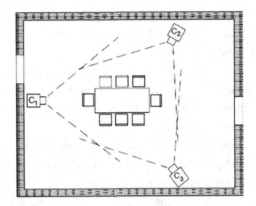

veilled scene is constantly covered by at least two cameras. The x, y, z measurements for the objects on the covered scene are made through analyzing these images. This method results in true three dimensional tracking in real time.

Traditional cameras capture flat images of three-dimensional space by focusing light rays directed toward a camera's lens on to digital sensor. Effectively, a camera records a two-dimensional array of colored dots or pixels corresponding to light rays directed towards the camera from objects in front of the lens. The Stanford Multi-Camera Array, shown in Figure 2 b), records the color, intensity, and direction of the light rays in a scene. These light rays collectively make up a scene's light field.

Three-dimensional rendering and ray tracing technique enables the generation of a light field for a synthetic scene made up of 3D models. A ray tracing renderer follows rays of light emitted from synthesized sources as they bounce from object to object, reflecting at varying angles depending on the surface qualities of an object.

Without knowing anything about the objects in a scene, however, the entire scene and the objects in it can be visually recreated if its unique light field is known.

Capturing images of the real world using multiple cameras and reconstructing those images

Figure 2. (a) System used for three dimensional tracking - in real time, (b) A multi-camera array built at Stanford to record light fields. (c), (d), (e) 3D reconstruction of a scene, from the image of a dancer captured by eight cameras, (f) anti-deception technology (Google, 2013).

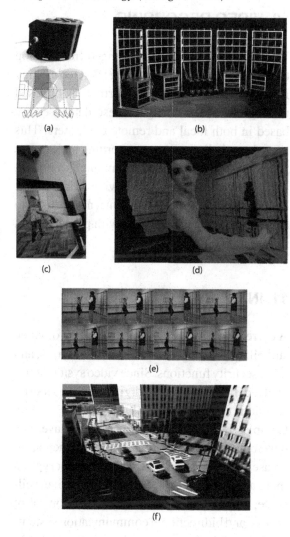

(a)

(b)

(c)

(d)

(e)

(f)

in 3D makes it possible to represent a scene or object in a different way. The three dimensional information about an object can be reconstructed and viewed from any perspective.

This technology can have a revolutionary impact on the creation of film and TV content by enabling the camera to be positioned anywhere. The possible viewpoint locations of a virtual camera, a device used to project a scene will be enabled and determined by this system.

Anthropometric identification systems will be using multiple cameras and three dimension images reconstruction in order to study persons' gestures and movements aimed at identifying and tracking individuals based on their dynamic biometric characteristics.

Another future application of multiple cameras and three dimension images reconstruction technology is in the design of the immersive and interactive television. The users will be able to control the devices like computer or television by using gestures without using a mouse, keyboard or remote control.

Recent computing advances have made this three dimensional compilation process possible.

8. HYBRID EYE CAMERA

A possible future hybrid eye camera would consist of one high-resolution central portion surrounded by a low-resolution outer segment.

Like a human eye, the hybrid eye camera would have a highly focused central field and a moderately focused periphery. While the periphery works to detect a moving target's motion, the pan/tilt function points the camera to a central point and ensures that the target is centered in the high-resolution part of the sensor.

The features of the hybrid eye camera are the following:

1. High resolution capability at center of field of view while retaining high angular field of view.
2. Increases intelligence information.
3. Provides variable magnification over lens field of view.
4. Possess high pixel density at center that allows high magnification with excellent resolution.

9. MONITOR DISPLAY TECHNOLOGY

9.1 Organic LED

The technology of organic light emitting diodes, or OLED, has seen much improvement over the last years and will eventually drastically reduce the cost of video displays while improving their performance.

Organic light emitting diodes' displays do not require as much power as equivalently bright screens since the light itself is emitted from the display. Other screens are back illuminated and the light is transferred through an liquid crystal display LCD matrix panel.

OLED technology allows for display mediums that are more adaptable and resilient than competing flat-panel displays.

9.2 Three-Dimensional Monitors

Three dimensional LCD liquid crystal display monitors come with different modes. When the monitor is switched off, the display acts as a regular two dimensional liquid crystal display monitor. When switched on, light passes through the main thin film transistor liquid crystal display and is directed so that odd pixel columns are sent to the left eye and even ones to the right eye.

Figure 3. Hybrid eye camera

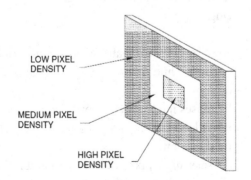

LOW PIXEL DENSITY

MEDIUM PIXEL DENSITY

HIGH PIXEL DENSITY

This is how three dimensional technology works: when the monitor directs different pixels at different parts of the eye, the human brain fuses the two into a complete three dimensional view.

10. VIDEO RECORDING

While video recording has changed from analog to digital, digital video recording DVR technology is currently developing into virtual, as opposed to tangible, video storage. These databases are based in both local and remote computers. This way, the only limitation on recording and storage is the capacity of the network computer's memory.

Local area network LAN, wide area network WAN, wireless WiFi, and the Internet are used to access these image databases with proper access information.

11. INTEGRATED SYSTEMS

A current development is the integration of video surveillance with general alarms, fire alarms, and other security functions. Since video systems have evolved from analog to digital, many security functions can be integrated into a single system. Completely integrated security systems have been developed thanks to software improvements, increase in transmission speeds, and data encryption innovations. These systems include video surveillance, fire and other security alarms, control of access, and bidirectional communication systems made possible through Local area network LAN, wide area network WAN and wireless WiFi.

"Integrated security systems" and "interoperability" are important new terms in the field. The platform upon which integrated security systems function consists of very powerful computers and multi-tasking software. This way, integrated sites can be controlled remotely, greatly increasing the usability of surveillance systems. Real-time video can be transferred long distances over fiber-optic networks, which also greatly increases surveillance systems' functionality.

In the near future, the combination of Internet and satellite transmission with global security installations will be common and expected.

12. REMOTE SURVEILLANCE

Consumer and business technologies have positively affected the video surveillance market. Consumer innovations include cell phones, digital networks, the Internet, and variations on WiFi protocol 80211x. The continuing development of these technologies allows for the upgrade of security installations' capabilities, specifically transmission methods. Ideally, groundbreaking new technologies allow for a globally connected remote video system that can be controlled and surveilled from anywhere in the world that has a wired or wireless connection.

13. TRANSMISSION

Wide area network WAN and wireless WiFi, the wireless video transmission formats, are the biggest challenge in new security technology. They are challenging because of limitations in range, QoS (quality of service), and security.

Wireless digital transmission greatly reduces cost while improving video coverage in comparison to wired networks. The next decade will see attempts to compensate for the current lack of reliability in wireless transmission with regard to QoS and security.

13.1 Range

IEEE 80211x protocols are currently improving, especially in terms of QoS over long ranges.

Ideally, range will be maximized and QoS will remain high. But generally QoS is reduced over a long distance.

MIMO transmission technology (multiple-in, multiple-out) doubles range using either single or diverse antenna systems.

13.2 Quality of Service

QoS is the measure of the quality of a wireless video signal as it is transferred over a wireless network.

The signal's strength can become low, fade, or be interrupted by other electronic signals and 80211x transmission devices. All of these outcomes cause either loss of signal or an intermittent signal.

A mesh transmission network can improve QoS because it overlaps multiple transmission paths, ensuring that at least one path will remain open for signal transmission.

This MIMO technology is currently being improved, having not yet reached a manufacture-ready standard. Multiple signals, both direct and multi-path, can be used between the transmitter and the receiver to improve the QoS. This technology is being developed.

Most multiple antenna wireless 80211x systems currently eliminate multi-path signals, whereas MIMO technology uses these multiple path signals to its advantage.

13.3 Security

WiFi video transmission does not yet guarantee the complete security of video images; ideally, only those with proper permission should be able to see the video.

Complete security through video encryption is a subject of much research and development. FIPS, AES, DES, and other encryption protocols are being advanced in order to improve security.

REFERENCES

3D The World Seen Through Multiple Cameras. *(n.d.). Retrieved from* http://www.upc.edu/saladepremsa/informacio/monografics/3d-el-mundo-visto-desde-multiples-camaras?set_language=en

Analog to IP Network. (n.d.). Retrieved from http://r3.cygnuspub.com/files/cygnus/image/SIW/2005/DEC/60 0x400/1135031175643_10560636.jpg

Bradski, G., & Kaehler, A. (2009). *Learning OpenCV*. Sebastopol, CA: O'Reilly Media, Inc.

Bulb. (n.d.). Retrieved from http://i00.i.aliimg.com/wsphoto/v0/638768082/-font-b-Tungsten-b-font-font-b-Halogen-b-font-font-b-Bulb-b-font.jpg

Camera Field of View. (n.d.). Retrieved from http://www.customs.gov.au/webdata/resources/images/fov-vs-focus.gif

Camera. (n.d.). Retrieved from http://mtxglobal.com/wp-content/themes/mtxglobal/images/fov.jpg

Camera View. *(n.d.). Retrieved from* http://www.google.com.hk/imgres?q=Multi-Camera+Three+Dimensions&um=1&hl=en&newwindow=1&safe=strict&sa=N&biw=1360&bih=673&tbm=isch&tbnid=rrqwfuUhbiaUwM:&imgrefurl=http://projects.washingtonpost.com/top-secret-america/galleries/gallery-technology/&docid=rhifFwxgaJRU-M&imgurl=http://media.washingtonpost.com/media/images/2010/07/15/07152010-63v_606x404.jpg&w=606&h=404&ei=ZRkuUe7wMInukgX98oDADA&zoom=1&iact=rc&dur=644&sig=117471693243402725643&page=1&tbnh=171&tbnw=266&start=0&ndsp=18&ved=1t:429,r:10,s:0&tx=1168&ty=366

Canon CX-1 Camera. (n.d.). Retrieved from http://www.canon-europe.com/Medical/Eye_Care/CX-1/

Caputo, A. C. (2010). *Digital video surveillance and security*. London: Elsevier.

CCTV Lens. (n.d.). Retrieved from http://ganpati-infosys.com/?page_id=108

CCTV Lenses. (n.d.a). Retrieved from http://www.goyooptical.com/products/cctv/manual.html

CCTV Lenses. (n.d.b). Retrieved from http://www.goyooptical.com/products/cctv/airis.html

CCTV Lenses. (n.d.c). Retrieved from http://img.directindustry.com/pdf/repository_di/29083/cctv-lenses-10334_1b.jpg

CCTV Lenses. (n.d.d). Retrieved from http://www.si-cube.com/Products/Lensassembly/7/

Damjanovski, V. (2005). *CCTV networking and digital technology*. London: Elsevier.

Eye Structure and Camera Structure. (n.d.). Retrieved from http://electronicimaging.spiedigitallibrary.org/data/Journals/ELEC-TIM/23509/033009_1_1.png

Field of View. (n.d.). Retrieved from http://ars.els-cdn.com/content/image/1-s2.0-S1077314211002384-gr10.jpg

Foresman, C. (n.d.). *Lytro's new light field camera lets you focus* after *you take a picture*. Retrieved from http://arstechnica.com/gadgets/2011/10/lytros-new-light-field-camera-lets-you-focus-after-you-take-a-picture/

Image Tracking System. (n.d.). Retrieved from http://www.tracab.com/technology.aspx

IP (Network) Digital Video Recording System. (n.d.). Retrieved from http://www.dynapost.com/index.php?page_no=33

Kruegle, H. (2007). *CCTV surveillance analog and digital video practices and technology* (2nd ed.). London: Elsevier.

Lens Field of View. (n.d.a). Retrieved from http://www.image-tmart.com/info_images/CCTV-Cameras-2.jpg

Lens Field of View. (n.d.b). Retrieved from http://www.videosurveillance.co.in/images/cctv%20view.jpg

Lens Geometry. (n.d.). Retrieved from http://ars.els-cdn.com/content/image/1-s2.0-S0926580511002251-gr2.jpg

Lens Size. (n.d.). Retrieved from http://www.elplanbg.com/EN/wordpress/wp-content/uploads/2012/10/CCTV_lens.jpg

Network System. (n.d.). Retrieved from http://embedded.communities.intel.com/servlet/JiveServlet/showImage/38-5444-3988/DSS+diagram.JPG

Network Video. (n.d.). Retrieved from www.axis.com

Network Video System. (n.d.). Retrieved from http://www.axis.com/products/video/camera/about_cameras/img/video_system.gif

Nilsson, F. (2009). *Intelligent network video - Understanding modern video surveillance systems*. Boca Raton, FL: CRC Press Taylor & Francis Group.

Rapid Eye Hybrid, H. D. *(n.d.). Retrieved from* http://www.honeywellvideo.com/products/recorders/pc/306064.html

Switched Digital Video. (n.d.). Retrieved from http://static.ddmcdn.com/gif/switched-digital-video-3.gif

Video Network. (n.d.). Retrieved from http://www.axis.com/products/cam_292/img/ipsurvnw.jpg

Chapter 20
Video Surveillance System Design

ABSTRACT

A video surveillance system design requires making decisions that demand knowledge of basic options and the rationale for selecting from different ones available on the market. One needs to face making the following key decisions: choosing the best video surveillance companies, camera types, camera connection to video management system, video management system types, storage type, video analytics type, surveillance video display, and integrating video with other systems.

1. CHOOSING THE BEST VIDEO SURVEILLANCE COMPANIES

The right choice of installed video surveillance system enables to the company that needs video surveillance system and its employees to be safer from the theft, accidents and vandalism.

Cooperation with the best video surveillance companies assists one to design a video surveillance system based on the company's needs – from a single video camera and monitor to more complex video surveillance system.

The most important characteristics of the best video surveillance companies are (Honovich, 2011):

1. Long and rich experience.
2. Resources to handle specific and more serious issues.
3. Previous experience with similar companies.
4. Open to on-site visits to their facilities and exposure of the way they operate.

5. Complete demonstration and education about the equipment's functions.
6. List of references that can be contacted.
7. Installation of the video system in the guaranteed time frame.
8. All the prices and installation details contained in the contract.

It is crucial to make a research on several different video surveillance companies, interview them and compare their offers before the final decision is made. This procedure will enable identification and cooperation with the best video surveillance company that offers all the desired features and services at the adequate price.

Experience is one of the most important virtues that should be required from a video surveillance company. Long lasting experience is a strong indicator of how reliable and stable the searched company will be in the long term. Only several years of experience in installing video surveillance systems for various companies can be a guaranty

DOI: 10.4018/978-1-4666-4896-8.ch020

that the chosen video surveillance company will be able to balance considerations about wiring, lighting, and optics. Also it is important to know that the provider will be active in future in case that problems with the installed video surveillance system occur or upgrade of the present system is needed as company grows.

It is also important to note that the best video surveillance companies have the resources to handle specific and more serious issues. They will visit the location to make its analysis and determine exact video surveillance requirements needed for that particular setting. Based on the performed detailed research and rich experience they will recommend the appropriate equipment and features that would be the most adequate.

The best video surveillance companies will be capable of providing a high quality installation.

They will also train and educate the employees how to operate with the equipment. Finally they will provide the detailed documentation for all the installed equipment.

2. CAMERA TYPES

Cameras represent the main input into the video surveillance system and the following is relevant to them:

1. **Physical position of used cameras:** Cameras have to be placed in critical areas in order to record relevant video. The critical places for proper camera placement are entrances, exits, hallway, driveways, etc in surveiled areas where there is a high density of people or vehicles. Also, camera placement can be related to the specific objects or areas that need security such as safes, merchandise areas, cash registers, parking spots, lobbies, banks, etc. Placing cameras at critical and adequate points is a very cost-effective way to document people and vehicles entering and exiting certain facility.

2. **The camera type being used.**
   a. A camera can be fixed when it is recording only one specific view or it can be PTZ camera that is moving left and right which is called panning, moving up and down which is called tilting and closer and farther away called zooming. PTZ cameras are generally used to cover wider fields of views. Most cameras used in video surveillance are fixed because they cost five to eight times less than PTZ cameras.
   b. Color cameras are used during day time and highly lighted areas. During night time and obscure and poorly illuminated areas infrared or thermal cameras are used that produce black and white images.
   c. Cameras can be standard definition or high definition cameras that provide up to 16 MP resolutions.
   d. There are analog and IP cameras. IP cameras digitize the video inside the camera and analog cameras used as surveillance cameras' recordings are digitized on computers. Megapixel resolution is only provided by IP cameras. Video surveillance systems usually mix and match a number of different camera types.

3. CAMERA CONNECTION TO VIDEO MANAGEMENT SYSTEM

The video captured by cameras has to be transferred to the module of the video surveillance system called video management system which is recording and managing access to that video. There are two types of connectivity:

1. Video can be transmitted over the computer network IP or it can be sent as analog video. Both IP cameras and analog cameras can

be transmitted over the computer network where IP cameras can connect directly to an IP network unlike analog ones that cannot directly connect to an IP network. In the case of analog cameras an encoder has to be installed in order to transmit analog video over IP. The encoder has an input for an analog camera video feed and outputs a digital stream for transmission over an IP network.

2. Depending whether IP or analog video camera is being used, the captured video can be sent over cables or though the air. Cables is generally the cheapest and most reliable way of sending video but, wireless is an important option for transmitting video as deploying wires can be cost-prohibitive for certain applications such as parking lots, fence lines, remote buildings, etc.

4. VIDEO MANAGEMENT SYSTEM

Video management systems are responsible for accepting the video captured by cameras, storing the video and managing video distribution to various viewers. Most video surveillance systems use one of four different video management systems:

1. Digital Video Recorder DVR is a security system device that records the video from surveillance cameras on a hard disk. The frame rate can be switched from real time to time lapse in order to save disk space. Digital recorders are more flexible than earlier analog VHS tape systems and the video can be easily transmitted over a computer network. DVRs combine software, hardware and video storage. They only accept analog camera feeds and support remote viewing over the Internet.

2. HDVRs are hybrid Digital Video Recorders that support IP cameras. They have all the functionality of a Digital Video Recorder listed above plus they add support for IP and megapixel cameras.

3. NVRs are network video recorder is a computer that records video transmitted over the network from multiple digital CCTV surveillance cameras. It only supports IP cameras. To support analog cameras with an NVR, an encoder must be used.

4. IP Video Surveillance Software is a software application that does not come with any hardware or storage. The user must load and set up the PC/Server for the software which provides much greater freedom and potentially lower cost but at the same time it comes with significant more complexity and time to set up and optimize the system. IP Video Surveillance Software is the most frequent choice for very large camera counts (hundreds or more).

5. STORAGE

Storage of the captured surveillance video is very important part of the video surveillance system. It is used for later retrieval and review of the surveillance video. The storage duration is determined by the cost of storage and the security threats an organization that is using the video surveillance system faces. For example, banks have great need for longer term storage because a major threat to it is the report of fraudulent investigations which are often reported 60 or 90 days after the incident. Unlike casinos that usually use much shorter storage duration for a few weeks because they know about issues right away.

Storage permanently holds digital data, until it is purposely erased. It is a repository that retains its content without power. Storage mostly means magnetic disks, solid state disks and USB drives. The term may also refer to magnetic tapes and optical discs like CDs, DVDs, etc.

Even though storage price is always decreasing, video surveillance system demands for amount of storage are increasing. Various techniques have been developed to optimize the use of storage because of its significant cost. There are three fundamental types of storage:

1. Internal storage represents the hard drives that are built inside of a digital video recorder, network video recorder or server. It is the cheapest storage but tends to be less reliable and scalable. It is used the most frequently in video surveillance and can provide total storage of 2TB to 4TB.
2. Directly Attached storage represents hard drives located outside of the digital video recorder, network video recorder or server. It is more expensive but has greater scalability, flexibility and redundancy.
3. Storage Clusters are IP based storage places specialized in storing video from large number of cameras. They provide efficient, flexible and scalable storage.

6. VIDEO ANALYTICS

Video analytics encompasses the following tasks:

1. **Optimize Storage:** Storage optimization is realized based on the detected motion detection. If the motion or moving object is detected in the observed scene the video management system can decide to store video or if it is not present in the scene not to store video or to store video at a lower frame rate or resolution. Cameras placed in hallways, staircases, buildings when they are closed, etc. capture long periods of inactivity. Motion analytics application can reduce storage consumption by 60%-80% relative to continuous recording.

2. **Identify Threatening Events:** Video analytics used to identify threatening events is what is proposed in this chapter. Typical examples of threatening events identification are perimeter violation, abandoned objects detection, people counting and license plate recognition. The goal of these types of video analytics is to pro-actively and automatically identify security incidents and to stop them while being in progress.

7. VIEWING VIDEO

Surveillance video captured by video surveillance systems is ultimately viewed by human beings, the most commonly used for historical investigations. Some surveillance video is viewed online continuously, generally in shops in order to catch shoplifters and in public surveillance to identify criminal threats. There are four different ways for video viewing:

1. Local Viewing directly from the digital video recorder, the network video recorder or servers is ideal for monitoring small facilities on site most commonly used in retailers, banks and small businesses.
2. Remote PC Viewing through standard remote PCs to view live and recorded video using an installed application, powerful web viewing or only using a web browser.
3. Mobile Viewing allows immediate check of the captured surveillance video. It has great potential in video surveillance systems. Mobile clients exist on the market for at least 5 years, but there are its implementation challenges with PDAs/phones. The introduction of the Apple iPhone has renewed interest and optimism related to mobile viewing.
4. Video Wall Viewing is typically used in large security operation centers that have

hundreds or thousands of cameras under their jurisdiction. Video walls provide very large screens so that a group of people can simultaneously watch captured videos from numerous cameras. Video walls generally have abilities to switch between feeds and to automatically display feeds from locations where alarms have been triggered.

8. INTEGRATING VIDEO WITH OTHER SYSTEMS

Video surveillance systems are usually used only by itself without integrating it with other systems but this is an inefficient and poor manner to perform security operations. Large organizations and those with more significant security concerns prefer an approach similar to the military's common operational picture where numerous security systems display on a singular interface. There exist three ways to realize integration with video surveillance:

1. **Access Control as Hub:** Most organizations have electronic/IP access control systems that have been designed to integrate with other security systems such as intrusion detection and video surveillance.
2. Physical security information management PSIM as Hub is specialized applications whose sole purpose is to aggregate information from security systems like video surveillance and provide the most relevant information and optimal response policies.

3. **Video Management System as Hub:** Video management systems are adding in support for other security systems and security management features.

The very first element in the video surveillance system is the device that captures the images, which is the camera. The next chapter is very important chapter in the book as it discusses the concepts of analog and digital cameras, its various designs, and camera specifications. Proper camera choice as well as setting is very important issue in video surveillance system installation and design.

REFERENCES

Bradski, G., & Kaehler, A. (2009). *Learning OpenCV*. Sebastopol, CA: O'Reilly Media, Inc.

Caputo, A. C. (2010). *Digital video surveillance and security*. London: Elsevier.

Damjanovski, V. (2005). *CCTV networking and digital technology*. London: Elsevier.

Honovich, J. (2011). *Video surveillance book*. IPVideoMarket.jnfo

Kruegle, H. (2007). *CCTV surveillance analog and digital video practices and technology* (2nd ed.). London: Elsevier.

Nilsson, F. (2009). *Intelligent network video - Understanding modern video surveillance systems*. Boca Raton, FL: CRC Press Taylor & Francis Group.

Section 7
Devices and Applications

The very first element in the video surveillance system is the device that captures the images, which is the camera. "Cameras" is very important chapter in the book as it discusses the concepts of analog and digital cameras, their various designs, and camera specifications. Proper camera choice as well as setting is a very important issue in video surveillance system installation and design.

The next chapter in this section is a summary of IP surveillance systems: basic functions, the advantages of network video, customizing surveillance applications, and possible legal concerns. The most important step one can take before installing an IP surveillance system is to define goals and requirements. Once these are determined, the video system can be set up. The required goals to be determined are the following: definition of the video surveillance system needs (installation plan, area of coverage, camera positioning, illumination conditions determination, camera cabling, the recording server positioning), network camera and/or video encoder selection (image quality, lens selection, network camera selection, Power over Ethernet [PoE], video motion detection, audio, accessories selection, testing), hardware (switches, additional light sources, power supplies, additional server for video management software, hard drives), software (software package selection, licenses, image quality and frame rate requirements, IP address range calculation, hard disk usage calculation, cameras configuration, video motion detection settings, user access definition), and maintenance.

The first five sections represent the foundation and offer various intelligent algorithms that are the basics for motion detectors and their realization. There are two classes of security system alarm triggers: physical motion sensor and visual motion sensors. Both analog motion detectors and digital motion detectors belong to the group of visual motion sensors. Digital motion detector systems should differentiate between activities that are acceptable and those that breach security. When security-breaching acts occur, the system should identify the individuals and instruct security personnel what to do. Motion detectors can surveil, detect, and assess, as well as analyze information and distribute information to security personnel. Motion detector systems drastically reduce the load of footage that guards must watch for a long period of time.

Automated motion detectors are now a standard for serious medium to large security installations; they are necessary for high detection capabilities. All security systems must have an alarming device to signal the guard of irregular motion in a scene, even systems that have a tiny or huge number of cameras.

The fact that video surveillance is such an effective system especially when one thinks of its widespread use attests to its low investment cost. The last chapter contains information about design guidelines, hardware information, specific examples, and necessary parameters to be addressed while designing representative security video surveillance system applications: protection of all assets and personnel, calculation of the overall cost of the video system, surveillance target (assets and/or personnel), surveillance timing schedule, type and number of cameras needed, camera placement, field of view required, console room monitoring equipment, number and types of monitors, number of displays per monitor, number and type of recorders, digital recording technology needed, type of video switchers, type of video printer, if additional lighting is required, if intensified or thermal IR cameras are required, if sensors at doors, windows, and perimeters that are integrated with video signals are needed, digital video motion detectors placement, IP cameras, type of signal and video transmission, type of digital transmission, type of 802.11 protocol, type of compression (MPEG-4 or H.264), and the necessity of encryption or scrambling.

Chapter 21
Cameras

ABSTRACT

The very first element in the video surveillance system is the device that captures the images, which is the camera. This is a very important chapter in the book as it discusses the concepts of analog and digital cameras, its various designs, and camera specifications. Proper camera choice as well as setting is a very important issue in video surveillance system installation and design.

1. INTRODUCTION

The notion camera stems from the Latin word camera which translates to room and when we go further into the origin of this word we come to the Latin expression "camera obscura", which means "dark room." "Camera obscura" was a lightproof room, of a box shape, where a convex lens was placed at one end and a screen that reflected the image at the other end of it. It assisted artists to produce paintings in the Middle Ages.

In the nineteenth century, "camera" referred to a device for recording images on film that consisted of a lightproof box, a lens through which light entered and was focused, a shutter that controlled the duration of the lens opening, and an iris that controlled the amount of light that passed through the glass.

The first negative film image was produced in 1826 by Joseph Nicéphore Niépce and it is considered to be the birth of photography.

The lens of a video camera first receives the light reflected from a focused scene and then concentrates it for the camera's image sensor. The image sensor functions by converting the image from the lens into a time-varying electronic signal. This signal is processed by the camera's electronics, and a transmitter (two-wire unshielded twisted-pair UTP, coaxial cable, fiber optics, or wireless) sends it to a monitor.

Figure 1 illustrates a simple system: camera, lens, and monitor.

Cameras (monochrome/color, solid-state/thermal IR) scan the vertical and horizontal pixels picked up by the camera's sensor.

These pixels are converted into a signal representative of the scene's color and light information as a function of time. The scene can then be recorded or reconstructed on a remote monitor.

Video cameras collect information about a scene point-by-point until they have one frame that shows a complete scene. This process differs from human eyes, film cameras, and low light level light intensifiers, which see an entire scene all at once.

Video cameras function much like typewriters: the element moves from left to right until it reaches the right corner, then returns to the left and begins a new line. Most video cameras work this way, adding a second "carriage return" after

DOI: 10.4018/978-1-4666-4896-8.ch021

Figure 1. The simplest configuration: one video camera and one monitor

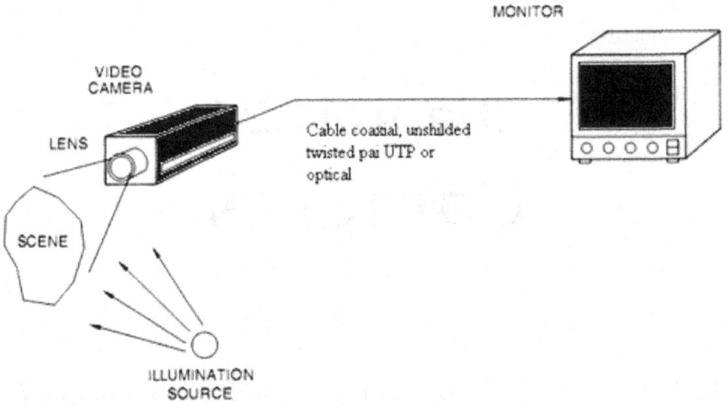

each line until the end of the page or bottom of the screen. This is how they complete one field, or half of the video image (Kruegle, 2007).

Then the scanner moves back up to the second line (the first blank line on the screen) and fills in all the remaining blank lines, completing the second field or a full video frame. This repeats for each frame. This process is called interlaced scanning. Some cameras, and also computer monitors, utilize progressive scanning, which fills in one line after another without skipping any.

Again, the camera sensor converts either an IR light image or a visual image into an image that the camera's scanner can read in a point-by-point or line-by-line fashion. It then creates a time-dependent electrical signal to represent the light intensity of the focused scene.

Color cameras require this process to be repeated three times in order to convert red, green, and blue inputs into an electrical signal.

Analog video cameras always include:

1. An image censor.
2. A synchronized electronic scanning system.
3. Timing electronics.
4. Electronics for amplifying and processing video.
5. Electronics for synchronizing and combining video signals.

The electronics for synchronizing and combining create a complete video output signal.

Scanning must be fast (at least 30 fps) to record scenes with movement.

Synchronizing signals must be adequate in order to produce stable displays and recordings.

Digital video cameras contain:

1. An image sensor.
2. Circuitry for reading horizontal and vertical pixels.
3. Digital signal processing DSP circuits.
4. Electronics for synchronizing and combining video signals (for a complete video output signal).

All solid-state, low light level and thermal cameras operate based on the following process:

1. The lens focuses an image on the censor.
2. "Linear" or "raster" scanning performs a readout of the sensor's image.
3. Electronics evaluate each pixel's light level in order to create a video picture.
4. The scene's intensity and color profile are expressed in each pixel; the resulting signal should represent the original scene.

2. THE SCANNING PROCESS

Each video frame has two fields.

Scanning processes vary globally. The National Television System NTSC Committee analog television system, used in the U.S., uses a 60Hz power line frequency and a speed of 1/30 seconds per frame (30 fps). Each frame has 525 lateral lines. In the European system, each frame has 625 lateral lines but operates on a 50Hz power line frequency and runs at 25 seconds per frame.

The output signal for tube cameras and for modern solid-state analog video cameras is the same. However, scanning methods have improved with time. Now cameras scan using the 2:1 interlace technique instead of random interlace, which decreases the flicker effect in the picture and also equalizes motion in the scene without requiring a bandwidth increase. Both 2:1 and random interlace techniques scan every other line of pixels; this is called two-field, odd-line scanning. The principle of interlace scanning is shown in Figure 2.

In the NTSC system, there are 262.5 television lines per field. 30 frames, therefore 60 fields, can be completed each second. Since there are 525 television lines per frame and 30 frames per second, the NTSC system handles 15,750 television lines per second.

The vertical blanking interval in an NTSC system utilizes 21 lines for each field – 42 lines in each frame. Since 525 lines minus 42 lines is 483, there are 483 picture lines that remain active in each frame.

Each time the camera's scanning function reaches the right side of the scene, it goes back to a point below its original starting point on the upper left corner. This period of time of the video signal is called the "horizontal blanking interval." Once the camera sensor reaches the bottom right of the image, one field is completed.

After the completion of one field, the sensor's readout pauses (the beam turns off again in a cathode ray tube CRT monitor) and goes back to the top left of the image. This is called the "vertical blanking interval." Then the camera sensor scans the lines in between the lines of the first field.

This interlacing method clarifies the image, reduces flicker, and uses the same amount of transmission bandwidth as progressive scanning does.

Upon completion of the second field, the scanning spot repeats the process, starting at the upper left corner.

In order for the individual pixels to transfer from a solid-state camera's sensor to the camera's electronics, they must be clocked out. These clocked-out individual pixels create a video signal, which then reproduces the same two interlaced fields.

In a tube camera, a scanning process like the cathode ray tube CRT is performed by a moving electron beam located in the camera's tube. The target is scanned twice starting at the top left in order to create a signal representative of the focused scene. The odd lines must be scanned first, completing one field of 262.5 lines. After the scanning of the second field, a full frame of

Figure 2. Interlace scanning

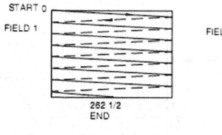
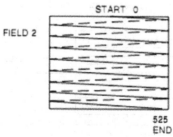

525 lines is produced. A complete frame is created every 1/30th of a second.

The signal then goes to the monitor, where the picture is reproduced inversely. The signal's voltage ranges from 0 to 1 volt peak to peak and is limited by an electrical bandwidth of 4-10 MHz. This factor depends on the resolution of the system.

Progressive scanning alternatively referred to as noninterlaced scanning is a way of displaying, storing, or transmitting images where all the lines of each frame are drawn in sequence. Figure 3 illustrates the process of progressive scanning.

The progressive scan makes that motion appears smoother and more realistic. There is an absence of visual artifacts associated with interlaced video of the same line rate, see Figure 4.

Frames have no interlace artifacts and can be captured still photos. There is no necessity in intentional blurring referred to as anti-aliasing of video in order to reduce interline twitter and eye strain. Progressive scanning offers clearer and faster results for scaling to higher resolutions than its equivalent interlaced video.

3. THE VIDEO SIGNAL

A video signal is a composite signal that consists of two elements: the light information (or scene illumination intensity) and time information (synchronizing pulses).

Standard pulses have a rise and fall time of 0.1 microseconds and have frequency components that go as high as 2.5 MHz.

When the focused image consists of high-contrast, high-speed small scenes, they are represented by approximately 4.2MHz, or a higher frequency that must be reproduced electronically for accuracy.

Extremely sharp synchronizing pulses and a wide bandwidth are necessary to produce accurate images.

To reproduce color, the sensor transmits a color signal along with a Y component (for luminance intensity), which contains a C, or "color burst" component (for chrominance).

A more basic method of color reproduction is RGB (red, blue, green), which all have waveforms like those of monochrome signals.

3.1 The Monochrome Signal

Monochrome camera signals represent the illumination absorbed by the sensor using intensity information.

All of this information is condensed into one signal, which has four components: lateral line synchronization pulses, setup (black) level, luminance (gray scale) level, and full field synchronizing pulses.

Figure 3. Progressive scanning

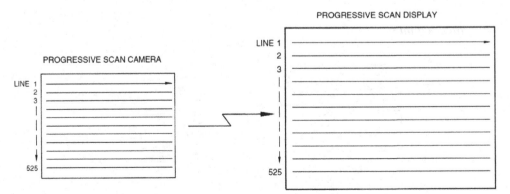

Figure 4. Interlaced video frame of a car wheel (Google, 2013)

3.2 The Color Signal

Video color signals have three parts: luminance (black and white), hue (tint and color), and saturation (color intensity). However, black and white signals include only the luminance factor. These three parts work together based on primary color information.

Red, green, and blue can be joined in multiple ways to create the colors seen in color bar test patterns. The colors' component parts are adjusted between full "on" and full "off" to create other colors, like a dimmer on a light switch.

In order to utilize these colors, a camera's color signal has to isolate the scene's illumination into RGB color components. This process is quite complex, so timing, spatial accuracy, and the frequency response of the electronics are much more important than they are for a monochrome signal.

Color video signals consist of seven crucial parts:

- Lateral line synchronizing pulses.
- Color synchronization ("color burst").
- Setup (black) level.
- Luminance (gray scale) level.
- Hue or tint.
- Saturation or vividness.
- Field synchronization pulses.

1. **Lateral Line Synchronization Pulses:** The composite video signal's first component is the lateral line synchronization pulse. It contains three parts:
   a. The front porch works to separate synchronization pulses from the previous line's picture inputs;
   b. The back porch separates synchronization pulses from the next line's picture inputs, and
   c. The horizontal line sync pulse enforces the correspondence of the monitor, receiver, or recorder to the video camera.

2. **Color Synchronization ("Color Burst"):** Each horizontal line's color information is used to synchronize the lines surrounding it. The horizontal blanking interval consists of the phases of the front porch, synchronization pulse, color burst, and back porch. During the back porch segment of the video signal, the color burst occurs, synchronizing the chrominance signal.

3. **Setup:** This black and white component shows the video signal's breadth under conditions of zero light.

4. **Luminance:** Shifts in light levels are reflected through the luminance component, which is the fourth part of a color video signal.

5. **Color Hue and Saturation:** The color image is produced by taking these two factors, along with setup and luminance, into account.

6. **Field Synchronization Pulse:** This is the component responsible for time synchronization and interlace. A composite waveform is formed by the above-listed seven components. Only chrominance and luminance are necessary for a video color signal's analog parts. These components are kept separate in order to prevent contact between chrominance and luminance. Such contact could lead to distortion within an NTSC system.

High-quality video security systems use the RGB output format. Most of the time, these three signals are encoded into one video signal representing all primary color information, including Y and C (intensity and color information).

This encoding process is done by a signal encoder. Standards for this process are controlled by the NTSC in the U.S., whereas in Europe and other countries, PAL (phase alternation line) or SECAM (sequential with memory) systems are used.

The NTSC system uses Y (luminance), or the black-and-white component, as a base for the color signal. Color tags onto the base Y signal.

It took years of experimentation to realize that an accurate version of the original color signal could only be obtained by combining RGB signals in a very specific way. This ratio is: 30% red, 59% green, and 11% blue. Saturation and hue are then added to the signal. In order to do this, two more combination possibilities of RGB signals were generated.

Within the NTSC limitations, hue and saturation are determined by the combination of I-modulating and Q-modulating levels, which consist of RGB signals in specific ratios. These ratios and relationships of the signals are expressed in degrees.

4. THE TYPES OF CAMERAS

There are a few generic types of video security cameras:

1. Analog.
2. Digital.
3. Internet.
4. Low light level LLL.
5. Thermal IR.

Monochrome, color, analog, digital, and IP cameras are used during the daytime. IP cameras are used for remote surveillance. Low light level LLL Intensified Charged Coupled Device ICCD (image intensified) cameras are used in low light and at night. Thermal IR cameras are used in times of very low light or no light.

4.1 Analog Camera

All security cameras were Complementary Metal Oxide Semiconductor CMOS and Charged Coupled Device CCD analog until 2000. Advances in circuit technology led to the development of digital signal processing (DSP), so digital cameras are now common.

CCD and CMOS image sensors tend to have wide light ranges, from 400-700 nanometers (the visible range) to 800-900 nm (the near-Infrared IR spectral region).

4.1.1 Monochrome Analog Camera

Near infrared IR light and IR light emitting diode LED illuminators affect only some monochrome cameras; these cameras do not utilize IR cutoff filters. Analog cameras are frequently overloaded when pointed at strong or bright near-IR light because of the sensitivity of their imagers. As a result, the monitor displays a band of bright light above and below the object.

When the scene includes sunlight, a car headlight, or any spots of IR radiation, an IR cutoff filter is necessary.

Most types of lighting can be picked up by monochrome cameras as long as there is enough light. Mercury vapor, metal arc, tungsten, and low- and high- pressure sodium tend to be used for monochrome cameras.

4.1.2 Single Sensor Color Analog Camera

The most common kind of analog camera used in security CCTV systems is the single color sensor analog. The three-sensor with prism analog camera is used less frequently.

The single-color sensor creates signals corresponding with red, green, and blue. It does this through its three optical filters, which create an overlay that produces all of the visible spectrum's colors.

Each filter accounts for one third of the scene's pixels, so the total number of pixels must be divided by three.

In order to create a single composite signal, the camera uses electronics and clocking signals. However, alternatives exist: a three wire RGB output signal and a two wire Y and C output signal. These systems produce a higher quality image.

A single-sensor camera reduces the camera's sensitivity by three, since the light entering the lens is split into thirds. The monitor's resolution elements are also made up of three colors, which further reduces resolution by 3. Despite this drawback, single-sensor cameras are still the most popular variety due to their availability and relatively low cost.

In order to deal with IR energy, which would just distort the monitor image since it provides no color information, color cameras are outfitted with IR filters. These blocking filters function by changing the CCD imager's spectral response to correspond with the visible color spectrum.

Light sources must fall within the range of 400nm and 790nm of energy in order for the video camera to properly rend images.

Thanks to IR blocking filters, the bandwidth that actually reaches the color sensor from IR sources must fall within this range. IR radiation from 800-1200nm prohibits the use of color cameras.

Color tube cameras and color CCD cameras used to have white-balance circuits and sensors to make up for changes in color. Modern solid-state color cameras have automatic white balance compensatory functions.

4.1.3 Color Monochrome Switchover Analog Camera

Cameras that can operate both during the day and at night are necessary for most purposes. For this reason, many cameras include an automatic conversion option from monochrome to color. A multiple-use camera is much more efficient than owning more than one camera.

The switchover from monochrome to color can be done either optically or electronically.

The optical method mechanically removes an IR filter from the camera's optical path to open up visible light and near-IR radiation for the color sensor. This switches from the daytime to nighttime mode. At the same time, the camera's three-part color signal condenses into one monochrome signal; typically, this increases the camera's sensitivity by a factor of ten.

4.1.4 Color Three Sensors Analog Camera

The physical components of a three-sensor color camera are a prism and sensors. A prism inserted between the lens and solid-state sensors splits beams into R, G, and B components.

Each of the three sensors uses its own video and timing electronics to recreate the scene via three separate but proportional video signals.

Compared to a single-sensor camera, the three-sensor camera's display is three times more detailed and accurate since there are three times as many pixels.

Advanced high-resolution security systems can utilize these cameras with the help of analog S-VHS, Hi-8 VCRs, and DVRs and DVDs.

These recorders use either Y (luminance) and C (chrominance) signals or RGB signals. YC and RGB are combined to create a composite output signal.

Although a three-sensor camera is much more expensive, it leads to a superior picture.

4.2 Digital Cameras

Video security was one of the last fields to move to the digital realm. Currently, all components of security systems are being converted to their digital versions. Digital signal processing DSP is the basic technology behind this drive. DSP cameras were the first venture into the digital world, followed by PC-powered switching devices, digital ID cameras, and Digital Video Recorders DVRs.

DSP cameras are becoming cheaper and cheaper, and their features are becoming more numerous and advanced. DVRs, as opposed to video cassette recorder VCRs, are more reliable, have a better picture quality, and are easier to search for records.

Digital color video is much more economical, practical, and effective: 70-80% of video camera sales are color cameras.

The average resolution of digital video cameras used in security systems is 512x576 active pixels, while high-resolution cameras are usually 752x582 active pixels. High-resolution digital cameras have a bandwidth of 6-7MHz and are the equivalent of SVHS analog video.

VHS quality is adequate for many security needs, so VHS format is still the standard. Following NTSC policies, the CIF (common intermediate format) is 352x240 pixels for the Y signal and 176x144 for U and V (chrominance signals). The CIF resolution format ensures sufficient image quality while decreasing the data load being transmitted.

Although CCD cameras are currently the most popular in digital systems, CMOS technologies tend to be cheaper, smaller, and more energy efficient and are catching up to CCD.

Some desire to continue using analog components to upgrade to a digital system, but this is unadvisable. One should invest in new digital components, especially if the resulting video signal will be sent over digital networks. This is because analog signals require a large amount of bandwidth, whereas digital signals can be easily transmitted in digital networks. Conversion of signals from analog to digital is possible but calls for specific converters. It makes more sense to purchase a complete digital camera for immediate signal transmission.

4.2.1 Digital Signal Processing

The advent of DSP cameras and digital technology required the video security industry to rethink its basic operations.

When talking about CCTV cameras, "digital" does not necessarily mean that the output signal is digital, just that the camera has some form of digital enhancers. Digitally enhanced cameras can improve:

1. Image quality.
2. Back-light.
3. Iris control.
4. Shutter speed and quality.
5. Electronic zoom.
6. Sensitivity to lighting variations and other issues.

The majority of surveillance cameras still use analog output signals. Digital signals can only be transmitted so far (a few hundred feet), whereas analog signals have a further reach.

Network cameras and equipment allow for the use of long-distance transmission via Local Area Network LAN, Wide Area Network WAN or Wireless Local Area Network WLAN, wireless WiFi, intranets, and the Internet. Digital Signal Processor DSP cameras tend use analog outputs via the aforementioned channels.

The signal-to-noise ratio (SNR) is better in DSP cameras than in analog cameras, so manufacturers can use AGC (automatic gain control) to improve amplification and create a better quality image despite bad lighting conditions.

Non-DSP cameras have an average SNR of 46-48dB. DSP cameras have an average SNR of 50-54dB. This is significant considering that a change of 3dB improves the signal strength by 50%.

New technology has improved camera performance, bringing it closer to the capacities of the human eye. This advancement was made in DSP signal processing, which now utilizes circuitry increasing image sensors' range to 64 times that of average CCD cameras.

Cameras with this DSP signal processing technology sees dark and bright light levels at the same time and digitally processes the images independently of one another. To achieve this, the dark parts of the scene are subject to a long exposure whereas the bright portions only require a short exposure. DSP then combines these signals into one image that includes the highest quality parts of each exposure. This image is condensed into an analog signal and sent to a recorder or monitor.

Analog signals can be altered much more easily than digital signals. Although digital signals are immune to more disturbances than analog, the signal disappears upon an overload of disturbances. This disappearance is called the "cliff effect," at which point the picture breaks up or goes blank.

4.2.2 Smart Cameras

Digital advances have introduced automated video security AVS. Whereas analog video systems required a security officer to make judgments about the scene on the monitor, cameras within AVS systems make decisions without human input. These cameras equipped with intelligence are called "smart cameras."

For example, in the past, a person walking in a restricted area would draw the attention of the guard on duty, who would sound an alarm to trigger an investigation of the activity. Now, smart cameras can distinguish between objects and movement using Video Moving Detection VMD algorithms. This way security personnel

can perform other tasks, trusting that the smart camera will alert her or him to unusual activity.

Smart cameras can also be used to complete basic tasks, like tallying the number of people who walked into a store in a certain period of time, or pinpointing the most popular sections of the store. This type of task is performed by the camera's DSP, which converts incoming video into a format used to analyze a scene and make decisions. The DSP's output is transmitted to separate devices for decision-making.

Image analysis must be performed within individual cameras if they are operating within a multiple-camera automated video security surveillance system. This is necessary in order to pinpoint elements of failure within the system. On-point analysis also increases the scalability of the AVS system because cameras can be added without affecting the central structure. Also, the camera has access to the unaltered video and can optimize it for the analysis algorithm.

Smart cameras are also beneficial in that they can decide what video should be transmitted from the camera to the central monitor or recorder and how to compress the video. This allows the automated video security system to work within its bandwidth limitations, and as a result, signals tend to be clear and uninterrupted.

DSP increases the intelligence of cameras. Now they can not only record but also analyze the event, eliminating the need for humans to constantly be monitoring footage. Camera-level processing allows for more accurate and high quality image capturing. Movement in a scene can be evaluated as inconsequential (a dog, a piece of paper blowing in the wind) or of importance (a person moving in the wrong direction).

Thanks to smart cameras, a single security officer can now monitor a much larger number of cameras than she or he used to be able to using an analog system, leading to a reduction in employee expenditures. Automated video security can also save money thanks to its ability to judge which scenes require a lower resolution, which saves bandwidth and storage space.

It is possible to manipulate compressed video, which leads to legal complications that must be considered when using automated video security footage for prosecution purposes. To avoid these complications, cameras should record uncompressed JPEG images at a high frame right in order to get the most accurate representation possible, eliminating the possibility of manipulation of compressed video. However, it would require human judgment to decide when to start recording the event in JPEG, at which point the event would have likely already taken place. Responsiveness of smart cameras could be improved by introducing intelligence that would allow them to make this decision. Then resolution and frame rate would increase automatically. Automatic zoom on a target would also be an improvement within the automated video security system.

4.3 Internet Camera

Since cameras must be identified within a CCTV network, each camera receives its own address and password. Any port connected to the Internet has the capability to access the camera. To view the camera's scene, a user must enter the camera's unique Internet address, camera ID, and password. The user, or security personnel, can command the camera to zoom, pan, and tilt from a remote location via an Internet connection.

Digital (IP) addresses allow IP cameras to be accessed both locally and remotely. Not only can the security personnel input commands for the camera, but also the camera sends the image back to the security personnel, making a two-way connection.

The industry of video security is making the switch to automated video security technology. Its benefits are numerous, including:

1. Can be accessed and controlled (pan, tilt, and zoom) from anywhere with an Internet connection.
2. Increased effectiveness through ease of access.
3. Reliable and economic.

4.3.1 Compression

Engineers have long recognized the necessity of compression color video signals. This was a priority even before the invention of digital video transmission. Original color systems were meant to be usable with monochrome video signals, which were already being used, so the color signals had to conform to the same bandwidth as the monochrome ones. Many sacrifices in color signal transmission were made in this process; they can only be overcome through digital video transmission.

Ideally, the three full primary red, green, and blue (RGB) channels would be sent in high resolution with their own separate color information and luminance. However, analog matrix coding compresses the color video signal even before it can be converted to digital and digitally compressed once more. High-resolution and high-quality computer digital video signals are not able to be sent via real-time standard video transmission systems. It would be like trying to transmit superior quality stereo signals via a telephone; it is impossible no matter what coding one uses.

Video disturbances in an analog system include graininess, smearing, and problems with contrast and brightness. These problems manifest themselves as tint/hue changes, breakup, and picture rolling.

While properly designed digital systems avoid the aforementioned problems, they do bring to the table another set of issues: jumpy motion, jagged edges, compression blurriness, aliasing, and if the bit or compression rate is low, general poor quality.

As of this writing, there is no standard way to compare video systems across the board. Video signal must be compressed within the camera and decompressed at the monitoring server. This allows for transmission of the video's wide bandwidth signal over a narrow communication channel.

Video compression methods get rid of extra signal and picture details intra-frame (in individual frames) and inter-frame (between frames). Some of these methods or algorithms – M-JPEG, MPEG-4, and H.264- were developed over time by the Joint Motion Picture Engineers Group, and they operate using frame-by-frame compression.

JPEG 2000 is another option; it was developed to succeed the original JPEG format from the late 1980s that was used for still frame video and photography. JPEG-2000 is a wavelet compression method. It was designed for static imaging applications such as e-commerce, image databases, digital photography, and cell phones, not live video transmission.

Video compression can be divided into types:

1. Lossy.
2. Lossless.

Lossy compression results in a final picture that is not exactly the same as the scene scanned by the camera sensor. High rates of compression generally lead to a lossy result. The more compression, the less resemblance to the original. This type of compression can range from 10 to 1 – 400 to 1 in reducing necessary bandwidth.

Compression can be described as a system that decreases the amount of redundancy in the data's language depicting the screen's pixels. It decreases each frame's size, whereas decompression converts the signal back into a form similar to the original signal.

The compression algorithm's power and quality determine the congruence of the compressed signal to the original.

Digital video engineers can employ two basic types of compression technique: inter- and intra-frame. Inter-frame, which happens between frames, relies on the fact that data does not usually change much from one frame to the next in most scenes. This technique only compresses the portions that are different from frame to frame.

4.4 Low Light Level Intensified Charged Coupled Device ICCD

Intensified Charged Coupled Device CCD, or ICCD cameras are the most sensitive of all the Low Light Level LLL cameras. The ICCD camera has largely replaced previous tube camera technology like the silicon intensified target SIT and the intensified silicon intensified target ISIT.

Monochrome CCD and CMOS cameras are similar to low light level cameras, but low light level cameras have been updated with light intensification that increases the power of the light in the scene. This way the camera can utilize light levels that are naturally much lower.

The ICCD is the most sensitive solid-state camera available and is generally used for capturing scenes that have extremely low light levels or are lit by the moon and stars. The ICCD and other low light level cameras join image intensifiers to solid-state sensors/imaging tubes in order to see from hundreds to thousands of feet away from the camera in low light conditions.

4.5 Thermal Infrared Camera

Thermal IR systems differ from low light level night vision systems in that they react only to heat emitted from objects. Low light level cameras react to all types of lighting and reflected light, even near-IR light.

The latest trend in IR security technology is room temperature functionality. The camera can operate at room temperate, reducing costs and setup requirements.

5. TYPES OF SENSORS

Bell Telephone Laboratories invented solid-state CCD sensors and their components in 1969. They tend to be durable, small, and energy efficient. General Electric invited the solid-state CID camera soon afterwards in the 1970s. This camera, using a solid-state sensor, can use any random sequence to scan an image; it is not confined to row and column scanning. This has not been a popularly used technology in the past but lately digital cameras have been utilizing it.

Visible light monochrome and color solid-state cameras are the most commonly used security installation cameras. Before the advent of solid-state cameras, video cameras' sensors were built with vacuum tube technology. Vacuum technology is still used today in low light level, silicon intensified target SIT, and intensified silicon intensified target ISIT cameras.

5.1 Basic Types

Before solid-state sensor cameras, tube technology was used for sensors while combined circuits and solid-state transistors did processing of signals. These predominantly monochrome tube cameras converted the scene's image into an electrical signal using a scanning electron beam.

This tube was made of a scanning electron beam kit, a target that was sensitive to light, and a clear window. To scan the area, the electron beam used electromagnetic coils that were situated outside of the tube. These coils refracted the electron beam vertically and horizontally. The electron beam was capable of extracting new images from the tube very quickly; the standard was each 1/30th of a second. These tube cameras came in ½ inch, 2/3 inch, and 1-inch sizes.

Since tube cameras were sensitive to light, they would quickly experience image burn-in, which decreased their lifespan to merely a few years.

Lenses work to take in a scene and focus it onto a surface in the camera after it passes through the sensor's window. The target area's back surface gets scanned by the electron beam and produces a signal that represents the scene's image. To continue the process, electronics amplify the electrical signal by one volt and then join it with synchronizing pulses to create a composite video signal. This composite signal represents three environmental factors: the light level and the vertical and horizontal pulses for synchronization. These tube monochrome cameras had a very high resolution because the camera treated the scene as one continuous, consistent surface. For example, a 2/3-inch small electron beam camera would be able to produce an image with a resolution of 500 to 600 TV lines.

Technology advanced to develop energy sensitivity (both visible and near-IR), which was incorporated into monochrome silicon and Newvicon cameras (the latter trademarked by Panasonic). These cameras had "night vision" since their silicon diodes were sensitive to red light and could be used in the dark provided an IR source was at the scene.

The silicon camera used to be the most sensitive tube camera, but it was also impervious to damage from strong light.

1. **Solid State–Visible:** Tube cameras were replaced by CCD sensors, which decreased cost, energy consumption, and size; overall, CCD sensors proved more reliable than tube cameras.

There are many differences between the operation of CCD and CMOS cameras and their predecessors. First of all, the modern cameras do not have an electron beam. Their solid-state sensors incorporate hundreds of pixels both horizontally and vertically, or close to several hundred thousand pixels in general. Pixels transform energy from light into an electrical charge and then to an electrical signal. They are the smallest sensory element found on the sensor. Pixels are arranged like a checkerboard; they have a predetermined number of columns and rows. The number of pixels decides the camera's resolution.

The two basic types of solid-state image sensors are CTD (charge transfer device) and CMOS. CCD and CMOS are the most frequently purchased types, since they have a huge range, proper sensitivity, anti-bloom and anti-smear abilities, low noise, and a standard 30 fps video rate.

a. **Charged Coupled Device CCD:** The charge in a CCD is transmitted through MOS capacitors from one storage device to another. The device arranges pixels into lines, then stacks them atop one another to produce an area array detector. The electron charge packets generated by pixels are created when a camera lens focuses illumination from the scene onto its corresponding pixel. The strength of each packet corresponds with the actual light levels at the scene. So, each pixel has a corresponding charge packet, and every line of pixels is a line of video information. If radiation turns into a focused image emanating from the optical lens system, then that array of pixels' charge packets is an accurate representation of the image. The "charge coupling" process consists of electrical charges being transferred all at once from CCD pixels to nearby storage devices using either clocking voltages or external synchronization. CCD sensors use synchronized pulses to emit the video signal line by line at a selected interval. The signal is thus "pushed" out of the silicon sensor.

Each pixel's charge depends on the scene's light levels, and it only represents one point in the scene itself. The CCD's scanning equivalent is performed by timed voltage that is applied to the sensor. This voltage forces the charge packets in each pixel to move out of their pixels to eventually be processed and transmitted. The image sensor only has 1/30th of a second in the NTSC system to produce a field of video information all at once. To do this, the sensor uses storage registers and horizontal and vertical clocking signals.

The benefits of a CCD include low energy consumption and low voltage operation. The sensors themselves can withstand bright light but the images can be saturated or include blooming in such conditions.

The most recent CCD devices have load-reduction functions such as anti-blooming geometry and electronic shuttering (for controlling exposure).

1/3-inch CCD sensors typically have the following dimensions: 768x494 for color cameras and 771x492 for monochrome cameras. While monochrome cameras have 570 TV lines, color cameras have 480.

Interline Transfer: Manufacturers use varying CCD sensor pixel architecture. These include ILT, or inter-line transfer, and FT, frame transfer. Overall pixel organization consists of photo sensors aligned with inter-linearly arranged vertical shift registers.

Variations in light level produce electronic emissions thanks to photo-sensor sites. Then these electronic emissions travel through vertical and then horizontal shift registers until they get to the sensor output amplifier. Camera electronics then process and augment the signal. The information must then be extracted out of the sensor. Eventually the inter-line transfer device is cleared by the clocking function, which reads all 525 lines to create a video frame. Eventually a constant video signal is compiled from repetition of this sequence.

Frame Transfer: The Frame Transfer CCD's 525 lines are stored for a short amount of time in a non-illuminated silicon buffer array after they are switched out of the light-sensitive array. The Frame Transfer CCD setup consists of a photo-plane and a companion memory component. After the photo-plane is first exposed to light, a charge is produced and transmitted to the companion memory component. Then the charge is read methodically, one line at a time, for a period of time that is the same as the frame time. During this process, the photo-plane is being prepared for the next image by exposure. While storage memory must account for all pixels in an image, having all the pixels exposed at once is a huge advantage. CMOS technology, conversely, keeps one line under exposure until its reading time comes. Then the line is switched to the output register. Because of this, each line's exposure time is different and pixels cannot be exposed all at once. When a scene contains motion, CCD is the most effective technology because its reading is methodical.

Frame Transfer CCD imagers have pixels that are organized into an X-Y matrix (rows and columns). Each of these pixels, or photo sites, contains two light elements: a light-sensitive photodiode alongside a charge site that lacks light. First the photodiode works to convert the light's photons into an electrical change, or electrons. The number of photoelectrons, or the intensity of the light, is the same as the number of electrons. The sensor takes in all of the light simultaneously and then transfers it to the adjacent storage spot, where every row is converted to a horizontal transfer register. Then the CCD reads out each row's charge packets chronologically, at which point a charge-to-voltage converter and amplifier sense the charge packets.

b. **Complementary Metal Oxide Semiconductor CMOS:** CMOS technology has challenged the two-decades long dominance of CCD sensors. NASA has researched CMOS, leading to the possibility of its commercial usage. CMOS used to be applicable only in low-resolution situations but now their pixels are plentiful enough to be useful in high-stakes security surveillance. Whereas CCD sensors are highly resolute and highly sensitive, CMOS is

more appropriate in most mainstream applications. Usually, a single CMOS chip contains the image sensor, timing and control mechanisms, and circuitry for post-processing, which led to it being called a "camera-on-a-chip."

While CCD and CMOS both share high picture quality, the CMOS sensor is less sensitive. This is because CMOS signals are read directly instead of line-by-line. CMOS sensors are advantageous because everything is included on the chip: analog to digital converters, timing circuits, clocks, and synchronization circuits. They are low-cost because they are produced using the same standards as regular computer chips – standard silicon processes. CMOS sensors are 80-90% more power efficient than CCDs. Whereas CCD sensors store digital signals, CMOS sensors transmit them immediately and do not require a DSP. Technology related to low light levels and the CMOS sensor has improved. CCD cameras usually can be used in lower light than CMOS.

Since CMOS sensors are manufactured at a lower cost and are more easily integrated into various circuitries, they are cheaper than CCD sensors. Also, they are an improvement on CCDs light sensitivity, as they are able to handle light overload and display much less blooming. For example, when pointed at a ceiling lamp, a CCD sensor takes in the image of a white blob, covering up the ceiling and fixture behind the lamp. CMOS cameras are able to pick up the fixture and the ceiling.

c. **Active Pixel Sensor APS:** Since its invention by California's NASA Jet Propulsion Laboratory, CMOS Active Pixel Sensor APS technology has drastically improved. Active Pixel Sensor itself was invited in the 1990s by Stanford University engineers. APS includes DPS (a digital pixel system) to create better quality images, and also includes an amplifier and an ADC (analog to digital converter) in each pixel. The pixels' analog to digital converter translate light signals into digital signals at the moment when light is captured. Since each pixel is equipped with its own analog to digital converter, each can be considered its own camera. So one can consider each sensor a collection of thousands of cameras whose combination leads to high-quality video.

However, analog to digital converter technology necessitates decreased sensitivity to light and noise. It also creates fixed patterned noise.

CMOS Active Pixel Sensor APS' advantages are that when areas of the scene are lit by a street light or automobile light, they are not saturated, so they do not bloom or smear. Its immunity to smearing makes it a useful technology for night-time highway surveillance and license plate identification. Local micro lenses for the increasing of sensitivity on the sensor is a common solution and is cheaply done. These micro lenses send light to the most sensitive parts of the pixel in order to increase responsiveness by two or three times. The pixel's saturation, or fill factor, is a ratio: illuminated part of the silicon area: total silicon area of the pixel.

d. **Active Column Sensor ACS:** Since the Active Pixel Sensor CMOS sensor is not ideal for sensitivity and noise, engineers have created Active Column Sensor CMOS sensors. Active Column Sensor ACS' contribution to the usefulness of CMOS for security purposes is that it makes gain uniform. That is, at each pixel, the Active Column Sensor CMOS imager uses a gain amplifier to make the pixels' gain constant. While Active Pixel Sensor APS technology has a 30% fill factor, Active Column

Sensor ACS works at a 70% fill factor. Since both Active Pixel Sensor and Active Column Sensor work at very high speeds, fast motion generates no smear. And since they have great anti-blooming mechanisms, they are suitable for use in both high- and low-light scenes. The video quality standard remains high, as well.

Thanks to Active Column Sensor, CMOS is now at the same quality level as CCD sensor technology. Both are suitable for Internet broadcasting, which requires great image quality and low cost to fit in with VGA (video graphics array) and common intermediate format resolutions.

Before Active Column Sensor ACS imaging, CMOS utilized Active Pixel Sensor technology, which required the placing of an amplifier in each pixel. Unfortunately, this technique reduces the percentage of the pixels that are filled, and thus the range and sensitivity of the sensor itself.

Unity gain amplifiers are the tool used by the Active Column Sensor imager to unify individual pixels, thus increasing fill factor and range.

The future of CMOS sensors means decreased limitations in terms of resolution, sensitivity, frame speed, and noise, especially compared to CCD sensors. While most CCD sensors operate at a signal-to-noise ratio up to 58 dB, CMOS arrays have caught up to this standard, with some even operating at a 66 dB sensitivity. Their resolution can be from 1024x1034 to 4096x4096.

2. Intensified Charged Coupled Device ICCD, Silicon Intensified Target SIT, Intensified Silicon Intensified Target ISIT – Visible/Near Infrared.

Only high-quality CCD cameras are capable of creating usable videos at dawn and dusk. Intensified Charged Coupled Device ICCD cameras are suitable for working under ¼ moonlight, while the Intensified Silicon Intensified Target ISIT camera can utilize merely starlight to illuminate a scene. These two low light level cameras are 100-1000 more sensitive than high-quality monochrome CCD and CMOS cameras.

Low light level cameras are light intensifiers as compared to CCD and CMOS, which only absorb light. ICCD cameras employ either micro-channel plate intensifiers or light intensifying tubes in order to amplify existing light at a predefined rate up to 50,000. The result is an extremely accurate image in a camera that is very small, power efficient, and lacks the blur of the SIT camera. This camera system can be used from either full sunlight to quarter moonlight.

ICCD cameras have automatic light level manipulation mechanisms that operate on a range of 100 million to 1. They also come with sensor degradation and overload protection. However, ISIT cameras operate on a range of 4 billion to 1, thus providing the best low-light scene recording capabilities. Although they are large, they are good solutions for critical low light level security situations. Equipped with an SIT tube and extra stage for light amplification, the ISIT camera is the most expensive and best-suited low light level camera on the market.

3. **Thermal Infrared:** Near IR or short-wave IR generally covers from 700 to 3000nm (075–3microns (m)), mid-wave IR from 3 to 5 microns, and long-wave IR from 8 to 14microns. This is an infrared spectrum.

Short-wave IR cameras are generally used when security situations need to use low light level radiation from moonlight, sky glow, or artificial sources such as IR LEDs and IR lamps. These systems utilize natural reflection of light off of targets.

Mid-wave IR cameras use thermal emissions, or energy from warm – hot sources. Some examples are lamps, fires, gun barrels, explosives, and extremely hot objects.

Long-wave IR cameras utilize radiation from objects that emit energy at room temperature. These can include humans, animals, buildings, ships and aircraft, and vehicles. Usually these objects must be hotter than their environments. When the previous cameras cannot detect differences, the IR thermal camera is the only solution. This is thanks to their capability of detecting in fog, smoke, and total darkness. This technology is based temperature contrast between objects and their backgrounds; images created with an IR thermal camera often have better contrast than ICCD cameras. The temperature difference between the object and its background does not have to be high to be detected by a thermal sensor.

While thermal IR cameras may look like video cameras, their lenses differ drastically in that they are made of germanium or other infrared transmitting materials. They are ten to one hundred times more expensive than other video cameras, but thermal IR cameras are easy to find and install. They should not be used for intricate detail detection because they have fewer pixels than other cameras. However, they often come with intelligence that can identify objects and activities in a scene. Also, IR cameras can employ electronic smoothing to increase the quality of the image.

In thermal IR systems, different colors represent different temperatures. These are called pseudo colors and can be very useful. While average systems have a resolution of 320x256, expensive high-resolution systems like those used in the military operate at a resolution of 640x512.

When viewed in the long-wave IR spectrum, the human body glows similarly to a 100-watt bulb. Most earthly objects glow at mid- and long-wave spectrum, since they are usually between 3 and 12m into the spectrum. When the human body is at 98 degrees Fahrenheit, its wavelength is 9m.

Infrared detectors can be either photovoltaic or thermal. Photovoltaic detectors respond to the number of photons on the detector itself by generating a proportional current.

Thermal detectors respond to change in a temperature-dependent factor in the scene. For example, as the temperature of light increases, the pixels change either in capacitance or resistance, which changes the detector's electrical circuit.

Detectors can also be a part of non-cooled thermal IR cameras. These detectors are either pyroelectric or bolometric.

4. **Sensor Fusion–Visible/IR:** An image from two different detectors that utilize different wavelengths can be shown on the same display, which is known as "multi-spectral imaging." This is becoming more popular in the security field because the more varied information about the scene, the better.

Multi-spectral imaging can address the issue of energy-level reversal, which often occurs in the 3-5 micron region. Normal single detector systems would overlook this energy reversal, making detection more difficult. However multi-spectral imaging notices and isolates this reversal.

Fusing visible and IR light can greatly improve visibility in adverse conditions. A technique combining light from an image-intensified camera and a thermal IR camera is one way to see in foggy, dusty, and smoky conditions, as does the combination of near- and far- IR cameras. Using both types of detection means that the image will be intensified and detected thanks to IR's contrast capabilities.

5.2 Camera Features

Analog cameras can only compensate for poor conditions using AGC and WB (automatic gain control and white light balance). However, DSP-equipped digital cameras come with many automatic compensation functions.

5.2.1 Video Motion Detection

Intrusion can be detected using two devices: pyroelectric infrared PIR and video motion detection VMD.

Digital video motion detection converts analog signals to digital signals using a specific device. Then, movement in the image recorded triggers a response from the digital signal processing DSP circuit. This movement must be recognized as corresponding to a preset controlled by the operator. The difference between detection and pyroelectric infrared and video motion detection is that pyroelectric infrared works with specific parts of a camera image whereas video motion detection senses an overall change in the camera scene.

Video motion detection modules can now be integrated into other video systems as a small piece or, if the module is sophisticated, connected between the camera and the monitor. Electronic interference and temperature change can trigger false alarms in pyroelectric infrared systems whereas digital video motion detection is more foolproof.

Previously, video motion detection had many issues related to false alarms, including those related to shadows, scene lighting, transmission noise, and more. However, the addition of CCD cameras and DSP circuitry makes for a reliable overall system. A large part of this is thanks to localized pixel analysis.

Recently, digital video motion detection has been improved through the addition of automatic algorithms to eliminate extremely fast and slow movements, such as those of clouds, small animals, debris, and birds that are not of interest. Now most video motion detection systems only respond to actual intruders, not to false alarms. Computers are not required to control a digital video motion detection system since they usually come with interfaces to take care of remote reporting and programming. Most users can easily navigate this interface provided they are comfortable with menu screens and computer mice. Video motion detection are usually modular units or plug-in boards that can be easily put in to extant camera systems.

5.2.2 Electronic Zooming

Zoom lens optics used to be the sole zoom option before the advent of DSP electronics. Electronic zoom was introduced in CCD and CMOS camcorders and still cameras and then ventured into surveillance cameras. It electronically magnifies the image by choosing one part of the sensor area and displaying just that part on the monitor screen. Depending on the sensor's resolution, electronic zoom can work from a ratio of 5:1 to 20:1. It is also possible to utilize panning and tilting at the same time as zooming. Physically, the camera and lens remain motionless while electronics do the panning and tilting.

5.2.3 Electronic Shuttering

Before shooting, consider the rule of thumb that the more lighting available, the less sensitivity required by the camera. DSP permits the electronic shutter to adapt the camera to the scene's existent illumination. DSP changes the sensor's sensitivity based on the light level. This technology, called electronic sensitivity control, is sensitive enough to detect differences in indoor situations like lobbies, hallways with windows, storage areas, and place where doors are frequently opened. In situations with large variation in light, like outdoor applications, automatic iris lenses should be used instead. Electronic sensitivity control can be used with manual iris lenses.

5.2.4 White Balance

When a camera is first turned on, it should be calibrated to a default white background, which requires an automatic white balance feature. Then the camera can adjust itself to the actual illumination at the scene. The white-balance circuits are constantly monitored and used to make compensations for changes in the scene's color spectrum. The light's color temperature is what color cameras respond to. This measurement is defined by a CRI or coloring rendering index. When different light sources have varying coloring rendering index, the exact color of an object cannot be replicated. This disparity is described by the term "color rendering," which also implies how well the camera can reproduce the color without errors.

Light sources consist of all of the spectrum's colors, and the light quality's white component is determined by color temperature. Lamps differ in ranges of white light, so cameras must compensate for these differences. This act is performed by the WB, or white balance, circuits.

Modern cameras come equipped with white balance electronics to switch between color temperatures that fall within the usable range of 2800 to 7600 K.

5.2.5 Video Bright Light Compression

DSP cameras now have back light compensation, or BLC. It can view both bright and dark areas of the scene at the same time, which improves the camera's dynamic range by over thirty times that of regular cameras. When light conditions highly contrast or change quickly, back light compensation is a very useful function. Cameras use back light compensation by employing two different rates by which digitize the signal. Faster-speed digitization captures bright areas whereas slow speed captures dark areas. Then they are combined into one signal before output. Before the advent of back light compensation, these types of scenarios called for high-end cameras that had a digital backlight masking function.

Back light compensation functionality can be used at entrances, exists, ATMs, and dark parking facilities in which there is high light contrast. More examples include casinos, loading docks, and jewelry counters. Thanks to back light compensation, quality surveillance can be performed in extreme conditions both indoors and outdoors without much sacrifice of image integrity.

5.2.6 Geometric Accuracy

Solid-state image sensors offer much more accurate pixel placement than their tube camera predecessors. CCD, CMOS, and thermal IR sensors are manufactured with pixel sites in place and can physically never move.

5.3 Camera Resolution/Sensitivity

Resolution and sensitivity are the two most important categories when classifying video cameras.

5.3.1 Resolution

Resolution is a measure of a picture's clarity and definition. Its unit of measure is TV lines–the more lines, the better the resolution and thus the better the picture. The number of pixels in the CCD chip directly determines resolution. Some data sheets have two types of resolution: horizontal and vertical.

Horizontal resolution is the number of lines is also related to vertical lines and is bandwidth dependent.

Vertical resolution is the same as the number of horizontal lines. It is limited by NTSC and CCIR standards, which determine that there must be either 525 or 625 lines of resolution, respectively.

5.3.2 Vertical Resolution

Analog scanning utilizes 504/525 scanning lines for its vertical resolution. Each line is then divided into 483 pieces. The monitor maintains a static width, and so do its scanning lines, so detail that falls between these scanning lines is generally lost. It is calculated that about 30% of any scene's information is lost. So to determine how much of the scene is actually visible, one can calculate that the 525-line NTSC TV system has 483 segments, multiplied by .07 gives you 340 actual vertical lines.

In a CCTV system, 350 vertical lines is the best possible resolution. And in a 625-line system, 408 TV lines is ideal.

In a digital system, vertical resolution is simply the number of vertical pixels on the sensor. But if the display method is analog, such as a cathode ray tube, then the resolution is still limited to the analog standards (350 or 408):

5.3.3 Horizontal Resolution

NTSC standards require 525 lines in the video frame, with the image's lines numbering 483 and 21 retrace lines that compose two vertical blanking intervals. The standard TV industry viewing format is 4:3 (width to height), whereas horizontal resolution is measured in TV lines per picture height. So the horizontal resolution of analog monitors' tubes solely depends on the speed of video signal changes. These changes occur as the signal draws its image on horizontal lines. When only one resolution is mentioned on a data sheet, it must be the horizontal resolution. It can be measured in several ways.

A video resolution chart can be used, which has vertical and horizontal lines representing the scene. The resolution itself is the point at which lines become blurred and cannot be separated. This measurement technique cannot be entirely accurate since it relies on human judgment and perception. The monitor's resolution must exceed that of the camera.

Horizontal and vertical wedge values refer to the smallest visible black and white transition margins in the wedge area. Analog security defines TV lines as the resolution constraints.

It is more accurate to measure horizontal resolution using the signal's bandwidth; this can be done using an oscilloscope. After obtaining the bandwidth measurement, multiply it by 80 TV lines or MHz and you will have the final resolution of the camera. Again, horizontal resolution is the maximum speed or bandwidth of the video signal and electronics. Vertical resolution is simply the number of pixels and lines chosen, so it is always constant at 525, at least under the NTSC standard. However, horizontal resolution is variable and dependent on the electronics of the camera, transmission system, and monitor itself.

Standard 6 MHz bandwidth cameras have a bandwidth of more than 450 TV lines, so the system's horizontal resolution has to be limited at around 80 lines or MHz.

However, solid-state systems measure resolution using pixels. If you only have the number of pixels and need to translate it into analog resolution, multiply the pixels by .75. Still photography cameras measure resolution using line pairs and cycles per millimeter.

These specific measures are confusing, but useful for noticing differences in varying technologies.

CCTV security systems use TV line resolution notation. Here are the equivalent measures for other technologies:

- One cycle equals one line pair.
- One line pair equals two TV lines.
- One TV line equals 1.25 pixels.

For more reference, a cycle is the same as a single black-and-white transition, which is the least amount of information needed to complete the most elementary parts of the image. Solid-state CCTV cameras take into account the total amount of pixels that are reproduced in an area. 380,000 pixels per 525-line image is an average CCTV measure.

Modulation Transfer Function, or MTF, is another parameter used for measuring system performance. It can predict overall performance when taking smaller components such as the transmission method, lens, camera, monitor, and recorder into account.

Modulation Transfer Function can define the performance of either one single component or all of them together.

Decent monochrome security cameras should have a resolution of about 550-600 TV lines, while decent color cameras should have 450-480 TV lines. However, manufacturers' data sheets often only state pixels, not TV line resolution. First you must convert pixels into TV lines before comparison. The very first monochrome solid-state sensor cameras had a 200-TV line maximum horizontal resolution; their pixel resolution was 288x394. Modern sensors have 400-600 TV line resolutions, or 510x492 pixels for medium resolution cameras and 739x484 for high resolution.

Increasing pixel density is the best way to improve resolution in solid-state sensors. The manufacturing of large-scale integrated VLSI components for computers has brought about the advances in pixel density. VLSI encompasses all image sensors.

5.3.4 Static and Dynamic Resolution

The preceding section dealt only with static resolution, or that of a stationary scene. Moving scenes call for a new type of resolution: dynamic. Cameras can read motion by either scanning or targeting the motion, and within these conditions intelligence depends on the resolution, detection, and identification of very fine detail. With solid-state cameras, one can resolve very quick movement without compromising the resolution independent of lighting conditions. Quick moving targets require high resolution. In these cases, solid-state cameras use an electronic shutter. Most solid-state cameras come with a shutter speed function, the most common of which being 1/60, 1/1000, and 1/2000. This function is the equivalent of film cameras' fast shuttering. This technology makes it so that action can result in a sharp image, whereas without shutter control, the image would be blurred. One must consider the amount of light in the scene when using an electronic shutter. Faster speeds mean less light coming in through the camera, so a scene must have adequate light to capture motion.

5.3.5 Sensitivity

Foot candles (FtCd) and lux are used to measure cameras' sensitivity. Sensitivity is the smallest amount of light needed to create a decent video image. Since "decent" is a matter of opinion, this measurement can be a confusing and misleading one. Most manufacturers take "sensitivity" to mean two things:

1. Sensitivity at the location of the sensor's faceplate.
2. Minimum amount of light at the scene.

While the first stipulation measures light only at the sensor chip, the second measures light at the scene.

When using the second definition of sensitivity, one must define the following parameters: scene reflectance, optical lens speed (f/#), automatic gain control, usable video, and shutter speed.

The majority of manufacturers use the standard of 89% or 75% reflectance as a minimum scene illumination. However, the manufacturers' data sheets generally do not exactly match the scene being captured. Materials have different reflection capabilities: snow is about 90%, grass at 40%, brick at 25%, and blacktop at 5%.

It follows that when a camera views a black surface such as a chalkboard, about 5% of the light in the scene is reflected to the camera. This means that about 15 times more light needs to be applied to the scene in order to meet the standard set by a white surface.

The on-chip lens (OCL) technique increases the CCD sensor's sensitivity to a level that two times better than what other devices can achieve. Since the sensor has tiny lenses on each pixel, the light is always focused on the areas of the photo sensor, which increases the camera's overall sensitivity.

Some CMOS sensors utilize the OCL technique plus the addition of lenses in between the pixels, thus getting rid of the areas between the tiny lenses that prove to be useless. This technology improves sensitivity by a factor of two; in addition, it decreases smearing possibilities.

5.4 Sensor Formats

Superior solid-state CCD sensor color cameras have hastened the development of color cameras for security purposes.

Solid-state security cameras are generally formatted for three image sizes: ¼ inch, 1/3 inch, and ½ inch.

EIA and NTSC standards determine that all sensors have a geometry of 4x3. ¼ inch formatting produces the smallest image whereas ½ inch produces the largest.

Intensified Charged Coupled Device ICCD cameras are the modern solid-state equivalent of intensified silicon intensified target ISIT tube cameras working within low light level circumstances, the former largely replacing the latter.

Camera sensors' formats define the lens format size, set the lens focal length, and determine the field of view. As a rule of thumb, a larger sensor means a larger lens diameter, which means that the lens will be larger and more costly. Whereas lenses designed for large formats can be used on small-format cameras, small-format lenses cannot be used with large-format cameras. The latter combination produces vignetting, which is a dark blemish surrounding the image.

5.4.1 Solid-State

Solid-state cameras equipped with CCD and CMOS sensors come in ¼-, 1/3-, and ½- inch formatting. Recently, the quality and sensitivity available within these smaller formats is comparable to what 2/3- and 1-inch solid-state and tube sensors were capable of providing.

The majority of color cameras in surveillance systems today include single-chip sensors with tricolor stripe filters. These cameras range in sensitivity from .5 to 2 FtCd for a full video, whereas their monochrome equivalents are about 10 times more sensitive. Low-res color cameras' horizontal resolution is around 330 TV lines, whereas high-res cameras hover around 480 TV lines.

5.4.2 Image Intensifier

ICCDs are the most frequently used image intensifiers; they use CCD image formatting and the same resolution as standard monochrome cameras. The format resolution tends to be about 500-600 assuming the use of a ½-inch sensor.

5.4.3 Thermal Infrared

Thermal IR cameras utilize a long-wave IR arrangement that is created based on manufacturing methods that vary drastically from those used with CCD and ICCD. IR sensors are comparatively challenging to create and yield far less than other solid-state sensors, so the number of pixels each sensor includes is far smaller. IR sensors usually have a TV line resolution of 280-320. Developments will eventually lead to IR sensors with resolutions similar to CCD and CMOS cameras.

The CCTV industry has a variety of camera-lens mounts, some of which can be switched out while others cannot.

The lens mounts and camera mounts absolutely must be congruent.

C and CS mounts are the most commonly used varieties.

10mm (.5mm pitch), 12mm (.5mm pitch), and 13 mm (1mm pitch) mini lens mounts are commonly used in small surveillance applications.

For specialized cameras and lenses, large bayonet mounts are often installed.

5.5 Lens Mounts

5.5.1 C and CS Mounts

Most cameras used to automatically use the standard C mount. As cameras and lenses got smaller, it became necessary to lessen the gap between the lens and the sensor. This smaller mount, specified for ¼-, 1/3-, and ½- inch sensor cameras, became known as the CS mount. While the diameter and thread of C and CS mounts are the same, the space between the lens' back mounting area and the sensor itself on the CS mount is .492 inches, or 12.5 mm. It is also .2 inches or 5 mm smaller than the C mount. So the lens can be made smaller since it is closer to the censor.

C mount lenses may be used with CS mount cameras as long as you add a 5mm spacer between the lens and camera itself. Also, the lens structure must be at least as big as the camera format size.

With a CS mount system, lenses are lighter, smaller, and cheaper than in a C mount system. Furthermore, a C mount lens can be used in a CS mount camera thanks to the creation of the 5 mm spacer. However, CS mount lenses will not work on C mount cameras.

5.5.2 Mini-Lens Mounts

Smaller lens and camera mounts have become a necessity as mini lenses and cameras have gotten more popular. The mounts specific to these devices have thread sizes of 10, 12, and 13 mm in diameter. Their thread pitches are either .5 or 1 mm. The most popular sizes are 10 and 12 mm mounts with .5mm pitches.

Figure 5. C and CS mount lenses

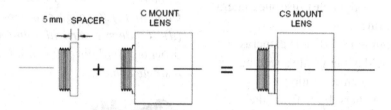

5.5.3 Bayonet Mount

Bayonet mounts have a diameter of 2.25 inches, which can be used in security settings, and in broadcast, industrial, and military situations. Their compatible cameras are three-sensor color cameras, low light level cameras, and focal length FL large lenses. The security industry uses them only occasionally.

5.5.4 Lens-Mount Interferences

The image can be out of focus when mechanical interference prevents a lens from being completely situated in a mount. This is a problem that most manufacturers have addressed by selling lenses and cameras that are compatible with one another. But since lenses are often switched around, consumers must be wary of the changes they undertake.

5.6 Zoom Lens–Camera Module

Zoom lens-camera modules combine these two components in a useful way. It developed out of a need for light, quick-response camera lenses that could be used in high-speed pan/tilt/zoom PTZ security installations, for example, in airports, malls, casinos, stores, etc. This module is configured in the shape of a cube. This way it can be integrated into a pan/tilt PT dome housing setup, able to be pointed in any direction at any speed.

The module setup consists of the following:

1.   Strong and compact mechanics that are appropriate for high-speed pan/tilt platforms.
2.   Great optical zoom ratio (16 or 20 to 1).
3.   Great electronic zoom ratio (8 or 10 to 1).
4.   1/4-inch solid-state color camera that has good sensitivity and resolution.

Module options are:

1.   Automatic focus.
2.   Image-steadying capacities.

Auto-focus is useful only when the camera is not operating at high speeds.

When a moving target enters the lens' field of view, the auto-focus follows the moving person no matter what direction they move in, blurring the surrounding scene. When the module is moving quickly, tilting, or panning, auto focus should not be used because the application will not know what to focus on.

Typical zoom lenses' focal length range is from 36-80mm. When set to wide-angle, the camera and lens can cover up to 54 angular horizontal field of view. When set to telephoto, it can cover 25 angular horizontal field of view.

5.7 Panoramic 360 Camera

The need to see an entire area at 360 degrees is a common one. In the past, this need was met by systems that included more than one camera, and then the scenes were combined on the monitor into split screen. The advent of panoramic lenses in combination with high-res digital cameras and DSP electronics make it possible to use one camera in a 360 degree setting.

Now, high-resolution solid-state cameras can draw a 360 by 90 field of view onto a rectangular monitor maintaining high resolution.

First, the lens gathers light from the panoramic scene and focuses the light in the shape of a donut onto the camera sensor. Then, the camera's electronics and preconfigured algorithms convert the panoramic image into a rectangular one that can be seen on a regular monitor. Usually, joysticks and computer mice are utilized to pan and tilt the camera; a segment of the 360 degree panoramic image can always be displayed on the monitor.

5.8 High Definition Television

High Definition Television HDTV runs the new format of 16x9 (horizontal by vertical) inches, which can display a much better resolution than the NTSC 4x3 standard format.

HDTV was created in order to:

1. Provide a higher resolution display.
2. Have the display conform to what the human eye actually sees, as it has a wider horizontal view.

Although HDTV was created for the consumer market, it will eventually be incorporated into the video security market thanks to its superior formatting and resolution. HDTV has not yet been standardized for security use. It has many variations. For example, horizontal lines and resolutions vary in HDTV images. Methods for drawing images onto monitors are also variable. Formats include 720p, 1080i, and 1080p/24. To decode these formats, use the following guidelines:

1. The first number is vertical resolution.
2. The first letter is either I (interlaced) or p (progressive), which refers to the scanning method.

Figure 6. (a) Lomography Spinner 360° Panoramic Camera; (b) 8 MP JPEG2000 HD 360° Pano Camera; (c) 360 degree camera lens attachment; (d) 360-degree vertical solution is designed to provide visual coverage of an entire room from a single camera.

3. The final number, which can be 24, 30, or 60, is the frame rate.

Progressive scanning draws the whole picture from top to bottom, while interlaced scanning first draws even lines and then odd ones, splitting the image into two fields. Progressive scanning is widely considered superior to interlaced.

NTSC video security systems that use the 4x3 format use the interlaced method, whereas computer monitors use progressive.

The finest current HDTV system is 1080i: it has an interlaced 30 frame/60 fields per second system comparable to NTSC, but has the 16×9 format of HDTV. Thanks to its wide aspect ratio, high resolution, and larger screen size, HDTV security installations are generally more intelligent. Also, the resulting videos are sharper and crisper.

The next chapter is a summary of IP surveillance systems: basic functions, the advantages of network video, customizing surveillance applications, and possible legal concerns. The most important step one can take before installing IP surveillance system is to define goals and requirements. Once these are determined, the video system can be set up.

REFERENCES

Bradski, G., & Kaehler, A. (2009). *Learning OpenCV*. London: O'Reilly Media, Inc.

Caputo, A. C. (2010). *Digital video surveillance and security*. London: Elsevier.

Damjanovski, V. (2005). *CCTV networking and digital technology*. London: Elsevier.

Intelligent Video Surveillance. (n.d.). Retrieved from http://www.3xlogic.com/xview

Interlaced Video Frame. (n.d.). Retrieved from http://en.wikipedia.org/wiki/File:Interlaced_video_frame_(car_wheel).jpg

Kruegle, H. (2007). *CCTV surveillance analog and digital video practices and technology* (2nd ed.). London: Elsevier.

Lomography Spinner 360° Panoramic Camera. (n.d.). Retrieved from http://www.bhphotovideo.com/c/product/711901-REG/Lomography_919_Spinner_360_deg_Panoramic_Camera.html/c/product/#inpage:IN+STOCK

8MP JPEG2000 HD 360° Pano Camera. (n.d.). Retrieved from http://www.google.com.hk/imgres?q=Panoramic+360+Camera&um=1&hl=en&newwindow=1&safe=strict&sa=N&biw=1360&bih=673&tbm=isch&tbnid=VgfgkptAgEusnM:&imgrefurl=http://avigilon.com/products/cameras/hd-panoramic/jpeg2000-hd-panoramic-camera/8-mp-360-jpeg2000-dome-panoramic/&docid=C603IZ-RG-BNR2M&imgurl=http://avigilon.com/assets/Uploads/JPEG2000-HD-Panoramic-Dome360Camera1140x640rev.jpg&w=1140&h=640&ei=qCsvUfP-J6uXiQe3_4HgDw&zoom=1&iact=rc&dur=565&sig=117471693243402725643&page=1&tbnh=152&tbnw=242&start=0&ndsp=18&ved=1t:429,r:7,s:0&tx=264&ty=362

Network Video System. (n.d.). Retrieved from www.axis.com

Nilsson, F. (2009). *Intelligent network video - Understanding modern video surveillance systems*. Boca Raton, FL: CRC Press Taylor & Francis Group.

The 0-360 Panoramic Optic. (n.d.). Retrieved from http://www.0-360.com/

Chapter 22
IP Video Surveillance System

ABSTRACT

The chapter is a summary of IP surveillance systems: basic functions, the advantages of network video, customizing surveillance applications, and possible legal concerns. The most important step one can take before installing IP surveillance system is to define goals and requirements. Once these are determined, the video system can be set up. The required goals to be determined are the following: definition of the video surveillance system needs (installation plan, area of coverage, camera positioning, illumination conditions determination, camera cabling, the recording server positioning), network camera and/or video encoder selection (image quality, lens selection, network camera selection, Power over Ethernet [PoE], video motion detection, audio, accessories selection, testing), hardware (switches, additional light sources, power supplies, additional server for video management software, hard drives), software (software package selection, licenses, image quality and frame rate requirements, IP address range calculation, hard disk usage calculation, camera configuration, video motion detection settings, user access definition), and maintenance.

1. INTRODUCTION

Security systems that utilize an Internet Protocol-based IP network such as the Internet or a Local Area Network LAN in order to allow users to observe scenes or record audio and video are IP-Surveillance systems.

Simple IP-Surveillance systems consist of network cameras (or analog cameras that have a video encoder), a network switch, and a computer equipped with software for video management. IP-Surveillance systems use IP networks to transmit information, unlike analog video systems' point-to-point cabling from the camera's physical location to the monitoring station (Kruegle, 2007).

Video monitoring and recording is possible from anywhere in the world provided that the location is enabled with a wired or wireless IP network.

Network video systems allow signals to be sent and received simultaneously; they are bi-directional. As a result, network video systems can be easily integrated into larger systems. Analog systems, however, are unidirectional: only one signal can be transmitted at a time. For example, a network camera is capable of both sending data (audio, video, SMS) to a user and receiving information (instructions, audio) from the same user. This type of activity can be used to perform multiple functions, like activating alarms or doors.

DOI: 10.4018/978-1-4666-4896-8.ch022

Network video systems are also more flexible than audio in that they can multitask and connect with multiple applications at once.

IP-Surveillance offers many benefits and advanced capabilities. Via IP-Surveillance, you have superior control over recorded video, live video, and alarm events, which makes a network video system a natural choice for surveillance applications.

Among the benefits are:

1. **Remote Accessibility:** Authorized users from around the world can view video footage at any time of day. If your company would like to contract out its security needs to a third party, remote accessibility is a huge advantage. Remote accessibility through an analog system would only be possible with the purchasing of extra equipment like network Digital Video Recorders DVRs and video encoders.

2. **Superior Image Quality:** In order to identify subjects in a video scene, the image must be clear. Network video systems' images are consistently sharp because no inessential

conversions are performed and distance between the scene and the remote monitor is not a factor. However, every time a video is converted in an analog system, its quality is degraded. Also, video signals become weaker with distance in an analog system.

a. Digital images are also of higher quality than analog because they are more easily stored and received. Networks cameras have the progressive scanning capability, which presents an image as one whole, thus creating a clearer image.

b. Large areas can be covered in more detail with megapixel network cameras. These cameras' images consist of at least 1 million pixels, which is greater than the capabilities of analog.

3. **Streamlined Integration:** Since network video components are built based on open standards, they can be assimilated into security and audio systems as well as made compatible with Ethernet-based and computer information, application and management software, and various devices. Network

Figure 1. IP surveillance video system

Figure 2. Analog surveillance video system

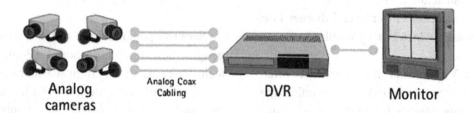

Figure 3. a) Progressive scan; b) Interlace scan

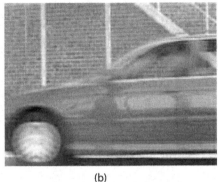

(a)   (b)

video cameras can be integrated with other software integral to a firm's livelihood, such as a Point of Sales system, to perform tasks, check for accuracy, and surveil the premises.

4. Scalability and flexibility enable that IP-Surveillance systems adapt to your needs. Adding and removing cameras will not affect the overall functionality of your system; in fact, you can install cameras in almost any location and protect your network to whatever extent you desire.

5. **Economical:** The overall costs of installing and maintaining an IP-Surveillance system are lower than those of an analog CCTV system. While analog systems run on DVRs, which are proprietary, IP-surveillance systems utilize open systems-based servers, and its storage methods and applications are industry standard. Also, IP transmission is much cheaper than the analog coaxial and fiber optics methods. IP signals are transmitted around the world using LANs and the Internet. An organization can use the extant IP infrastructure for other applications, and can also access Power over Ethernet PoE technology, which is not possible for analog systems.

6. **Smart Video:** Surveillance systems often produce too much video to examine the footage thoroughly. Intelligence can be built

in to advanced network cameras and video encoders to solve this problem. Intelligence isolates interesting events using motion detection, audio detection, tampering alarms, I/O connections, and alarm management, and through a chain of responses, reports the events to security personnel.

a. Analytics performed at the camera-level is desirable because both network bandwidth usage and storage needs are reduced since the amount of video sent to the recording server is decreased. Also, there is less demand on the recording server.

b. Intelligence can be customized on the network video product user interface or using a piece of management software. More specifically, users can set when and how triggers will be set and what the responses will be. For example, a user can define if one or multiple sites will be recorded; if external devices like lights, doors, and alarms will be activated; and if messages notifying users will be sent.

Security personnel are in place to safeguard people, assets, and property. IP-surveillance technology can greatly improve their ability to do so. IP-surveillance systems can be found indoors and outdoors, both in private and in public. Some

Figure 4. Power over Ethernet video system

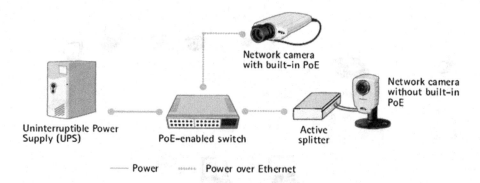

common uses are in airports, public transport hubs, factories, warehouses, banks, schools, government offices, childcare centers, homes, and stores.

2. OVERVIEW

IP-surveillance systems range from basic to complex. A basic system hinges on the ownership of a PC with which one can record and view video. An Ethernet cable is also needed to connect the PC and the network switch (a piece of equipment that enables devices of all types to share an Internet connection or communicate), and a separate cable for connecting the network switch to the camera itself. Additionally, there must be a camera for capturing video and sending the data over a network. The camera can be network-enabled or analog with a video encoder. This can also be called a video server.

Network cameras and analog cameras with video encoders are advantageous because they directly join a network instead of using a PC as an intermediary, like web cameras. Users can connect to a network camera or analog camera with a video encoder using an Internet connection remotely, or simply on a local PC. Video management software becomes necessary when using more than one camera at once.

In summary, IP-surveillance systems are very scalable; doing so is straightforward and cost-effective. Components within the system are customizable, which means that an IP-surveillance system is a flexible and effective security solution.

2.1 Network Camera/Video Encoder

The surveillance market offers network cameras and video encoders of all types. Cameras can be used indoors or outdoors, and have different options: fixed to pan/tilt/zoom camera bodies are available, as well as domes that are either fixed or can pan, tilt, and zoom. Additional functions, like vandal resistance, built-in wireless support and varying megapixel resolutions, are also available.

Network cameras and video encoders may include the following:

1. Multiple synchronized video streams operating with varying video compression formats to create the optimal image quality and bandwidth usage. These formats include H.264, MPEG-4 Part 2, and Motion JPEG.
2. Input/output ports to connect cameras to alarms, sensors, and other devices.
3. Motion and tampering detection software and other intelligence.
4. Management functions for communication with outside devices and applications at the same time. They are also used to send individual video streams to different places, at varying frame rates and resolutions.

Figure 5. IP video surveillance system

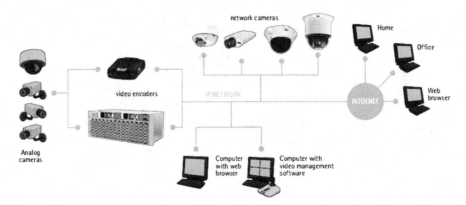

5. Audio support mechanisms.
6. Power over Ethernet PoE which utilizes one Ethernet cable to transfer both power and data.

2.2 Network

IP-Surveillance networks can be devised and protected in multitude of ways. They can be wireless, wired, or some combination of both, and their size can vary based on your needs. Adding bandwidth to your network requires only the simple installation of switches and routers. Using the appropriate technology, you can also enhance your bandwidth usage.

Wired networks are beneficial because they can use Power over Ethernet PoE. This leads to simpler camera installation methods and saves money.

2.3 Hardware

IP-Surveillance systems utilize hardware that already exists. An average PC (equipped with a Windows operating system and a Pentium processor), using video management software, can handle footage from 1-50 cameras. If and when a server runs out of storage space for video footage, it is simple to add hard disk space and improve the

hard disk's flexibility and reliability. Hard drives with a lot of storage space are becoming cheaper.

2.4 Software

To prepare, install, and administer an IP-Surveillance system, one can use many types of software. Some companies offer tools that estimate the amount of bandwidth a network video system will demand, and other software tools simplify the process of locating, installing, and configuring cameras and other pieces of hardware on the network. There is also video management software, which enables managing and arranging network video cameras to suit the site needs.

2.5 IP Video Surveillance System Specific Application

Before implementing a video surveillance system, the important step of determining the system's goal must be taken. It is advisable to define the purposes of video surveillance (for example, identification of individuals, counting customers, etc.) and then map out the locations where the surveillance will take place. Having determined these basics, the number of cameras and other components to be installed can be planned, and get an idea of how much the system will cost.

2.6 Legal Considerations

Laws dealing with video surveillance vary all over the world. You should check your region's laws before installation in order to make decisions about the following:

1. **License:** Especially in public places, authorities may require that you register your surveillance system or purchase a license.
2. **Equipment:** Ensure that your hardware meets the local standards.
3. **Equipment Positioning:** Does your surveillance system monitor only your property, or will you have to ask surrounding property owners to impede on their space? Also, video surveillance is sometimes prohibited in spaces like toilets and dressing rooms.
4. **Notification:** Signage may be required to alert the public that they will be in an area under video monitoring.
5. **Image Quality:** Courts may determine that only images meeting a certain standard can be used in courts as evidence.
6. **Video Format:** The police and other authorities may only be able to work with certain video formats.
7. **Information in the Video:** A time and date stamp, among other information, is sometimes required in order to be used in courts.
8. **Image Processing:** Rules defining how long an image can be kept, who can see the images, and where they can be seen, are sometimes in place. Also, an audit log is sometimes necessary. You may also have to draw a diagram of where cameras are installed.
9. **Training of Personnel:** Operators of surveillance systems may have to be trained in privacy issues, policies of disclosure, and general security.
10. **Third Party Access:** This type of access may be restricted. Video released to the media may have to be edited, blurring individuals' faces.
11. **Sound Recording:** Recording sound may require a permit.
12. **System Maintenance:** Companies should do regular system checks to ensure their equipment's proper operation; local guidelines may exist.

2.7 Component Considerations

The following sections outline the important parts of an IP-Surveillance system and give advice on how to choose the equipment:

1. Network camera.
2. Video encoder.
3. Network switch.
4. Server hardware.
5. Software for video management.

3. NETWORK CAMERA

Network cameras consist of a camera enhanced with computer components and technology. They have an operating system, a compression chip, a web server, an FTP (file transfer protocol) server, an FTP client, alarm management, an e-mail client, and more. While web cameras must be attached to a PC in order to transmit the video signal, network cameras are directly connected to an IP network. They can be installed anywhere that has access to wired or wireless networks. Authorized users can view, record, and manage live images either locally or remotely that are sent from the network camera using an IP-based network configuration.

A great many types of network camera are on the market today. Both network and analog cameras are available for many functions, but network cameras have more benefits such as flexibility of installation and superior image quality. Wireless setups and situations that call for extremely high-resolution images can only be serviced by network cameras.

There is the broadest variety of professional network cameras available today on the market that are available for both indoor and outdoor usage.

Automatic iris lenses are a necessary component of outdoor cameras because they control how much light the camera receives. Housings to shield outdoor cameras from the elements are often necessary. Some cameras come with built-in protective enclosures. Indoor cameras can also be equipped with housings in order to protect the camera from dust, humidity, tampering, and vandalism.

3.1 Network Camera Types

There are several mobility types of network cameras:

1. Fixed.
2. Fixed dome.
3. PTZ (pan/tilt/zoom).
4. PTZ dome.

Fixed Cameras: Fixed cameras do not move or swivel once mounted to one spot. This is the traditional surveillance camera. In situations that call for a highly visible and consistent camera, a fixed camera is the best choice. Interchangeable lenses are an advantage of this type of camera. Both indoors and outdoors, the camera can be protected by housings.

Fixed Dome Cameras: Frequently called mini domes, fixed dome cameras come pre-installed in a dome-shaped housing. This way, the camera has the ability to point in all directions. It is often chosen because its design is inconspicuous and because passersby cannot tell where the camera is pointing. It is also resistant to tampering.

PTZ Network Cameras: These cameras pan from side to side, tilt up and down, and zoom in and out under manual or automatic control. They can be mechanical or non-mechanical.

Mechanical PTZ Cameras: Mechanical PTZ cameras perform all of the tasks listed above and are usually mounted on walls and ceilings. A manual operator uses a PTZ camera for functions like trailing a shopper in a store. They are most often used in an indoor setting alongside a human operator, where the camera's viewing angle is appropriate. Mechanical PTZ cameras usually have an optical zoom range from 10x to 26x.

PTZ cameras lack the 360-degree full pan capability that PTZ dome cameras possess. A mechanical stop in PTZ cameras blocks circular movement. As a result, non-dome PTZ cameras cannot always consistently follow objects of interest. Some cameras have the possibility of a 180-degree flip motion that allows it to pan past its zero point. This way it can follow people and objects no matter the direction they are moving.

PTZ cameras are not optimal for nonstop automatic functioning, whereas domes are able to perform these "guard tours."

Non-Mechanical PTZ Cameras: Non-mechanical PTZ cameras do not have moving parts, which means that there is no damage from long-term use. To make up for its lack of movement, its lens can range from 100 to 180 degrees or wider, and it enables the camera's operator to use the zoom function immediately without motorized movement.

PTZ Dome Network Cameras: PTZ dome network cameras cover an extremely wide area and can pan 360 degrees, tilt to 180 degrees, and zoom. These versatile cameras are optimally used in inconspicuous setups: their discreet design, mounting capabilities, and the fact that the camera's viewing angle is often obscured thanks to clear or smoked dome coverings make it so that they often go unnoticed. This type of camera can constantly jump between presets, so it is ideal for 24-hour monitoring situations in "guard mode." PTZ dome network cameras can do the work of 10 fixed cameras in guard tour mode.

3.2 Feature Considerations

3.2.1 Image Sensor

Charge-coupled device CCD and complementary metal-oxide semiconductor CMOS are the two types of image sensor technology available on today's network camera market. They are useful in different situations.

CCD censors are reliable; they have been on the market for over 20 years and have many advantages like high light sensitivity. Unfortunately, they are more difficult than CMOS sensors to install in a camera and likely use more power.

The image quality that results from CMOS sensors has almost reached CCD levels thanks to recent technological advances. They are less costly than CCD sensors because they already have all of the logics necessary for building cameras up around them. CMOS technology also allows higher functionality and greater possibilities of integration. Thanks to CMOS sensors, companies can create smaller cameras. Most image sensors are ¼- and 1/3-inches and use either progressive or interlace scan technology.

A great deal of megapixel sensors is congruent with the sensors in VGA 640x480 resolution cameras, which means that megapixel sensors have smaller, more numerous pixels. As a consequence, megapixel sensors are not as sensitive to light as non-megapixel sensors.

3.2.2 Progressive Scan

Sensors use this technology to present a whole image at once instead of splitting into two fields. This is done progressively, without skipping any lines during the scanning process. Objects in motion on a video will be presented more clearly on a PC if captured using the progressive scanning technique because this is the technology PC monitors already use. On the other hand, the interlace technique will present a blurry image because the separate fields are not optimal for PCs. Except

for a few PTZ dome cameras, all of the network cameras that Axis produces use progressive scan technology.

3.2.3 Lens

Network cameras can utilize three types of lenses:

1. Fixed that have a fixed horizontal field of view FoV or focal length.
2. Varifocal where the focal length can be manually adjusted.
3. Zoom where when zooming is on a scene, the camera remains focused.

The latter two lenses' focal lengths fall on a spectrum from telephoto to wide angle.

Irises regulate the amount of light entering the camera. Indoor camera lenses' irises can be adjusted manually, whereas automatic adjustment is preferred for outdoor cameras. Either the camera's processor or a video signal controls automatic iris lenses.

Lens Changeable: Camera lens mounts come in two types: C or CS. In order to use other lenses, like wide angle or telephoto, you must know the mount type of the original lens. Nowadays, CS-mount lenses are by far the most common.

The size of the image sensor is also an important factor when purchasing a new lens. If the sensor is too big for your new lens, black image corners will result. And if the sensor is too small for your new lens, some of the image input will be lost outside of the sensor, resulting in a smaller angle of view than the lens' default angle.

Automatic Day/Night Function: Certain outdoor cameras have this function, allowing the infrared IR cut filter, which exists to prevent color alteration, to be removed automatically when needed. In conditions of sufficient light, the cut filter is enabled, producing color video; in dark scenes, the filter is removed in order to use the scene's near-IR light. The result is IR-sensitive black and white video.

Figure 6. Different camera types

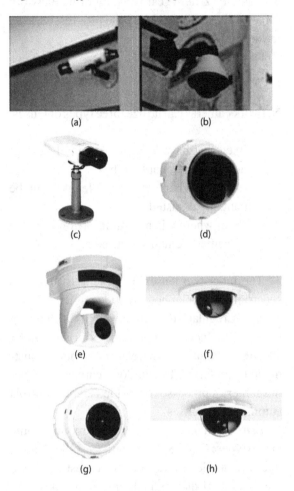

(a)   (b)

(c)   (d)

(e)   (f)

(g)   (h)

Figure 7. a) CCD image sensor; b) CMOS image sensor

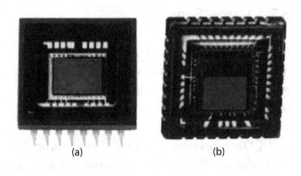

(a)   (b)

be compared when examining cameras' light sensitivity, since manufacturers use different qualifications.

3.2.4 Type of Video Compression

Today one can find three video compression standards:

1. Motion JPEG.
2. MPEG-4 Part 2 or simply MPEG-4.
3. H.264 or MPEG-4 Part 10/AVC.

Each works to decrease the amount of data that must be transferred and stored within a system, using different techniques.

The H.264 standard is quickly becoming the latest industry compression standard. It reduces bandwidth and storage demands by over 80 percent more than Motion JPEG and up to 50 percent more than MPEG-4 Part 2. If your network video product supports H.264 and MPEG-4 Part 2, make sure that a license fee is included in the original price, as these standards are licensed. They are more functional than Motion JPEG in that they can manage synchronized audio. Motion JPEG is unlicensed. As of now, it is ideal to integrate network video products that are capable of supporting more than one compression standard, in order to build a flexible network video surveillance system.

In the outdoors or in other situations in which artificial light cannot be used freely, day/night cameras are advantageous. This includes surveillance situations that must be discreet.

Minimum Illumination/Light Sensitivity: The term "lux" refers to network cameras' sensitivity to light. It matches the level of luminance at which a camera is capable of generating a quality image. If a lux number is low, the camera is enabled to capture images in poor light conditions. The lux specification means that images can be produced at that specific luminance level, but may be low quality. For example, a 1 lux camera can create an image at level 1 luminance, but it is probably not of high resolution. 200 lux is considered the standard image illumination for the production of a decent quality image. Captured images should

3.2.5 Video Resolution

Computer screens' resolution is measured in Video Graphics Array VGA and multiples of VGA. VGA resolution is 640x480 pixels. 4CIF is another resolution format, measuring 704x480 pixels in a National Technical Systems NTSC system and 704x576 pixels in a Phase Alternating Line PAL standard system. In applications that demand detail or a large monitoring area, megapixel cameras are used, thanks to their high resolution (at least 1280x960 pixels).

Frames Per Second: Different resolutions usually call for different frame rates. The NTSC video standard, found in North America and Japan, calls for 30 frames per second. The European PAL standard is 25 frames per second. The majority of video surveillance applications do not require cameras' top frame rate. In order to reduce storage demands, network cameras use intelligence to determine when frame rates can be lowered (one to four frames per second) and when they should be higher, recording and sending important data. Video management software can be set up to alter its video stream and increase its frame rate upon the signal of an alarm, which alerts built-in intelligence of motion detection or the activation of an external sensor.

3.2.6 Multiple, Individually Configurable Streams

To allow for varying compression levels and formats, frame rates, and resolutions within the same system, network video products are outfitted the capability to configure multiple streams at once. As an example, the first stream can be assigned the maximum compression rate and a low frame rate in order to decrease storage demand; the second stream can be transmitted with a greater frame rate and less compression in order to decrease transmission lag; and the third stream can be highly compressed with a low resolution in order to optimize it for use with mobile phones.

3.2.7 Audio Support

Network cameras generally come with either an input for an external microphone or an integrated microphone. The speakers may also be external or integrated. Audio-equipped cameras allow users to listen to the scene and transmit instructions, requests, or commands to those within the field of audio transmission. Intelligence can also use audio detection to trigger alarms and video recordings.

Audio modes come in three varieties:

1. Simplex where either the operator or the camera sends the audio transmission.)
2. Half duplex where the audio stream is sent in both directions at once, but only by one party at a time.
3. Full duplex where the audio is sent to and from the operator at the same time.

After compression and incorporation into the video stream, the audio is conducted over a network in order to be scrutinized or recorded.

Network video systems use four different standards for audio compression: the only licensed technology is AAC-LC, whereas G.711, G.726, and G.722.2 (Adaptive Multi-Rate Wideband standard) are non-licensed.

Video and audio are sent across networks in two individual packets. These packets must have a time stamp in order to allow for perfect audio-video harmonization. However, network cameras do not always allow Motion JPEG technologies to time stamp. So H.264 and MPEG-4 Part 2 compression methods are the only acceptable ones to use it if synchronization is necessary.

3.2.8 Input/Output (I/O) Ports

These allow peripheral products to be used with a network camera. Inputs such as infrared motion detectors, shock and glass break sensors, and door contacts give the camera the capability of responding to events at the scene. After recognizing an event, the camera then starts recording and sending video based on its presets. Outputs, like alarm activation, triggering of door locks, generation of smoke, or the switching on of lights, allow the camera to control peripheral devices.

I/O ports are an integral part of the conservation of storage space. Since a high-resolution image of each person who enters a store is usually unnecessary, input and output ports allow for the camera to capture and transmit only necessary data (for example, only when the door opens).

3.3 Video Motion Detection

When a change occurs in a surveillance camera's field of view, video motion detection generates an alarm. Motion detection can be a function of either the network camera itself or the management software. This function is more bandwidth efficient when used directly with the network camera, as the video will only be delivered after motion is detected. Motion detection comes with many network cameras available in the market.

Active Tampering Alarm: Some network video products come with an intelligent video analytics application. It triggers notifications and recordings at the moment a camera is physically manipulated: for example, when it is damaged, covered, spray-painted, blocked, or accidentally redirected.

Alarm and Event Management: This management application triggers events based on video motion detection, audio detection, tampering alarm, temperature, I/Os, schedule, etc. Network cameras' image buffers record and send images that were collected by buffers both before and after an alarm event. After the camera detects of events and alarms, notifications are sent through HTTP, TCP, and e-mail. Images can also be uploaded via HTTP, FTP, and e-mail. Image uploads are not video streams, but single JPEG files. In order to capture a video stream based on an alarm trigger, the camera should use H.264, MPEG-4, or Motion JPEG compression formats at a high frame rate and image quality. These settings should result in a higher quality video than general surveillance

footage, meaning that recording settings will likely be different.

3.4 Power over Ethernet

Using this feature, cameras can send data and receive power using the same cable. It is beneficial for saving money and reducing the amount of cables involved in an installation.

3.5 Wireless

Wired setups using cables to connect LANs and cameras can be impractical and costly. Sometimes a setup with a wireless-supported network camera is a better solution. Wireless cameras can be used outdoors, in places in which the installation of cables would be intrusive (like historical buildings), and when cameras must be moved frequently (like in a grocery store). Wireless network cameras must be compatibility with IEEE 802.1X security protocols and WPA/WPA2 WiFi Protected Access in order to provide proper network security.

3.6 Management and Security

Video surveillance network cameras should allow varying levels of password-protected access to their controls and outputs. While very few can manage all of the network camera's settings, some can have access as operators, while a greater number of users may be able to merely see images from specific cameras without being able to change any settings. Higher levels of network camera security than simple password protection are available. For example, a camera can have HTTPS encryption, IP address filtering, IEEE 802.1 for the network access management, and a log of user access.

Network Management Features: Quality of Service QoS is a feature that conserves network resources in the case of a critical surveillance mission. Other features include Internet Protocol version 6 IPv6 support and IPv4 addresses.

3.7 Criteria Used to Choose a Network Camera

First, the goals and the environment to which they pertain must be defined. Then it will be easier to decide which type of network camera is appropriate and how many to obtain.

It should be considered:

1. **The Environment:** Choose between outdoor and indoor, select tamper and vandal proof features, and determine whether you need special housings. Also, is your scene's lighting appropriate to produce an image of decent quality? Should you install additional light sources? Do you need a light-sensitive camera?
2. **Area of Coverage:** Fixed network cameras can cover less area than PTZ and dome cameras. Generally, the larger the area, the greater the quantity of cameras required.
3. Application:
   a. Should covert or overt surveillance be conducted?
   b. Are general images or close-ups needed to identify objects and people?

To determine the camera's placement, type, features, and lens, you must first decide the purpose of surveillance. PTZ and dome cameras can be used to monitor large areas and are quite versatile in terms of images they can capture. However, sometimes many different cameras can be utilized within the same network for the fulfillment of different needs: one camera can supply an overview in order to catch larger actions, while a camera appropriate for close-ups can identify objects and people.

Image quality, open application programming interface API, free upgrades, global product support are important parameters to refer to when choosing the appropriate network camera for the certain application.

4. VIDEO ENCODER

If you do not wish to replace your CCTV analog components with the all-digital components of an IP-based surveillance system, you may simply connect a video encoder (or video server) to analog cameras. The job of the encoder is to switch analog signals to digital video and transmit them via an IP network. This way, users can observe the cameras from far distances and record and store video on PC servers.

Video encoders allow for new possibilities, such as remote monitoring, management of events, ease of incorporation to other security systems, and scalability. Also, it renders extra equipment like analog monitors, digital video recorders, and coaxial cabling obsolete. Video encoders are used not only with standard network video cameras, but also with specialized cameras: black and white sensitive cameras, microscope or miniature cameras, fixed, dome, indoor, outdoor, and PTZ analog cameras. One encoder can usually work as a connection between one and four analog cameras to the network, and can also function as an Ethernet port to connect to the IP network.

The encoder, like a network camera, has an integrated web server, an operating system, a chip for compression, and processing power to fuel built-in intelligence. Video encoders not only turn analog signals into digital ones; they also incorporate many other functions: intelligence in forms like video motion detection, audio detection and an active tampering alarm, digital I/O (used to activate alarms and devices), and one or many serial ports to transmit serial data and manage PTZ cameras and devices. Using image-buffering technology, video encoders make pre- and post-alarm footage available.

Some video encoders are enabled to use PoE, so the encoders and their correspondent analog cameras can transmit data through the same cables from which they get power. This reduces costs by removing the need for separate power cables. Also, transportation of the surveillance system

Figure 8. Video encoder

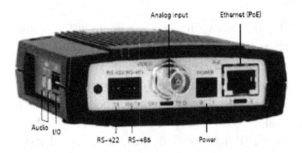

is much easier without as many cables. Another benefit of PoE is that if it is connected to a backup power source, the camera or video encoder can still function in the conditions of a power failure.

When a system contains a lot of analog cameras that are connected to the control rom via coaxial cables, it is beneficial to have rack-mounted video encoders or blades (another name for video encoders that lack casings). Racks can include a variety of video encoder blades; Axis offers blades with one, four, and six channels. They come with three ports: network, serial, and I/O, and can power all of the blades.

When using certain racks, it is unnecessary to turn off the power while putting in or removing the blades. This process is called hot swapping.

Up to 84 analog cameras can be hooked up to one 19-inch rack, digitizing the footage and transmitting multiple streams from every station.

If your system does not require coaxial cabling, standalone video encoders placed close to analog cameras are the best signal conversion method. They do not call for the installation of new coaxial cables, instead sending video and PTZ commands via the IP network. This way installation costs remain low and image quality is not reduced as it would be if the video had to be transmitted over long distances through cables. Digital images maintain their integrity over long distances.

When selecting a video encoder, the following should be considered:

1. **Image Quality:** Some encoders deinterlace digital video, which means that they remove the horizontal lines that the analog interlace scanning technique imposes, with the result of a higher quality image.

2. **Frame Rate/Resolution:** The most common resolutions are CIF (352x240 NTSC, 352x288 PAL), 4CIF (704x480 NTSC, 704x576 PAL), and D1 (702x480 NTSC, 720x576 PAL), the highest available resolution.

3. **Video Compression:** Most encoders offer multiple compression formats, including Motion JPEG, MPEG-4, and H.264. H.264 proves the most efficient as it saves a lot of bandwidth and storage.

4. **Multiple, Separately Configurable Streams:** Some encoders can offer more than one video stream coming from every video channel. These streams can have different configurations, such as compression format, compression level, frame rate, and frame resolution.

5. **Power over Ethernet PoE:** If PoE would be useful in your setup, look for an encoder that comes with PoE support.

6. **Audio:** Most encoders include integrated audio, which can be joined to a microphone or other line-in equipment. Audio detection can be used either to improve surveillance capabilities by picking up sounds, or to trigger security events.

Figure 9. Rack that can accommodate 84 analog cameras

7. **Rack Solution:** Racks can manage many analog cameras at once. Consider your system's channel needs and the types of network it can support.

8. **Intelligent Video and Event Management:** Think about what types of features your system would benefit from. I/Os and built-in intelligence (motion and audio detection and tampering alarms) generally decrease bandwidth and storage needs since they allow only necessary data to be transmitted.

9. **Advanced Security/Network Management:** Video encoders can ensure secure access to video streams and footage. Available features include password protection on multiple levels; IP address filtering (offers or withholds access based on IP address); HTTPS encryption (secures the channel between the application and the video encoder); and, to manage network access, IEEE 802.1.

For network management, some video companies offer Quality of Service (QoS), which ensures that the appropriate amount of bandwidth is always on hand for streaming and commanding needs.

10. **Video Management Software:** There are many pieces of software supported by video encoders.

5. NETWORK

Network specification is a very important parameter. Network switches are necessary for communication and sharing (sometimes of an Internet connection) between network cameras, servers, and PCs. Networks can take many shapes and have varying levels of security and performance. In order to determine which specifications to make, the goal of the network should be defined and information about LAN or WAN's traffic levels obtained.

For small surveillance systems (8 to 10 cameras), a basic network switch of 100-megabits should be appropriate. Since this setup does not require much bandwidth, most firms can install such a surveillance system on their extant network.

For more than 10 cameras, the following rules of thumb to assess the network's load can be used: If a camera is configured to produce images of high quality at high frame rates, it will need about 2 to 3 megabits of bandwidth. If you have 12-15+ cameras, a switch equipped with a gigabit backbone is advisable. Gigabit-supporting switches call for the installation of gigabit network adapters on the server that manages the video management software.

To determine whether more bandwidth capacity should be installed, congestion levels should be analyzed over a period of time. If traffic drops at night or on the weekends, bandwidth may not need to be added to the network because those may be the times to use the surveillance system. The existing infrastructure can be used if it will be able to withstand the surveillance system's bandwidth demands, or an IP-surveillance network can be added if necessary.

Even if more capacity is necessary, more cabling will likely not have to be installed; just adding a switch or reengineering the patch panel may be a sufficient solution.

5.1 Wireless Networks

In situations in which a wired network is not ideal, wireless access points (called WAPs, device bridges, or wireless routers) are a great option. Wireless networks are advantageous in places where cable installation would be detrimental, like in historical buildings. It is also frequently used in outdoor installations and in places where cameras are often moved, like grocery stores. To connect sites without a costly ground cabling operation, wireless technology can be utilized.

5.2 Security in Wireless Networks

Wireless networks must be secured, or else anyone within the coverage zone can access the network and use its services. WEP, or Wireless Equivalent Privacy, is today's most frequently used security standard. It implements RSA RC4-based communication encryption, which requires that each person who wishes to access the network must have a key. However, since this key itself lacks encryption, RSA RC4 provides only basic security. WPA (WiFi Protected Access) encryption is more secure because it improves upon WEP's weaknesses, including encryption of the key.

Keep the following in mind when utilizing wireless cameras in a surveillance system:

1. Authorize username and password login within the cameras themselves.
2. Ensure that encryption is running in the wireless cameras and router.
3. Do not connect more than four or five cameras to a single WAP because its bandwidth capacity is not sufficient.

6. STORAGE NEEDS

Servers and PC hard drives can store video much like they save documents and other files, which means that no special hardware is necessary.

However, video storage hardware, which much process large amounts of data, may be pushed to its limits in situations in which video streams are constantly running.

6.1 Calculating Storage Needs

Some elements should be taken account when determining your network surveillance system's storage requirements:

1. Amount of cameras.
2. Amount of time per day the cameras will be operating.
3. Timespan of data storage.
4. Necessity of intelligence (such as triggers for motion detection and continuous recording).

Frame rate, compression type, image quality and the scene's amount of motion are also considerations. Storage calculations can also be affected by video compression formats. H.264 is definitely the most efficient compression technique since it reduces video files by over 80 percent more than Motion JPEG and 50 percent more than MPEG-4 Part 2 technologies. H.264's efficiency means it creates higher quality video using less bandwidth and storage space. While H.264 and MPEG-4 both determine storage requirements based on bit rate, Motion JPEG's corresponding storage requirements are dependent on degree

Figure 10. Network

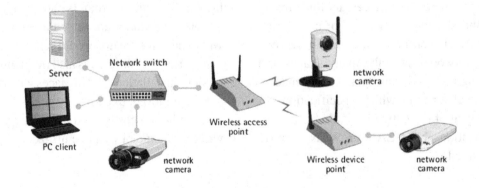

of compression, frame rate, and resolution. As a result, it is easy to calculate Motion JPEG's storage requirements because each image has one file. The other two compression methods are more complex to calculate because bit rate is affected by many outside variables.

6.1.1 H.264 Calculation

Bit rate / 8(bits in a byte) x 3600s = Kilobyte (KB) per hour / 1000 = Megabyte (MB) per hour.

MB per hour x hours of operation daily / 1000 = Gigabyte (GB) per day.

GB per day x planned period of storage = Final storage need.

6.1.2 MPEG-4 Calculation

Bit rate / 8(bits in a byte) x 3600s = KB per hour / 1000 = MB per hour.

MB per hour x hours of operation daily / 1000 = GB per day.

GB per day x planned period of storage = Final storage need.

In the previous two calculations, the amount of motion at a scene is not taken into account. However, this factor can have a huge affect on storage needs.

6.1.3 Motion JPEG Calculation

Size of image x frames per second x 3600s = KB per hour/1000 = MB per hour.

MB per hour x hours of operation daily / 1000 = GB per day.

GB per day x planned period of storage = Final storage need.

6.2 Storage Options

The storage PC or server determines what kinds of storage options are available. Since hard drives are continuously decreasing in cost, video storage is becoming more cost effective. Hard disk storage can be done in two ways:

1. Direct-attached storage keeps video on the server that is running the video management application.
2. Network-attached storage (NAS)/Storage area network (SAN) separates the video from the server.

Most small surveillance outfits use direct-attached storage (the PC contains both the video management software and the storage hard disk). The power of the PC and its hard disk storage capability determine the storage it can support. The average PC supports two to four hard disks. Assuming that each disk has a storage capacity of 300 GB, a PC can store about 1.2 terabytes of data in total.

7. VIDEO MANAGEMENT SOFTWARE

Video management software offers more customizable and effective management options than the general interfaces that come with most network video products. It is a must-have in any IP-surveillance system. Management requirements are reliant upon platform preferences, performance criteria, number of cameras in the system, and integration with other systems. Video management software is available for smaller operations, which sometimes require only one PC in their surveillance installations, to vast operations with thousands of cameras and multiple users accessing the system at once.

Video management software is optimized for use with video encoders and network cameras, enabling the user to manage events, view multiple cameras, access superior quality recording, utilize the playback function.

Some of video management software offers the following:

1. View and store video from multiple cameras simultaneously. For example, in a retail store, a surveillance system can be used simultaneously to investigate store traffic and monitor for security events.

2. Choose between many recording modes. They include manual, continuous, triggered upon alarm, and other video intelligence features. To schedule specific recording times, switch to continuous or triggered mode. Recordings can be compressed with H.264, MPEG-4, and Motion JPEG to suit your quality and bandwidth needs. The software's multi-view playback function creates a complete representation of an incident using synchronized footage from different cameras. Video management is enhanced by customizing search preferences (by external alarm and motion triggers, for example) and including the option of viewing recording instances via timeline. The software includes export capabilities, as well.

3. **Manage Alarms:** Functions like I/Os, schedule, video motion detection, and other video intelligence can trigger events. The number of pre- and post-alarm stream buffers that should be sent before and after alarm events by video encoders or network cameras can be established. As soon as the software program recognizes an event, it is capable of emailing an alarm notification requesting that a network video component transmit a video stream (including its specific recording settings).

4. **Control Frame Rates:** Users can create different settings, for example, for regular operations and for alarm conditions. One may also want to manipulate frame rates for recording and viewing purposes based on the recipient of the footage.

5. **Manage the Camera:** All management tasks can be performed from the same interface. These tasks include camera detection, IP address management, resolution settings, security, and compression levels.

Video management software can allow each camera access to its interface and can automatically distribute updates to firmware. Especially when cameras are hard to reach, this function is practical and useful. It is not necessary to upgrade each camera on location.

Various video management software systems are capable of managing very large number of cameras in one installation. If there are more than limit determined number of cameras, as many pieces of the software may be installed as needed.

Since video management software systems are mostly based on a PC server platform, they ensure fully scalable system by allowing cameras to be installed one at a time without a limit. The only limitation lies in your PC or server's storage capacity, not in the software. Individual pieces of hardware can be selected and purchased nearly anywhere since they are compatible with "off-the-shelf" components.

Video recordings are stored on the hard drive(s) of the same PC that has video management software system installed. This software is mostly Windows-based and contains a Windows client program for local and remote viewing, administration, and playback. All cameras are configured based on settings from the management software, so the server containing the software can be installed anywhere, including basements and server rooms.

Via the video management software, users can alternate between servers that have this software installed. This way, video can be managed at remote points or through a vast system.

The software runs as a background service so that it can still run in the background even when users are logged off of the computer. It can be added to different systems like Point of Sale, building management, industrial control, access control, and tracking systems like radio-frequency identification. Data from other systems activates functions like recording upon specific events. Operators will find this common interface advantageous for the administration of various systems.

8. MOUNTING SURVEILLANCE CAMERAS

Here are some guidelines on how to produce the best-quality surveillance video considering environmental and positioning factors:

8.1 Surveillance Objective

Remember the type of image needed to be capture. If a general overview is needed, a camera and mounting position that will perform this task should be used. For identification of specific objects or people, cameras that can perform high-detail identification work are necessary. Higher positions are advantageous if tampering is an issue in your installation, whereas placing the camera lower might increase its ability to identify detailed objects.

Police and security authorities may be able to assist you in surveillance camera placement.

To test an installed camera's perception of detail, a letter chart like the one used at an optometrist's can be used. To test for movement, a spinning Rotakin device is used.

8.1 Housing

Cameras that are mounted outdoors require a protective covering, or housing. These are available in various qualities and sizes, sometimes with extra features like fans and heaters. Vandal-resistant cameras are protected by casing and include a heater and fan. Cameras like this do not require extra protection.

8.2 Reflections

If glass obstructs the path between a camera and the scene it observes, the lens must always be close to the glass to avoid reflections that destroy the integrity of the image. A special coating may also be applied to glass that obstructs a lens in order to reduce this distracting reflection.

Secure Support: Since a camera body should not move, it is advisable to use stable supports. PTZ cameras' movement can also harm the final image if its mounting is not secure. Strong winds can always interfere with outdoor installations, so outdoor cameras should be especially secure.

Adding Light: Light deficiency is the most frequently cited reason for bad quality images. As a rule of thumb, more light results in better images; without light, the images are often dull and blurry. Powerful lamps can be used indoors and outdoors as an easy and cheap way to improve light conditions. 200 lux is the minimum amount of light that can result in a high quality

Figure 11. A spinning Rotakin device used for movement testing

Figure 12. Outdoor casing

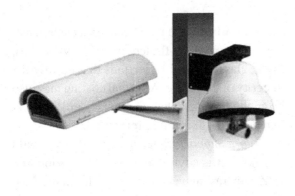

image. Although superior cameras may have a lux specification of 1, the image captured at 1 lux may not be sufficient.

It is challenging to compare cameras' light sensitivities because manufacturers tend to use different standards. To overcome this problem, cameras should be tested and the results compared.

Shadows and reflections should be avoided when using artificial lighting in outdoor situations. If artificial light is not desirable (in a covert situation, for example), IR-sensitive black and white cameras or automatic day/night cameras should be selected. Day/night cameras produce color video during the day and black and white video during the night, utilizing near-infrared light at the scene. A camera's nighttime capabilities can be enhanced by IR illuminators, which create infrared light.

Stay Away from Direct Sunlight: Pointing the camera into direct sunlight has long-term consequences: it decreases the image sensor chip's performance, thus blinding the camera. Try to stand in a position in which the sun in shining behind you.

Avoid Bright Areas in the Images: Overexposure (bright white) leads to objects looking too dark in the final image. This often happens when target objects are located in front of windows. You can reposition your camera or close the window blinds to address this issue.

Contrast: When shooting outdoors, large amounts of sky in the frame may create too much contrast. The camera usually adjusts itself to the level of the sky, as a result, so the actual object of interest will be depicted as too dark. You can address this issue by mounting the camera on a pole high above the ground. Camera operators can adjust which parts of the camera image are exposed using advanced network cameras.

Lenses: Outdoor shooting always requires an auto iris lens to regulate the amount of light reaching the image sensor. The lens' regulatory function both shields the sensor from sun damage and improves image quality.

Adjust Camera Settings: White balance settings should be changed based on environment's light, paying attention to qualities like fluorescence, brightness, and sharpness.

Rapid movement in a scene and a high frame rate both call for fast shutter speeds (or shorter exposure times). Longer exposure times, while improving image quality, generally decrease the frame rate, often creating motion blur.

Some network cameras contain an automatic setting that regulates exposure, which means that the amount of light determines whether the frame rate will increase or decrease. As the amount of light decreases, either artificial light must be added or priority over image quality or frame rate decided.

9. SERVER SELECTION

This section addresses the following:

1. Recommendations for servers.
2. Selection of a hard disk.
3. Network-attached storage.
4. RAID.

Example of General Server Recommendations for IP-Surveillance system using AXIS Camera Station as the video management software:

tTable 1 lists suggestions for server requirements in order to implement IP-Surveillance systems. These are not the minimum requirements to run the software.

1. These numbers were compiled based on Motion JPEG compression technology and using the viewing/recording standard of a 25 percent compression rate and a 640x480 resolution. If frame rate, resolution, and image quality are a priority, then server requirements increase.
2. This recommendation for CPU usage has been made based on Intel Dual Core processing. If Xeon Dual processors are used, the CPU requirement may be smaller.
3. To reduce hard drive storage demand and bandwidth, use H.264 or MPEG-4 compression.
4. Storage method affects the quality of recordings. For performance and stability, implement a high performance network storage method or use local hard drives.
5. Opt for hardware-based RAID controllers over software-based as the latter often results in bottlenecking. With fast disks, hardware

RAID controllers can safely store your recordings.

6. Ensure that at least 1 GB of disk space is free for log files.
7. A graphics adaptor that has at least 256 MB of memory and supports DirectX 9.0C is necessary.

9.1 Hard Disks

If you have multiple cameras that are sending a continuous stream to your server, your hard drive will have a bigger load than standard PC servers. There are three types of hard drives regularly available:

1. SCSI.
2. Serial ATA.
3. IDE.

While SCSI is the most reliable, it is also the most expensive. Serial ATA is the second most reliable, followed by IDE. The latter two options are meant only for office desktop computers, not for the continuous monitoring that most surveillance systems require. Considering that Serial ATA and IDE disks' lifespans are hard to predict, they should be installed in a place in which they are easily removable.

Table 1. Server and client recommendations

Number of cameras	Server				Client		
	Hard discs	Bandwidth	CPU [GHz]	RAM [GB]	Graphics	CPU [GHz]	RAM [GB]
10	1	100	Dual Core 2.0	1	256	Dual Core 2.0	1
20	2	1000	Dual Core 3.0	2	512	Dual Core 3.0	2
30	2-3	1000	Dual Core Quad	2	512	Dual Core Quad	2
40	3	1000	Dual Core Quad	3	512	Dual Core Quad	3
50	4	1000	Dual Core Extreme	4	768	Dual Core Extreme	4

9.2 Network Attached Storage NAS

NAS is often used by video management software to store footage. First, the software records video to the hard disk. The video stays on the disk for the specified number of days, a setting that can be controlled during configuration. You must indicate how much storage space will be needed for each drive used for video recording.

Video management software program automatically removes the oldest recording if ongoing recordings exceed the disk space available. It is also necessary to specify the amount of time that recordings will be stored for every camera. This configuration has an "unlimited" option. If you specify unlimited storage, then the video will be stored for as long as the disk maintains free space. At this point, the oldest recordings are deleted first. Remote disks and NAS both require an allotted amount of bandwidth for the transfer of video from the video management software program server to archival drives.

While data is moved to the NAS, the camera's live streams are still functioning.

9.3 The Redundant Array of Independent Disks RAID Setup

RAID is used to make recordings and system configurations secure; it is the arrangement of hard drives in a way that forces the operating system to view them as a single logical hard disk. RAID 1 and 5 call for information to be recorded twice on two hard disks (both primary and mirror disks). Since the writing process is doubled, performance is necessarily slowed. RAID controllers use buffers to manage the data load and allocate it to hard disks when being used with more than one camera. Bottlenecks can occur because the hard disk write is multiplied by two, sometimes overloading the setup. RAID setups must be handled correctly. This is usually done in three ways:

1. Certain software can combine two or more hard disks into one RAID setup. However, for video surveillance systems, this is very slow and inappropriate.
2. The RAID setup is built in to the CPU. Since the hardware has been altered, this solution is not extremely reliable.
3. RAID controls are handled separately from the full hardware setup. This remains the only advisable RAID method.

It is important to choose a reputable RAID technology because it is an integral part of the surveillance system.

9.4 Hard Disk Cleanup

To prevent the hard drive from filling up, there are maintenance programs alongside the recording engine as part of video management software. These procedures can:

1. Remove images that have been stored past the date designated to the camera ("days to record").
2. Free up hard drive space for new recordings. Emergency cleanups, which run when the remaining space on the primary hard drive is less than what the configuration calls for, delete the oldest footage from all cameras.

10. VIDEO MANAGEMENT SOFTWARE INSTALLATION AND CONFIGURATION

The process of installing and configuring video management software includes the following:

1. Registration.
2. Camera setup.
3. Recording options.
4. Bandwidth control.
5. Security.

This software should only be installed on an individual PC whose sole task is managing network cameras and video encoders.

10.1 Setting up a Network Camera/Video Encoder

After completing the software installation, the software must be configured to meet the specifications of the video encoders and network cameras. Upon the first configuration, a built-in search will find and install all available encoders and network cameras. The procedure will be unsuccessful if there is no sufficient number of licenses for cameras.

Users can tweak settings like quality, frame rate, streaming format, and size for live video on individual cameras. If one view combines nine or more cameras, the settings must be static to allow for optimal PC performance.

10.2 Recording Methods

Each camera can record three ways:

1. Continuously.
2. Motion- or alarm-triggered.
3. Manually.

The former two options can operate on a schedule. Each camera has specifiable recording settings (quality, frame rate, streaming format, and size). Adjusting these settings will affect bandwidth and storage space available on the network.

Most of network cameras and encoders come integrated with motion detection technology, which video management software uses for triggered recording. Local motion detection decreases the server's processing load and bandwidth usage. For I/O triggered recording, one can determine and select the trigger that will activate specific cameras to record. To change the pre- and post-alarm image buffers, one can denote the amount of time that a camera should be recording both before and after the alarm trigger. These buffers

add context and complexity to a scene. Compared to constant recording, shooting footage only when alarms and motions are detected preserves quite a bit of hard drive space.

When a surveillance system running video management software starts up, so does the software's background service. This service ensures that recording continues after a user logs out.

10.3 Event Handling

Event handler is integrated into the recording device. This event handler helps users determine which actions will occur upon the triggering of certain events. These triggers are categorized as either video motion detection or input/output.

When video encoders and cameras perceive motion, the video motion detection function is triggered. This action is completed by the encoder, meaning that the server that runs software does not expend bandwidth on motion detection.

Devices that are attached to I/O ports can also trigger actions. These devices include glass break detectors, door contacts, and passive infrared detectors.

Other video intelligence can be incorporated into an IP-surveillance system, including camera tampering detection. This intelligence must first be configured to stimulate the video product's output port.

10.4 Calculating Hard Disk Requirements

The configuration of network video components determines how much bandwidth they will use. The following five stipulations affect bandwidth usage:

1. **Resolution of Images:** More bandwidth is required for high resolution.
2. **Compression Method:** H.264 is the most bandwidth-efficient, followed by MPEG-4 and Motion JPEG.

3. **Compression Rate:** As compression increases, bandwidth usage decreases.
4. **Frame Rate:** As frame rate increases, so does bandwidth.
5. **Image Intricacy:** Bandwidth usage increases as the scene becomes more active.

These factors can be controlled by video management software, the network video camera, or the encoder.

To decrease bandwidth usage and storage space, the following steps should be taken:

1. Continuous recording.
2. Recording only upon trigger.
3. Using H.264 or MPEG-4 compression.

10.5 Security Aspects

Video management software can allow for very high security controls. The operator can offer or block access to any user when connected to the local Windows user database. This way, extant database can be utilized without creating a new one.

After user definition, the user's access level can be selected out of three options:

1. **Administrative:** Complete access.
2. **Operative:** Access to functions and recorded events, but no access to configuration pages.
3. **Viewing:** Simply view live video.

Each user's camera access can be determined by the administrator. Specific functions, like PTZ and audio control, can be individually blocked by user and camera.

10.6 Video Motion Detection

When the motion detection feature notices action in a scene, it triggers an alarm. Users can specify an area within an image where they want motion to be detected ("included" windows) and also areas that can be ignored ("excluded"). Users can also

manipulate the viewing window's size to specify for motion detection. To control for object size, users can adjust sliders on the configuration screen. These sliders can also control history (the time-sensitive reference point for triggering detection) and sensitivity (the percentage of pixel change that is required to trigger alarms). Colored peaks in the activity window indicate detected motion. Software starts recording when the colored peaks reach the level specified in the network camera or video encoder. Since the camera and encoder do all the processing work, the video management software server is left to function regularly and efficiently.

10.7 Daily Operation

Some video management software options can be utilized on a day-to-day basis:

1. Event search.
2. Live image viewing.
3. Log files.
4. Configuration check.
5. Remote connections.

Events Search: This function searches within footage collected by an alarm trigger or that was manually recorded. It can play back up to four cameras at once, resulting in a complete picture of an event. Searching involves the selection of a camera and the date and time of interest. Then the software will show sample images of the events that match your criteria.

The events can also be viewed chronologically on a timeline. This is beneficial because users can select a specific period of time and see which recordings occurred and what type they are.

If necessary, recordings can be locked using the log search interface. This guarantees that the recording will remain on the system even if it is older than the specified number of days for which it was supposed to be held. Until the event is unlocked, it stays on the hard drive. Playback also allows users to zoom in and remain zoomed in.

10.8 Live Images, PTZ, and Audio Controls

An observed scene can be viewed in four ways by most video management software:

1. Split screen.
2. Single camera.
3. Full screen monitor mode.
4. **Sequence:** Specify cameras to be utilized in a "tour" of a surveillance system.

Pan/tilt/zoom functions could also be controlled by video management software using the following tools:

1. Display Keypads.
2. Mouse (click to maneuver within the image and use the scroll wheel to zoom.)
3. JOYSTICK.

When viewing a live scene, digital PTZ is a possibility. Even when using a fixed camera, zooming and steering within the specified area of a camera is an option.

The audio functionality built into some cameras can also be controlled.

10.9 LOG Files

Most software offers three different log files: alarm, event, and audit. Alarm logs show system messages and pre-configured alarms. Event logs list server and camera events sorted by source, type, date, and time of the events. This way you are able to search for when motion is detected or there is an error. Audit logs show a list of user actions according to camera used, type of activity, time, and user.

Most video software allows for simple installation of additional cameras into the surveillance

system, and the client application enables easy management of more than one video management Server.

While installing more than 10 cameras, pay close attention to the network load. Take the following into consideration:

1. Cameras that are configured to produce high-quality images with a high frame rate probably use 2 or 3 MB of bandwidth.
2. Motion JPEG uses a large amount of bandwidth; H.264 and MPEG-4 are more efficient options.
3. A switch equipped with a gigabit backbone should be used if the system has more than 12 cameras.
4. In such cases, also should be ensured that the server has a gigabit network adapter.

Quality of Service QoS can improve your system functionality. It reserves network capacity and arranges surveillance by priority (critical surveillance missions are the most reliably and securely recorded).

10.10 Server Considerations

It should be made sure that the server's CPU is not overtaxed when installing additional cameras. An average hard drive can store footage from six to eight cameras. Two hard drives should be used when there are more than 12 cameras. For more than 50 cameras, an additional server is used, as well.

10.11 Storage Considerations

Network-attached storage NAS and storage area networks SANs take over for direct attached storage when data and management requirements go over direct storage's limitations. NAS and SANs not only offer more space, but increase recoverability and flexibility.

NAS is attached to a LAN and provides storage for all products on the network. NAS devices are easy to add and manage; they are low-cost and efficient. On the other hand, they operate on only one network connection, so the amount of data that can be input is limited. NAS devices are not ideal in high-performance situations.

SANs are connected to one or multiple servers using fibers. They are very fast and can be used for many purposes. Using the surveillance servers, one can gain access to any storage product on the SAN, which can hold up to hundreds of terabytes. Administration needs are reduced using SANs' centralized storage capabilities; furthermore, they are high-speed and adaptable to more than one server. Files are generally stored on more than one hard drive in a block by block fashion. Data transfers are performed at 4GB/second using Fiber Channel technology. SAN hard disk configuration is highly scalable and multi-purpose. Very large amounts of recording can be stored.

Redundant Storage: Redundant storage systems exist to enable video to be stored in more than one location. In other words, multiple copies of the same file exist for recovery purposes. Redundancy is included in SAN systems. To utilize this layer of storage, you can use RAID, data replication, clustering servers, and multiple video recipients.

Redundant Array of Independent Disks RAID: Redundant Array of Independent Disks formatting arranges average hard drives in a way that appears as one large hard disk to the computer's operating system. RAID proves useful because it distributes data equally over all available hard drives so that one disc failure does not affect the integrity of stored data. RAID spans from almost no redundancy to fully mirroring a system. A fully mirrored system guarantees that hard drive failure does not result in data loss.

Data Replication: Network file servers are setup to back up one another's data in the case of a server failure. Data replication is a common feature.

Server Clustering: Two servers can work with a RAID system or similar storage method so that upon the failure of one server, the other server can step up. Since it is configured identically, their settings are the same and they share the same IP address. A server failure or "fail-over" goes unnoticed to users.

Multiple Video Recipients: A network video system can be set up to send video to separate servers in two locations in order to ensure recovery from potential failure. Furthermore, these servers can have RAID, clusters, or data replication built in. This solution is especially advantageous in situations in which surveillance systems are out-of-reach and hazardous, like in industrial facilities and public transit systems.

Since there are so many ways to store data in an IP-surveillance system, you must first consider how the data will be utilized and how it should be saved in the long term.

Thanks to the rapid advancement of hard disk technology, it is important to use open standards and platforms so that technology does not become obsolete. Open standards mean that the system will remain scalable. The storage devices should also be built on open standards so that quickly-advancing IP surveillance methods like intelligent algorithms will continue to be valid as time passes.

The first five chapters provide the feed into the next chapter nine. They are the foundation and provide the intelligent algorithms which realize and enable motion detectors. Motion detector systems drastically reduce the load of footage that guards must watch for a long period of time. The advancement in DSP allows for the integration of intelligence into digital motion detector technology. Motion detector systems equipped with intelligence utilize complex DSP algorithms to make them responses to changes in the scene instead of presenting false alarms. This is a huge improvement upon previous technologies. Automated motion detectors are now a standard for serious medium to large security installations; they are necessary for high detection capabilities.

REFERENCES

Bradski, G., & Kaehler, A. (2009). *Learning OpenCV*. Sebastopol, CA: O'Reilly Media, Inc.

Caputo, A. C. (2010). *Digital video surveillance and security*. London: Elsevier.

Damjanovski, V. (2005). *CCTV networking and digital technology*. London: Elsevier.

Kruegle, H. (2007). *CCTV surveillance analog and digital video practices and technology* (2nd ed.). London: Elsevier.

Network Video. (n.d.). Retrieved from www.axis.com

Nilsson, F. (2009). *Intelligent network video - Understanding modern video surveillance systems*. Boca Raton, FL: CRC Press Taylor & Francis Group.

Chapter 23
Motion Detectors

ABSTRACT

The first five sections represent the foundation and offer various intelligent algorithms that are the basics for motion detectors and their realization. There are two classes of security system alarm triggers: physical motion sensor and visual motion sensors. Both analog motion detectors and digital motion detectors belong to the group of visual motion sensors. Digital motion detector systems should differentiate between activities that are acceptable and those that breach security. When security-breaching acts occur, the system should identify the individuals and instruct security personnel what to do. Motion detectors can surveil, detect, and assess, as well as analyze information and distribute information to security personnel. Motion detector systems drastically reduce the load of footage that guards must watch for a long period of time. Automated motion detectors are now a standard for serious medium to large security installations; they are necessary for high detection capabilities. All security systems must have an alarming device to signal the guard of irregular motion in a scene, even systems that have a tiny or huge number of cameras.

1. INTRODUCTION

There are two classes of security system alarm triggers. One class is the physical motion sensor: simple contact switches and pyroelectric infrared PIR sensors. These systems recognize only movement, but are varied in terms of their technologies and operations. The other class is visual motion sensors: human guards count in this category, as well as both analog motion detectors AMVD and digital motion detectors DVMD.

Digital motion detector systems should differentiate between activities that are acceptable and those that breach security. When security-breaching acts occur, the system should identify the individuals and instruct security personnel

what to do. In order to accomplish these tasks, a digital motion detectors system utilizes physical monitors or real-time/time-lapse video cassette recorders VCRs and digital video recorders DVRs.

Video security systems are necessarily comprised of these four components:

1. Surveillance.
2. Detection.
3. Assessment.
4. Response.

Motion detectors can inform all four of these components, even the response mechanism. They can surveil, detect, and assess, as well as analyze information and distribute information to secu-

DOI: 10.4018/978-1-4666-4896-8.ch023

rity personnel (Kruegle, 2007). Additionally, the motion detector encourages security personnel to train and develop their response philosophies.

Automated motion detectors are now a standard for serious medium to large security installations; they are necessary for high detection capabilities.

Innovations in the digital signal processing DSP field have made motion detectors much more available and affordable, and have also improved the quality and capabilities of simple, first generation analog motion detectors.

In short, the advancement of DSP allows for the integration of intelligence into digital motion detector technology. Digital motion detector systems are a combination of motion detection and the visual representation thereof. Motion detector systems equipped with intelligence utilize complex DSP algorithms to make them responses to changes in the scene instead of presenting false alarms. This is a huge improvement upon previous technologies.

For example, digital motion detectors with intelligence can come with a huge amount of presets, such as the overlooking of tree branches, rain, dust, and other environmental factors that would have thrown off previous motion detector systems. Security footage that is deemed useful is often of moving objects, vehicles, and people, or otherwise captures activities with motion. This is the type of information that is eventually shown on a security monitor.

All security systems must have an alarming device to signal the guard of irregular motion in a scene, even systems that have a tiny or huge number of cameras.

Although motion detector systems drastically reduce the load of footage that guards must watch, medium and large security video installations often generate too much video for one security guard to watch for a long period of time.

Video multiplexers address this issue: they decrease the number of physical monitors to which the guard must be paying attention, which increases the guard's capability to react in real-time. Ultimately it is the motion detector that analyzes the camera footage for alarm-worthy events, which alert the security officer. This technology frees the security guard for other tasks while it monitors the scene at which it points. It alerts the guard of suspicious situations.

These systems work within the camera's field of view FoV in order to detect abnormalities in the area. This task is performed by analyzing the difference between pixel light levels from one frame to the next; the motion detector system notices significant changes.

Analog motion detector systems, which are simpler and cost less compare larger areas in a frame to the preceding frame. These systems are satisfactory in situations that have consistent lighting and few changes. This type of scene is almost always found indoors.

Analog systems are not recommended for outdoor installations because they are extremely sensitive to changes in light, natural objects passing through the field of view FoV, animals, water movement, and general vibration. Digital motion detectors should be used outdoors instead.

Digital motion detectors, which are based on DSP, are capable of analyzing thousands of different types and locations, even maintaining its low false-alarm rate in extreme conditions (changes in light-level, a lot of environmental movement, etc.).

Traditional digital motion detectors cannot be used in applications that require pan, tilt, and zoom. Digital motion detectors that have the most modern learning algorithms and image processors are capable of performing such functions, but are more expensive and less available.

One must take the environment into account when choosing the type of digital motion detector system he or she is using outdoors. For example, the digital motion detector system should be as securely mounted as possible because it can only tolerate a little bit of camera vibration. Common light changes, such as those that occur when a cloud passes in front of the sun, do not cause false alarms in digital motion detectors; however, drastic light changes may affect it. Some of them are capable of ignoring common motions like leaves, flags, and trees that wave. This way they do not trigger a false alarm. Others can even choose portions of the scene to sensitize or desensitize to prevent false alarms. Areas become desensitized when an object is in constant motion and is unlikely to be a source of important activity.

Once the digital motion detector notices and classifies an object, it then follows the object around the scene as it moves from one camera's field of view FoV to another's. Now it is possible to find a system that shows images from far-off locales depicting objects in motion. These systems notice, identify, locate, and follow objects and people that fall within the camera's field of view.

System operators have a display of the site that is mapped, that has highlighted icons that specify types of targets like personnel, cars, and gates. This digitized map allows guards to see icons of the moving target as it moves. These systems are also capable of tracking the path of vehicles, synthesizing the different footage in the monitor display and presenting it as one path. If the operator clicks on a moving icon, the video footage itself can be viewed. This type of system is often found in large, high-traffic transportation environments like seaports and airports.

A motion detector is basically an analog device capable of reacting to movement of a specific type and timestamp that takes place within the specified coverage area. Motion detectors were originally designed assuming that the background would be stable while the target moved. These detectors used pyroelectric infrared technology and were pyroelectric. While pyroelectric infrared sensors could sense general change in a scene, they could not provide intelligence about the movement's origins or history. Cameras can operate as alarm sensors provided they have sufficient motion detector processing electronics.

These electronics memorize the video picture moment-by-moment, and as time passes, if the scene changes by a preset amount, an alarm signal is generated. Then either a guard acts or a video recorder is switched on.

Figure 1 shows how analog motion detectorss and digital motion detectorss connect to a video system. First, a person walks into a room, and the technology begins recording the person's motions. Motion detectors will highlight the person on the screen, either simply detecting their motion or alerting a security officer of their presence.

There are two types of motion detector electronic processing: first-generation analog and second-generation digital. While more costly, digital motion detector is significantly more advanced and can perform more functions.

Any scene can be surveilled using video cameras that are placed at the proper junctions and angles to detect intruders and objects. These cameras should be positioned in a way that provides a view of all of the parts of a scene that are of interest.

Figure 1. Motion detector

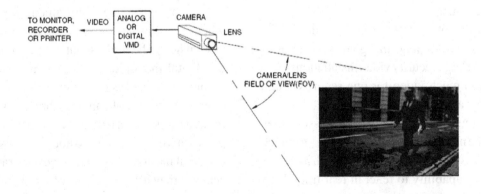

Figure 2 depicts where the motion detector fits into a video surveillance system.

Digital motion detector systems were available by the 1980s. These systems were very expensive, not to mention large and complex, and their electronic workings were such that each video image was divided into zones. Motion could be monitored in each zone. The zoning breakthrough was pivotal in that it was the first time targets could be localized. In the analog motion detector system, this was impossible. The systems could additionally analyze each zone's light level.

Only the government and large corporations could afford to buy digital motion detector systems in the 1980s and early 1990s. By the mid-1990s, most security applications could afford digital motion detector technology and it became widespread. It was a more refined technology in that it was the beginning of actually identifying the intruders in the scene. Digital motion detectors provided more intelligence information to the security guard or personnel.

The earliest analog systems did not have access to color technology, so only recorded in monochrome. Also, they could not be used outdoors because inconsistent lighting, weather events, and various motion interferences were too much for analog systems to handle. The late 1980s advent of the CCD camera in combination with the prevalence of color cameras in the 1990s spurred completely new advances in motion detector.

However, this was not enough to make analog motion detectors reliable and useful outdoors.

The advances of the late 1990s were what finally brought on highly reliable motion detector: digital motion detectors plus CCD cameras that had DSP. Digital motion detectors became widespread thanks to the availability of solid-state memory and digital circuitry. This new technology can actually analyze the scene pixel-by-pixel, not just frame-by-frame, which allows for the complex examination of a scene's motion. New digital motion detectors can reliably manage alarms, detect intrusion, and automatically record the events of an intrusion.

Digital motion detectors are usually used in very open areas, which allow guards to monitor from afar instead of performing the boring task of walking up and down hallways, parking lots, rooms, and parking garage levels that may be empty. They can now be trusted to monitor scenes without the constant supervision of a guard because they have been shown to be reliable, sensitive, and capable of analysis.

A newly emerging technology is that of "specific act recognition." It is a type of motion detection that can identify certain acts and motions that may be unwanted or part of a larger unwanted pattern. These acts include shoplifting, physical violence, and natural phenomena like fire. In fact, video smoke detectors are already on the market.

In order to identify and process license plates or other numbers without a human presence, motion

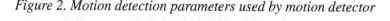

Figure 2. Motion detection parameters used by motion detector

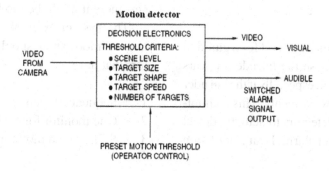

detectors are being equipped with alpha-numeric character recognition and biometric recognition. Even some facial recognition programs are making their way into mainstream surveillance systems.

1.1 Functional Operation

The location and qualities of an environment should be considered before applying analog motion detectors and digital motion detectors to a scene. Indoor light levels tend to remain constant or at least consistent. Motion detector depends on the identification of light-level changes based on a location within the scene, whereas overall light-level changes tend to occur naturally. The software must differentiate between the two. When only users control a scene's light, analog motion detectors can be used because its features will be sufficient.

1.2 Surveillance

In general, surveillance can only be truly accomplished when cameras and lenses are placed appropriately in order to gather complete intelligence; it must avoid getting only fragments of a scenario.

Cameras act in conjunction with alarms and remote eyes to present a complete image of an area which is also a source for alarm input.

Large areas like parking lots require motion detectors that can be equipped with:

1. Wide-angle lenses.
2. Multiple cameras.
3. A dual-lens, split screen.

Wide-angle lenses make it hard for a guard to notice an intruder because the intruder appears very small on the monitor, especially if the intruder is only present for a few moments. This technology relies on motion detectors to actually detect the object and trigger an alarm. If an installation has multiple cameras, the field of view is divided up among the cameras, so each camera must have its own motion detector.

When using a split-screen technique, one of the lenses can be medium or narrow while the other is wide-angle. In regular split-screen systems, the guard him or herself must do the physical manipulation of the PTZ function in order to find the source of the alarm. This is risky since the source might be gone by the time the guard could locate it. So more advanced systems the PTZ functionality is triggered by the source of the alarm and will work independently to isolate the source.

1.3 Detection Probability

Outdoor scenarios are the most difficult to surveil. No matter how advanced the technology, all motion detector systems experience false alarms outdoors because natural phenomena and premeditated artificial alarms cannot be controlled. Outdoor cameras sometimes have seismic sensors, which can have false alarms during episodes of wind, when vehicles pass by, and in many other situations. Also, microwave sensors are susceptible to false alarms created by blowing papers or leaves and moving animals. Outdoor security systems must always include actual video footage to check the alarms, making sure that they are not false.

Alarms imply a disturbance in an area, but without seeing the area, one cannot determine the nature of the alarm or its location. And if there is no video camera, guards must be sent to investigate the alarm, which means that by the time the guard gets there it might be too late.

The system available to guards monitoring large outdoor areas should include many monitors that have:

1. Sequenced scenes.
2. One monitor for each camera.
3. Split-screen monitors.

Also, the lens magnification must be high enough that the details of an intruder's face are visible to a guard, and the guard can attract the intruder's attention. The use of multiple cameras is the best way to address this issue.

The guard must also know that the alarm is real, and that there is an actual threat, the details of which are made clear by the motion detector and corresponding intelligence. However, the only guaranteed function of the motion detector is to display intrusion alarms on the monitor; this does not require the intervention of humans. The guard makes a decision based on information on the monitor.

The motion detector system, besides giving accurate and timely information, should also:

1. Be responsive to changes in the camera's field of view FoV.
2. Be capable of activating an alarm to monitor the guard of abnormalities.
3. Transmit the scene in question to the monitor.

In addition, the system should have an audio or video alarm, and be able to activate a recorder (video cassette recorder or digital video recorder) and a video printer. For larger operations, the system should be able to transmit the video over a network. That which is displayed on the monitor should show not only the specific location within the scene, but also give the guard precise information about the location, movement pattern, and nature of the security event. Hiding intruders will trigger flashing patterns of the intruder's path, from point of entrance to hiding spot. The probability that an event will be detected is determined by the cameras' placement and also the design of the system.

Ideally, systems would guarantee 100% detection rates and have zero false alarms and equipment failure. The highest reliability rates are from 95-99% if equipment and placement are proper.

In the time it takes for the guard to identify the cause of the alarm scene, intelligence assesses the scene as well. Using motion detector, a security guard is not required to identify the camera at hand or even find the movement on the screen since the monitor itself indicates the location and cause of the alarm via a flashing map. If it is indeed an intruder, the guard can respond because he or she will know where the person will be and some details about his or her identity. If the guard can tell that it is not a legitimate alarm, he or she can press the alarm resent button and continue to the next alert.

Video motion detectors are useful not only for their triggering of video responses but also because they hold much independent information themselves. In some situations, only motion detector systems are capable of detecting activities; other cameras and alarms would not be able to perform the task. Motion detectors equipped with mapping display capabilities can actually map the path taken by the intruder, an invaluable part of some surveillance installations.

1.4 Assessment of Motion

The person sitting behind and using the security console must be able to assess, or identify and evaluate, the original cause of the alarm. There are two reasons that this step is one of the most important parts of a security operation:

1. The security guard must be able to respond immediately if the alarm is real.
2. If the alarm is invalid, the guard must be able to make that distinction almost immediately and then cancel the alarm.

Some digital motion detector systems contain a random access memory RAM module which records the alarm locations in a separate location (alarm map memory or AMM). When the alarm is activated, the alarm map memory contents are displayed on the video monitor in the form of an array of alarm points that flash and are highlighted. This is a key feature for assessing most alarms.

Alarm map memory allows the responsible person to instantaneously know the exact location of the disturbance and also gives an assessment of the nature of the alarm itself.

After the security guard decides which response to make, he or she should press the reset switch, which returns the monitor to its default blank condition. Such a precise and quick assessment elevates the response force.

If another alarm happens before the first one can be reset, these scenes are displayed in a cause-and-effect type scenario, in sequence on the main monitor, at a definable rate. However, if a lot of cameras are in an alarm condition at the same time, it could lead to an assessment problem. The result of an assessment problem could be that by the time the operator sees the last video the intruder has already left, leaving only the map behind.

Digital motion detector controls this effect by producing video in real-time at a rate of 30 fps while the guard watches the monitor. This process continues until the guard presses the reset button. As soon as a guard realizes that a group of people is attempting to intrude, he or she can replay the intrusion alarm map in order to determine the cause of the alarm and the direction in which the people are going. Alarm assessment capacity is very high in these types of situations using an intrusion map. The guard does not have to exit his or her station while an alarm is in progress unless there is a need to physically respond to a real intrusion. Progress is mapped almost immediately as it happens, which can be observed by the guard.

1.5 Illumination Conditions

Since motion detector technology operates based on changes in the scene, it is important that the scene's illumination is appropriate. Motion detector equipment should compensate for average scene lighting variations during the day and also for artificial lighting at night. All motion detector-operable scenes are illuminated by either infrared or visible light.

Outdoor environments are more variable: sunlight, clouds, lightning, and other objects change the scene's luminance frequently and cannot be controlled. Although a large number of digital motion detector systems can work well in outdoor conditions, they are less capable when it is snowing or raining heavily. Other types of systems that utilize different sensors should be used in heavy precipitation. Digital motion detectors in an outdoor environment are more likely to have false alarms because of clutter and changes in lighting. As a result, the digital motion detectors must be preset to have algorithms that can handle these changes in brightness in illumination as well as quick movement across the camera's field of view. Movement must be detected while it is in the scene or else it will go unnoticed. So if updates to the scene happen too slowly, a security officer watching the lagged video will not have time to react to a situation. To decide whether or not a target is a real object of interest, the equipment itself should be able to determine the target's speed, shape, and size. Digital motion detectors are the only motion detecting method that is usable in outdoor applications.

1.6 Testing

When there is an intruder, an alarm signals the security operator to evaluate the alarm. Before the alarm occurs, the CCTV monitor is blank. The CCTV monitor shows the intruder and his or her location, which is represented by a flashing light on the exact location.

Analog motion detectors, digital motion detectors, and recorders can be used by management to do a test run of security plans and responses. Afterwards, management evaluates the performance of both the guards and the security system itself. If a system has motion detectors built in, security personnel can practice for events so that when a real event occurs, both the guard and the system can rely on previously determined plans of action. A planned response is optimal in a surveillance installation. The motion detector training method enhances the personnel's plan, the response times of individual guards, and security in general.

2. ANALOG MOTION DETECTORS

Analog motion detectors have been in use for several decades. Although it is quite successful used indoors thanks to consistent conditions, outdoor environments remain out of the analog motion detector's reach.

Its successor, the digital motion detectors, along with its component digital video recorders and multiplexers, has made motion detector in general an essential part of the monitoring process.

Analog motion detector is quite simple: it alerts guards to any change that occurs in the video signal it receives. The downside of analog motion detector is that it is very susceptible to unimportant environmental changes that affect light levels. More specifically, false alarm are caused by:

1. General changes in scene lighting. This can be caused either by humans turning lights on and off, or natural light changes, be them sudden or simply fluctuations.
2. One flash of light that changes contrast in the scene.
3. Smaller light incidents such as cigarette lighters, neon signs, and flames.
4. A cloud obstructing the sun.
5. Debris flying through the camera's field of view.
6. Animals and birds in the scene.
7. Precipitation or other weather events.
8. Continuous motion, like revolving doors, escalators, water ripples, waves, water fountains, etc.

Because these types of environmental factors are omnipresent, analog motion detector is not an all-purpose solution. It is usually only used in very small indoor systems.

Technology: Analog motion detectors are a time-tested technology that is inexpensive and capable of detecting simple, one-time motion. They are best used indoors, where the environment and lighting are controlled. They should never be used outdoors. The most basic analog motion detector systems operate on analog subtraction. This is the process of subtracting the frame in which motion occurred from a general reference frame, which, if the difference is significant, triggers an alarm. As previously stated, analog subtraction can easily fall victim to false alarms and should never be used outside. Digital motion detectors are more suitable for outdoor use.

Most motion detectors allow for the detection of two types of activity:

1. Motion.
2. The presence and absence of objects.

If desired, these two types of activity can be configured separately and independently, making it possible to combine them in the same field of view. The motion windows that the motion detector utilizes should be able to detect movement within and in between their detection zones. Even if an object moves into a window and remains still within the window, the system should be able to detect it.

However, one can program the digital motion detectors to time out after an object stays still for a certain amount of time. this type of configuration allows the digital motion detectors to return to standby mode, avoiding constant alarm mode.

Motion windows specifically check for big changes in the image's contrast or pattern of movement within a detection zone. Motion windows will not trigger a false alarm when very tiny objects that are likely debris cause contrast.

When the system is working in the mode of object presence and absence, the monitor only displays those objects that are expected to remain still, if they move. The monitor ignores and does not display the surrounding, undesignated movement.

If the system is in place to protect a specific object or area, an operator using the motion detector can select that area. Then, even when a person moves through the field of view an alarm will not be triggered because the motion detector is focusing only on the object within the tight selection window. However, both modes involve the augmentation of individual windows in order to monitor significant light changes in the background scene. Sudden light changes trigger an alarm in almost any surveillance system.

Every analog motion detector comes equipped with a detection of motion zone DMZ that is adjustable; it selects a specific portion of the monitor. The detection of motion zone is especially sensitive to changes in movement and light, and when changes occur, it triggers one of four possible alarms:

1. Audible inner alarm.
2. Signal light on the front panel.
3. An auxiliary signaling device hooked up through an AC or DC outlet.
4. An isolated terminal relay contact or path by which the alarm activates security devices like recorders, bells, printers, and other devices used for security.

Most analog motion detectors equipment has a front panel with controls to adjust the shape, size, and location of the active detection of motion zone area. The detection of motion zone depends on what the surveillance application's options are.

Figure 3 shows some area of interests or detection of motion zones marked in the screen examples: split-screen, square, rectangle.

First, one chooses the sensitive areas in a location. These surround the part of the scene where motion will likely occur. The detection of motion zone itself provides the operator with the ability to sensitize certain portions of the field of view, but the entire scene is always revealed. In this case, an alarm happens only if motion occurs within the detection of motion zone. Detection of motion zone is usually shown on the monitor using an extra-bright window or frame, which can be adjusted in the front panel. However this display varies based on the equipment. If desired, the extra-bright window or frame can be turned off so that the view is representative of the scene at hand. The detection of motion zone will still remain active. It can cover from 5 to 90% of the camera's field of view. The default setting for analog motion detectors sensitivity is 25% if the video changes by 25% in 1% of the actual picture frame, an alarm is activated.

The analog motion detector analyzes the analog video signal and determines the extent to which the scene has changed over the current range of frames. Once a system has committed a standard reference value to its memory, it compares the scene at hand in the detection of motion zone to the standard reference. If all preset values are the same when comparing the detection of motion zone to the standard reference, the system's electronic circuitry decides that no motion occurred and therefore an alarm is not necessary. However, if a moving object, intruder, or light-level disturbances

Figure 3. Area of interests or detection of motion zones marked in the screen

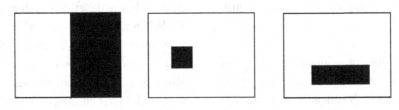

changes the scene by more than the prescribed amount (about 10-25%), the electronic circuitry kicks in an alarm signal. The alarm signal then produces audiovisual alarms or turns on a printer.

Analog motion detectors themselves operate completely separately from video monitors and other equipment in the surveillance system, so there is no worry of system interference.

3. DIGITAL MOTION DETECTORS

Analog motion detectors may be time-tested, but they have proven to be relatively useless in outdoor scenarios; they only function in consistently lit areas. Outdoor applications require a much more complicated electronic digital system for reliability.

The digital motion detectors must be able to recognize and account for lighting variations, movement of targets, and background electrical disturbances that external sources cause. Only recently has the digital motion detectors graduated from its traditional use in large government installations and nuclear power plants to commercial installations. This is due to the decreasing cost of high-density memory and the advancement of computer technology.

Digital motion detectors enable users to split the monitor into smaller areas called windows, which can be manipulated for viewing and sensitivity. These windows can be so small as to depict a few pixels at a time. Using windows, users can select areas of specific interest. Each window can be programmed for sensitivity and alarm triggering levels. In order to set an alarm algorithm, one must designate a window in the given area. Areas that are excluded from windows or zones cannot be manipulated, evaluated, or triggered by any means.

For example, a building's doors can be one monitoring zone whereas outside factors, like a car's headlights, can be ignored. When regular light changes occur, the digital motion detectors system updates its settings and reference levels to fit each video input. The scene as a whole is also evaluated in terms of its light. Small changes and full image changes (like clouds, lightning, etc.) are considered. They do not trigger alarms, but are an important part of setting each zone's reference levels, which allows the digital motion detector's intelligence to remain valid.

Each window's sensitivity is controlled by a user. More advanced digital motion detectors systems divide the scene automatically into hundreds or thousands of zones, which are then converted into digital signals. These are called elemental detection zones.

After they are converted to a signal, the system's processor examines the zones one-by-one in order to determine whether or not to activate an alarm. These complex digital motion detector systems are more reliable because they take more information into account thanks to microprocessors.

Digital motion detector systems make their decisions primarily based on light level changes, which can be determined after comparison with previously stored values. This comparison is done on a percentage basis, or ratio-metrically. Alarm decisions are made only on the basis of incremental change, not gross change, thanks to ratio-metric thresholding. Also, only small portions of the picture are analyzed, not the whole thing. A camera scene can have as many as 10,000 zones or windows, and within each zone a calculation or subtraction is performed, comparing the steady scene with the motion scene. When the threshold is reached in just one or more than one zone, the whole system enters alarm mode.

The process of changing a signal from analog to digital then dividing it into a large number of zones leads to a very sensitive motion detector device. This way, false alarms are not mistaken for real intruders, making the system more reliable, especially outdoors. Users select the zones where motion seems most likely or expected. Zones or windows can cover entrances, exists, parking lots, perimeters, fences, and assets that require protection. Sensitivity can be changed on a zone-by-zone basis depending on the user's expectations for a zone. The larger the alarm threshold, the less likely the system is to produce a false alarm because of unrelated changes of contrast.

Digital motion detectors are drastically more sensitive than analog motion detectors.

3.1 Mode of Operation

First, the digital motion detector processor converts analog signals to digital codes. Then it performs digital signal processing DSP in order to make the code respond to motion in the camera scene. This process can be observed in Figure 4.

Each camera can have its own pattern of detection either selected by a user or programmed into the camera. This pattern consists of parts of the camera image or the whole thing. Within this image, there are sample points. Sample points' location and number depend on the manufacturer of the digital motion detector system.

A camera's reference image is converted from analog to digital at a specific rate, and then the digital code is stored in the motion detector's temporary memory. The base image is updated at different rates, compensating for small changes in the scene, for example, the disappearance of daylight, that should not cause alarms. At a later time, the images from the camera are transformed into a digital format, and then intelligence compares them with the stored and frequently changing reference image. If intelligence notices variation in a preset number of sample points, then an alarm will be triggered.

Irrelevant actions such as the movement of small animals and birds will not trigger a digital motion detector's alarm, whereas people opening and closing windows and doors will trigger the alarm.

The system's manufacturer and model as well as the operator's preferences control how many sample points are designated within a view and also how much change it takes to initiate an alarm.

Motion detectors can process 1, 10, 16, 32, or 62 cameras. They can also be sampled chronologically, for example, from 1 to 10 and then back again. They can also process cameras simultaneously instead of serially, reacting to the data all at once and producing the necessary actions.

Motion detector alarm output can be used in many ways. It can:

1. Display the alarm view on the monitor.
2. Use an audiovisual signal to alert a guard.
3. Record the alarm.
4. Send the alarm signal to a far-off site.
5. Activate time-lapse video cassette recorders or digital video recorders to switch their modes from time-lapse to real-time.

Whereas analog motion detector only works with a small number of zones at once, digital motion detectors can analyze up to thousands of zones of a video signal, providing details like where the picture is located and where the motion occurred. Its output results in audiovisual alarm signals, a map showing the intruder's path, and also a recording of the events of the intrusion.

Figure 4. Block diagram of digital motion detector

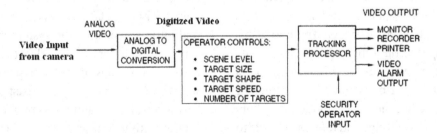

Normally, when the scene is static, the motion detector stores the motionless frames' video signals as reference points and uses them to compare to the previous scene. Only motion will trigger an alarm. Differences in the standard scene value and the new scene value produce alarms and outputs.

However, outdoor situations must always inspire caution in their observers, as light, distance, movement, camera position, water, and distractions are a constant and inevitable feature of outdoor installations. These problems are central to handling outdoor security applications. Digital motion detector systems sometimes come with automatic algorithms to address these environmental factors, excluding their input from signals of interest.

One of the biggest problems is defining the size of a scene's target. From a distance, targets always seem smaller than they are. As they approach the camera, targets increase in size, which confuses the camera sensor. Perpendicular movement is usually much easier for motion detectors to identify than targets moving towards and away from the camera. The best way to mount an outdoor motion detector is to ensure that targets will be moving perpendicularly in their field of view.

The latest additions to digital motion detector processors in outdoor operations are the following:

1. Multi-directional detection.
2. Three dimensional 3D perspective analysis.
3. Auto-adjust capabilities for environmental changes.

The first category, advanced multi-direction detection, allows the camera to determine in which direct the object is moving (towards or away). This is especially useful when the target is at a distance.

Automatic adjustments take away the need to change the camera's settings manually based on environmental fluctuations. If a system does not have an automatic adjustment option, it must constantly be manually recalibrated, which is extremely inconvenient.

Video images are converted to digital format, at which point that converted image's specific information becomes a "stored digital value." This value changes as the scene changes. Complicated algorithms are utilized to find patterns in the changing digital values of the image. This is "video content analysis." These algorithms are a function of software and can be programmed onto the chips that come with cameras, digital video recorders, standalone modules, and computer processors.

Digital motion detectors can also be installed as software in consumer computing applications. Some algorithms actually reduce the number of monitors that must be observed. In order to do this, scenes are averaged and filtered in order to get rid of objects that do not fit in the general pattern of important motion. Also, these objects must not be a threat to the scene. As soon as an object is detected by the system, the system uses algorithm tests in order to categorize the object. It must take shape, size, height to width ratio, and location into account in order to make an accurate categorization. If the object is deemed to be of possible importance, it is then submitted to more tests to identify the object and report it to personnel.

Digital motion detector monitors every single pixel of every image on its own and as a group. Each pixel's light levels are memorized and stored so that they can be compared with subsequent pixels. This is the basis of determining light-based alarm situations.

Algorithms help identify objects based on their individual pixels. Examining the pixels, algorithms can match them with its predefined notions of shape, size, and movement to determine the type of object. To ensure that false alarms do not occur, certain items can be filtered out based on direction, speed, color, pattern, and size.

Sizes are difficult to determine because the camera's depth perception is not ideally accurate. Because of this, in order to determine an object's size, one must also know its shape and movement patterns. Direction is easily determined because pixels in the object's path are activated; the censor keeps track of left-to-right and up-and-down motion.

Sometimes color is an important characteristic to know and is very easy to determine with current technologies. This is useful, for example, when a target is known to be wearing a certain color. The color parameter can be set to follow this person. Also, a car's color might be its key identifying trait, which a motion detector can be set to track.

However, precipitation often causes haziness in target recognition. Precipitation can make motion detector less useful over longer ranges. So the combination of pattern recognition and motion is often an appropriate way to identify an object, since it is likely that at least one of these measures will be accurate.

Movement and gait algorithms have also been developed. Most digital motion detector systems know if a person is walking or crawling and can recognize a dog's movement. Abnormalities in human motion, such as a suspicious gait, also register as alarm material. These types of motion can be stored into the camera's memory so that they can be accessed and used to identify new targets.

Setting reasonable speeds for different types of objects also helps identify targets. If an object moves slower or faster than a certain speed, it can be disregarded as a false alarm.

Motion detectors sometimes contain libraries storing information on unique movement patterns like those of birds, paper, leaves, and ripples.

The digital motion detectors can eliminate constant motion from its frame of view, such as rainstorms, snow, hail, sleet, water, waves, etc. Those algorithms that are stored in the motion detector memory filter out these "constant motion" instances. However, the system can still identify items moving within the "constant motion," like an intruder walking through a rainstorm.

Digital motion detectors digitize each camera's frames into zones or windows that correspond with the monitor screen's exact locations. The amount of digital zones can be from a few hundred to a few thousand. The digital motion detector system gives each zone a gray-scale value or light level, and then records these values in its random access memory RAM along with the zone location. Each of the video camera channels goes through this process. The range of digitization is from 16-256 light levels, so it is possible for the digital motion detectors to store each image as a very accurate representation.

After the reference scene is stored in RAM, the digital motion detector works to analyze subsequent camera scenes (after digitizing frames), comparing them zone-by-zone to the reference scene. Alarms are activated if light levels are more than two shades different.

A majority of today's digital motion detectors are equipped with regular menu screens that monitor and react to alarm states. Regular keyboards and mice can be used to program, adjust, and operate the system. While most digital motion detectors do not need a PC to operate, they do come with RS-232 interfaces just in case the operator wants to integrate the system into a personal computer to allow for remote reporting and programming. RS-232 interfaces are user-friendly and offer full control of digital motion detectors.

On their own, digital motion detectors run on proprietary signal processing algorithms, easily integrating themselves into extant video surveillance systems. Many camera inputs already have resolutions of 768x480 pixels and 8 bits, or 256 levels, of light or gray-scale. Images are always shown at 30 frames per second, or 60 fields per second.

When an alarm occurs, the camera that recorded it is easily identifiable and can be isolated to record the scene to a digital video recorder. Also, if a camera loses power or a video signal, the camera alarms personnel and remains in an alarm state until the issue has been addressed.

Although only one monitor is necessary for most viewing situations, a lot of digital motion detector systems have two based on user preference. One of these monitors can be used to view real-time footage and navigate between cameras, while the other is often used in digital mode in order to examine zones or windows that are in an alarm state.

When more than one camera at once is in an alarm state, the operator should use a sequence mode to switch between these cameras at a pre-defined rate. Also, the operator can switch one monitor to view 4, 9, or 16 views on the same screen, and can put all alarms on the screen at once. Alarmed cameras are indicated in a special way on the display.

Most cameras are set up to remain focused on alarm scenarios for at least 5-10 minutes, but these settings can be defined by the user. The user can also freeze alarmed images for any period of time from a few second to many minutes. Freeze frame mode allows the video to be frozen in the same position on a full screen. If another alarm event begins right after the freeze frame time elapses, the video automatically switches back to live mode, allowing the operator to monitor the action.

To play back images, the video cassette recorder or digital video recorder can display the footage on one or both monitors. This way, one monitor can work with real-time footage and alarms while the other one reviews past footage.

3.2 Programming Digital Motion Detector

Digital motion detectors use the RS-232 interface, which offers users either front-panel controls or a mouse to setup the system. Definition of sensitivity, size, and window placement are simple using both methods.

It is possible to assign a name and timestamp to certain cameras and decide whether or not that data will be displayed in the final video. This information can be placed anywhere on the screen depending on which areas must be visible and which can be obscured.

Digital motion detectors have pull-down menus for the programing of split-screen sequence rates, titles, and camera ID information.

There are also sensitivity and scene area pixel balance menus to control alarms.

Some digital motion detectors offer lost object detection along with intruder detection.

Intelligent digital motion detector setups can handle a lot: even when there are many objects moving at once in the same field of view, they can dismiss rapid environmental changes as unimportant factors for surveillance.

3.3 Setup Procedures

Physical symbols are used to represent motion sensitivity settings in a digital motion detector system, which makes setup a bit simpler. Among these symbols can be flashing cursors and text prompts. Certain areas of the scene can be totally disabled to motion detection capabilities as defined by the user.

This is not the same thing as the enabling and disabling of zones and pixels. Disabled zones likely include some of the following factors: trees, unimportant directional motion, and reflections. These alarm zones are usually assigned colors for the purposes of identification.

Alarm sensitivity is often represented by a bar graph. The graph shows a red line for sensitivity. One black line goes from bottom of the bar to the top, showing how motion and activity in the scene have changed. Once the black line touches the red line, the alarm is activated. The user can control the sensitivity by selecting a number between 1 and 10 on the designated interface.

Operators should simultaneously watch the footage from a scene while monitoring the motion graph in order to have a good idea of what sensitivity the scene and camera should have. Operators perform this procedure for each camera upon setup.

Motion detection sensitivity can be set from level 1 to level 10. Sensitivity is determined from camera to camera, and the settings apply to all of the zones in one camera's scene. Within each zone, color is distinguished based on 256 gray-scale levels. 1 is the lowest sensitivity, whereas 10 is the most sensitive to motion. Sensitivity settings are decided based on a bar graph.

Following are some rules of thumb for setup:

1. Reduce sensitivity if it seems that motion detection is activated randomly.
2. Select the very highest setting that does not frequently give false alarms when deciding the sensitivity level.
3. The higher the sensitivity level, the more likely it is that accidental or unimportant motion will be flagged as intrusive.
4. Sensitivity levels of 8-10 call for environments absent of false motions like frequent tree movements and reflections. In these types of environments, high sensitivity levels will result in many false alarms.

Digital motion detectors are used as sensors that can activate alarms. The result is a motion-based alarm sensor input. In this type of situation, the digital motion detector system treats inputs and external alarm sensors such as switches and glass break detectors as the same.

3.4 Hardware

It is possible for digital motion detectors to monitor up to 32 cameras at once. These are managed through sampling and sequential sharing of information. Each camera's detection of motion zone is different and adjustable individually so that the camera is optimized for the scene at hand. In the same way, each camera is assigned a specific amount of zones to match the operator's expectation and assessments.

For example, if a single camera is looking upon a large area for smaller intrusions, the alarm zone should be set to a small size. A small scene with

potentially large intrusions should be set for large alarm zones, and so on.

Each manufacturer has different setup guidelines, but there are a few constants when it comes to the installation of digital motion detectors hardware. These controls include:

1. **Channel Mode Control:** You can use a switch to choose a mode for each video channel. The down position, which is INHIBIT, disables the channel against alarms. The middle position, or NORMAL, enables the camera for motion detection and alarms. The up position, SET, allows the operator to manually choose cameras from the monitor. The default position for the switch is NORMAL.
2. **Alarm Area Control:** Using this set of controls, the operator can adjust the size and position of the zone that is ready for alarms. They can also desensitize specific zones within the field of view to ensure that normal movement does not bring on a false alarm. In this case, for example, a waving flag would be desensitized so that its movement would not cause an alarm.
3. **Refresh Control:** The time it takes for RAM to memorize a reference frame and then store it before the reference frame is once again updated is called the refresh rate. Refresh rates are usually 1/30th of a second to a few seconds. Operators fully control the refresh rate based on information about the number of cameras and the expected types of alarms.
4. **Ranging Control:** The majority of systems have analog-to-digital A/D converters with adjustable electronic analog dynamic ranges. The A/D converter works to change the analog electronic signal to a digital one. Since each camera should be outfitted with optimal resolution, the operator should adjust the white-to-black levels in the output digital signal.

5. **Masking Control:** This control enables the operator to select areas on the camera's field of view that do not require alarm sensitivity. The operator does this by superimposing square, rectangular, and circular masks onto the said area. This can also be done with a light pen. Light pens allow operators to draw irregular shapes on the CCTV monitor that represent the masked areas.

Detection zones in motion detector systems are often divided into more than one area and are of various shapes, compliant with all types of detection requirements. These zones can be switched on and off one-by-one in order to accurately surveil entrances, exits, hallways, and parking areas.

For example, a zone covering a frequently used can be turned off when access through this door is authorized. Also, a zone that covers a specific file cabinet can remain off during the day when it is frequently used. However, at night, when it should not be touched, the zone gets switched on.

Digital motion detector systems can include such complex functions as 16-step independent zone sensitivity, signal integration and retention, and multilevel digital filtering. These functions greatly increase motion detection while minimizing the likelihood of false alarms. Predetermined periods of rebalancing allow the system to adjust to slow changes in lighting. While the system is functioning, cells are stimulated by variations in the video content of serial image fields. When set to a higher retention level, auto rebalancing is delayed a bit in order to better detect slow changes and objects that move slowly. An operator can adjust both the sensitivity (video change) and retention (rebalancing time) of a single zone if needed. A single activated cell will activate the entire zone and thus the entire video channel.

Digital motion detector systems come with video switches that have dual video outputs and an RS-232 port. This enables the digital motion detectors to work independently of the other components in a surveillance system.

Audio outputs alert the operator of alarm situations and a relay circuit starts the recording of the involved video channels. RS-232 ports give these channels a path in which to move; they provide input and alarm output. They also allow for the system to be controlled remotely. There are two on-screen presentation modes that track an object through a surveillance system:

1. Normal mode.
2. Trace mode.

Normal Mode: While working in normal mode, each activated cell is represented by a bright dot in the monitor. If the system has manual reset, the dot will be lit until the channel is reset by an operator. If the system has auto reset, the dot will disappear 16 seconds after the activation of the first cell. So an intruder will be physically manifested as a series of dots that represent activated cells. The intruder leaves this trail of dots for either 16 seconds or until the system is reset.

Trace Mode: When working in trace mode, the cells are represented by bright dots, as well. However trace mode has the additional function of a bright burst of flashes precisely 8 seconds after its corresponding cell is activated. If the system should be manually reset, then the flashing trail will remain on the screen until the operator decides that there is no longer a threat. Under automatic reset, there is only one burst of flashes before the cell is reset automatically. This functionality greatly assists operators to track and find an intruder.

Large surveillance sites call for more monitors and cameras as well as a more advanced digital motion detector system. High-speed microprocessors work to examine motion that has been detected for position, size, and rate of movement in order to decide whether or not the target is an intruder or simply an environmental byproduct. Then, once the intrusion is verified, the alarm signals are activated.

The alarmed cameras' video channel is hooked up to the alarm monitor's outputs, which records the position of intruders. Standalone output relays allow external devices to be controlled. An included serial switcher allows all cameras to be viewed based on their distinct outputs. Some systems include light pens that are used to identify active areas. These zones can also be deactivated in order to prevent false alarms that would go off upon sensing insignificant motion. These systems also have the intelligence to discriminate between targets.

Operators can program individual cameras to enhance their intelligence based on anticipated traits of potential intruders, like rate of movement, size, and environment. Zones in which motion has been detected are represented by highlighting on the video monitors.

A microprocessor in the system examines the individual cells' data and then eliminates unnecessary background information in order to efficiently analyze for significant changes. Then the intelligent components of the digital motion detector system analyze the motion, direction, speed, and distance of a target in order to match the target to a potential label: human intruder, environmental factor, or simple disturbance. The identification of a human intruder signals an alarm. The target is then represented on the monitor by a specific set of graphics. Upon setup, an operator chooses which graphics will represent certain situations.

Target discrimination is performed based on contrast, speed, target size, and direction.

In order to control for false alarms, target tracking double checks the detection of the target before activating the alarm system. System operators should create well-planned and well-defined detection zones for each camera. These can be manipulated to compensate for distance, which is often a challenging factor for digital motion detection systems to handle.

Digital motion detectors of different types and sizes can be found, see Figures 5, 6 and 7.

Figure 5. Various digital motion detectors

Figure 6. Passive Infrared motion detector used for outdoors

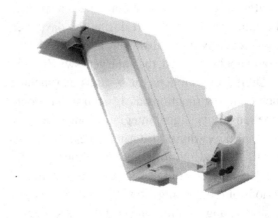

A set of products for one or four channels is on the market. They are equipped with DSP and microprocessors that allow for the analysis of an entire scene operating at 30 fps. Each preset update of the reference frame triggers a measurement of the change in gray-scale at the pixel level (a.k.a. light intensity). This type of digital motion detector system is small, easily installed, and has a user-friendly interface for programming. They are secure, as well; they come equipped with password protection and access codes that prevent unauthorized persons from accessing the system.

Figure 7. Digital motion detectors (Google, 2013)

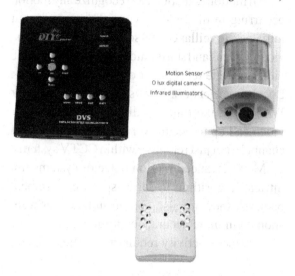

Digital motion detector systems are prepared for 99 levels of sensitivity; they can be used in many types of lighting. Units made for 4, 9, and 16 channels come with serial switchers and also give video and alarm output from the relevant cameras. These alarm outputs can activate time lapse TL video cassette recorder and digital video recorders, quads, video printers, matrix switches, and video transmission devices.

One type of system can cascade up to 16 distinct channel items using a single host RS-232 serial port. It is shown in Figure 8.

One of the digital motion detectors makes up to 16,000 zone locations in each scene of the up to 16 camera scenes, digitizing the scene itself. Since this process leads to incredibly high resolu-

Figure 8. Digital motion detector cascades up to 16 of the single channel units via a single host RS-232 serial port

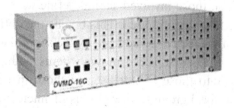

tion, the system is now able to notice an intruder that is only occupying .01% of the camera's field of view. With a blank monitor, the digital motion detectors can still operate normally. The monitor will be switched on automatically upon the digital motion detector's detection of a motion. Then the digital video recorder is activated and records and reviews the scene.

The digital motion detector scales the intruder up to a size the guard can see despite the actual ratio of field of view. Even if the intruder is hiding, the guard will know where he or she is hiding since the system provides a lit path on the monitor. Bright flashes illuminate the places where the intruder has been. The operator of the system is privy to information not only about the intruder's path, but also his or her exact location at the exact moment. The operator or guard can then decide which plan of action to take.

Although there is no industry standard design of analog motion detectors and digital motion detector systems, they do share some common features that are discussed in the text below.

Graphic Site Display Maps: Illuminated graphic displays with an overlaid diagram of the monitored site are a very useful way to display motion detector information. The overlaid map displays the location of the sensors and cameras and also flashes upon intrusion. In case of multiple motions or intrusions in a scene, all footage is recorded by a video cassette recorder or digital video recorder. These machines record the scene, the target, the path of the target, and a graphic alarm map if possible. If many alarms occur in one recording system, the recorder focuses on one scene for an amount of time that is predetermined by the system operator before focusing on the next scene. If it is a non-video sensor that notices an alarm situation, the system then triggers the relevant cameras and recorders. This information allows the operator to make quick decisions and report information about the scene to his or her colleagues. Modern digital motion detector systems are about 20 times more capable than a human guard of detecting intrusions.

Storage: Digital motion detectors access scene data through solid-state RAM. Storage requires about 33 milliseconds to complete, and the whole process involves the sampling of a picture (which can have up to 16,384 different locations), measuring the locations' brightness on a scale of 1-256, and then storing the address, which is the pixel location, along with its brightness number. All of a scene's zones go through this process.

After storage of brightness and location data, the system compares the camera's live footage (generated 20 times per second) to a stored representation of the scene. Any discrepancies in brightness are noted and stored based on the pixel's location and zone.

Environmental factors such as electric noise, blowing trees, leaves, and flags are not considered to be alarms so are processed out of the alerting system. Operators should mask out all zones that do not require motion detection. When changes occur in a specified number of zones, alarms are activated. Comparison occurs 30 times per second across the whole scene.

Alarm conditions are triggered by calculating the total number of locations that have varied values; when a predefined threshold is reached (often 1 in 8), alarms go off. Each time a new storage process occurs, the previous count gets cleared.

Operators also control how often memory gets refreshed. This can range anywhere from 1/15th of one second to several seconds. This refresh process ensures that false alarms do not occur. When a scene is deemed an intrusion, the camera's signal is shown on a monitor. Often the monitor is blank before the alarm because there is no point in showing a motionless scene.

3.5 Features

Since motion detector technology is not standardized, it is important to understand all available features and your own requirements in order to make an educated selection.

All motion detection can recognize any motion occurring in the field of view. Then one output initiates surveillance personnel to monitor the video screens and starts automatic recording to the video cassette recorder or digital video recorder. Local area network LANs, wide area network WANs, and the Internet all made it possible for video call up to occur over long communication channels, not just remotely within CCTV systems.

More advanced motion detector systems use intricate algorithms to define specific movement patterns; they are also able to initiate alarm responses in more accurate conditions.

Advanced activity requirements are:

1. Intruder ID.
2. Environmental compensation (the recognition and dismissal of unimportant environmental factors.)
3. Counting objects.
4. Direction (specifying which ones are unauthorized and triggering alarms upon such motion.)
5. Item recognition (acknowledgement of specific items in an field of view.)
6. Tracking subjects.
7. Tracking multiple subjects.

Those in charge of a facility's security and those who are knowledgeable about motion detector installations should first ask the following questions before beginning a project:

1. What is capable of movement within this video image?
2. What details do we want to find out about its movement?

First, those involved should define what can move in a specific area. This begins the definition of the area to be covered by the surveillance system. Then separate moving items within a scene into those of interest and those that are merely background noise. Items of interest are generally in motion and require identification. They can include:

1. Vehicles.
2. Unauthorized personnel entry and exit.
3. Unattended baggage.
4. Personal property.
5. Suspicious individuals.
6. Employee behavior at work.

The following events should also be under scrutiny:

1. Intruders.
2. Leaks and other mechanical problems.
3. Flame, fire, and smoke.
4. Erratic, violent behavior.
5. Movement in an unusual direction.

After personnel decide on what type of movement they are scanning for, they should figure out what, if any, responses will be undertaken upon detection. If the event requires a quick reaction, personnel must be equipped to understand they image they are seeing, and they must also be knowledgeable about the steps they should take in each situation.

If the video is usually used for documentation, litigation, and prosecution, the camera's field of view should change as rarely as possible, since the footage should be extremely reliable. The more cameras, it is the better. Video must be compressed, stored, and enhanced with great discretion in order for it to remain valid in a court of law.

The fact that video surveillance is such an effective system especially when one thinks of its widespread use attests to its low investment cost. The tenth and the last chapter contains information about design guidelines, hardware information, specific examples, and necessary parameters to be addressed while designing representative security video surveillance system applications.

REFERENCES

Bradski, G., & Kaehler, A. (2009). *Learning OpenCV*. Sebastopol, CA: O'Reilly Media, Inc.

Caputo, A. C. (2010). *Digital video surveillance and security*. London: Elsevier.

CBR Motion Detector. (n.d.). Retrieved from http://www.google.com.hk/imgres?q=motion+detector&hl=en&newwindow=1&safe=strict&biw=1360&bih=630&tbm=isch&tbnid=blOdA3Iptmc2HM:&imgrefurl=http://www.haines.com.au/index.php/datalogging/cbr-motion-detector.html&docid=2GabYelHm80wjM&imgurl=http://www.haines.com.au/media/catalog/product/cache/1/image/902f33c22afdec0ceb057adbcc4c9bb7/D/A/DATA-TEXAS-INSTR-MOTION.jpg&w=800&h=1143&ei=5JoxUY-bCoj_iAf9xoGICA&zoom=1&ved=1t:3588,r:32,s:0,i:182&iact=rc&dur=4093&sig=117471693243402725643&page=2&tbnh=193&tbnw=137&start=16&ndsp=27&tx=86&ty=76

Damjanovski, V. (2005). *CCTV networking and digital technology*. London: Elsevier.

Digital Motion Detection. (n.d.). Retrieved from http://www.asia.ru/en/ProductInfo/1128085.html

Infrared Motion Detector. (n.d.). Retrieved from http://www.google.com.hk/imgres?q=motion+detector&hl=en&newwindow=1&safe=strict&biw=1360&bih=630&tbm=isch&tbnid=WiH_jJQX7VLd6M:&imgrefurl=http://www.directindustry.com/prod/optex-sec-division/passive-infrared-motion-detectors-for-outdoors-24435-380999.html&docid=W2m-_JfUh1j0GM&imgurl=http://img.directindustry.com/images_di/photo-g/passive-infrared-motion-detector-for-outdoors-24435-2679839.jpg&w=844&h=900&ei=5JoxUY-bCoj_iAf9xoGICA&zoom=1&ved=1t:3588,r:30,s:0,i:176&iact=rc&dur=1363&sig=117471693243402725643&page=2&tbnh=193&tbnw=181&start=16&ndsp=27&tx=81&ty=120

Kruegle, H. (2007). *CCTV surveillance analog and digital video practices and technology* (2nd ed.). London: Elsevier.

Motion Detector. (n.d.). Retrieved from http://www.google.com.hk/imgres?q=motion+detector&hl=en&newwindow=1&safe=strict&biw=1360&bih=630&tbm=isch&tbnid=Y7RnprCu9VdA6M:&imgrefurl=http://en.wikipedia.org/wiki/File:Motion_detector.jpg&docid=hdMoZ4owPjoYvM&imgurl=http://upload.wikimedia.org/wikipedia/commons/2/2e/Motion_detector.jpg&w=1352&h=1740&ei=5JoxUY-bCoj_iAf9xoGICA&zoom=1&ved=1t:3588,r:46,s:0,i:224&iact=rc&dur=1027&sig=117471693243402725643&page=3&tbnh=168&tbnw=144&start=43&ndsp=27&tx=63&ty=71

Motion Sensor. (n.d.). Retrieved from http://www.securitycameraking.com/securityinfo/wp-content/uploads/2010/07/Wireless-16-Camera-Motion-Detector-Security-Systems-300x236.jpg

Network Video. (n.d.). Retrieved from www.axis.com

Nilsson, F. (2009). *Intelligent network video - Understanding modern video surveillance systems*. Boca Raton, FL: CRC Press Taylor & Francis Group.

Sensor. (n.d.). Retrieved from http://ecx.images-amazon.com/images/I/31fwdkOmfYL._SL500_AA300_.jpg

Chapter 24
Video Surveillance
System Applications

ABSTRACT

The fact that video surveillance is such an effective system especially when one thinks of its widespread use attests to its low investment cost. This chapter contains information about design guidelines, hardware information, specific examples, and necessary parameters to be addressed while designing representative security video surveillance system applications: protection of all assets and personnel, calculation of the overall cost of the video system, surveillance target (assets and/or personnel), surveillance timing schedule, type and number of cameras needed, camera placement, field of view required, console room monitoring equipment, number and types of monitors, number of displays per monitor, number and type of recorders, digital recording technology needed, type of video switchers, type of video printer, if additional lighting is required, if intensified or thermal IR cameras are required, if sensors at doors, windows, and perimeters that are integrated with video signals are needed, digital video motion detectors placement, IP cameras, type of signal and video transmission, type of digital transmission, type of 802.11 protocol, type of compression (MPEG-4 or H.264), and the necessity of encryption or scrambling.

1. INTRODUCTION

The fact that video surveillance is such an effective system especially when one thinks of its widespread use attests to its low investment cost. This chapter is contains the following information: design guidelines, hardware information, specific examples, and necessary parameters to be addressed while designing representative security video surveillance system applications.

The facilities, surveillance and institution area covers wide range including:

1. Small and large retail stores.
2. Government/industrial/business agencies.
3. Banking and financial institutions.
4. Correctional institutions.
5. Lodging and casino establishments.
6. Airports, seaports, and highway surveillance, and many others.

The applications are concerned with three generic-type systems:

1. Analog systems.
2. Combined analog and digital systems.
3. Digital systems.

When designing a video surveillance system regardless of its specific application the following parameters should be considered:

DOI: 10.4018/978-1-4666-4896-8.ch024

1. Protection of all assets and personnel.
2. Calculation of the overall cost of the video system.
3. Surveillance target: assets and/or personnel.
4. Surveillance timing schedule.
5. Type and number of cameras needed.
6. Cameras placement.
7. Field of view span.
8. Type of cameras: fixed or pan/tilt/zoom.
9. Type of cameras: overt or covert.
10. Type of cameras: color or monochrome.
11. Type of cameras: day or night.
12. Console room monitoring equipment definition.
13. Number of monitors.
14. Types of monitors: CRT, LCD, or plasma.
15. Number of displays per monitor.
16. Number and type of recorders.
17. Digital recording technology required.
18. Type of video switchers.
19. Multiplexer or video quad splitter.
20. Type of video printer: monochrome or color; Inkjet, thermal, or laser.
21. If additional lighting is required.
22. If intensified or thermal IR cameras are needed.
23. If sensors at doors, windows, and perimeters that are integrated with video signals are required.
24. Digital video motion detectors placement.
25. IP cameras.
26. Type of signal and video transmission: coaxial cable, UTP, fiber optic, RF, or microwave analog transmission.
27. Type of digital transmission: LAN, intranet, Internet, WiFi digital transmission.
28. Type of 802.11 protocol.
29. Type f compression: MPEG-4 or H.264.
30. The necessity of encryption or scrambling.

The application scenarios described below a single and multiple site video surveillance systems, as well as a portable rapid deployment video system. All the preceding chapters have served as a basis for understanding the design requirements and hardware that enables a practical video security system. A layout of various security problems shows, explains and offers solutions regarding equipment locations and system requirements.

Eight case studies, i.e. possible video surveillance system application scenarios are analyzed (Kruegle, 2007):

1. Two analog systems.
2. Three combination of analog/digital systems.
3. Three digital systems.

These eight specific applications are analyzed to teach the user the methodology in designing a video system.

1.1 Analog System

Two of the eight applications are legacy-based analog video systems. The case studies analyzed are the following:

1. Analog Three Camera Video Lobby Surveillance System.
2. Analog Six Camera Video Elevator Cab and Lobby System.

Currently there is a large base of video surveillance installed with equipment using legacy cameras, analog transmission means tube monitors, and magnetic tape–recording equipment. Much of this equipment will be in use in the future, but is currently being augmented and will be replaced by digital equipment. Wired and wireless digital networks will replace present legacy systems now interconnected by analog video transmission means. This will serve to provide multiple site monitoring.

1.2 Analog/Digital System

Three of the eight applications are based on the analog and digital video combination system components. The case studies analyzed are:

1. Analog/Digital Six Camera Office Video System.
2. Analog/Digital Eight Camera Showroom Floor Video System.
3. Analog Wired/Wireless Rapid Deployment Video System.

Integration of legacy analog equipment with digital video makes use of local area networks LAN, as well as other networks including the Internet and intranets. Interface equipment integrates the analog cameras and Internet protocol (IP) cameras into the digital system. Installed analog systems, new installations, and new rapid deployment of portable systems show good scenarios for this type of equipment.

Digital, wired and wireless WiFi video transmission has the technical means to transmit the video over long distances and from site to site.

1.3 Digital System

Three applications are based on the latest digital video hardware techniques. The case studies analyzed are:

1. Digital Wireless Twelve Camera Parking Lot Video System.
2. Digital Video Surveillance at Warehouse.
3. Digital Video and Control over Internet to Remote Sites.

The systems use digital IP cameras and digital transmission for video, multiplexing, and recording, communications, control, and digital switching. They provide the most versatile means for intelligent video and automatic video surveillance.

Most systems use wired networks including the intranet and Internet; however many make use of WiFi using the many 802.11x transmission protocols and compression and encryption algorithms to transmit video images to multiple sites. The video images are monitored on PCs, personal digital assistants, laptops, and on digital video recorder equipment or via virtual digital recording.

1.4 Video Surveillance Applications

The eight case studies listed above are only a few of the many video security applications. The following are important applications that are not analyzed as case studies but reviewed to provide insight into the particular requirements. These applications include:

1. Banking and financial institutions.
2. Lodging and casino surveillance.
3. Correctional facilities.
4. Airports, seaports.
5. Highway surveillance systems.

Each has unique requirements. A brief analysis of each provides insight into how to optimize video surveillance solutions.

Banking and financial institutions have special ways for protecting documents and money from thieves. Special requirements encompass monitoring cashiers, money counting rooms, and safes. Quick response systems for intercepting holdups and provisions has to be provided for communicating with internal security and outside law enforcement personnel in real-time.

Hotels and motels demand 24/7 surveillance of many facility locations including outdoor parking areas, indoor lobbies, hallways, reception areas, cashier areas, elevators, and elevator lobbies.

Casinos require specialized smart camera equipment to perform identification of customers to prevent unacceptable individuals from gambling. These video systems are used in: iris scan, retinal scan, and facial recognition.

Correctional facility institutions require additional higher level of physical protection from physical harm for facility guards and intentional vandalism to equipment. Other special requirements include observing inmates while sleeping and those prone to suicide or other personal physical harm. Video surveillance system with this application provides the quick response and communications to security guards to prevent an outbreak of violence and stop offenders in real-time.

Airport and seaport terminal facilities require large video systems that transmit and operate over long distances and between many buildings.

Highway surveillance requires transmission over very long distances. Each application has its unique requirements.

Video systems may additionally be used to identify personnel requesting entry to or exit from a facility. A security person may view the face of the person requesting entry/exit and comparing it with a stored image. With the use of video digital image analysis algorithms as well as retina scanning, facial profiling, and iris scanning, the equipment automatically identifies or rejects the person. Fingerprints and hand geometry represent biometric features that can be used for personnel identification.

Analog and digital video equipment is used extensively to train security personnel. It is a convenient, cost-effective, and powerful visual tool to get new personnel acquainted with physical facilities, security and safety procedures, as well as the management.

A professional installer or installing company is crucial in the successful implementation and effective operation of any security system. A professional maintenance program is equally as important.

In designing the video system, how one chooses the camera equipment depends on whether it will be used indoors or outdoors. In indoor applications such as elevators, lobbies, stairwells, stockrooms or computer rooms, minimum and low environmental protection is required.

However, outdoor equipment can be subjected to various environmental factors including extreme temperature and humidity, high winds, precipitation (rain, sleet, and snow), dirt, dust, chemicals, and sand. The outdoor equipment must be designed to be durable under all these adverse environmental conditions. To maintain proper operation of cameras and lenses in outdoor environments, thermostatically controlled heaters and/or fans are essential to the maintenance of the interior of the housing for the appropriate temperature range of the camera and lens equipment. Periodic maintenance of the pan/tilt mechanisms must be performed, including lubrication of moving parts and checkups for deterioration or wear of flexing or exposed wires.

If it is to be used for daytime and nighttime surveillance, the equipment may need to operate under large variations in light levels. Video equipment in outdoor applications operates under extreme variations in light level, from low levels (produced by artificial lighting for nighttime use) to bright sunlight and snow, sand or sun-reflected scenes. This often represents a one-million to-one decrease in light levels for which the camera system must compensate.

Video cameras and lenses are installed in indoor and outdoor environments through a couple of different means by using:

1. A simple camera bracket.
2. A camera housing and bracket.
3. A recessed mounting in the ceiling or wall.

Camera brackets can fix the camera and lens at a location but do not protect them from vandalism or environmental damages.

Indoor and outdoor video equipment consists of the following:

1. Camera mountings.
2. Camera housings.
3. Cameras, lenses.
4. Pan/tilt mechanisms.
5. Domes.
6. Visible or IR illuminators.
7. The cable that transmit the power and control signals to the equipment and then transmit the video signals, as well as any other communication.

The security room equipment consists of the following items: Cathode ray tubes CRT monitors, switchers, multiplexers, time/date, camera ID, Liquid Crystal Display monitors LCDs, VCRs, DVRs, message generators, hard-copy video printers, etc.

2. ANALOG LOBBY VIDEO SURVEILLANCE SYSTEM

A common surveillance place is the entrance lobby to a facility. The lobby contains a front entrance door and one or more internal doors and is usually occupied by person whether it is a receptionist, a security guard, some visitors (business or public), as well as employees of the facility. The security

functions that the video system performs for the receptionist and security staff include:

1. Observing the lobby area.
2. Monitoring and controlling personnel entry and exit.
3. Monitoring and controlling material movement through the main entrance.
4. Guarding the receptionist.

Figure 1 shows video security application of monitoring people entering and leaving the front lobby of a building, as well as the surveillance of the reception area.

One camera C1 is located in the lobby close to the ceiling and looks down on the entrance door and lobby with a lens having a wide field of view, wide enough to see at least half of the lobby, the receptionist, and the front door. The second camera, placed on the opposite wall C2 views the other half of the lobby and the internal access door. The third camera is covertly mounted in a clock, C3.

After choosing the equipment, choosing the camera locations is most important aspect. The camera/lens should not be pointed in the direction of a bright light, the sun, or even toward an outside door or window. If sunlight enters the camera lens directly, blooming (white areas in scene)

Figure 1. Analog lobby video surveillance system

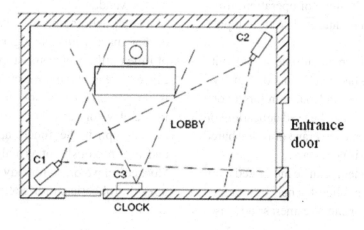

can obliterate part of the scene. CMOS or CCD cameras use automatic-iris lenses or electronic shuttering to compensate for light-level changes but do not always accurately compensate for a bright spot in a scene. A person under surveillance who is back-illuminated by light from an outward facing window or door is usually seen on the monitor as a black silhouette and are unable to be identified. Some cameras have automatic back-light compensation.

The video signals from the two overt video cameras and the covert camera in the lobby are transmitted to one or two monitors located at the remote security guard station. The two overt cameras overlook people entering and exiting through the front entrance door, most of the lobby, the receptionist, and the internal access door. The third covert camera provides backup in the event the overt cameras are rendered inoperative.

Accompanying each hardware component is a list of parameters that must be identified in order to define it. First the following aspects should be taken into account:

1. The number of cameras needed to cover all important areas.
2. Illumination conditions: light level constant or cameras exposure to the direct sunlight.
3. Type of lenses: automatic-iris lens or manual lens.
4. Necessity for covert cameras as a backup to the overt cameras in case they are inoperative.
5. Video recorder's mode of operation: time-lapsed, manual or automatic (alarm input).

The cameras can be monochrome or color with automatic-iris lenses because of outside windows and doors. A multiplexer and four monitors, or one monitor and a switcher can be used depending on whether 100% full-time coverage or time-shared (switched) coverage is necessary.

The two overt cameras can be integrated camera lens-housing assemblies that may be mounted directly on brackets, or can be cameras and lenses

installed in housings and then bracket-mounted (depending on the vandalism/environmental issues). In a typical console, the monitor(s) are usually around 9 inches diagonally, but possibly larger for optimum viewing capacities.

The multiplexer is an 8-channel system permitting display of all four cameras in a quad format, or for each individual camera. The switcher, if used, is a four-position, alarming sequential type.

The digital video recorder or video cassette recorder should be programmed to record the pictures sequentially, in a time-lapse mode coming from all three cameras. In the event that an alarm input goes off, the recorder automatically switches to real-time recording. The video printer is available in order to make hard-copy prints of any video scene from the recorder or monitor.

3. ANALOG ELEVATOR VIDEO SURVEILLANCE SYSTEM

In recent years, elevator crime has increased drastically; this threat is a potential liability to the owner of the building. The use of video surveillance in elevators and the lobbies in which people wait for them decreases the likelihood that elevator passengers will be the victims of crime. Since elevators are quite an investment, installing a video camera is a good way to protect this investment. Surveillance decreases the possibility that passengers themselves and also the elevator will be vandalized.

People getting into an elevator are "locked in" to that space with a stranger for a short period of time until the elevator stops on another floor. Since there are no more elevator operators, there is no person to monitor passengers' behavior inside elevator cabs. The elevator operator used to accomplish the function, both consciously and unconsciously, of visual monitoring in the "locked" elevator, so nobody was ever alone. As a result, robberies, molestations, and vandalism were prevented. Obviously placed video and audio surveillance takes the place of elevator operators.

Vandalism costs building managers and owners a vast amount of money per year: they spend thousands of dollars to renovate elevator cab interiors that have been vandalized and defaced. Studies show that installing video monitoring systems in open facilities considerably reduces elevator cab vandalism and personal crime.

Elevator video surveillance systems must be able to see a picture of the complete elevator interior from a remote video location. The image should amplify the facial view of the occupants of the elevator, and the image quality and resolution of the camera should be high enough to identify individuals and their activities. Using a wide field of view lens and camera in an appropriate housing system ensures that 100% of the elevator will be visible from the remote monitor. Real-time surveillance is actually performed in the building's lobby or in a manager's office, where the video signal is streamed to a monitor.

If the monitor is in the lobby, potential passengers can assess the situation to determine that the elevator is safe before entering. The fact that everyone is aware that surveillance is happening is an additional safeguard that reassures passengers.

Figure 2 shows examples of a wide field of view camera placed in a ceiling corner, which has been shown to be the most effective elevator setup.

The camera system ought to have a 90 degree horizontal field of view by about a 70 degree vertical field of view. Also, the camera/lens optical axis ought to be focused 45 degrees from each wall and 45 down from the ceiling. This viewing setup has an outcome of 100% exposure of the elevator's contents while also offering the tremendous likelihood of occupants and activities being identified. Cab video camera systems should also be very unobtrusive and small since space is of high demand in such a confined environment.

Since the camera is necessarily in the cab itself, it must be housed and protected against vandalism. Figure 3 shows durable and heavy duty housing.

Figure 2. Elevator video surveillance

Figure 3. Heavy duty corner elevator housing (Google, 2013)

Elevator video camera systems should also have:

1. A tamper-proof, hinged encasing.
2. Easily accessible lens and camera (for maintenance).
3. Unbreakable window.
4. An easily detachable camera lens setup (for maintenance).

The detachable observation window is most often made of mar-resistant polycarbonate and is .25 inches thick. One can also use tempered glass instead of polycarbonate as it is scratch- and chemical-resistant. Numerous other camera/lens/ housing arrangements are accessible for direct mounting into the elevator cab's ceiling corner.

The back of the camera/lens housing is formed to correspond directly to the shape of the ceiling corner, avoiding the jutting of the façade into the main area of the elevator.

Elevator camera systems tend to have wide-angle lenses which give a 90 degrees horizontal by 75 degrees vertical field of view.

Covert video camera installations use:

1. Small video cameras.
2. Small remote-head camera.
3. Right-angle optics.

A small camera only shows the front of its lens to passengers when installed inside elevators. Remote-head cameras equipped with wide field of view lenses can be installed in an elevator cab and only the lens will show. The right-angle optical system permits a full-size camera to be installed parallel to the elevator ceiling, avoiding vignetting which is reduction of an image's brightness or saturation at the periphery compared to the image center. . This is possible through a redirection of the image by 90 degrees.

High-resolution camera systems can be used in elevators with only the lens visible. The lens adapter and camera body are located above the ceiling itself. Although this is the least conspicuous camera option, it has the worst facial viewing capabilities. In most situations, all these types of lenses can simply be hidden behind windows that are treated to be semitransparent and then the installation is completely covert.

Analog Six Camera Video Elevator and Lobby Surveillance System

Figure 4 shows an elevator cab equipped with six cameras; the surveillance system is located in the lobby.

The system has:

1. A video camera/lens and housing assembly in each elevator cab, making four total.
2. Two cameras/lens assemblies in the lobby.
3. Four cables from the cameras to the console room for video transmission purposes.
4. A video switcher, quad splitter or multiplexer.
5. Two monitors in the console room and two in the lobby.
6. Digital video recorder equipped with time-lapse and alarm technology.
7. A video printer.

The four pictures from the four elevators can be split onto two monitors in the elevator lobby. The images from all six cameras are then displayed

Figure 4. Analog six-camera video elevator and lobby surveillance system

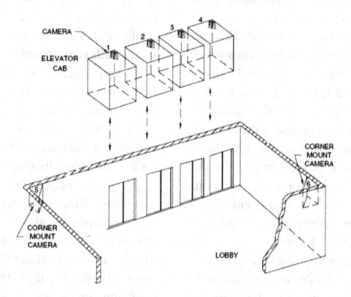

in the security console on two separate monitors. The time-lapse digital video recorder or video cassette recorder records the video signals from the elevator and lobby and they are then printed out in hard copy as needed.

To operate, cameras 1, 2, 3, and 4 in the elevator takes in an image of the elevator cab and sends it to the quad splitter/combiner component and the video switcher. From there the signal travels to the monitors, record, and printer.

Then the video output is conducted through cables. Every time the elevator cab moves, the cables will twist and bend, so the cable must be very flexible and durable. Fiber-optic cables are advantageous because they are immune to noise interference; elevators are very noisy due to their motors, relays, switches, and electronics. Fiber optics also insures that there will be no electrical interference. Digital wireless systems have recently emerged as an alternative to previous wired systems.

The usual six-camera elevator surveillance system uses only analog technology in both the cabs and the lobby.

The following issues should be considered when trying to design a security system that deters crime and does not intimidate passengers:

1. Type of camera operation:
   a. Overt systems are ideal because they can sometimes deter a criminal in the first place.
   b. In a covert situation, a guard may be more able to respond immediately. Concealed camera systems are not as offensive as overt ones.
2. Lenses with wide field of view are necessary. Ideally the system points 45 degrees downwards and has a 90 degree horizontal field of view with a 70 degree vertical field of view.
3. The elevator should offer no hiding spots.
4. Camera housing must be durable and vandal proof. Vandal proof locks and tamper proof screws are an integral part of this expectation.
5. Lighting should be good enough for CCD or CMOS conditions.
6. Monitor installation positions.
7. Permanent documentation of the monitor picture is suggested.

Cameras inside elevators can possibly be CCD format or CMOS format with a CS/mini lens mount. Luminance levels change on each floor, so these surveillance systems must have a manual or auto iris lens, or an electronically shuttered camera. Stainless steel housing is the best, most durable choice for housing in an elevator. The housing is mounted on holes that are drilled in the elevator cab and then the camera/lens setup is installed.

To allow for anyone in the lobby to see the faces of people in the elevator, the monitors in the lobby should be very large and mounted visibly on brackets. The security room should have 9-inch CRT or 15-inch LCD monitors so that the guards have the maximum possible resolution.

The digital video recorder has four channels with which to record the cab images. If the images are recorded onto a video cassette recorder, it is done in S-VHS format.

Video printers are useful because they produce a hard copy of a potential target for distribution to security personnel. If planning to use the hard copy as evidence in a court of law, it must be dated and marked with the time.

4. ANALOG/DIGITAL OFFICE VIDEO SURVEILLANCE SYSTEM

Maintenance contractors and employees steal millions of dollars worth of goods every year from government, business, and industrial facilities. Calculators, telephones, PC and laptop computers, personal digital assistants, and fax and copying machines are the main targets of theft. Sometimes company software and data files are copied or removed without permission.

Installing a covert video system in the area is the best thing a company can do to reduce these losses. The following section discusses obscured video camera/lens surveillance systems for the purposes of an office environment.

Covert video surveillance can be used for those who are behaving normally as well as for those who are committing crimes. A video system ought to help guards apprehend and prosecute those who are being unlawful. Covert systems can also act in conjunction with an overt system in case the overt system falls victim to vandalism or technical error.

Covert cameras should be concealed inside an office in unexpected places. Since covert systems have small lenses and cameras they can be put in ceilings, walls, and other fixtures. Specifically, cameras can be put in exit signs, pictures, lamps, radios, emergency lights, cabinets, computers, etc.

Existing analog cameras can be used in a digital system by adding an analog to IP interface adapter. In general, new installations can be either analog or digital. The video signals are then transmitted via fiber optics, coaxial or UTP cables, or wireless (analog) or wireless digital networks. Wireless installations are easier and quicker to install. Analog wireless cameras utilize analog transmitters or a receiver pair. Digital systems utilize IP cameras and a transmission means like a LAN.

The following should be considered when designing analog/digital office video surveillance system:

1. Temporary or permanent installation, if temporary the type of power supply should be determined.
2. Types of cameras, wired or wireless.
3. Type of video surveillance system, analog or digital. Remote sites require digital surveillance.
4. If an immediate response from the guards is needed.
5. If video is required to be recorded for later events and uses.
6. The personal in charge of the covert video system installation – security, management, or outside security sources.

Covert cameras are sometimes disguised as water sprinklers in the ceiling of an office, which provides the best possible view from above. One version of this system involves a pinhole lens that is either straight or at a right angle. It is mounted onto a camera that has a faux sprinkler head and a beam-directing mirror that positions the camera field of view appropriately. The small mirror and the sprinkler head are the only visible parts of the installation. The mirror is able to be adjusted to many angles from completely horizontal down to -60 degrees. Lenses that point directly down are also acceptable. Most observers will not be able to notice the mirror behind the sprinkler head in the ceiling.

In a second variety, a combined sprinkler-head camera involving a single board camera is attached to the ceiling using magnetic supports if the camera must be dropped, or using a mechanical attachment if the contraption is directly attached to the ceiling.

If the installation of cables proves too difficult, analog video transmission can be performed by low-power analog RF, microwave, and IR transmitters from the camera to the monitor. To transmit the video image digitally, one must use a digital WiFi transmitter or receiver pairs.

Some areas of offices are more susceptible to theft than others, including computers, cabinets, copies, fax machines, software, records, and vaults.

For example, two of three ceiling-mounted cameras can be undercover as sprinkler heads, and the third can have a 360-degree panning ability in order to increase coverage and to follow moving targets. The last three cameras can be hidden in a wall clock, an exit sign, and an emergency lighting fixture.

Dome cameras are considered semi-covert because although passersby are aware of its presence, they do not know in which direction it is pointing. Dome cameras can pan 360 degrees using a zoom lens. The camera inside the exit sign can see anyone entering or leaving the manager's office as well as anyone trying to enter the fault.

The camera/lens combination stored in the manager's clock is an extremely small CCD/CMOS camera that has offset mini lens optics for the viewing of files and the office door. The "sprinklers" on the ceiling can be fixed and monitor the manager's computer terminal and desk. The file

room has a wall-mounted light fixture that monitors the fax machine, copier, files, and computer. Two ceiling-mounted cameras can monitor front office personnel, the office entrance, the vault, and the file cabinet and stacks.

Hard-wire, fiber optics, and wireless methods are used to transmit signals from cameras, lenses, and panning units. Monitors, a recorder, and a video printer are also necessary in the installation.

5. ANALOG/DIGITAL MERCANTILE ESTABLISHMENT VIDEO SURVEILLANCE SYSTEM

Video should lend "remote eyes" to management and security departments. It is the best tool to use in mercantile establishment security systems. Strategically placed video should make it possible for security to see many locations within the store from the management consoles. These cameras should focus on cashiers, point-of-sale terminals, merchandise, high-end products, and entrances and exists.

Both overt and covert operations are appropriate in a retail setting, as long as they are equipped with pan/tilt/zoom functionality when necessary. Video domes are very useful in this setting.

The system should also be capable of signaling the guard to action through motion detectors, alarms, and physical signals from personnel in the area. Video cassette recorders and digital video recorders should be in place to record and store camera scenes either live or after the fact. When triggered by alarms, recorders should be able to switch automatically to real-time mode. Video printers are a good solution when an instantaneous response is required.

While monochrome cameras are the most sensitive and resolute, color cameras make it easier to identify objects and people.

Video systems are much cheaper to implement than an entire crew of security personnel.

Small Retail Stores

Experts claim that most theft occurs at the point of sale. It happens at this point about three times as often as any other time in a shopping experience. It can also occur through employee and outside vendor theft, trafficked out the back door.

When data from the point-of-sale system is recorded along with an image and employees are held accountable for their transactions, theft dramatically decreases. Cash register displays should have the transaction number, register number, operator name, date, time, items purchased, total cost, the amount tendered, and the amount of change. Employee theft at the register is the foremost cause of inventory shrinkage in convenience stores.

Video surveillance has been shown to decrease this loss. Video footage in combination with accurate register readouts means that the manager can see every detail and have them confirmed with a visual record. Equipment not unlike that used in lobbies is also used in small retail environments. To ensure employee accountability, the register must be electronically able to associate a transaction with a specific employee via an interface.

Large Retail Stores

Functional security systems in retail stores must integrate video, alarm sensors, intrusion detections, and personnel coordination in order to see response procedures through. There must be an atmosphere of teamwork. In order for security officers, sales force members, and console staff to communicate there must be a two-way radio connection. This enhances the system already provided by the video system. The head guard and the management monitor the sales floor through the video footage, on the watch for systemic violations and shoplifting. When a violation occurs, the operator contacts the floor officer who then apprehends the perpetrator or questions people at the scene. Officers can keep a physical eye on the door, radioing the console operator when they see something suspicious that should be tracked via security camera. Floor officers, the console operator, and management work together to surveil the premises.

Obviously placed cameras tend to nip any desire to shoplift in the bud. Those who are professional thieves bank on the fact that many large retail stores are simply too big to monitor the entirety. They keep track of where overt cameras are pointing. In order to prevent this, stores can implement optical domes or other features like sprinkler heads that will disguise the camera.

Plastic domes conceal the whole setup, which prevents observers from seeing which way the camera is panning, tilting, and zooming. This way they cannot know whether they are being observed. However, a dome reduces visibility and light loss by about 50%. It is possible to install dummy domes that do not even include cameras. They simply deter customers from potential theft. Cameras can be installed at a later date.

Overt Showroom Floor Surveillance

Overt video surveillance's main advantage is that it deters theft on the part of both customers and employees. When cameras are highly visible, they enable employees to keep guard over expensive merchandise. The main sales floor is generally monitored by ceiling-level color cameras.

PTZ dome cameras are capable of monitoring very large spaces; security operators review the footage in order to track potential violations. Dome cameras generally have magnification functions that are powerful enough to identify not only stolen merchandise but also the facial details of the person in question. With small jewelry, extremely high magnification color cameras are able to notice the smaller, characteristic features necessary for identifying the jewelry that monochrome cameras cannot capture. These color cameras can identify jewelry, small items, and disparities in skin color, hair, and clothing. Digital video motion detector functions help cameras decide on which aspects to focus.

To focus on a high-traffic area of a store, security personnel can draw a window around this section, triggering an alarm when there is any motion in this area.

In a small shop, fixed cameras can cover the entire area.

In summary, the primary function of overt video surveillance in a retail setting is deterring crime in the first place. When crime does take place, the surveillance system helps officers identify the person in question and the items at hand.

The third most important function is that of monitoring employee performance and adherence to procedures. Employees are often monitored for breaking procedures like the following: leaving the doors to a showcase open, showing too many items at once, and leaving keys in locks.

Covert video assists with the location and apprehension of the thieves and employees who were not deterred by the overt system. Since the thief cannot see the covert video, he or she cannot get past it; video cameras are usually hidden within the building itself. Small covert cameras can be easily installed or removed, making them suitable for internal store investigations.

There are many concealment options for cameras in a store. One of the most useful techniques is hiding a lens and camera within a ceiling-mounted sprinkler head. This is a good hiding spot since most stores are legally required to have overhead sprinkler systems. The camera does not interfere with the functionality of the fire-suppression system. Customers do not notice the sprinkler cameras because they are too far up and well disguised. The whole assembly of camera lens and sprinkler head rotates in the direction it needs to, and a small mirror tilts the camera to the right angle. More advanced sprinkler installations include a 360-degree pan function controlled remotely.

Analog/digital eight-camera showroom floor video system is the example video surveillance system that is both covert and overt, see Figure 5. Before installing the video surveillance system in showroom floor the following is important to assess:

1. Surveilled areas.
2. Prime camera locations.
3. Type of covert transmission: wireless or wired.

Figure 5. Analog/digital eight-camera showroom floor video system

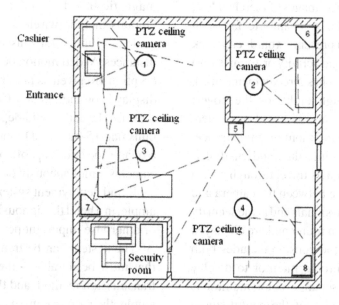

4. The best fit and location of high-speed dome cameras.

5. Fixed camera position for the purpose of consistently surveilled areas.

6. Type of cameras: analog or digital.

7. Monochrome camera locations.

8. Color camera locations.

9. Cameras enclosed in a dome or enabled with pan/tilt/zoom or pan/tilt platforms.

10. Application of electronic or electro-optical registers/point-of-sale.

Five color overt cameras are placed on the sales floor, whereas three monochrome cameras are hiding to monitor more specific activities. There is one fixed camera that utilizes IP technology. Four speed-dome cameras utilize PTZ control alongside IP video transmission. These four cameras can scan very quickly from their dome since the camera and zoom lens module is mounted on a high-speed PT platform. The dome is tinted for more covert operation. CCD cameras emit digital IP video signals, at which point the pan/tilt platform and zoom lens signals are sent to the lens itself.

It can be seen in Figure 5 that the four color cameras that are mounted on quick-moving pan/tilt platforms are equipped with zoom lenses to provide very high quality images of merchandise, activities, and individuals. Thanks to fast-scan technology and certain presents, guards can track potential thieves or illegal activity or zoom in on a location that the camera has already memorized.

Cameras six through eight, or the covert monochrome cameras, are mounted in corners inconspicuously. Camera 7 monitors the entrance.

Controls such as panning, tilted, and lens directing as well as video signals travel through a hard wire or fiber optic cable between the camera and security console. Video signals end at the security console; they enter via a router and are displayed on monitors. Usually the console includes both a color and a monochrome monitor to display the covert scenes. A separate color monitor is designated for the display of the pan/tilt/zoom cameras' images. It is possible to display all eight of the images on a color monitor, record them on a digital video recorder and print them on a thermal video printer. The color pan/tilt cameras and their functions and presents are controlled remotely.

The zoom lens, focus, and camera iris can be easily remotely controlled or preset thanks to their detailed parameters. The pan/tilt platform is also highly controllable and can be manipulated for the four color camera in order to easily track targets.

6. ANALOG/DIGITAL VIDEO RAPID DEPLOYMENT SYSTEM VIDEO SURVEILLANCE SYSTEM

The video rapid deployment system consists of video surveillance cameras hooked up either through wires or wirelessly to the security console. They are used to trigger a very quick response in order to protect specific assets or personnel. Rapid deployment system is specific to certain tasks and situations. Equipment should be contained in watertight cases to ensure safe transport. This is a portable system that provides temporary surveillance. It can be monitored remotely or locally. The video system consists of cameras with convenient mounting options including clamps, magnetic-based tripod accessories (pan/tilt). Options include wireless color cameras having analog or digital transmission over short or long distances. Video motion detection and video encryption are given as possibilities as well. Video display is on individual LCD monitors built into the case. Usually rapid deployment system contains one 15-inch LCD monitor that comes with a quad processor capable of displaying the four cameras simultaneously or individually.

Rapid deployment system can be used, for example, in a hotel that is housing visiting diplomats or otherwise important personas.

The system can be transported in two cases that must be durable – they hold the cameras, transmission method, and the display. In this example, the system consists of two wired and two wireless cameras and LCD monitor for the display of the signals. The system also includes analog cameras that can use digital motion detectors and encrypt said signals.

When designing the rapid deployment system video surveillance system the following is important:

1. Number of cameras.
2. Type of cameras: analog, IP, wired, or wireless.
3. The distance between the camera and the monitor.

7. DIGITAL PARKING LOT VIDEO SURVEILLANCE SYSTEM

There are quite a few factors to take into account when installing an outdoor system: it should monitor the perimeter, the fence, the parking lot, the building's façade, and the loading dock. This can be done with just a few cameras or require a very large system with many cameras.

To surveil a whole parking lot, an entire exterior, driveways around the facility, and an entire fenced perimeter, cameras should be mounted on poles or on the roof of a building. In order to avoid installing cables underneath a parking lot, cameras should be mounted on poles and connected to the control room via two-way wireless transmission capabilities. The electricity that is already going to the lights on poles powers the system. Ideally, such an outdoor installation would use digital IP color cameras with a WiFi digital transmission system.

Twelve camera outdoor parking lot surveillance system is the example where at least a couple of cameras should be mounted to poles, pedestals, and fence posts in order to notice intrusion around the perimeter of the facility. These cameras only view external components of the facility like the entrances, exits, parking lots, and loading docks. Building cameras improve their accuracy. Cameras surveilling a parking lot should also have a very

wide field of view, up to 360 degrees, while also being able to zoom in very quickly and provide a lot of detail through resolution. It is necessary that the lens and camera tilt from 0 to -90 degrees in order to see a scene close up and far away.

The solution to the requirement that the camera must see with both wide and narrow precision can be addressed in four ways:

1. Use cameras on pan/tilt platforms that have zoom lenses, or use speed-dome cameras.
2. Multiple cameras can fragment a wide field of view into narrow field of view.
3. Use pan/tilt cameras that have two fixed focal length lenses, one that is wide and one that is narrow.

A pan/tilt system makes it so that video cameras and lenses can rotate in any direction, examining scenes that would normally be outside the reach of the field of view. The scope of fixed focal length lens and camera systems that are placed on stationary platforms is limited by the camera lens' field of view and sensor format.

Zoom lenses that are either in domes or on pan/tilt platforms are more useful than fixed focal length lenses in that they can see any part of the scene either automatically or thanks to operator control. Focal length variable zoom lenses have varied field of views that can cover large areas in a low-resolution mode and smaller areas in high-resolution mode. However, the zoom lens installation almost always has a "dead zone" as a result of the time it takes for the camera to switch positions and foci. The camera cannot be examining all locations at once, so the time in between foci is called the dead zone.

This dead zone can be eliminated by certain system presets which imply static vs. dynamic field of views of stationary and pan/tilt systems. This arrangement is especially suitable for use in outdoor parking lots and fence lines (perimeters).

Even though the camera with pan/tilt option and zoom lens' instantaneous and dynamic field of view adjustment represent the complete angular coverage, the monitor can only show a certain amount of the surveilled area; in fact, most of it goes undisplayed. When a person is hiding from the camera, the camera's pan/tilt mechanism can sometimes be hidden so that the person cannot know where the camera is pointing. When used by a fence line, the pan/tilt function in its default position pointing at a gate only assures motion detector when it occurs within that narrow field of view. At the same time, the use of a wide field of view lens ensures that there will be no dead zone.

When designing digital wireless twelve-camera parking lot and perimeter video system the following has to be taken into consideration:

1. The position of fixed focal length, zoom, and bi-focal lenses.
2. Dead viewing zones problem.
3. Position and placement of color and monochrome cameras.
4. Cameras housing or concealing.
5. The need for fans, heaters, and window washers.
6. Low light level cameras versus adding artificial light.
7. Transmission mode type: UTP, fiber optics, digital wireless, coaxial cable, microwave, RF, IR.

In this setup, eight cameras are mounted on a pedestal and use a speed dome along with pan/tilt/zoom functionality for complete coverage of the entire area. There are also two covert cameras monitoring the building and its entrance. The last two cameras are mounted on fixed platforms to monitor the loading dock and its surrounding areas using vari-focal lenses.

All video signals are sent to the security room. UTP or fiber optic cable is used to transmit the digital video signal in order to get rid of the possibility that machinery, lightning, and other phenomena will not cause electrical interference. From the console room, output travels to the monitors, a digital video recorder, and a printer.

The speed dome cameras lining the perimeter should be digital IP cameras that are equipped for day and night, color and monochrome, using automatic switchover technology and integrated motion detection. CCD cameras have automatic iris zoom lenses and/or electronic shuttering for all conditions. When operating in monochrome mode, the CCD can see in lower light levels than in color mode. When there are no artificial lighting options for low-light situations, the following may be done:

1. Add pole lighting or IR illumination technology to the camera
2. Buy a more expensive Intensified CCD camera
3. Employ a thermal IR camera

Outdoor housings should come equipped with heaters and fans to fit local weather. Also, an automatic window washer can improve image consistency. Antifreeze should be added to the washer solution in cold climates. The rating of the pan/tilt platform should exceed the weight of the housing, camera, lens, and accessories, plus take into account wind power and a 10% safety buffer.

Fiber-optic cables are the optimal video transmission method; they can be buried or located in a conduit. Coaxial cable can be used, but only in places where there are guaranteed to be no storms.

Pan/tilt/zoom cameras that are mounted on a building can be either color or monochrome. Color makes it easier to identify people, equipment, and cars, whereas monochrome cameras are better in situations that require close attention to a narrow field of view, such as a loading dock.

Choose the best combination of features so that the highest amount of scene components will be visible and identifiable on your security monitor. Insufficient lighting can be compensated for by artificial lighting installations or an low level light camera.

Figure 6. Digital wireless twelve-camera parking lot and perimeter video system

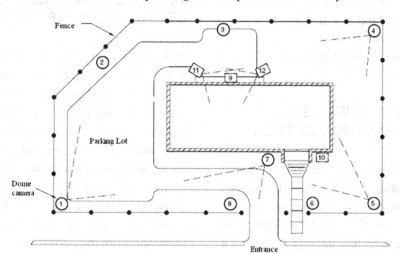

8. WIRED AND WIRELESS SINGLE SITE VIDEO SURVEILLANCE SYSTEM

Digital video technology is rapidly replacing analog technology in video surveillance installations. This is largely due to the low cost and availability of personal computers and gadgets. As a result, digital IP cameras, multiplexers, and digital video recorder equipment is newly installed on a daily basis.

Since the rise of digital equipment, digital signal transmission means have also overtaken analog methods (UTP, fiber optic, and coaxial transmission) using technology such as wide area network WAN, local area network LAN, Intranet, and WiFi Internet. Special software allows operators to view scenes from video cameras and manage the cameras from far away, being able to switch, display, and record scenes in various combinations.

The following is the example of a single site eight-camera warehouse digital video surveillance system that is using internal intranet networks and WiFi transmission that monitors the perimeter, parking lot, and loading area of a single facility. It should also monitor the warehouse entrance to the office, the back docking area, and the general interior of the warehouse.

Four outdoor speed dome pan/tilt/zoom cameras view the outdoor scenes of the facility. They are mounted along the fence looking towards the building, not outward. The main function of these cameras is to observe vehicles going in and out of the gate, monitor the parking lot and various loading and unloading operations. On the pedestals near the fence, four pan/tilt/zoom IP outdoor color cameras are mounted. In the back of the warehouse, two indoor cameras have been placed so they can observe the loading dock and trucks' interiors. In order to identify people, activities, and products, these two cameras are equipped with day/night and IR illumination technology. Meanwhile, the warehouse office and general floor are monitored by two indoor cameras in order to provide very general oversight of activities and personnel. Indoor cameras utilize LAN digital networks for the transmission of video signals to the security console. The signals get sent to multiplexers, then switchers, computers, displays, and finally recorders. WiFi transmits the four outdoor cameras' digital and PTZ control signals to the monitoring security console.

LCD monitors and keyboards for the viewing of camera images are supplied to security, operations, and management officials.

The following should be assessed prior to this video surveillance design:

1. The number of outdoor cameras.
2. The number of indoor cameras.
3. Illumination conditions.
4. Type of cameras: overt or covert.

9. WIRELESS MULTIPLE SITE VIDEO SURVEILLANCE SYSTEM

The proposed application requires both single- and multi-site monitoring via LANs and the Internet in order to perform inter-site transmitting, control, and communications. This way, video images are visible to anyone who has Internet access on a laptop, PC, personal digital assistants PDA, and other devices. Digital recording in the central control center can also be done with network video recorder NVR.

All wireless transmission should have appropriate encryption levels in order to deter eavesdropping and increase security.

In this example the enterprise is divided into three separate sites, each with its own control room and remote control center. These sites are all within the same city, whereas the security center's headquarters is in another city. Since the sites are distanced from one another and the control center, it is absolutely necessary that surveillance is performed at real time and transmitted as quickly as possible to the remote sites. The surveillance network can also be accessed through mobile devices and gadgets.

The previous example's hardware and equipment is similar to the gear in this case. The headquarters use this type of equipment as well. The hardware and software must also be able to communicate and transmit data between all of these sites; each camera in each site must be equally accessible. The following should be kept in mind: type of digital recording, level of security, the best kind of encryption.

10. VIDEO SURVEILLANCE OF CORRECTIONAL FACILITY

Video is the primary means by which guards can monitor and control inmates from afar in a large correctional facility. Guards can also check the movement patterns of visitors, vendors, employees, contractors, and inmates themselves.

Cameras observe inmates at the beginning of their sentences, then continue while the inmates are in their cells and doing activities. Overt security installations are especially useful in correctional facilities because they deter inmates from trying to escape from the perimeter.

Video systems should have advanced graphics display abilities in order to be of real help to security personnel on a daily basis. Large-screen color monitors are able to show facility maps that were previously stored, outlining entrances and exits, alarms, and the locations of security cameras. This physical information in combination with the video information is invaluable to guards' decision-making capabilities, especially when it comes to opening and closing doors, calling for backup, and in general, ensuring the safety of everyone on the premises.

Video systems must come equipped with a backup electrical power system because they are so crucial to the functioning of the facility and the safety of the staff.

The most critical cameras are recommended to have a backup transmission path and system, hopefully wireless, in the case their cabled main transmission path is interrupted or severed.

Obvious, overt operations are located everywhere in the correctional facility. It both deters inmates from performing unwanted actions and monitors them 24/7. Video systems equipped with alarms are installed at all perimeter locations in order to track the movement patterns of vehicles and site personnel. Personnel are identified based on the technologies of iris scanning, retinal scans, and facial scans, which can be integrated into a security system. These make sure that each person entering a facility is identified and recorded.

Via pan/tilt/zoom video equipment, including video motion detectors, a correctional facility's perimeter can be monitored. Other intrusion detection technology includes seismic, E-field, microwave, and RF detectors.

Digital motion sensing is the best way to detect motion in an outdoor environment; it also ensures low rates of false alarms. In order to function correctly, perimeter surveillance must be outfitted with nighttime lights. This way, people, activities, and procedures can still be accurately monitored and matched to the results of the video motion detector system.

Durable, strong camera housings, as well as light fixtures and luminaries, are necessary in case of attack or natural factors that could interfere with the hardware. If sufficient lighting cannot be provided, use Intensified CCD and thermal IR cameras.

Low level light monochrome or color cameras are used to monitor cells, cell blocks, and activity centers. Color is desired because it can more accurately identify inmates. Depending on the scene's location and requirement, both fixed cameras and high-speed pan/tilt/zoom cameras can be used. If more than one cell must be monitored by a single camera, wide-angle systems with 90 degree horizontal field of view can be installed. Holding cells require 24-hour supervision, which is improved by the addition of IR illuminators to the camera, allowing them to "see" at night.

While overt surveillance both deters unwanted activities and monitors, covert surveillance is used to discover clandestine, secretive acts. The areas that most call for covert surveillance are cells that hold disturbed inmates, drug dispensaries, and in places that would be helpful to staff during emergency situations. Most correctional facilities have many places in which covert equipment can be concealed.

To surveil at night, IR illuminators and monochrome cameras can be used.

11. VIDEO SURVEILLANCE OF BANKING AND FINANCIAL INSTITUTIONS

Banks and financial institutions very frequently use video surveillance. Increasing government regulation calls for integrated security systems using video. Video also allows banks to protect assets and staff, as well as survive and make assessments about disasters or crimes. Not only people and assets must be monitored, but also telecommunications, data, and computers.

Advanced video surveillance systems control the restriction of access to certain acts: money counting, vault storage, sensitive data processing, and confidential communications. ATMs also require the use of video surveillance cameras in order to link customers with the transactions they are performing. Money withdrawal and check cashing are now more accurate thanks to this technology. Similarly, drive-in banking utilizes video monitoring to link customers and transactions as well as to keep a general eye on things.

The main parts of a bank that require surveillance are the main floor and the safe deposit room. Video cameras are often installed in the same area as the bank tellers so that the customer's face can be recorded and matched with account information. Often, one camera monitors two teller stations. An automatic time and date function comes with the camera, marking the date and time of each transaction. There are also holdup cameras, which must be very high quality and accurate in order to provide information about crime in the bank.

Digital video recorders like digital video recorders and virtual digital recorders must replace the analog S-VHS video cassette recorders.

The most sensitive areas of a bank must be digitally and remotely controlled. The combination of electronic intelligence and video control allows full security of data and assets. Video identification is a necessary supplement since electronic access control and PINs do not ensure complete security. Ideally, a video storage and retrieval system is put in place.

Covert video should also have a place in banking environments in order to identify those who perform holdups or employees who may be stealing.

Banks' profitability is highly reliant on customer check identification. This should occur in two ways:

1. The customer's face along with an image of the check and the time and date should be recorded.
2. The employee should positively identify the customer him- or herself.

The first situation calls for the video surveillance system recording images of the face and check, and then annotating the date, time, and transaction number on the image frame itself. Prepackaged countertop video systems can meet this demand. High-resolution digital video recorders should be in place to record this video footage just in case it should ever be used in a court of law. The customer can be positively identified assuming accuracy of the hard disk video storage system.

In practice, the bank employee first enters a customer's name, data, and other identifying information onto a digital storage medium, and then assigns the image of the face to the same file. Then every time the customer comes into the bank to have a check cashed, one piece of data is entered, and the rest of the information pops up on the teller's screen to be used for proper identification.

This video retrieval system can operate via fiber optic/LAN wired connections, or intranet or Internet wireless communications for long distance transmission of data and video, potentially to other branches of the bank.

ATM security involves the recording of a customer's face along with manual entry of a PIN number. Then this information is recorded in a log along with the transaction time and date, the terminal number, and the transaction number. If a customer disputes a charge that was imposed by an ATM transaction, the financial institution

itself must provide the necessary evidence for or against the claim. A message annotator enables all of the information of the transaction to be recorded as a single visual record, with the data being combined with the person's picture in one image. This video camera also records footage of holdups and unauthorized withdrawals.

Drive-in banking is a common feature that banks provide for their customers. While in some setups, the teller can directly see the customer in his or her car, most of the time the customer's face is not visible to the teller. In any case, the customer's face, documents, and license plate should be recorded by video cameras and monitors.

12. VIDEO SURVEILLANCE OF LODGING AND CASINO SURVEILLANCE AREAS

Due to their size and complexity, hotels, motels, and casinos are often targeted for theft and vandalism. They also play host to many personal injuries (of staff and guests). Large surveillance setups are necessary in such environments. The following areas should be surveilled: lobbies, hallways, elevators, parking lots, entrances, gambling rooms, casino floors. Access control can also be performed by the surveillance system in locations including sensitive data and equipment, money-counting rooms, and security rooms themselves.

Since hotels, motels, and casinos are often casual, they attract people who may be amateur or professional offenders. Because of this, both overt and covert security should be used.

Video equipment should fully monitor hallways and corridors, showing the directions in which people are walking, among other details. Both color and monochrome overt and covert cameras can perform this function. Since the intersections of lobbies and hallways are often very angular, dome cameras or tri-split lenses should be used to reduce the number of cameras necessary. Often a three-lens, one-camera system is attached to the ceiling in a low-profile housing. This sends three images to one monitor.

Casino floors are complex environments to surveil because the system must satisfy not only staff and management, but also gaming officials on the state and local level. Large computer-controlled switchers and multiplexers control a vast array of equipment, including monochrome/color, overt/covert, fixed-position, pan/tilt/zoom systems. The most commonly used equipment is fixed-dome and speed-dome cameras. They are placed in order to see all slot machines, money counting rooms, cage and chip rooms, cashier cages, bars, vaults, and gambling tables. Often they are disguised behind one-way glass in the ceiling or camouflaged in plastic domes. They can also be disguised as sprinkler heads. Speed-dome and pan/tilt/zoom cameras are usually right at the ceiling level or above it in order to be unobtrusive. These installations also tend to be decorated in the style of the casino as to avoid detection. Their resolution is high enough to count chips and read cards.

When large casinos use hundreds of cameras, monitors, and recorders, they implement video matrix switching systems for ease of operation. This way, the operator has full control over each camera view, monitors, and recording devices. When video motion detectors and alarm sensors are added, they help detect and follow unauthorized paths or movements. The security guard is then cued by these motions and their subsequent alarms.

13. VIDEO SURVEILLANCE OF AIRPORT, SEAPORT, AND HIGHWAY SURVEILLANCE

The use of video surveillance equipment at seaports and airports has increased significantly over the last years because of the threat of terrorism. Airport cameras are both covert and overt because criminals will bypass overt cameras that they notice. At this point, covert cameras kick in and do the backup recording.

Usually the security control centers in airports and seaports are located far away from the site. Since distances are usually long and there is a high chance of interference from other communication devices in the area, transmission is usually performed by hard-wire fiber optic cables, shielded and isolated copper, and some digital wireless methods. This applies to both airports and seaports.

Highway surveillance is implemented to track traffic patterns and also traffic jams and car accidents. Cameras tend to be placed atop the poles and traffic signs that already exist along the highway or street. Cameras can run off of power that is already directed to the pole because the poles often host lights and other transmission equipment. Smart cameras with video motion detectors and intelligent algorithms give law enforcement officers the information they need to quickly assess a situation and then choose a plan of action.

14. ACCESS CONTROL THROUGH VIDEO SURVEILLANCE SYSTEM

Access control can also be done via video. Video must be added to electronic access control system if personnel must be identified correctly before accessing an area or object. Electronic access control card readers can only identify a card, never a person. Personal identification numbers (PINs) increase this security by adding a human element. However, unless photo identification or barometric methods are imposed, identification is never 100% guaranteed. Video systems can be useful for: image ID system and storage and retrieval of images and video.

The split-screen photo ID system simply shows the person's photo ID card on one half of the screen and the face of the person asking for access on the other. This type of identification is used when electronic access control systems enhanced with PINs are already useful.

The ID system is mounted to a door and contains optics and lights for the proper viewing of a person's face and ID card. A guard can communicate with the person using a call button and two-way intercom.

Each time a new person requests access, the system restores his or her information either magnetically or optically so that it can later be retrieved. If a person who has already been logged in the system asks for access, the system then grabs the image of the person that it already has. The human guard compares the two pictures – recorded and live – and makes a judgment. This human factor ensures that identification will be positive and accurate. A person can receive access using their name, ID number/PIN, or an electronic ID card.

These units can also be attached to a turnstile, which ensures that people will not be able to "tailgate" or enter immediately behind an authorized person. In this case, an overhead camera monitors the turnstile and its confined area. The guard should make sure that only person at a time is in the turnstile area and gaining access to the restricted area. This system can be joined with both an electronic access control system and a video image storage and retrieval system to ensure even greater security and positive identification of individuals who want to entre a restricted area.

When turnstiles cannot be used, a portal or mantrap is a suitable alternative. This two-door portal also prevents tailgating, but might more adaptable to some environments' security or architectural needs. Since this portal is larger, it allows other types of identification electronics (biometric and electronic) and is also accessible to physically disabled personnel. In order to positively identify personnel, this portal is often used in combination with video storage and retrieval systems and video identification equipment.

Video Vehicle Control

Vehicles must often enter facilities, for many reasons ranging from simple transportation to the transfer of goods. For less stringent control, electronic ID cards and keys can be used to access motorways, parking lots, and loading decks. This is simply an electronic access control system.

To ensure that the driver is positively identified, video image storage and retrieval or video photo ID systems must be implemented.

Video ID systems that are mounted on pedestals can be used for cars and vehicles of similar height. Housing should take the environment into account; this housing is equipped with heaters and fans that respond automatically to outside temperatures.

The system that works with varying heights utilizes color cameras and lights that reside at many different heights in order to see any vehicle's occupant. Small cars and even large tractor-trailers can fit through this system.

Video Facial Recognition

Facial recognition technology uses specific facial features to identify a person. It is a non-contact passive digital video system. In this system, facial features are the personal descriptors by which a person can be identified. The first time a person enters the system, their face is digitally recorded with their characteristics and features being stored in a separate data file. Later, that file can be accessed by its address, and then it is used for digital comparison to the person who wants to enter a facility. Manufacturers of this technology claim an accuracy of 90% and a false acceptance of only 1%.

Video Iris and Retina Personnel Identification

Iris and retina identification systems examine the very specific features of a person's eye. The eye is a perfect identifier because each person's irises and retinas are absolutely unique. A positive identification is possible. Iris systems choose parts of the iris that are rarely obstructed by eyelids. Retinal systems illuminate the retina (with a safe beam of light) just enough so that a beam will be reflected back into the video camera. This information forms an image of the retina that is truly unique to each individual.

REFERENCES

Bradski, G., & Kaehler, A. (2008). *Learning OpenCV*. Sebastopol, CA: O'Reilly Media, Inc.

Caputo, A. C. (2010). *Digital video surveillance and security*. London: Elsevier.

Corner Camera. (n.d.). Retrieved from http://www.securitycameraworld.com/Accessories/FB-1303.asp

Damjanovski, V. (2005). *CCTV networking and digital technology*. London: Elsevier.

Dismantling Elevator Camera. (n.d.). Retrieved from http://www.google.com.hk/imgres?q=security+camera+in+elevator&hl=en&newwindow=1&safe=strict&biw=1360&bih=673&tbm=isch&tbnid=GNU1OwHHyU3kZM:&imgrefurl=http://www.myspace.com/jerkface99/photos/6110094&docid=-TbmklutRL4BtM&itg=1&imgurl=http://a4.ec-images.myspacecdn.com/images01/48/6f55aef9812ff629e1bc05f72af46f10/l.jpg&w=500&h=375&ei=8MMyUdipHImTiAebmYGAAw&zoom=1&ved=1t:3588,r:20,s:0,i:146&iact=rc&dur=4262&sig=117471693243402725643&page=2&tbnh=185&tbnw=244&start=16&ndsp=23&tx=124&ty=103

Elevator Camera. (n.d.). Retrieved from http://www.google.com.hk/imgres?q=security+camera+in+elevator&hl=en&newwindow=1&safe=strict&biw=1360&bih=673&tbm=isch&tbnid=TgXcjBV1kyMV3M:&imgrefurl=http://www.brooklynpaper.com/stories/31/48/31_48_mm_pizzafiti.html&docid=nswx9pfw2pLjWM&imgurl=http://www.brooklynpaper.com/assets/photos/31/48/31_48_pizzagraffiti01_z.jpg&w=500&h=361&ei=8MMyUdipHImTiAebmYGAAw&zoom=1&ved=1t:3588,r:13,s:0,i:117&iact=rc&dur=803&sig=117471693243402725643&page=1&tbnh=176&tbnw=264&start=0&ndsp=16&tx=77&ty=70

Elevator Security Camera. (n.d.a). Retrieved from http://www.google.com.hk/imgres?q=security+camera+in+elevator&hl=en&newwindow=1&safe=strict&biw=1360&bih=673&tbm=isch&tbnid=Zoo1176I97kbLM:&imgrefurl=http://www.turbosquid.com/3d-models/3ds-max-elevator-security-camera/505146&docid=W_CSfjyBsUlFRM&imgurl=http://preview.turbosquid.com/Preview/Content_2009_12_20__01_42_59/elevator_door_closed_a_small.jpgb1388bec-37da-46f4-a921-499d00315bc3Larger.jpg&w=600&h=450&ei=8MMyUdipHImTiAebmYGAAw&zoom=1&ved=1t:3588,r:0,s:0,i:78&iact=rc&dur=880&sig=117471693243402725643&page=1&tbnh=189&tbnw=248&start=0&ndsp=16&tx=133&ty=118

Elevator Security Camera. (n.d.b). Retrieved from http://www.google.com.hk/imgres?q=security+camera+in+elevator&hl=en&newwindow=1&safe=strict&biw=1360&bih=673&tbm=isch&tbnid=cMEo7fwm1ilzIM:&imgrefurl=http://tobyschachman.com/&docid=T-q5xUYAEe2gwM&imgurl=http://tobyschachman.com/transpiration/security.jpg&w=580&h=435&ei=8MMyUdipHImTiAebmYGAAw&zoom=1&ved=1t:3588,r:6,s:0,i:96&iact=rc&dur=760&sig=117471693243402725643&page=1&tbnh=172&tbnw=255&start=0&ndsp=16&tx=126&ty=67

Kruegle, H. (2007). *CCTV surveillance analog and digital video practices and technology* (2nd ed.). London: Elsevier.

Nilsson, F. (2009). *Intelligent network video - Understanding modern video surveillance systems*. Boca Raton, FL: CRC Press Taylor & Francis Group.

Conclusion

The terrorist attacks of 9/11 as well as the Boston marathon incident that happened more recently raised the public awareness of security issues as well as tremendously increased the importance of intelligent automated video surveillance systems applied in public, commercial, law enforcement, and military domains.

Computerized video processing and analysis implemented in a variety of fields, such as governmental institutions, various businesses, municipalities, agencies, educational institutions, mass transportation centers, financial institutions, utility plants, medical centers and industries, is typically associated with analysis of video streams captured by surveillance systems. It performs video real-time analysis for immediate detection of events of interest as well as analyzes pre-recorded video for the purpose of extracting events and data that is known as forensic analysis.

As the use of video surveillance systems becomes more widespread and the quantity of recorded video increases, the need to go through recorded video data and extract specific segments and events of interest is growing. Very often in such cases, time is of the essence, and such review must be undertaken efficiently and rapidly. When done manually by human operators this represents a very time consuming, inefficient, and tedious task. Considering various research studies and real-life incidents indicate that an average human operator employed in an analog video surveillance system, tasked to observe video screens, cannot remain alert and attentive for more than 20 minutes and that the operator's ability to monitor the video and effectively respond to events is significantly compromised with time, operators show to be a costly resource with limited alertness and attention. This makes intelligent automated video surveillance systems to automatically monitor cameras and alert for events of interest very attractive and popular.

The benefit from a video surveillance system is significantly increased when it is accompanied by intelligent video analysis. Intelligent automated video surveillance systems make practical and effective use of the surveillance systems. The application domains of the intelligent automated video surveillance systems are numerous: security applications and intrusion management where it ensures perimeter control for sensitive or restricted areas such as permit parking and limited-access buildings where security officers are alerted to automatically detect and track burglary or to a suspicious individual loitering in the parking lot; urban surveillance applications where it measures traffic flow, detects accidents on highways, monitors pedestrian congestion in public spaces; crowd management where it compiles consumer demographics in shopping malls and amusement parks, monitors for the build-up of crowds in public areas based on occupancy measurements, ensuring that customers are not impacted by uncomfortable and potentially unsafe crowds; industry applications where it performs quality control or count the number of products on the production lines; various military applications include patrolling national borders, measuring the flow of refugees in troubled areas, providing secure perimeters around bases and embassies, battlefield surveillance applications, real-time moving object detection and tracking from stationary and moving camera platforms, recognition of objects like humans and different types of vehicles, human gait analysis, human activity recognition, vehicle tracking and counting, airborne surveillance, etc.

Numerous advantages of automated intelligent video surveillance systems caused an increased number of cities, schools, districts, workplaces, apartment buildings, garages, stores, banks, restaurants, and public housing to apply surveillance systems to monitor movement, detect illegal activity, and protect the public. The survey conducted in 1997 showed that only 13 city police departments in the US used CCTV video surveillance systems, primarily to monitor pedestrian traffic and to catch cars running red lights. After 9/11, this number significantly increased. Every city in America now has its share of private surveillance cameras that monitor public areas such as sidewalks, parking lots, freeways, and traffic lights, many of which are integrated with the Internet so that real-time video of people in public places can be observed online. Thousands of Web cameras in every corner of the world distribute images of street scenes, famous landmarks, and allow the Internet observer to control who, what, and how closely the target subject is observed.

Besides the US, many countries employ public video surveillance to monitor population movements in order to prevent crime and potential terrorism like Singapore, Canada, the US, Australia, China, UK, and other European countries that installed thousands of cameras in public settings. The United Kingdom is by far the international leading country in the matter of applied CCTV video surveillance as according to one source the average Briton is photographed by 300 separate cameras in a single day.

All the advantages of the video surveillance systems raise other questions and concerns that are conflicting with its beneficial side like: privacy issues, its philosophical or theoretical considerations, policy issues related to video surveillance, its social and legal dimensions, cost, rate of return of investment, quality assurance, etc. (Nieto, Johnston-Dodds, & Simmons, 2002; Bharucha, London, Barnard, Wactlar, Dew, & Reynolds, 2006; Collins, et al., 2000; Scherr, 2007).

An intelligent automated video surveillance system is tireless and permanently records everything without ever getting distracted. Recorded digital videos and images are permanently stored and can be viewed at any time, from any place, as many times as desired. The arising problem is that this data can be modified and used beyond the original intent of either the image collector or the subject. This is why the public, some government officials, and various organizations are increasingly concerned about protecting individual privacy.

For three decades, until the late 1990s, continuous video surveillance was mainly considered by courts and legislators to be a form of "passive" surveillance, which was not considered to be an intrusion upon an individual's privacy and did not present a significant legal obstacle. Within the last years, the rapid increase in the application of intelligent video surveillance systems have significantly impacted the appropriate use of video and related surveillance technologies and their implications for civil liberties and privacy rights.

The speed at which video surveillance systems evolve challenges the ability of judicial and legislative system to enact and enforce policies that protect the public's security and right to privacy. The newly opened questions that are inevitably imposed are global use of emerging surveillance technologies, law enforcement, national security interests, and the privacy rights of citizens. Apart from being defined as the "right to be let alone," the legal concept of privacy encompasses three categories: physical privacy, informational privacy, and decisional privacy, which are all tackled by video surveillance systems.

According to some polls, American citizens are willing to give up some privacy for better security but at the same time are concerned about the possibility that information obtained from video surveillance could be abused by government agencies, employers, or businesses, as well as about the potential false identification caused by computer errors.

The ethical implications of surveillance technologies on the privacy of citizens and the pragmatic approach to the central ethical concern about privacy and confidentiality protections and relevant issues of the informed consent process as well as the question about setting the appropriate balance between law enforcement, national security, and civil liberties are far beyond the scope of this book and are left to be addressed by professionals in those fields like sociologists, legislators, lawyers, philosophers, psychologists, etc.

The book, *Video Surveillance Techniques and Technologies*, offers various original methods and algorithms that automatically analyze video with the goal to detect, track, and identify moving objects based on sequence of images. It also includes biometric algorithms for anthropometric measurements, military aircraft radar ISAR image analysis, and iris recognition. The book is primarily aimed for graduate students and professionals in the field of signal and image processing applied in static/moving object detection, tracking, and identification, but I hope that others who are also in the field of video surveillance and security can profit from its content as well. The targeted readers' group can benefit from its educational and informational content, and the wider audience can perceive and get the idea through this book about the algorithms and intelligent software that represents the main core of intelligent automated video surveillance systems.

The main value of this book lies in its practical implementation in numerous domains and wide spectra of applications like video surveillance, homeland security, military applications, healthcare, quality control, industry, safety, etc. The described mathematical algorithms are employed in security video surveillance systems with wide variety of applications, some of them having very high priority and importance: homeland security and national defense. These algorithms could be further extended to perform other functionalities like identification, behavior analysis, or other forms of situation-awareness, which is the scope of my future research.

Vesna Zeljkovic
New York Institute of Technology, Nanjing Campus, China

REFERENCES

Bharucha, A. J., London, A. J., Barnard, D., Wactlar, H., Dew, M. A., & Reynolds, C. F. III. (2006). Ethical considerations in the conduct of electronic surveillance research. *The Journal of Law, Medicine & Ethics*. doi:10.1111/j.1748-720X.2006.00075.x PMID:17144185

Collins, R. T., Lipton, A. J., Kanade, T., Fujiyoshi, H., Duggins, D., & Tsin, Y. …Wixson, L. (2000). A system for video surveillance and monitoring (CMU-RI-TR-00-12). Pittsburgh, PA: The Robotics Institute, Carnegie Mellon University.

Nieto, M., Johnston-Dodds, K., & Simmons, C. W. (2002). *Public and private applications of video surveillance and biometric technologies*. Berkeley, CA: California Research Bureau, California State Library.

Scherr, C. (2007). You better watch out, you better not frown, new video surveillance techniques are already in town (and other public spaces). *I/S: A Journal of Law and Policy for the Information Society*.

Compilation of References

3D The World Seen Through Multiple Cameras. *(n.d.)*. *Retrieved from* http://www.upc.edu/saladepremsa/informacio/monografics/3d-el-mundo-visto-desde-multiples-camaras?set_language=en

8MP JPEG2000 HD 360° Pano Camera. (n.d.). Retrieved from http://www.google.com.hk/imgres?q=Panoramic+360+Camera&um=1&hl=en&newwindow=1&safe=strict&sa=N&biw=1360&bih=673&tbm=isch&tbnid=VgfgkptAgEusnM:&imgrefurl=http://avigilon.com/products/cameras/hd-panoramic/jpeg2000-hd-panoramic-camera/8-mp-360-jpeg2000-dome-panoramic/&docid=C603IZ-RG-BNR2M&imgurl=http://avigilon.com/assets/Uploads/JPEG2000-HD-Panoramic-Dome360Camera1140x640rev.jpg&w=1140&h=640&ei=qCsvUfP-J6uXiQe3_4HgDw&zoom=1&iact=rc&dur=565&sig=117471693243402725643&page=1&tbnh=152&tbnw=242&start=0&ndsp=18&ved=1t:429,r:7,s:0&tx=264&ty=362

Abaza, A., Ross, A., Hebert, C., Harrison, M. A. F., & Nixon, M. S. (2013). A survey on ear biometrics. *ACM Computing Surveys*, *45*(2). doi:10.1145/2431211.2431221

Abdelkader, B., & Chiraz, Y. Y. (2010). Statistical estimation of human anthropometry from a single un-calibrated image. Abu Dhabi, UAE: New York Institute of Technology.

Adler, F.H. (n.d.). *Physiology of the eye, clinical applications*. London: C. V. Mosby.

Analog to IP Network. (n.d.). Retrieved from http://r3.cygnuspub.com/files/cygnus/image/SIW/2005/DEC/600x400/1135031175643_10560636.jpg

Arkin, E. M., Chew, L. P., Huttenlocher, D. P., Kedem, K., & Mitchel, J. S. B. (1991). An efficiently computable metric for comparing polygonal shapes. *IEEE Transactions on Pattern Analysis and Machine Intelligence*, *13*(3). doi:10.1109/34.75509

Avis, D., & ElGindy, H. (1983). A combinatorial approach to polygon similarity. *IEEE Transactions on Information Theory*, 29.

Babaud, J., Witkin, A., Baudin, M., & Duda, R. (1986). Uniqueness of the Gaussian kernel for scale-space filtering. *IEEE Transactions on Pattern Analysis and Machine Intelligence*, 8. PMID:21869320

Ballan, L., Bertini, M., Del Bimbo, A., Dini, F., Lisanti, G., Seidenari, L., & Serra, G. (n.d.). *Recent research activities in video surveillance*. Florence, Italy: University of Florence, Multimedia Integration and Communication Center.

Ballard, D. H., & Brown, C. M. (1982). *Computer vision*. Englewood Cliffs, NJ: Prentice-Hall.

Barnsley, M. (1993). *Fractals everywhere*. San Francisco, CA: Morgan Kaufmann.

Berry, W. M., Drmac, Z., & Jessup, J. R. (1999). Matrices, vector spaces, and information retrieval. *SIAM Review*, *41*(2), 336–362. doi:10.1137/S0036144598347035

Berry, W. M., Dumais, S. T., & O'Brien, G. W. (1995). Using linear algebra for intelligent information retrieval. *SIAM Review*, 37, 573–595. doi:10.1137/1037127

Bovik, A. (2005). *Handbook of image & video processing* (2nd ed.). London: Elsevier.

Bracewell, D. B., Lobo, D. V. N., & Shah, M. (2001). *Obtaining body measurements for human identification*. Pennsylvania: The Pennsylvania State University CiteSeer Archives.

Bradski, G., & Kaehler, A. (2009). *Learning OpenCV*. Sebastopol, CA: O'Reilly Media, Inc.

Bulb. (n.d.). Retrieved from http://i00.i.aliimg.com/wsphoto/v0/638768082/-font-b-Tungsten-b-font-font-b-Halogen-b-font-font-b-Bulb-b-font.jpg

Camera Field of View. (n.d.). Retrieved from http://www.customs.gov.au/webdata/resources/images/fov-vs-focus.gif

Camera View. (n.d.). Retrieved from http://www.google.com.hk/imgres?q=Multi-Camera+Three+Dimensions&um=1&hl=en&newwindow=1&safe=strict&sa=N&biw=1360&bih=673&tbm=isch&tbnid=rrqwfuUhbiaUwM:&imgrefurl=http://projects.washingtonpost.com/top-secret-america/galleries/gallery-technology/&docid=rhifFwxgaJRU-M&imgurl=http://media.washingtonpost.com/media/images/2010/07/15/07152010-63v_606x404.jpg&w=606&h=404&ei=ZRkuUe7wMInukgX98oDADA&zoom=1&iact=rc&dur=644&sig=117471693243402725643&page=1&tbnh=171&tbnw=266&start=0&ndsp=18&ved=1t:429,r:10,s:0&tx=1168&ty=366

Camera. (n.d.). Retrieved from http://mtxglobal.com/wp-content/themes/mtxglobal/images/fov.jpg

Canny, J. (1986). A computational approach to edge detection. *IEEE Transactions on Pattern Analysis and Machine Intelligence*, 679–698. doi:10.1109/TPAMI.1986.4767851 PMID:21869365

Canon CX-1 Camera. (n.d.). Retrieved from http://www.canon-europe.com/Medical/Eye_Care/CX-1/

Cao, F., Lisani, J. L., Morel, J. M., Muse, P., & Sur, F. (2006). *A theory of shape identification*. Berlin: Springer.

Caputo, A. C. (2010). *Digital video surveillance and security*. London: Elsevier.

CBR Motion Detector. (n.d.). Retrieved from http://www.google.com.hk/imgres?q=motion+detector&hl=en&newwindow=1&safe=strict&biw=1360&bih=630&tbm=isch&tbnid=blOdA3Iptmc2HM:&imgrefurl=http://www.haines.com.au/index.php/datalogging/cbr-motion-detector.html&docid=2GabYelHm80wjM&imgurl=http://www.haines.com.au/media/catalog/product/cache/1/image/902f33c22afdec0ceb057adbcc4c9bb7/D/A/DATA-TEXAS-INSTR-MOTION.jpg&w=800&h=1143&ei=5JoxUY-bCoj_iAf9xoGICA&zoom=1&ved=1t:3588,r:32,s:0,i:182&iact=rc&dur=4093&sig=117471693243402725643&page=2&tbnh=193&tbnw=137&start=16&ndsp=27&tx=86&ty=76

CCTV Lens. (n.d.). Retrieved from http://ganpatiinfosys.com/?page_id=108

CCTV Lenses. (n.d.a). Retrieved from http://www.goyooptical.com/products/cctv/manual.html

CCTV Lenses. (n.d.c). Retrieved from http://img.directindustry.com/pdf/repository_di/29083/cctv-lenses-10334_1b.jpg

CCTV Lenses. (n.d.d). Retrieved from http://www.si-cube.com/Products/Lensassembly/7/

Chang, S. G., Yu, B., & Vetterli, M. (2000). Spatially adaptive wavelet thresholding with context modeling for image denoising. *IEEE Transactions on Image Processing*, *9*(9), 1522–1531. doi:10.1109/83.862630 PMID:18262990

Cieszynski, J. (2003). *Closed circuit television: CCTV installation, maintenance and operation* (2nd ed.). Newnes.

Conejo, A. N., & Hernandez, D. E. (2006). Optimization of aluminum deoxidation practice in the ladle furnace. *Materials and Manufacturing Processes*, *21*(8), 796–803. doi:10.1080/10426910600837764

Corner Camera. (n.d.). Retrieved from http://www.securitycameraworld.com/Accessories/FB-1303.asp

Corrall, D. (1991). *VIEW: Computer vision for surveillance applications*. London: IEE.

Cox, P., Maitre, H., Minoux, M., & Ribeiro, C. (1989). Optimal matching of convex polygons. *Pattern Recognition Letters*, (9): 327–334. doi:10.1016/0167-8655(89)90061-5

Damjanovski, V. (2005). *CCTV networking and digital technology*. London: Elsevier.

Daugman, J. G. (1994). *Biometric personal identification system based on iris analysis* (U.S. Patent No. 5,291,560). Washington, DC: US Patent Office.

Daugman, J. G. (1993). High confidence visual recognition of persons by a test of statistical independence. *IEEE Transactions on Pattern Analysis and Machine Intelligence*, *15*(11), 1148–1161. doi:10.1109/34.244676

Daugman, J. G. (2001). Statistical richness of visual phase information: Update on recognizing persons by iris patterns. *International Journal of Computer Vision*, *45*(1), 25–38. doi:10.1023/A:1012365806338

Daugman, J. G. (2003). The importance of being random: statistical principles of iris recognition. *Pattern Recognition*, *36*(2), 279–291. doi:10.1016/S0031-3203(02)00030-4

De Floriani, L., & Spagnuol, M. (2007). *Shape analysis and structuring*. Berlin: Springer.

Digital Motion Detection. (n.d.). Retrieved from http://www.asia.ru/en/ProductInfo/1128085.html

Dismantling Elevator Camera. (n.d.). Retrieved from http://www.google.com.hk/imgres?q=security+camera+in+elevator&hl=en&newwindow=1&safe=strict&biw=1360&bih=673&tbm=isch&tbnid=GNU1OwHHyU3kZM:&imgrefurl=http://www.myspace.com/jerkface99/photos/6110094&docid=-TbmklutRL4BtM&itg=1&imgurl=http://a4.ec-images.myspacecdn.com/images01/48/6f55aef9812ff629e1bc05f72af46f10/l.jpg&w=500&h=375&ei=8MMyUdipHImTiAebmYGAAw&zoom=1&ved=1t:3588,r:20,s:0,i:146&iact=rc&dur=4262&sig=117471693243402725643&page=2&tbnh=185&tbnw=244&start=16&ndsp=23&tx=124&ty=103

Dobeš, M., & Machala, L. (n.d.). *Iris database*. Retrieved from http://phoenix.inf.upol.cz/iris/

Douglas, K., & Douglas, S. (2003). *PostgreSQL-A comprehensive guide to building, programming and administering PostgreSQL databases*. Sams Publishing.

Duda, R., & Hart, P. (n.d.). *Pattern classification and scene analysis*. Hoboken, NJ: John Wiley and Sons.

Dunckley, L. (2003). *Multimedia databases: An object-relational approach*. Pearson Education.

Elevator Security Camera. (n.d.a). Retrieved from http://www.google.com.hk/imgres?q=security+camera+in+elevator&hl=en&newwindow=1&safe=strict&biw=1360&bih=673&tbm=isch&tbnid=Zoo1l76I97kbLM:&imgrefurl=http://www.turbosquid.com/3d-models/3ds-max-elevator-security-camera/505146&docid=W_CSfjyBsUlFRM&imgurl=http://preview.turbosquid.com/Preview/Content_2009_12_20__01_42_59/elevator_door_closed_a_small.jpgb1388bec-37da-46f4-a921-499d00315bc3Larger.jpg&w=600&h=450&ei=8MMyUdipHImTiAebmYGAAw&zoom=1&ved=1t:3588,r:0,s:0,i:78&iact=rc&dur=880&sig=117471693243402725643&page=1&tbnh=189&tbnw=248&start=0&ndsp=16&tx=133&ty=118

Elevator Camera. (n.d.). Retrieved from http://www.google.com.hk/imgres?q=security+camera+in+elevator&hl=en&newwindow=1&safe=strict&biw=1360&bih=673&tbm=isch&tbnid=TgXcjBV1kyMV3M:&imgrefurl=http://www.brooklynpaper.com/stories/31/48/31_48_mm_pizzafiti.html&docid=nswx9pfw2pLjWM&imgurl=http://www.brooklynpaper.com/assets/photos/31/48/31_48_pizzagraffiti01_z.jpg&w=500&h=361&ei=8MMyUdipHImTiAebmYGAAw&zoom=1&ved=1t:3588,r:13,s:0,i:117&iact=rc&dur=803&sig=117471693243402725643&page=1&tbnh=176&tbnw=264&start=0&ndsp=16&tx=77&ty=70

Eye Structure and Camera Structure. (n.d.). Retrieved from http://electronicimaging.spiedigitallibrary.org/data/Journals/ELECTIM/23509/033009_1_1.png

Farid, H., & Simoncelli, E. P. (2004). Differentiation of discrete multi-dimensional signals. *IEEE Transactions on Image Processing*, *13*(4), 496–508. doi:10.1109/TIP.2004.823819 PMID:15376584

Fathy, M., & Siyal, M. Y. (1995). An image detection technique based on morphological edge detection and background differencing for real-time traffic analysis. *Pattern Recognition Letters*, (16): 1321–1330. doi:10.1016/0167-8655(95)00081-X

Field of View. (n.d.). Retrieved from http://ars.els-cdn.com/content/image/1-s2.0-S1077314211002384-gr10.jpg

Foresman, C. (n.d.). *Lytro's new light field camera lets you focus after you take a picture*. Retrieved from http://arstechnica.com/gadgets/2011/10/lytros-new-light-field-camera-lets-you-focus-after-you-take-a-picture/

Foresti, G. L., & Regazzoni, C. S. (1994). A change detection method for multiple object localization in real scenes. In *Proceedings of IEEE Conference*, (pp. 984-987). IEEE.

Foresti, G. L. (1998). A real-time system for video surveillance of unattended outdoor environments. *IEEE Transactions on Circuits and Systems for Video Technology*, 8(6), 697–704. doi:10.1109/76.728411

Foresti, G. L., & Regazzoni, C. S. (1994). *A change detection method for multiple object localizations in real scenes*. Bologna, Italy: IEEE. doi:10.1109/IECON.1994.397923

Frank, T. (2007). Face recognition next in terror fight. *USA Today*.

Fruehan, R. J. (1998). *The making, shaping and treating of steel (steel making and refining)*. AISE Steel Foundation.

Garcia, E. (2005). *Patents on duplicated content and re-ranking methods*. San Jose, CA: SES.

Gittoes, M., Bezodis, I., & Wilson, N. C. (2009). An image-based approach to obtaining anthropometric measurements for inertia modeling. *Journal of Applied Biomechanics*, (25): 265–270. PMID:19827477

Gohringer, C. (n.d.). Advances in face recognition technology and its application in airports. *Allevate Limited*.

Gonzales, R. C., & Woods, R. E. (2002). *Digital image processing* (2nd ed.). Upper Saddle River, NJ: Prentice Hall.

Grady, L. (2004). *Space-variant computer vision: A graph-theoretic approach*. (PhD thesis). Boston University, Boston, MA.

Grady, L., & Schwartz, E. L. (2003). *The graph analysis toolbox: Image processing on arbitrary graphs*. Boston: Boston University.

Grossman, D. A., & Frieder, O. (2000). *Information retrieval: Algorithms and heuristics*. Kluwer Academic Publishers.

Haritaoglu, I., Harwood, D., & Davis, L. (2000). W4: Real-time surveillance of people and their activities. *IEEE Transactions on Pattern Analysis and Machine Intelligence*, 22(8), 809–830. doi:10.1109/34.868683

Hatfield, K., & Garnham, J. (2001). The application of image analysis to improve permeability prediction. *Petrophysics*, 42(5), 457–467.

Haywood, B., Anderson, W. C., Morris, J. T., & Kyprianou, R. (1997). Generation of point scatterer models for simulating ISAR images of ships. *Radar*, 97, 700–704.

Heseltine, T., & Whitehead, N. (n.d.). Facial recognition – Finding a reliable system that works in all conditions. *Ingenia, 48*.

Hong, J., & Tan, X. (1988). *The similarity between shapes under affine transformation*. Washington, DC: IEEE.

Hong, J., & Wolfson, H. J. (1988). *An improved model-based matching method using footprints*. Rome, Italy: Pattern Recognition.

Honovich, J. (2011). *Video surveillance book*. IPVideoMarket.jnfo

Hubbard, B. B. (1998). *The world according to wavelets-The story of a mathematical technique in the making* (2nd ed.). Wellesley, MA: A. K. Peters, Ltd.

Hummel, A. (1986). *Representations based on zero-crossings in scale-space*. In *Proceedings of IEEE Computer Vision and Pattern Recognition Conf.*, (pp. 204-209). IEEE.

Hummel, A. (1987). *The scale-space formulation of pyramid data structures in parallel computer vision*. New York: Academic Press.

Huttenlocher, D. P., & Kedem, K. (1990). *Computing the minimum hausdorff distance for point sets under translation*. In *Proceedings ACM Symposium for Computational Geometry*, (pp. 340-349). ACM.

Iguchi, M. et al. (2004). Spout eye area in ladle refining process. *ISIJ International*, 44(3), 636–638. doi:10.2355/isijinternational.44.636

Image Tracking System. (n.d.). Retrieved from http://www.tracab.com/technology.aspx

InfraredMotionDetector.(n.d.).Retrievedfromhttp://www. google.com.hk/imgres?q=motion+detector&hl=en&new window=1&safe=strict&biw=1360&bih=630&tbm=isc h&tbnid=WiH_jJQX7VLd6M:&imgrefurl=http://www. directindustry.com/prod/optex-sec-division/passive-infrared-motion-detectors-for-outdoors-24435-380999. html&docid=W2m-_JfUh1j0GM&imgurl=http:// img.directindustry.com/images_di/photo-g/passive-infrared-motion-detector-for-outdoors-24435-2679839. jpg&w=844&h=900&ei=5JoxUY-bCoj_iAf9xoGICA &zoom=1&ved=1t:3588,r:30,s:0,i:176&iact=rc&dur= 1363&sig=117471693243402725643&page=2&tbnh= 193&tbnw=181&start=16&ndsp=27&tx=81&ty=120

Inigo, R. M. (1989). Application of machine vision to traffic monitoring and control. *IEEE Transactions on Vehicular Technology, 38*(3), 112–122. doi:10.1109/25.45464

Intelligent Video Surveillance. (n.d.). Retrieved from http://www.3xlogic.com/xview

Interlaced Video Frame. (n.d.). Retrieved from http://en.wikipedia.org/wiki/File:Interlaced_video_frame_(car_wheel).jpg

IP (Network) Digital Video Recording System. (n.d.). Retrieved from http://www.dynapost.com/index.php?page_no=33

Iqbal, Q., & Aggarwal, J. K. (1999). Applying perceptual grouping to content-based image retrieval: Building image. In *Proceedings of IEEE Int'l Conf. on Computer Vision and Pattern Recognition* (pp. 42-48). IEEE.

Jain, R., Militzer, D., & Nagel, H. (1977). *Separating nonstationary from stationary scene components in a sequence of real world TV images*. Cambridge, MA: IJCAI.

Jolliffe, I. T. (2002). *Principal component analysis* (2nd Ed.). Springer Verlag. Retrieved from ftp://pets.rdg.ac.uk/

Kang, Y. J., Yu, L., & Sichen, D. (2007). Study of inclusion removal mechanism around open eye in ladle treatment. *Ironmaking & Steelmaking*, (34): 253–261. doi:10.1179/174328107X168101

Kim, K.-T., Seo, D.-K., & Kim, H.-T. (2005). Efficient classification of ISAR images. *IEEE Transactions on Antennas and Propagation, 53*(5), 1611–1621. doi:10.1109/TAP.2005.846780

Kimmel, R. (2004). *Numerical geometry of images: Theory, algorithms, and applications*. Berlin: Springer. doi:10.1007/978-0-387-21637-9

Koenderink, J. (1984). The structure of images. In *Biological Cybernetics*. Springer-Verlag.

Kotas, P., Praks, P., Válek, L., Zeljković, V., & Vondrak, V. (2012). Automated region of interest retrieval of metallographic images for quality classification in industry. *Advances in Electrical and Electronic Engineering Journal, 10*(1).

Kotas, P., Praks, P., Zeljković, V., & Válek, L. (2010). *Automated region of interest retrieval of metallographic images for quality scoring estimation*. Houston, TX: IEEE. doi:10.1109/IAS.2010.5615510

Kovesi, P. (n.d.). *Video surveillance: Legally blind*. Crawley, Australia: School of Computer Science & Software Engineering, The University of Western Australia.

Krawiec, K., & Bhanu, B. (2007). Visual learning by evolutionary and coevolutionary feature synthesis. *IEEE Transactions on Evolutionary Computation, 11*(5), 635–650. doi:10.1109/TEVC.2006.887351

Krim, H., & Yezzi, A. Jr. (2006). *Statistics and analysis of shapes (modeling and simulation in science, engineering and technology)*. Boston: Birkhauser. doi:10.1007/0-8176-4481-4

Krishnapisharody, K., & Irons, G. A. (2008). An extended model for slag eye size in ladle metallurgy. *ISIJ International, 48*(12), 1807. doi:10.2355/isijinternational.48.1807

Kroon, D. (2009). *Numerical optimization of kernel based image derivatives*. Eschedne, The Netherlands: University Twente.

Kruegle, H. (2007). *CCTV surveillance analog and digital video practices and technology* (2nd ed.). London: Elsevier.

Labský, M., Svátek, V., Praks, P., & Šváb, O. (2005). *Information extraction from HTML product catalogues: Coupling quantitative and knowledge-based approaches*. Wadern, Germany: Semantic Web. Retrieved from http://www.smi.ucd.ie/Dagstuhl-MLSW/proceedings/labsky-svatek-praks-svab.pdf

Lai, W.-H., & Li, C.-T. (2006). *Skin colour-based face detection in color images*. Sydney, Australia: IEEE.

Latecki, L. J., & Lakamper, R. (1999). Convexity rule for shape decomposition based on discrete contour evolution. *Computer Vision and Image Understanding, 73*(3), 441–454. doi:10.1006/cviu.1998.0738

Lens Field of View. (n.d.a). Retrieved from http://www.image-tmart.com/info_images/CCTV-Cameras-2.jpg

Lens Field of View. (n.d.b). Retrieved from http://www.videosurveillance.co.in/images/cctv%20view.jpg

Lens Geometry. (n.d.). Retrieved from http://ars.els-cdn.com/content/image/1-s2.0-S0926580511002251-gr2.jpg

Lens Size. (n.d.). Retrieved from http://www.elplanbg.com/EN/wordpress/wp-content/uploads/2012/10/CCTV_lens.jpg

Li, Q. (2007). *Study of monopulse radar target three dimensional imaging and recognition*. (Ph.D dissertation). Xidian University.

Lomography Spinner 360° Panoramic Camera. (n.d.). Retrieved from http://www.bhphotovideo.com/c/product/711901-REG/Lomography_919_Spinner_360_deg_Panoramic_Camera.html/c/product/#inpage:IN+STOCK

Lu, J.-M., & Wang, M. J. (2008). An intelligent system for customized clothing making. In *Proceedings of Conf. On Computational Intelligence, Man-Machine Systems and Cybernetics*, (pp. 171-174). IEEE.

Lv, F. T., & Zhao, N. R. (2006). Camera calibration from video of a walking Human. *Journal of Biomechanics*, 1513–1518. PMID:16929736

Machala, L., & Pospíšil, J. (2001). Proposal and verification of two methods for evaluation of the human iris video-camera images. *Optik (Stuttgart), 112*(8), 335–340. doi:10.1078/0030-4026-00066

Machala, L., Praks, P., & Snášel, V. (2004). *Two methods for iris recognition using mutual information*. Brno, Czech Republic: Znalosti.

Mallat, S. G. (1989). A theory for multiresolution signal decomposition: The wavelet representation. *IEEE Transactions on Pattern Analysis and Machine Intelligence, 11*(7), 674–693. doi:10.1109/34.192463

Manikandan, J., Venkataramani, B., & Jayachandran, M. (2007). Evaluation of edge detection techniques towards implementation of automatic target recognition. In *Proceedings of Conference on Computational Intelligence and Multimedia Applications*, (vol. 2, pp. 441-445). IEEE.

Marques, I., & Grana, M. (2010). *Face recognition algorithms*. Proyecto Fin de Carrera.

Martorella, M., & Giusti, E. et al. (2008). Automatic target recognition by means of polarimetric ISAR images: A model matching based algorithm.[RADAR.]. *Proceedings of Radar, 2008*, 27–31.

Maskall, G. T. (2002). An application of nonlinear feature extraction to the classification of ISAR images. *RADAR, 15*(17), 405–408.

Mazumdar, D., & Evans, J. W. (2003). Some considerations concerning empirical correlations for plume (spout) eye area in slag covered metallic melts. *ISIJ International, 43*(12), 2076–2078. doi:10.2355/isijinternational.43.2076

Mecocci, A. (1989). Moving object recognition and classification in external environments. *Signal Processing*, (18): 183–194. doi:10.1016/0165-1684(89)90049-2

Meunier, P., & Yin, S. (2000). Performance of a 2D image-based anthropometric measurement and clothing sizing system. *Applied Ergonomics*, 445–451. doi:10.1016/S0003-6870(00)00023-5 PMID:11059458

Motion Sensor. (n.d.). Retrieved from http://www.securitycameraking.com/securityinfo/wp-content/uploads/2010/07/Wireless-16-Camera-Motion-Detector-Security-Systems-300x236.jpg

Motion Detector. (n.d.). Retrieved from http://www.google.com.hk/imgres?q=motion+detector&hl=en&newwindow=1&safe=strict&biw=1360&bih=630&tbm=isch&tbnid=Y7RnprCu9VdA6M:&imgrefurl=http://en.wikipedia.org/wiki/File:Motion_detector.jpg&docid=hdMoZ4owPjoYvM&imgurl=http://upload.wikimedia.org/wikipedia/commons/2/2e/Motion_detector.jpg&w=1352&h=1740&ei=5JoxUY-bCoj_iAf9xoGICA&zoom=1&ved=1t:3588,r:46,s:0,i:224&iact=rc&dur=1027&sig=117471693243402725643&page=3&tbnh=168&tbnw=144&start=43&ndsp=27&tx=63&ty=71

Munkres, J. (1999). *Topology* (2nd ed.). Upper Saddle River, NJ: Prentice Hall.

Network System. (n.d.). Retrieved from http://embedded. communities.intel.com/servlet/JiveServlet/showImage/38-5444-3988/DSS+diagram.JPG

Network Video. (n.d.). Retrieved from www.axis.com

Niemann, H. (1990). *Pattern analysis and understanding.* Berlin: Springer-Verlag. doi:10.1007/978-3-642-74899-8

Nieto, M., Johnston-Dodds, K., & Wear Simmons, C. (n.d.). *Public and private applications of video surveillance and biometric technologies.* Berkeley, CA: California Research Bureau, California State Library.

Nilsson, F. (2009). *Intelligent network video - Understanding modern video surveillance systems.* Boca Raton, FL: CRC Press Taylor & Francis Group.

O'Rourke, J., & Washington, R. (1985). Curve similarity via signatures. *Computational Geometry*, 295–318.

Oikawa, K., Sumi, S.-I., & Ishida, K. (1999). The effects of addition of deoxidation elements on the morphology of (Mn, Cr)S inclusions in stainless steel. *Journal of Phase Equilibria*, *20*(3), 215–223. doi:10.1361/105497199770335749

Oliver, N. M., Rosario, B., & Pentland, A. P. (2000). A Bayesian computer vision system for modeling human interactions. *IEEE Transactions on Pattern Analysis and Machine Intelligence*, *22*(8), 831–843. doi:10.1109/34.868684

Perona, P., & Malik, J. (1990). Scale-space and edge detection using anisotropic diffusion. *IEEE Transactions on Pattern Analysis and Machine Intelligence*, *12*(7), 629–630. doi:10.1109/34.56205

Petrak, S., & Rogale, D. (2006). Systematic representation and application of a 3D computer-aided garment construction method. *International Journal of Clothing Science and Technology*, 179-187.

Pflug, A., & Busch, C. (2012). Ear biometrics: A survey of detection, feature extraction and recognition methods. *IET Biometrics*, *1*(2), 114–129. doi:10.1049/iet-bmt.2011.0003

Pokrajac, D., & Latecki, L. J. (2003). *Spatiotemporal blocks-based moving objects identification and tracking.* Nice, France: IEEE.

Praks, P., Černohorský, J., & Briš, R. (n.d.). *Human expert modelling using numerical linear algebra: A heavy industry case study.* IOS Press.

Praks, P., Dvorský, J., & Snášel, V. (2003). *Latent semantic indexing for image retrieval systems.* Williamsburg, VA: SIAM. Retrieved from http://www.siam.org/meetings/la03/proceedings/Dvorsky.pdf

Praks, P., Dvorský, J., Snášel, V., & Černohorský, J. (2003). *On SVD-free latent semantic indexing for image retrieval for application in a hard industrial environment.* ICIT. doi:10.1109/ICIT.2003.1290365

Praks, P., Grzegorzek, M., Moravec, R., Válek, L., & Izquierdo, E. (2008). Wavelet and Eigen-space feature extraction for classification of metallography images. In *Information Modelling and Knowledge Bases XIX.* IOS Press.

Praks, P., Kučera, R., & Izquierdo, E. (2008). *The sparse image representation for automated image retrieval.* ICIP. doi:10.1109/ICIP.2008.4711682

Praks, P., Machala, L., & Snášel, V. (n.d.). On SVD-free latent semantic indexing for iris recognition of large databases. In V. A. Petrushin, & L. Khan (Eds.), *Multimedia data mining and knowledge discovery.* Berlin: Springer Verlag.

Prasad, L., & Iyengar, S. S. (2007). *Wavelet analysis with applications to image processing.* Boca Raton, FL: CRC Press.

Praus, P., & Praks, P. (2010). Hierarchical clustering of RGB surface water images based on MIA-LSI approach. *Water S.A.*, *36*(1), 143–150. doi:10.4314/wsa.v36i1.50922

Prickett, M. J., & Chen, C. C. (1980). *Principles of inverse synthetic aperture radar imaging.* Arlington, VA: Electronics and Aerospace Systems.

Rao, G., Amarantini, D., Berton, E., & Favier, D. (2006). Influence of body segments' parameters estimation models on inverse dynamics solutions during gait. *Journal of Biomechanics*, 1531–1536. doi:10.1016/j.jbiomech.2005.04.014 PMID:15970198

Rapid Eye Hybrid, H. D. *(n.d.). Retrieved from* http://www.honeywellvideo.com/products/recorders/pc/306064.html

Remagnino, P., Jones, G. A., Paragios, N., & Regazzoni, C. S. (Eds.). (2002). *Video-based surveillance systems.* Kluwer Academic Publishers. doi:10.1007/978-1-4615-0913-4

Rosenfeld, A., & Thurston, M. (1971). Edge and curve detection for visual scene analysis. *IEEE Trans. Compu.,* (C-20), 562-569.

Ross, A., & Byrd, R.C. (n.d.). *Advances in ear biometrics.* Academic Press.

Rourke, A., Bell, M. G. H., & Hoose, N. (1990). *Road traffic monitoring using image processing.* London: Road Traffic Control.

Scharr, H. (2007). *Optimal second order derivative filter families for transparent motion estimation.* Poznan, Poland: IEEE.

Schwartz, J. T., & Sharir, M. (1984). *Some remarks on robot vision.* New York: New York University.

Schwartz, J. T., & Sharir, M. (1987). Identification of objects in two and three dimensions by matching noisy characteristics curves. *The International Journal of Robotics Research, 6*(2), 29–44. doi:10.1177/027836498700600203

Scin Colors. (n.d.). Retrieved from http://www.stiletto-moody.com/faq/how-do-i-match-my-skin-color/how-do-i-find-the-numerical-value-rgb-for-my-skin-color.html

Sensor. (n.d.). Retrieved from http://ecx.images-amazon.com/images/I/31fwdkOmfYL._SL500_AA300_.jpg

Shapiro, L. G., & Haralick, R. M. (1982). Organization of relational models for scene analysis. *IEEE Transactions on Pattern Analysis and Machine Intelligence, 4*(6), 595–602. doi:10.1109/TPAMI.1982.4767312 PMID:22499633

Singhal, A., Buckley, C., & Mitra, M. (n.d.). *Pivoted document length normalization.* Ithaca, NY: Cornell University.

Skifstad, K., & Jain, R. (1994). Illumination independent change detection for real world image sequences. *Computer Vision Graphics and Image Processing,* (46): 387–399.

Stancic, I., Supuk, T., & Cecic, M. (2009). Computer vision system for human anthropometric parameters estimation. *WSEAS Transactions on Systems,* 430-443.

Stauffer, C., & Grimson, W. E. L. (2000). Learning patterns of activity using real-time tracking. *IEEE Transactions on Pattern Analysis and Machine Intelligence, 22*(8), 747–757. doi:10.1109/34.868677

Subagyo Brooks, G. A., & Irons, G. A. (2003). Spout eyes area correlation in ladle metallurgy. *ISIJ International, 43*(2), 262–263. doi:10.2355/isijinternational.43.262

Switched Digital Video. (n.d.). Retrieved from http://static.ddmcdn.com/gif/switched-digital-video-3.gif

Tameze, C., Vincelette, R. B., Melikechi, N., Zeljković, V., & Izquierdo, E. (2007). *Empirical analysis of LIBS images for ovarian cancer detection.* WIAMIS. doi:10.1109/WIAMIS.2007.40

Tan, P. N., Steinbach, M., & Kumar, V. (2005). *Introduction to data mining.* Reading, MA: Addison-Wesley.

The 0-360 Panoramic Optic. (n.d.). Retrieved from http://www.0-360.com/

Vailaya, A., Figueiredo, M. A. T., Jain, A. K., & Zhang, H.-J. (2001). Image classification for content-based indexing. *IEEE Transactions on Image Processing, 10*(1), 117–130. doi:10.1109/83.892448 PMID:18249602

Vespe, M., Baker, C. J., & Griffiths, H. D. (2006). *Outline structural representation for radar target classification based on non-radar templates.* Paper presented at the CIE 2006 International Conference. New York, NY.

Video Network. (n.d.). Retrieved from http://www.axis.com/products/cam_292/img/ipsurvnw.jpg

Vincelette, R. B., Tameze, C., Savic, M., & Zeljkovic, V. (2007). Efficient shape recognition method using novel metric for complex polygonal shapes. In *Advances in Applied and Computational Mathematics* (Vol. 2). New York: Nova Science Publishers.

Wang, P., & Xu, C. (n.d.). *Robust face recognition via sparse representation.* Academic Press.

Wang, Y.-N., Chen, L.-B., & Hu, B.-G. (2002). *Semantic extraction of the building images using support vector machines.* Beijing, China: IEEE.

Watchareeruetai, U., Takeuchi, Y., Matsumoto, T., Kudo, H., & Ohnishi, N. (2011). Redundancies in linear GP, canonical transformation, and its exploitation: A demonstration on image feature synthesis. *Genet Program Evolvable*, *12*, 49–77. doi:10.1007/s10710-010-9118-x

Webb, A. R. (2002). *Statistical pattern recognition*. Chichester, UK: John Wiley & Sons Ltd. doi:10.1002/0470854774

Williams, M. (2007). *Better face-recognition software*. Academic Press.

Witkin, A. (1983). *Scale-space filtering*. Karlsruhe, Germany: IEEE.

Wolfson, H. (1987). *On curve matching*. Miami Beach, FL: IEEE. O'Rourke, J., & Washington, R. (1985). Curve similarity via signatures. *Computational Geometry*, 295–318.

Woodward, J., & Horn, C. (2003). *Biometrics a look at facial recognition*. Academic Press. Frank, T. (2007). Face recognition next in terror fight. *USA Today*.

Wren, C., Azarbayejani, A., Darrell, T., & Pentland, A. P. (1997). Pfinder: Real-time tracking of the human body. *IEEE Transactions on Pattern Analysis and Machine Intelligence*, *19*(7), 780–785. doi:10.1109/34.598236

Wright, J., Yang, A., Ganesh, A., Sastry, S., & Ma, Y. (2009). Robust face recognition via sparse representation. *IEEE Transactions on PAMI*, *31*(2), 210–227. doi:10.1109/TPAMI.2008.79 PMID:19110489

Xu, Y., Weaver, J. B., Healy, D. M. Jr, & Lu, J. (1994). Wavelet transform domain filters: A spatially selective noise filtration technique. *IEEE Transactions on Image Processing*, *3*(6), 747–758. doi:10.1109/83.336245 PMID:18296244

Yeadon, M. R. (1990). The simulation of aerial movement-II: A mathematical inertia model of the human-body. *Journal of Biomechanics*, 67–74. doi:10.1016/0021-9290(90)90370-I PMID:2307693

Yuasa, G., Yajima, T., Ukai, A., & Ozawa, M. (1984). Refining practice and application of the ladle furnace (LF) process in Japan. *Transactions of the Iron and Steel Institute of Japan*, *24*(5), 412–418. doi:10.2355/isijinternational1966.24.412

Yuille, A., & Poggio, T. (1986). Scaling theorems for zero crossings. *IEEE Transactions on Pattern Analysis and Machine Intelligence*, 8. PMID:21869319

Zarandi, M. H., & Ahmadpour, P. (2009). *Fuzzy agent-based expert system for steel making process. expert systems with applications*. Elsevier.

Zeljković, V., & Dragovic, R. (2004). *Software solution for moving object detection in video sequence independent of the scene illumination*. Zabljak, Serbia and Montengro: IT.

Zeljković, V., & Mousa, W. (2011). *An algorithm for petro-graphic colour image segmentation used for oil exploration*. Paper presented at the High Performance Computing & Simulation Conference: Workshop on Pattern Analysis and Recognition. New York, NY.

Zeljković, V., & Trpovski, Ž. (2004). *Illumination independent moving object detection in real sequence*. Sombor, Serbia and Montengro: DOGS.

Zeljkovic, V., Abu-Khamis, N., & Al Qahtani, H. (2011). *Algorithm for automatic body dimensions and skin colour detection used in homeland security systems*. Jeddah, Saudi Arabia: Ministry of Higher Education Second Scientific Conference.

Zeljkovic, V., Dorado, A., & Izquierdo, E. (2004). A modified shading model method for building detection. In *Proceedings of the 5ᵗʰ Int. Workshop on Image Analysis for Multimedia Interactive Services*. WIAMIS.

Zeljkovic, V., Pokrajac, D., Dorado, A., & Izquierdo, E. (2005). Application of the improved illumination independent moving object detection algorithm on the real video sequence. In *Proceedings of the 6ᵗʰ International Workshop on Image Analysis for Multimedia Interactive Services*. WIAMIS.

Zeljković, V., Praks, P., & Husar, I. (2010). *Monitoring the impact of the intensity of blowing of an inert gas to the visual character of the molten steel surface*. Paper presented at the IEEE International Energy Conference and Exhibition. Washington, DC.

Zeljković, V., Tameze, C., & Vincelette, R. B. (2010). *Algorithms for radar image identification and classification*. Paper presented at the High Performance Computing & Simulation Conference: Workshop on Pattern Analysis and Recognition. New York, NY.

Zeljkovic, V., Trpovski, Z., & Senk, V. (2003). Improved illumination independent moving object detection in real world video sequences. In *Proceedings of the 4th EURASIP Conf. focused on Video/Image Processing and Multimedia Communications*. EURASIP.

Zeljkovic, V., Vincelette, R. B., & Savic, M. (2006). *Novel object identification algorithm.* Paper presented at the 6th Conference Digital Speech and Image Processing DOGS. New York, NY.

Zeljkovic, V. (2010). *Illumination independent moving object detection in image sequences.* LAP Lambert Academic Publishing GmbH & Co. KG.

Zeljković, V., Dorado, A., & Izquierdo, E. (2004). *A modified shading model method for building detection.* Lisbon, Portugal: WIAMIS.

Zeljković, V., Dorado, A., & Izquierdo, E. (2004). Combining a fuzzy rule-based classifier and illumination invariance for improved building detection. *IEEE Transactions on Circuits and Systems for Video Technology, 14*(11), 1277–1280. doi:10.1109/TCSVT.2004.835145

Zeljkovic, V., Dorado, A., Trpovski, Ž., & Izquierdo, E. (2004). Classification of building images in video sequences. *IEE Electronics Letters, 40*(3), 169–170. doi:10.1049/el:20040128

Zeljković, V., Li, Q., Vincelette, R. B., Tameze, C., & Liu, F. (2009). *Aircraft identification by unions of ISAR images.* MOBIMEDIA. doi:10.4108/ICST.MOBIMEDIA2009.7904

Zeljković, V., Li, Q., Vincelette, R. B., Tameze, C., & Liu, F. (2009). *Automatic algorithm for ISAR images recognition and classification.* IET Radar, Sonar, and Navigation.

Zeljkovic, V., & Pokrajac, D. (2006). *Improved spatial-temporal moving object detection method resistant to noise.* ICEST.

Zeljkovic, V., & Pokrajac, D. (2006). *Motion detection based multimedia supported intelligent video surveillance system.* ELMAR. doi:10.1109/ELMAR.2006.329512

Zeljkovic, V., Pokrajac, D., Dorado, A., & Izquierdo, E. (2006). *Application of the improved illumination independent moving object detection algorithm on the real video sequence.* Montreux, Switzerland: WIAMIS.

Zeljkovic, V., Pokrajac, D., & Latecki, L. J. (2005). *Noise robust spatial-temporal algorithm for moving objects detection.* XLIX ETRAN.

Zeljković, V., & Popović, M. (2000). *Illumination independent moving object extraction from video sequences.* Soko Banja, Yugoslavia: ETRAN.

Zeljković, V., & Praks, P. (2007). *A comparative study of automated iris recognition using the biorthogonal wavelets and the SVD-free latent semantic methods.* Ostrava, Czech Republic: VSB-Technical University of Ostrava.

Zeljković, V., Praks, P., Vincelette, R. B., Tameze, C., & Válek, L. (2009). *Automatic pattern classification of real metallographic images.* Houston, TX: IEEE. doi:10.1109/IAS.2009.5324864

Zeljković, V., Tameze, C., Vincelette, R. B., & Izquierdo, E. (2008). *Nonlinear diffusion filter and triangle method used for noise removal from polygonal shapes.* Xi'an, China: VIE. doi:10.1049/cp:20080306

Zeljković, V., Tameze, C., Vincelette, R. B., & Izquierdo, E. (2009). *Different nonlinear diffusion filters combined with triangle method used for noise removal from polygonal shapes.* IET Image Processing.

Zeljković, V., & Trpovski, Ž. (2002). *Moving object localization applying change detection.* Novi Bečej, Yugoslavia: DOGS.

Zeljković, V., Trpovski, Ž., & Šenk, V. (2003). *Improved illumination independent moving object detection in real world video sequences.* Zagreb, Croatia: EURASIP. doi:10.1109/VIPMC.2003.1220508

Zeljkovic, V., Vincelette, R. B., & Savic, M. (2006). *Efficient shape recognition method using novel metric for complex polygonal shapes.* MOBIMEDIA. doi:10.1145/1374296.1374321

Zhang, L., et al. (2000). Effect of bubble size on the liquid steel flow in air-stirred ladles. *Selected Papers of Engineering Chemistry and Metallurgy,* 145-157.

About the Author

Vesna Zeljkovic is a researcher in the field of signal and image processing with more than 15 years of experience developing mathematical models and novel algorithms for the analysis of images that have applications in video surveillance, analysis of complex optical spectra, public health, homeland security, industry, and national defense. This work is reflected in more than 60 published scientific papers, 1 book chapter, as well as 1 published book in these fields. She has taught engineering courses at undergraduate and graduate level in 5 countries on 3 different continents.

Index